# *Freedom in the Arab World*

A preoccupation with the subject of "freedom" became a core issue in the construction of all modern political ideologies. Here, Wael Abu-ʿUksa examines the development of the concept of freedom in nineteenth-century Arab political thought, its ideological offshoots, their modes, and their substance as they developed the dynamics of the Arabic language. Abu-ʿUksa traces the transition of the idea of freedom from a term used in a predominantly non-political way, through to its popularity and near ubiquity at the dawn of the twentieth century. Through this, he also analyzes the importance of associated concepts such as "liberalism," "socialism," "progress," "rationalism," "secularism," and "citizenship." He employs a close analysis of the development of the language, whilst at the same time examining the wider historical context within which these semantic shifts occurred: the rise of nationalism, the power of the Ottoman court and the state of relations with Europe.

DR. WAEL ABU-ʿUKSA is a Polonsky Fellow at the Van Leer Jerusalem Institute and an assistant professor in the Political Science department at the Hebrew University of Jerusalem. He is also the author of *Liberalism and Left in Arab Thought after 1990*.

# Freedom in the Arab World

## Concepts and Ideologies in Arabic Thought in the Nineteenth Century

WAEL ABU-ʿUKSA
*The Hebrew University of Jerusalem*

CAMBRIDGE
UNIVERSITY PRESS

**CAMBRIDGE**
**UNIVERSITY PRESS**

University Printing House, Cambridge CB2 8BS, United Kingdom

Cambridge University Press is part of the University of Cambridge.

It furthers the University's mission by disseminating knowledge in the pursuit of education, learning and research at the highest international levels of excellence.

www.cambridge.org
Information on this title: www.cambridge.org/9781107161245



First published 2016

Printed in the United Kingdom by Clays, St Ives plc

*A catalogue record for this publication is available from the British Library*

ISBN 978-1-107-16124-5 Hardback
ISBN 978-1-316-61382-5 Paperback

*To my mother, Nayfi,*
*and in memory of my father, Nasrat*

# *Contents*

# *Acknowledgments*

This book builds on research I have carried out between October 2012 and April 2015 after completing my PhD. This project was made possible by the support of the Center for Middle Eastern Studies at Harvard University, the Fulbright Scholarship program, and the Polonsky postdoctoral program at the Van Leer Jerusalem Institute.

During the work on the manuscript, I received many suggestions, comments, and words of advice from friends, colleagues, and teachers. I owe a great debt of gratitude to Professor Baber Johansen, whose discussions and meetings in the CMES at Harvard were very helpful for the formation of the conceptual framework of the book. I wish to express my special thanks to Professor Fruma Zachs for her invaluable comments on the manuscript's various stages. Her suggestions helped in shaping the book into its present form. I would like to convey my sincere appreciation to Professor Avraham Sela, who painstakingly read and commented on the complete manuscript. His unwavering support before, during, and after my PhD studies also continued through the writing of this book. I am forever grateful. I am also indebted to Professor Efraim Podoksik, Professor Shukri Abed, and the readers who were consulted by Cambridge University Press for their valuable suggestions.

Many people have helped indirectly to get this work done, even though they might not be aware of the importance of their contributions. I wish to convey my special gratitude to Dr Anat Lapidot-Firilla for her assistance and support in the crucial stage of my academic career after my PhD, as well as to Dr. Yoav Di-Capua, Professor Butrus Abu-Manneh, and Professor Reuven Amitai, whose support has made this book possible. I am also grateful to my language editor, Deborah Schwartz, for her excellent and hard work on the text. Needless to say, all errors are entirely my responsibility.

A very heavy burden fell on my family during the writing of this book. I wish to acknowledge with thanks the help I received from Sally in organizing and categorizing part of the papers and the devoted effort of Bshara, a promising young scholar who helped in collecting part of the materials. Above all, my thanks to Vivian, who sacrificed so much of her time to make the work on this book possible, and to my mother Nayfi and my late father Nasrat, to whom I dedicate this book.

# *Note on Translation and Transliteration*

All translations in this book, unless otherwise noted, are by the author. Arabic is transliterated in accordance with the system commonly used in the field of Islamic studies. Diacritics appear in all Arabic transliterations, except in authors' names, where only the *ʿain* and *hamza* are retained. Names in book or journal titles are written using full diacritics. The Arabic definite article, when used with "and," as in *wa-ʾal* or *wa-ʾil*, is abbreviated to *wal-*, and the first letters in Arabic titles are capitalized. To reduce the length of the notes and because of the frequent lack of complete information, nineteenth-century newspaper and periodical references are cited without the name of the author or the title of the article. Places of publication in Arabic sources are written in English: for example Cairo, not al-Qahira, is used. Arabic terms in the text are italicized, with the exception of words widely used in English, such as Qurʿan, ʿulama, and Tanzimat.

# Introduction

The French political philosopher Montesquieu published, in 1748, an elaboration of his exploration of the concept of liberty. In one of his most insightful notes, he wrote: "No word has received more different significations and has struck minds in so many ways as has liberty."[1] Montesquieu's insight came before the profound, accelerated transformations of the second half of the century took place, with the outbreak of the great revolutions that shaped the politics of modern history, beginning with the American and French revolutions. His note preceded the modern ideological discourse of the nineteenth century that witnessed the formation of central concepts such as liberalism, socialism, and communism, which to a large extent dominated modern political thought. Had Montesquieu composed his note a century later, he might well have outlined the same content with more emphasis on the increased complexity and refinement reflected in the term "liberty" following the dramatic effects that the Enlightenment had on the nineteenth century and its attendant political events.

Although the philosophical preoccupation with the political aspects of freedom is strongly connected with the civilizational and historical legacy that is often presented as integrated in the "West," the concept "freedom" is strongly considered central to modern political thought in the Mediterranean countries. The vigorous claims for freedom dominating the slogans of twentieth-century political and social movements in the eastern and southern Mediterranean manifest the pivotal position that this concept occupied in the political and social systems of values. The transformation of freedom in modern philosophy to an inalienable attribute of the value of individuals and nations contributed significantly to the empowerment and intensification of its political influence. The focal function of these conceptions left a

[1] Charles de Secondat Montesquieu, *The Spirit of the Laws* (Cambridge: Cambridge University Press, 1989), 154.

mark on all modern ideologies: freedom of nations from foreign rule, freedom of individuals from the oppression of political authority and from conformity to the social majority, freedom of religion or from religion, emancipation of slaves, of women, of the working class, and so on.[2]

## Rationale

The fertile cultural, social, and economic background against which modern political ideas took shape in the eastern and southern Mediterranean was formed mainly during the nineteenth century. During this period scholars, journalists, and politicians not only founded a new epistemic background that was later referred to as *nahḍa* (revival) but also shaped the themes and language that preoccupied and articulated the sociopolitical discourse of the twentieth century. As part of these transformations, the semantics of freedom inflated significantly, which made the task of outlining all its manifestations almost impossible. The following chapters focus on the history of the political aspects of freedom, especially those that evolved in two categories – the social and the individual – in the cultural space that is confined to the Ottoman Arabic-speaking provinces. Despite the title, which relates to the whole of the nineteenth century, this research illuminates the history of this idea in the Arabic-speaking areas during the period that ranges from the French invasion of Egypt in 1798 through the British invasion of Egypt in 1882, relying on the assumption that Egypt constituted during this period the central country producing knowledge in Arabic. In general this book examines the transition of the idea of freedom from its frequent nonpolitical use prior to the nineteenth century, through its political semantic inflation at the beginning of the nineteenth century, to the stage where it became a signifier in Arabic for ideological affiliations.

The hypothesis underlying this inquiry assumes that the mental preoccupation with the subject of freedom became a core issue in the construction of modern ideologies, which makes the disassociation between the history of the concept and the structure of these ideologies nearly impossible. All modern ideologies evolved against

[2] Takashi Shogimen, "Liberty," *New Dictionary of the History of Ideas* (Detroit, MI: Charles Scribner's Sons, 2005), 1272–1279.

the background of certain preoccupations and interpretations of the issue of freedom: Nationalism relies on the collective, liberalism on the individual, and socialism on the class or the social aspects of freedom. These different interpretations of the same concept turned freedom into an inextricable component of various, sometimes contradictory, views of politics and society that might sustain intersecting meanings and sometimes might carry antithetical interactions.

Using conceptual history, this work aims to describe internal aspects of the emergence of modern ideologies by addressing the linguistic dynamics, the inconsistencies, and the dissonances that accompanied the construction of "freedom." By studying the particularity of the formation of modern ideas in a non-Western sphere, this approach emphasizes a frequently neglected aspect of research. Following the school of conceptual history,[3] the analysis of ideas is underlined by the premise that concepts maintain internal temporal structures. These structures encapsulate the full extent of historical experience, which can provide an illuminating perspective on the transitions of ideas. Concepts embed different meanings that transform over time and therefore evade any concrete definitions. Nietzsche articulated this insight by stating: "Only that which has no history is definable."[4] Concepts are expressed in semantic fields, and the scope of meaning is disclosed by the interconnections between words and associated concepts. Two lines of inquiry that constitute the core of conceptual history will be under scrutiny. The first makes use of synchronic analyses of language that focus on time frame and the interpretation of temporality of meaning. This aspect of the investigation aims to reveal stable structures of

[3] The history of concepts was developed by leading theoreticians of history such as Reinhart Koselleck, Otto Brunner, and Werner Conze. For further details see Iain Hampsher-Monk, Karin Tilmans, and Frank Van Vree, "A Comparative Perspective on Conceptual History – An Introduction," in *History of Concepts: Comparative Perspectives*, ed. Iain Hampsher-Monk, Karin Tilmans, and Frank Van Vree (Amsterdam: Amsterdam University Press, 1998), 2; Melvin Richter and Michaela W. Richter, "Introduction: Translation of Reinhart Koselleck's 'Krise' in Geschichtliche Grundbegriffe," *Journal of the History of Ideas* 67, no. 2 (April 2006): 348.

[4] Friedrich Nietzsche, "On the Genealogy of Morals," in *On the Genealogy of Morals; Ecce Homo*, trans. Walter Kaufmann (New York: Vintage Books, 1989), 80; Jorn Leonhard, "From European Liberalism to the Languages of Liberalisms: The Semantics of 'Liberalism' in European Comparison," *Redescriptions: Yearbook of Political Thought and Conceptual History*, no. 8 (2004): 38.

concepts that exceed the meanings of individual words. The second line of inquiry uses diachronic analyses, which follow changes in concepts over time and disclose their multiple layers by illuminating temporal differences between chronological units. This line of historical interpretation seeks to reveal the evolving semantics of "freedom" in the Arabic language and to identify the chronological frame in which freedom evolved into a consistent set of political principles or ideologies. Because of the chronological framework, the historical analysis in the following chapters briefly discusses the concepts prior to the eighteenth century. Certain concepts that might have sustained vibrant, vigorous states in the past were extinguished and lost their luster with time and thus fell into a static state. Assuming that these ideas underwent significant invigoration by the end of the eighteenth century, the historical analysis emphasizes the points of transition in the history of the concepts under scrutiny, especially in relation to their near-past state in the eighteenth century.

## Survey of Literature and the Study's Contribution

The period between the early 1800s and the 1860s is considered in prominent works of scholarship to be early for the formation of modern ideas. Some of these works, which outline the emergence of modern political and religious thought in Arabic, evade the investigation of this period. Majid Khadduri begins his survey in his work *Political Trends in the Arab World* late in the second half of the nineteenth century.[5] Similarly, in his work *Arab Intellectuals and the West*, Hisham Sharabi identifies the years between 1875 and 1914 as the "formative period" of modern ideas in Arabic.[6] The scant interest in this period, as compared to interest in the end of the nineteenth century or the twentieth century, among many historians is justifiable: The years that preceded the inauguration of private journalism produced a minor amount of intellectual activity. Furthermore, many of the modern political concepts were not yet linguistically stable, a state that made the sphere of ideas most ambiguous. The following chapters, however, attempt to explore the uncertainties attached to the understanding of ideas during this period, arguing that the emergence of modern political concepts,

[5] Majid Khadduri, *Political Trends in the Arab World: The Role of Ideas and Ideals in Politics* (Baltimore, MD: Johns Hopkins Press, 1970), 1–9.
[6] Hisham Sharabi, *Arab Intellectuals and the West: The Formative Years, 1875–1914* (Baltimore, MD: Johns Hopkins Press, 1970), x.

or the "formative period," took place earlier than 1875, and especially between the years 1820 and 1860. In this period, which witnessed cultural acculturation unprecedented in the history of the encounter between *dār al-Islām* (abode of Islam) and "Christendom," Arabic evidenced not only the creation of political vocabularies that to a large extent constitute the political lexicon of modern Arabic but also major conceptual shifts that involve the increased politicization and abstraction of concepts. Some of the concepts that prior to these years were largely static gradually gained dynamic retrospective and prospective dimensions and were frequently used to describe processes.

Beyond the discussion of time frame, the modern concept of freedom in Arabic has not received much attention in scholarship. Other than in an encyclopedia entry composed by Bernard Lewis,[7] the semantic history of *ḥurriyya* (freedom) has not been studied extensively – certainly not in the larger context that outlines its interconnections with other associated concepts. By using similar methodology, Mourad Wahba explores the early history of the concept of socialism in a short article, concluding that the formation of the Arabic term *ishtirākiyya* (socialism) took place only toward the end of the nineteenth century.[8] A pioneering work that explores political ideas through investigating the evolution of Arabic in overlapping time frames is Ami Ayalon's *Language and Change in the Arab Middle East*.[9] Ayalon's book, which makes broad use of primary sources, including early journalism, covers early transformations of ideas such as "subjects," "citizens," and concepts derived from forms of government and the structure

[7] In another short article Lewis uses linguistic methodology to explore the idea in Turkish. See Bernard Lewis, "Ḥurriyya: The Ottoman Empire and After," *The Encyclopedia of Islam* (Leiden: E. J. Brill, 1991), 589–594; Bernard Lewis, *Political Words and Ideas in Islam* (Princeton, NJ: Markus Wiener Publishers, 2008), 11–17.

[8] Prominent historians of the idea of socialism in the Middle East begin their discussion of the history of the concept at the end of the nineteenth century. See Mourad Magdi Wahba, "The Meaning of Ishtirakiyah: Arab Perceptions of Socialism in the Nineteenth Century," *Alif: Journal of Comparative Poetics*, no. 10 (1990): 42–55; Donald Reid, "The Syrian Christians and Early Socialism in the Arab World," *International Journal of Middle East Studies* 5, no. 2 (1974): 177–193; Panayiotis J. Vatikiotis, "Ishtirākiyya: The Arab Lands," *The Encyclopedia of Islam* (Leiden: E. J. Brill, 1978), 125–126; Ilham Khuri-Makdisi, *The Eastern Mediterranean and the Making of Global Radicalism, 1860–1914* (Berkeley, CA: University of California Press, 2010), 35–59.

[9] Ami Ayalon, *Language and Change in the Arab Middle East: The Evolution of Modern Political Discourse* (New York: Oxford University Press, 1987).

of communities. The following pages make extensive use of Ayalon's work, extending the research to concepts that were not under its focus. Additionally, this work emphasizes the early history of concepts such as liberalism, socialism, anarchism, and communism, utilizing a broad approach that reveals the interdynamics between all the vibrant political concepts that temporarily played an active part in shaping the political worldviews in the Arabic-speaking regions during the 1860s and 1870s. Another work that utilizes the "linguistic turn" and explores the realm of ideas from the perspective of the symbolic expression of language is Yasir Suleiman's *The Arabic Language and National Identity*. Although this work covers later periods, mainly the end of the nineteenth century and the beginning of the twentieth, the approach Suleiman employs found very relevant to this study.[10]

In addition to the attempt to cover the early history of central concepts in political discourse, perhaps the most significant contribution this work aims to make is in the field of the history of political and religious thought. Viewing the construction of political ideas through linguistic lenses brings into focus the confusion that beleaguered the meaning of ideologies in the same cultural realm. The unexplored early history of Arabic ideological idioms left scholarship with a variety of narratives that address the same political idea but that did not necessarily have the same ideational content. Thus, questions involving the genealogy, history, and particular features of ideas such as "liberalism," "socialism," "constitutionalism," "republicanism," "secularism," "progress," and "democracy" in the cultural space of Arabic remained extremely vague.

Because of the centrality of "liberalism" in studying and understanding the state of political thought in the nineteenth century, the next pages of this introduction focus only on its use, outlining the paradoxes of meanings that arose from the way it was employed in scholarship. This frequent use of "liberalism" in a way that preserved a state of detachment between the language of historiography and morphological history is used as a case study that clearly presents the dissonance that intellectual history generated in the field of the history of modern ideas in a non-Western context.

[10] Yasir Suleiman, *The Arabic Language and National Identity: A Study in Ideology* (Washington, DC: Georgetown University Press, 2003).

Use of the word "liberalism" is widely accepted in research to describe the history or the political atmosphere in a few Arab countries during the first half of the twentieth century, especially during the century's second and third decades.[11] It is reasonable to assume that this near consensus among historians regarding the use of "liberalism" might be derived from the fact that at this time Arabic witnessed not only the use of this term as a neologism and in its Arabized form but also its significant theorization and employment in politics, especially in Egypt. A prominent contribution to the domestication of this term was made by Egyptian politician Ahmad Lutfi al-Sayyid in the years prior to World War I. On the pages of his newspaper *al-Jarīda*, he championed the ideas of *madhhab al-ḥurriyya* or *madhhab al-ḥurriyyīn* (school of freedom or liberalism), perceiving it as the most appropriate ideology for contemporary Egyptian politics.[12] With the establishment of the Liberal Constitutional Party (*ḥizb al-aḥrār al-dustūriyyīn*) in 1922, al-Sayyid hoped to apply his liberal orientation to Egyptian politics, arguing that the party should change its name to *al-ḥurriyyīn*

[11] For a selected biography that employs "liberalism" to indicate a political category during the first half of the twentieth century (or part of it), see the following sources. The subject of the decline of liberal thought stood at the center of scholarly discussion, especially in the Egyptian context where a few scholars argued that Egyptian liberalism underwent a "crisis of orientation" in the 1930s. For more details see Baber Johansen, *Muhammad Husain Haikal: Europa und der Orient in Weltbild eines Ägyptischen Liberalen* (Beirut: In Kommission bei F. Steiner, Wiesbaden, 1967), 61–75; Panayiotis J. Vatikiotis, *The Modern History of Egypt* (London: Weidenfeld and Nicolson, 1969), 204–235; Israel Gershoni, "Egyptian Liberalism in an Age of 'Crisis of Orientation': al-Risala's Reaction to Fascism and Nazism, 1933–39," *International Journal of Middle East Studies* 31, no. 4 (November 1999): 551–576; Abdeslam Maghraoui, *Liberalism without Democracy: Nationhood and Citizenship in Egypt, 1922–1936* (Durham, NC: Duke University Press, 2006); Meir Hatina, *Identity Politics in the Middle East: Liberal Thought and Islamic Challenge in Egypt* (London: Tauris Academic Studies, 2007), 13–29; Katerina Dalacoura, *Islam, Liberalism and Human Rights: Implications for International Relations* (London: I. B. Tauris, 2007), 76–113; Christoph Schumann, "Introduction," in *Liberal Thought in the Eastern Mediterranean: Late 19th Century until the 1960s*, ed. Christoph Schumann (Leiden: Brill, 2008), 1–11; Israel Gershoni and James P. Jankowski, *Confronting Fascism in Egypt: Dictatorship Versus Democracy in the 1930s* (Stanford, CA: Stanford University Press, 2010), 3–13.

[12] See his article titled "*al-Ḥurriyya wa-Madhāhib al-Ḥukm*" (Freedom and ideologies of governance), which he published in December 1913 in *al-Jarīda*: Ahmad Lutfi al-Sayyid, *Turāth Aḥmad Luṭfī al-Sayyīd*, vol. 1 (Cairo: Maṭbaʿat Dār al-Kutub wal-Wathāʾiq al-Qawmiyya, 2008), 424–427.

*al-dustūriyyīn* because he felt the phrase more accurately identified the ideological platform that he advocated.[13] When works on the intellectual history of the Arabic-speaking countries examine the years prior to World War I, the use of "liberalism" becomes highly controversial, expressing a deep ambiguity that is characterized in some cases by paradoxes. A quick glance at the state of research reveals the linguistic dissonance generated by the use of "liberalism." It is important to emphasize that many of the works of scholarship that used this term were written in the 1950s and 1960s. It is reasonable to assume that these two decades, which witnessed military coups in important Arab states, the foundation of republican regimes, the destruction of the parliamentary systems, and the spread of the single-party model by the influence of Nassirism and Baʿthism, left a deep impact on the state of scholarship and on the perception of pre–World War II politics. In the antiliberal, anti-Western, and anticapitalist revolutionary sphere that was dominated by socialism and pan-Arab nationalist slogans, many scholars regarded "liberalism" as the most suitable concept for depicting the early political norms that preceded Cold War politics.[14] Wilfred Cantwell Smith, who published his work in 1957, uses the combined term "Islamic liberalism" to designate – "perhaps ineptly" and in a "deliberately broad sense" – an inconsistent intellectual phenomenon that reinterprets Islam predicated on three intellectual traditions: Sufism, rationalism, and Western thought. For him liberal Islam is not an established system of ideas and probably not a consistent ideology; rather it is a wide-ranging phenomenon supported, in the Arabic-speaking countries, by scholars such as Muhammad ʿAbdu and Taha Hussain.[15] Jamal Ahmed, Albert Hourani's student, whose *The Intellectual Origins of Egyptian Nationalism* was published in 1960, follows Smith's approach by using the combination "Islamic liberalism" to portray the intellectual biography and

[13] ʿAbas Mahmud al-ʿAqad, *Rijāl ʿAraftuhum* (Cairo: Nahḍat Miṣr, 1992), 191.

[14] See, for instance, the influence of this historical context on Albert Hourani's 1962 publication. In introductions to later editions of his book, Albert Hourani elaborated the impact of Cold War politics on content. See Albert Hourani, *Arabic Thought in the Liberal Age, 1798–1939* (Cambridge: Cambridge University Press, 1983), vii.

[15] Wilfred Cantwell Smith, *Islam in Modern History* (Princeton, NJ: Princeton University Press, 1957), 55–73.

the thought of Muhammad ʿAbdu.[16] Nadav Safran, who published his book *Egypt in Search of Political Community* in 1961, makes a distinction between "reformist Islam," which is represented by intellectuals such as Muhammad ʿAbdu and Rashid Rida, and "liberal nationalism," which evolved with the generation of Mustafa Kamil and Ahmad Lutfi al-Sayyid.[17] A comparison of these works, which address the same concept, reveals that their use of "liberalism" presents inconsistencies related to both the narrative this concept came to demarcate and its intellectual content. This conclusion is illustrated especially when addressing questions about the identity of the adherents of ideas described as "liberal" and in the alleged correlation between the intellectual streams of Islamic reformism and liberalism.[18]

The most influential work to contribute to the dissonance created by the use of "liberalism" in publications on nineteenth-century intellectual history is Albert Hourani's *Arabic Thought in the Liberal Age, 1798–1939*, published in 1962.[19] Hourani's book, which probes Arabic thought through analyzing biographies of the most prominent Arab scholars, thinkers, and intellectuals, brought to the historical scholarship broad discussions of focal stations in the evolvement of Arabic thought. Hourani's immense knowledge of the early modern social, cultural, and political history of the region equipped his analysis of ideas with comprehensive historical depth and makes his book frequently cited. His masterpiece, which covered almost a century and a half of streams of Arab thought, served for many generations as the fundamental source for the study of modern ideas. Although Hourani's

[16] Jamal Ahmed, *The Intellectual Origins of Egyptian Nationalism* (London: Oxford University Press, 1960), 35–48.
[17] See chapters 5 and 6 in Nadav Safran, *Egypt in Search of Political Community: An Analysis of the Intellectual and Political Evolution of Egypt, 1804–1952* (Cambridge, MA: Harvard University Press, 1961).
[18] For additional early works on intellectual history, see Charles C. Adams, *Islam and Modernism in Egypt: A Study of the Modern Reform Movement Inaugurated by Muhammad Abduh* (London: Oxford University Press, 1933); Raʾif Khuri, *al-Fikr al-ʿArabī al-Ḥadīth* (Beirut: Dār al-Makshūf, 1943); Hamilton A. Gibb, *Modern Trends in Islam* (Chicago: University of Chicago Press, 1947).
[19] For the vast influence of Hourani's book on scholarship as compared to other works on intellectual history published before 1970, see Donald Reid, "Arabic Thought in the Liberal Age: Twenty Years After," *International Journal of Middle East Studies* 14, no. 4 (November 1982): 549–550.

work largely shaped the methodological approach to the study of Arab liberalism, the hope is that after the passage of over fifty years, questioning the methodological approach of his book would be making a contribution to the field.

Hourani uses the combination "liberal age" to indicate the intellectual history of the Arab regions (predominantly in the Levant and Egypt) between the years 1798 and 1939. After Hourani's book, the combination "liberal age" and consequently "liberalism" came into widespread use in Western historiography for describing the intellectual atmosphere or political streams of certain defined historical categories not only in Egypt but also in the other Arab countries. Perhaps one of Hourani's most important contributions was that he firmly planted the methodological foundations for conceptualizing the political ideology "liberalism" in research.

Many historians criticized Hourani's use of the term "liberal age" and wondered if it could be accurate to designate an age that witnessed despotic rulers such as Muhammad ʿAli, ʿAbd al-Hamid II, and the Young Turks as "liberal." Other comments addressed the methodology that blends the study of systematic thinkers with the study of journalists and politicians.[20] Subsequent work criticizes the "arbitrary" chronological frame that Hourani chose to demarcate the beginning and end of the liberal age.[21] Additionally, one might question the book's conceptual anachronism, which uses "liberal" to describe a historical period that was only partly acquainted with the morphology or the ideological principles of liberalism. In the same sense, encompassing under one political category socialist-positivists such as Shibli Shumail, pan-Arab nationalists such as Satiʿ al-Husari, and early apostles of Islamism such as Rashid Rida might raise questions about the justification for narrating the intellectual history of these scholars

[20] For selected early criticism, see Elie Kedourie, "Arabic Thought in the Liberal Age, 1798–1939," *The Political Quarterly* 34, no. 2 (1963): 217–219; Peter M. Holt, "Arabic Thought in the Liberal Age, 1798–1939," *Bulletin of the School of Oriental and African Studies* 27, no. 1 (1964): 222–223; Malcolm Kerr, "Arabic Thought in the Liberal Age, 1798–1939," *Journal of the American Oriental Society* 84, no. 4 (1964): 427–429; Hisham Sharabi, "The Burden of the Intellectuals of the Liberal Age," *Middle East Journal* 20, no. 2 (1966): 227–232; Reid, "Arabic Thought in the Liberal Age: Twenty Years After," 550.

[21] Christoph Schumann, "Introduction," in *Nationalism and Liberal Thought in the Arab East: Ideology and Practice*, ed. Christoph Schumann (London: Routledge, 2010), 2.

under the book's title. Beyond these questions, the ambiguity of the term "liberal age" attracted the attention of leading historians who endeavored to explore the logic beyond the choice of title. For Elie Kedourie the title came to indicate "the reception of European thought in the Arabic-speaking world."[22] Malcolm Kerr suggested that "the subject is not exactly 'the age of Arabic liberal thought,' but rather Arabic thought of various liberal and illiberal kinds during an age in which the liberal spirit was predominant in European civilization and in which, in turn, Near Eastern intellectual life was heavily under the spell of Europe's presence."[23] To these illuminating comments on content, one might add that these attempts at clarification cannot ignore that the period the book covers was not entirely liberal even in Europe. This same period witnessed the rise of all modern ideologies, including anarchism at the end of the nineteenth century and communism, fascism, and Nazism in the first half of the twentieth century.

The generalization that characterizes the designation of the "liberal age" was questioned later by Hourani, who reassessed his use of the term in later editions of his book. In the expanded introduction for the 1970 edition, he indicated that

> were I able to rewrite the book now I should make some fundamental changes. I think now that the title (chosen at the last minute to replace another) is not a good one: the word "liberal" does not adequately describe all the ideas which came into the Arab world from Western Europe in the nineteenth century, and it may be misleading if it is taken to imply that all Arab reactions to those ideas were themselves "liberal" . . . But I am content to leave the book as it stands, in the hope that other scholars will cover the same ground in a more thorough way, and that they will not find my work an obstacle in their path.[24]

The repercussions that arose from the dissonance generated between the language of liberalism and the intellectual history of liberalism was therefore known to Hourani. He hoped, as quoted, that this title would not be an obstacle to future research. However, whether this controversial point was stressed enough or not, "liberal age" as a general and

[22] Kedourie, "Arabic Thought in the Liberal Age, 1798–1939," 218.
[23] Kerr, "Arabic Thought in the Liberal Age, 1798–1939," 427.
[24] Albert Hourani, *Arabic Thought in the Liberal Age, 1798–1939* (London: Oxford University Press, 1970), viii.

"open" term that indicates certain phenomena was rooted in scholarship in subsequent years.

Obviously, Hourani's theme was not liberal thought but the reception of all modern ideas in the Arabic-speaking regions. Earlier scholars used the term "modern trends" to describe the variety of these ideas without ascribing specific political features to their subject of study. As such it is the pioneering work of Hamilton Gibb that employs the combination "modern trends" to depict inconsistent ideas and intellectual streams in Islam during the nineteenth century.[25] Malcolm Kerr, Hamilton Gibb's student, followed the same logic and used the terms "modern," "modernist," and "reformist Islam" to portray the intellectual thought of Muhammad ʿAbdu and Rashid Rida.[26] Political concepts such as "Western," "liberal," "enlightened," "secular," and "modern" are widely used in research as synonyms, although they embed broad differences in notion, genealogy, and history. Needless to say, that which is considered "Western," "secular," "enlightened," or "modern" does not necessarily mean "liberal."

This short glance at the state of the concept "liberalism" in scholarship leads us to three conclusions. First, the historical research on the subject of liberalism has produced many historical narratives about "liberalisms" that addressed the same subject but not necessarily the same intellectual content. Second, at the core of the uncertainties and the ambiguity that beleaguered the meaning and use of the concept lies the dissonance between the terminology of historiography and the temporal language that is constructed in particular cultural realms and specific units of time. The third conclusion is that under the spell of Western cultural domination, intellectual history leans toward extensive use of local terminology in investigating a non-Western environment, resulting in an anachronistic or inaccurate use of concepts.

Given all this, the broader aim of this work is to contribute to the de-metaphysization of the use of political idioms, such as liberalism, secularism, progress and socialism, in the language of historiography. The methodology of conceptual history suggests overcoming the gap between the terminology of historiography that is often employed as

[25] Gibb, *Modern Trends in Islam*, 63–84.

[26] His book was based on his PhD dissertation, which was under the supervision of Majid Khadduri and Hamilton Gibb. See Malcolm Kerr, *Islamic Reform: The Political and Legal Theories of Muḥammad ʿAbdu and Rashīd Riḍā* (Berkeley: University of California Press, 1966).

a heuristic device and the temporal language (in Arabic, in this case) that is constructed in particular cultural realms in a given time. In that sense conceptual history constitutes a continuous demand for contextualization that discloses the language of liberalism, nationalism, and socialism as a precondition for narrating the history of these concepts. In addition, the relation between language and ideas will be explored by emphasizing two stages of inquiry: the first stage, in which ideas are formulated as certain morphological signifiers in the language, and the second stage, in which ideas are politicized and turned into words that are used in political confrontation. This last stage manifests the domestication of ideas by acquiring a sociopolitical function in the examined discourse.

The following chapters display the semantic evolvement of "freedom," as well as its ideological offshoots, their modes, and their substance, as it developed in the dynamics of language and the topographies of content. The first chapter underscores the history of the extreme politicization that the concept of freedom underwent between the time of the French invasion of Egypt and the second decade of the nineteenth century. This arbitrary chronological unit attempts to cover the evolution of "freedom" before the spread of the revolutionary technology of modern printing and before the institutionalization of the cultural acculturation with France. The second chapter focuses on the emergence of the ideas of progress and civilization (*tamaddun*, *taqaddum*), arguing that these concepts underpin modern ideological thinking in Arabic because of their embedding of a perception of new time. The chapter examines the integration of freedom into the comprehensive paradigm of progress around the 1820s, outlining the processual dimension that freedom had acquired. This chapter shows how the impact of the emergence of progress generated conflict between two comprehensive categories: "tradition" and "progress." The third chapter explores the semantic extension that freedom underwent, for the most part between 1820 and 1860, with the institutionalization of cultural acculturation by state projects that included translation (mainly from French) and dispatching student missions to Europe. Presenting the reorientation of influence on Arabic from the domination of Turkish to other Mediterranean languages – mainly French, but also to Greek and Italian – this chapter addresses the emergence of individual and collective conceptions of freedom. This last subject receives greater focus by extending the historical inquiry to the manifestations of the language of national liberation prior to 1882. The fourth chapter focuses on the years 1860–1882, recounting the emergence of ideological appellations after the launch of the private Arabic press. This chapter traces the transition that the meanings of "freedom" underwent – from signifying libertarian political streams to specific idioms that capture distinct ideologies. The final section of this chapter outlines intellectual thought through emphasizing the different and sometimes contradictory interpretations of "freedom."

Anticipating the premise underpinning the following discussions, the first chapters stem from the hypothesis that the idea of freedom underwent a conceptual shift around the turn of the nineteenth century, which can be regarded as a profound shift from the past meanings that the word carried. The change in concept was characterized by two primary features: The concept had been heavily burdened by overpoliticized content, and it had transformed more rapidly than it had in the past. The acquired structures of freedom were validated by extensive and reciprocal interactions with associated concepts, which together maintained complex, comprehensive structures of meaning. The events that took place around the beginning of the nineteenth century stimulated long-term processes of transformation in the concept of freedom, whose implications greatly affected the formation of modern ideologies.

The preceding argument relies on the assumption that freedom attained a certain kind of usage in language that semantically inflated around the turn of the nineteenth century and afterward. In his research Franz Rosenthal presents important insights in this regard. Rosenthal, who explored the semantics of the word *ḥurr* (free) prior to the nineteenth century by employing the methodology of classical philology, concluded that the word "free" was frequently used in Arabic in three main categories. The first and most common category was legal and indicated a legal status that is contrasted with slavery.[27] The second category was metaphysical and theological, and it focused on the nature of the relations between man and God.[28] The third category was ethical and was associated with honor and nobility.[29] Rosenthal discusses the political concept of freedom as the term is used in Arabic

[27] Franz Rosenthal, *The Muslim Concept of Freedom Prior to the Nineteenth Century* (Leiden: E. J. Brill, 1960), 29–34.

[28] Ibid., 25–28, 106.

[29] Equivalent to gentleman; free from the domination of greed, nature, or environment; self-control. Ibid., 10, 28, 82.

philosophical works, including Ibn Rushd and al-Farabi's philosophies, and concludes that the political concept did not go beyond the theoretical thought or develop practical applications. "Arabic did not possess a truly workable term to express the full force of the concept of 'freedom' until, in modern times, Western influence gave a new meaning to old *ḥurriyya*."[30] He expresses his doubts regarding whether the concept of freedom prior to the nineteenth century was acknowledged in Islamic history as "the most basic human attribute."[31]

It is worth noting that the thesis regarding the conceptual state of "freedom" in Islamic civilization prior to the nineteenth century was not confined to publications in the field of oriental studies but was rather part of Western scholarship and its view of non-Western cultures. Arguments made by scholars who support this thesis rely on the idea that the concept of civil liberties was the essence of the particularity of the "West." "Enlightenment," "liberalism," and "citizenship" are presented in early works as key concepts for the exceptionality of the West as compared to other civilizations. Earlier echoes of this conception of the state of the East are expressed in Georg Hegel's comment from the beginning of the nineteenth century: "The East knew and to the present day knows only that *One* is Free [that is, the despot]."[32] In a similar and more comprehensive approach, Max Weber argued in the beginning of the twentieth century that the concept of citizenship is particular to the West. Weber's argument went beyond Islamic civilization, including the cultures of India and China in his discussion. Other contemporary social scientists theorized these perceptions and used them to explain the "European Miracle," according to Eric Jones's designation.[33]

[30] Rosenthal indicates that Muslim philosophers such as Ibn Rushd "may have dreamed" about civil forms of freedom, but he argues that these dreams remained marginal and were never practiced in the history of Islam. Ibid., 11, 101.

[31] Bernard Lewis agrees with Rosenthal's approach. See ibid., 34, 56, 120–122; Bernard Lewis, *The Emergence of Modern Turkey* (London: Oxford University Press, 1968), 54–55; Lewis, "Ḥurriyya: The Ottoman Empire and After," 589–594; Lewis, *Political Words and Ideas in Islam*, 15.

[32] Georg W. F. Hegel, *The Philosophy of History*, trans. J. Sibree (Kitchener: Batoche Books, 2001), 121.

[33] Max Weber, *Wirtschaft und Gesellschaft: Grundriss der verstehenden Soziologie* (Tübingen: J. C. B. Mohr, 1976), 727–741; Eric Jones, *The European Miracle: Environments, Economies, and Geopolitics in the History of Europe and Asia* (Cambridge: Cambridge University Press, 1981).

Recent studies have challenged the essentialist views about the "Western" experience using a variety of methods. Through examining the language of liberalism, conceptual historian Jorn Leonhard contextualizes the phenomenon of liberalism in western Europe within the historical circumstances of the nineteenth century by illustrating how the word "liberal" was transformed and extremely politicized.[34] In the eighteenth century the word "liberal" in English frequently had aristocratic and nonpolitical social implications such as in "liberal education," or "liberal gentleman." Up until 1818 or 1819, English writers employed non-English spellings for the word "liberal" (the Spanish *liberales* or the French *libéraux*) to indicate its foreign roots and to describe the politics on the continent, while using the words Whig, Troy, or Radical to refer to the political orientations and parties in Great Britain. Use of the word in British politics to indicate "British liberals" took place only toward the end of the second decade of the nineteenth century. The reform-oriented Whigs employed the English word "liberal" as a positive and progressive indicator from the 1820s onward. Parallel development took place in German and Italian political language.[35] Conceptual history, in that sense, broke the ahistoric essence in favor of historicized narrative that relies on the analysis of the changes in language in concrete contexts and their impact on the realm of ideas. Additionally, the idea of Western exceptionalism that influenced Rosenthal's work on medieval Islam was challenged from domestic historical perspectives that reconsider the state of freedom in medieval Arab Islamic civilization.[36]

[34] Leonhard, "From European Liberalism to the Languages of Liberalisms," 17–51. A similar conceptual analysis was applied to the concept of democracy. Works using the linguistic approach to the study of ideas show that democracy was re-imagined, received its modern content, and was perceived as relevant to contemporary circumstances only after the French Revolution. See this collection: Joanna Innes and Mark Philp, eds., *Re-imagining Democracy in the Age of Revolutions: America, France, Britain, Ireland, 1750–1850* (Oxford: Oxford University Press, 2013).

[35] Leonhard, "From European Liberalism to the Languages of Liberalisms," 23–26, 33–36.

[36] Many scholars criticized Rosenthal's work from different perspectives. Some of the main comments were that Rosenthal's work ignores exploring fields that might contain perceptions of civil and social freedom such as the "five principles" of Islamic law and theological discussions about determinism and free will (*al-jabr wal-ikhtiyār*), ignoring social practices that embed challenges to political authority such as tribes and bedouin traditions. Others criticized

Regardless of the controversies around the content of "freedom" in medieval times, the argument that the Arabic concept had transformed and undergone extreme politicization during the nineteenth century is indisputable. By exploring the textual evidence between 1798 and 1820, the first chapter sheds light on the political semantics that the word "freedom" had acquired and thus provides an empirical content to the changing formation of freedom in the Arabic-Islamic context.

Rosenthal's methodology, which explores the meaning of freedom through isolating the word from its historical context. For reviews and criticism, see Radwan al-Sayyid, "Taqdīm," in *Mafhūm al-Ḥurriyya fī al-Islām: Dirāsa fī Mushkilāt al-Muṣṭalaḥ wa-Ab'āduhu fī al-Turāth al-'Arabī al-Islāmī* (Beirut: Dār al-Madār al-Islāmī, 2007), 8–10; Ernest Gellner, "The Muslim Concept of Freedom Prior to the 19th Century," *Philosophy* 39, no. 147 (1964): 85–86; Elmer Douglas, "The Muslim Concept of Freedom by Franz Rosenthal," *Middle East Journal* 15, no. 4 (1961): 470–472; 'Abd Allah al-'Arawi, *Mafhūm al-Ḥurriyya* (Casablanca: Al-Markaz al-Thaqāfī al-'Arabī, 1981), 11–25.

# 1 *The Politicization of Freedom, 1798–1820*

"They [the French] made a long decorated pillar and placed it in al-Azbakiyya [park] . . . They [the French] said: this is the tree of freedom, but the people of Egypt said: this is the sign of the stake that impaled us in the occupation of our kingdom."

(Niqula al-Turk, *Dhikr Tamalluk Jumhūr al-Faransāwiyya al-Aqṭār al-Miṣriyya wal-bilād al-Shāmiyya*, 47)

## France in Egypt and the Levant, 1798–1801

For contemporaries, the beginning of the nineteenth century was a vibrant arena for imagination, ideas, and challenges. Three geographical points of direct encounter between different cultures, beginning in Cairo in 1798 and later in Paris and Beirut, stimulated unprecedented change in the Arabic language. Arabic witnessed, during the following decades, intensive alterations in concepts: Political and social vocabularies rapidly transformed, absorbed new meanings, and acquired varying forms.

Systems of meaning that developed around the word "freedom" were organized in a variety of ways and inaugurated the age of modern ideologies.[1] Associated concepts such as equality (*taswiyya* and later *musāwā*), citizen (*sitūyyān*, *waṭanī*, and later *muwāṭin*) and citizenship (*jinsiyya*, *muwāṭana*), constitutional and constitutionalist (*qānūn* and *qānūnī*, *dustūr* and *dustūrī*, *sharṭa*), natural rights (*ḥuqūq ṭabīʿiyya*, *sharīʿa ṭabīʿiyya*, *ḥuqūq bashariyya*, and *ḥuqūq al-ʾādamiyya*), social contract (*ʿaqd al-tʾānus wal-ijtimāʿ*, *wathīqa*

[1] Ideology in this context means a comprehensive and consistent set of ideas and expectations for social, political, and economic order. It is worth mentioning that in the Western/European context, the word "ideology" was coined in 1796 by French philosopher Antoine Destutt de Tracy to indicate the "science of ideas." For further details, see Emmet Kennedy, "'Ideology' from Destutt De Tracy to Marx," *Journal of the History of Ideas* 40, no. 3 (1979): 353–354.

*ijtimā'iyya*, *'aqd ijtimā'ī*), secularity and secularism (*dunyawiyya*, *ṭabā'i'iyya*, *dahriyya*, *'almāniyya*, *'ilmāniyya*, *madaniyya*), tolerance (*tasāhul*, *tasāmuḥ*), republic (*jumhūr*, *mashyakha*, *jumhūriyya*, *fawḍa*), revolution (*qiyām*, *fitna*, *'āmmiyya*, *thawra*), parliament (*mashūra*, *shūra*, *ahl al-ḥall wal-'aqd*, *barlamān*), reforms (*tanẓīmāt*, *iṣlāḥāt*), society (*ijtimā'*, *hay'a*, *mujtama'*), progress (*taqaddum*, *taraqqī*), and many others acquired altering signifiers with unstable forms. Some of this vocabulary is the child of the nineteenth century, and some was recruited from medieval Arabic and absorbed new meanings, whereas other words were borrowed as neologisms. The topography of these concepts incorporates multiple layers that constitute a full range of historical meaning that illustrates the particularity of Arab modernity.

Many generations of Arab scholars designated the profound cultural, political, economic, and social alterations that occurred in the beginning of century by the term *nahḍa* (revival). The scholars who employed this term assumed the existence of a division between two eras, and two separate times. The logic that lay in this outlook was not confined to Arab thought; the sense of new time pertained to a wider event that was generated by the challenge of the Enlightenment and that was universalized with the imperial expansion of the West. Given that the French invasion of Egypt and other changes took place in the Ottoman Empire, it is widely acceptable among historians to mark the end of the eighteenth century as the beginning of the "new time" of modernity.

Close observation of the history of freedom in primary texts from around 1800 discloses the simplicity of this outlook. To a large extent the word maintained its previous, and frequently nonpolitical medieval, semantics.[2] In early nineteenth-century historical sources,

[2] The word had very rare political use, as was the case prior to nineteenth-century lexicons of Arabic to Western languages and Arabic lexicography – including the tenth-century *al-Ṣiḥāḥ*, eleventh-century *al-Muḥkam wal-Muḥīṭ al-A'ẓam* and *al-Qāmūs al-Muḥīṭ*, twelfth-century *Shams al-'Ulūm*, thirteenth-century *Lisan al-'Arab*, fifteenth-century *al-Ta'rīfāt*, seventeenth-century *al-Kulliyyāt*, and eighteenth-century *Kashāf Iṣṭilāḥāt al-Funūn wal-'Ulūm* and *Tāj al-'Arūs*. The eighteenth-century Indian scholar 'Abd al-Nabi bin 'Abd al-Rasul al-Ahmadnakri classifies freedom in his work into two kinds: "*ḥurriyyat al-'āmma*" (freedom of the common people) and "*ḥurriyyat al-khāṣa*" (freedom of the notables). The first means being free from instincts, and the second means being free from existence by unification with God (which is the Sufi perception).

the nonpolitical use of the word *ḥurr* was most common when any political implication was still very rare. A representative case of this infrequency appears in the monumental work of ʿAbd al-Rahman al-Jabarti, one of the most important historians of Egypt during the French expedition there (1798–1801). In his voluminous history the semantic field of the word *ḥurr* refers to its legal aspects, as in *aḥrār* (free, not slaves);[3] ethical and social aspects, as in *ṣaḥāba aḥrār* (notable companions of the Prophet); or *bikul ḥurriyya* (free choice)[4] as well as to the economic, as in *al-māl al-ḥurr* (pure tax).[5] Aside from this frequency in the use of *ḥurr*, there is limited textual evidence from the end of the eighteenth century that presents additional layers in the concept of freedom. Al-Jabarti and other contemporary chroniclers incorporate in their works complete French proclamations that made use of the word *ḥurriyya*.[6] In the first French proclamation, about 4,000 copies of which were distributed in July 1798 among the Egyptian population, the word *ḥurriyya* was used in a political context.

Neither combination has political implications. See Franciscus Raphelengius, "Ḥurr, Ḥurriyya," *Lexicon Arabicum* (Leiden: Ex Officina Auctoris, 1613), 89; Jacobus Golius, "Ḥurr, Ḥurriyya," *Lexicon Arabico-Latinum* (Lugduni Batavorum: typis Bonaventurae and Abrahami, Elseviriorum, prostant Amstelodami apud Johannem Ravesteynivm, 1653), 591; Francisco Cañes, "Libre," *Diccionario Español-Latino-Arabigo* (Madrid: Impr. de A. Sancha, 1787), 369–370; John Richardson, "Ḥurriyya," *A Dictionary, Persian, Arabic, and English: with a Dissertation on the Languages, Literature, and Manners of Eastern Nations* (London: William Bulmer, 1806); ʿAbd al-Nabi bin ʿAbd al-Rasul Ahmadnakri, "Ḥurriyya," *Jāmiʿ al-ʿUlūm fī Iṣṭilāḥāt al-Funūn al-Mulaqqab bi-Dustūr al-ʿUlamāʾ* (Beirut: Muʾassasat al-Aʿlamī lil-Maṭbūʿāt, 1975), 33–34.

3 ʿAbd al-Rahman al-Jabarti, *ʿAjāʾib al-Āthār fī al-Tarājim wal-Akhbār*, vol. 1 (Cairo: Dār al-Kutub al-Miṣriyya, 1998), 41, 606; ʿAbd al-Rahman al-Jabarti, *ʿAjāʾib al-Athār fī al-Tarājim wal-Akhbār*, vol. 2 (Cairo: Dār al-Kutub al-Miṣriyya, 1998), 174; ʿAbd al-Rahman al-Jabarti, *ʿAjāʾib al-Āthār fī al-Tarājim wal-Akhbār*, vol. 3 (Cairo: Dār al-Kutub al-Miṣriyya, 1998), 172, 229; ʿAbd al-Rahman al-Jabarti, *ʿAjāʾib al-Āthār fī al-Tarājim wal-Akhbār*, vol. 4 (Cairo: Dār al-Kutub al-Miṣriyya, 1998), 473.

4 Al-Jabarti, *ʿAjāʾib al-Āthār fī al-Tarājim wal-Akhbār*, 1:607; al-Jabarti, *ʿAjāʾib al-Āthār fī al-Tarājim wal-Akhbār*, 4:41.

5 Al-Jabarti, *ʿAjāʾib al-Āthār fī al-Tarājim wal-Akhbār*, 4:328, 349; Abd al-Rahman Jabarti, *ʿAbd al-Raḥmān al-Jabartī's History of Egypt: ʿAjāʾib al-Āthār fī ʾl-Tarājim Waʾl-Akhbār*, ed. Thomas Philipp and Moshe Perlmann, vol. 5 (Stuttgart: Franz Steiner Verlag, 1994), 349.

6 For the political employment of *ḥurriyya* in al-Jabarti, see al-Jabarti, *ʿAjāʾib al-Āthār fī al-Tarājim wal-Akhbār*, 3:4; al-Jabarti, *ʿAjāʾib al-Āthār fī al-Tarājim wal-Akhbār*, 4:81.

The proclamation that addressed the "Egyptian nation"[7] (*al-umma al-Miṣriyya*) stated that:

> [From the] French [state] that is built on the basis of freedom [*ḥurriyya]* and equality [*taswiyya*] . . . In the eyes of God, all people are equal, except in reason [*ʿaql*], virtue, and sciences [*ʿulūm*]. The Mamluks [the former rulers of Egypt] had neither reason nor virtue, and they have no special features that make them qualified to rule Egypt alone . . . but from now on no Egyptian shall worry about not being able to take part in high positions [of the state].[8]

The major political intention that stood behind this proclamation was to present the French hold on the country in conciliatory terms in order to keep the Egyptian Muslims neutral in the French struggle with the Mamluks. Against the background of this endeavor, the French presented their political principles, and "freedom" was used in association with other words that together comprise interconnected content referring to a variety of categories ranging between sociopolitical (equality), epistemic (reason, science), and collective identity (the Egyptian nation). Freedom combined with equality when indicating the two political principles that underpinned the French regime.

On the sociopolitical level the attempt to convey the French temporal meanings of *liberté*, *égalité*, *nation*, *raison*, and *science* in Arabic was not an easy task. All these words embed rich historical traditions that were acquired during the early modern history of France and Europe. In eighteenth-century Europe equality was diverse and comprised many concepts: the natural equality between individuals (Thomas Hobbes, d. 1679), all men being equal by reason and by rights (John Locke, d. 1704), and equality of economic opportunity (Adam Smith, d. 1790). In the French temporal context, the combination of *liberté* and *égalité* was formulated by Jean-Jacques Rousseau (d. 1778) in his philosophy and probed the question of freedom by emphasizing the economic aspects of equality. Rousseau, who criticized the inequality of the "Ancien Régime" and argued that freedom and equality exist in the natural state, contended that social institutions and customs undermine freedom and equality, and they corrupt human beings. Economic inequality, he argued, threatens individual freedom

[7] Al-Jabarti, *ʿAjāʾib al-Āthār fī al-Tarājim wal-Akhbār*, 3:6; Juan Cole, *Napoleon's Egypt: Invading the Middle East* (New York: Palgrave Macmillan, 2007), 31.

[8] Al-Jabarti, *ʿAjāʾib al-Āthār fī al-Tarājim wal-Akhbār*, 3:4–5.

and subverts the social contract. He associated the reconstruction of natural rights, including freedom and equality, with asserting popular sovereignty.[9]

In France, especially after 1792 (the establishment of the republic), the intimate combination of freedom and equality became rooted in the republican tradition. The quest for freedom evolved against the background of economic inequality, and it was crystallized by consistent attempts to eliminate the privileged social strata of the aristocratic order. The implied meanings of equality and freedom were, therefore, predominantly associated with economic, political, and legal rights that concern the state of both the individual and the collective. All these ideas were part of a comprehensive philosophy that is rooted in the legal and metaphysical theory of natural rights. The French Revolution slogan, "liberty, equality, and fraternity," and the universal Declaration of the Rights of Man and of the Citizen articulated this spirit.[10]

At the end of the eighteenth century, Arabic-speaking scholars found these concepts confusing and sometimes ambiguous. Equality and freedom had different implications in the Arabic-speaking provinces than they did in France. In the Ottoman Empire, religion was the main defining line between groups, both socially and politically. Religious identity received official recognition by the millet system that reproduced the religious sociopolitical bonds and boundaries. The state assimilated these relations by maintaining hierarchic order; the empire was governed by Muslims who maintained the divine religious laws of Islam. The state and the Muslim community emphasized the boundaries between the religious communities by practicing a hierarchic balance between "true" faith and recognized faith of the "people of the book." The concept of law was based on personal religious rather than territorial affiliation; the religious laws of each millet governed many particular, including personal, aspects of life when Islamic norms were dominant. Inequality between Muslims and non-Muslims had many faces, beginning with distinctive clothing, special requirements for repairing and building churches, special taxes, the ineligibility to

[9] Gregory Streich, "Equality," *New Dictionary of the History of Ideas* (Detroit, MI: Charles Scribner's Sons, 2005), 694–708; Shogimen, "Liberty," 1273–1275.

[10] Streich, "Equality," 694–708; Shogimen, "Liberty," 1273–1275.

serve in the armed forces, and difficulties in rising to high administrative posts. In the beginning of the nineteenth century, the concept of equality before the law and the concept of citizenship that combines equal rights and duties were not part of the Ottoman norm.[11]

The reception of these ideas was formulated against this particular background. Al-Jabarti, who systematically refuted the content of the French proclamation, commented on the assumption that "all people are equal" as follows: "This is a lie, ignorance and fatuity. How could that be right when God favored [certain] people over others."[12] Another chronicler, Haydar al-Shihabi (d. 1835), the ruler of the region of Shuf in Lebanon, quoted the formal Ottoman reaction from 1799 that in the same spirit attacked the faulty French assumptions that "all humans are equal in humanity and participate in the same mankind." The French, it was said, founded their principles on this basis and destroyed the laws of all religions.[13] Similar responses were evident among Turkish chroniclers.[14]

The primary Muslim reaction to these ideas reflects a different interpretation of the concepts, which was distinct from that of the French. Despite the fact that "equality" was presented by the French in the same phrase as "freedom," the response of Muslim scholars did not preserve this combination; while the idea of equality was perceived as a challenge and therefore attracted a reaction, freedom apparently did not. A partial explanation for these nuances in the function of freedom in the French and Arabic Islamic discourses can be found in the temporal notion of governance. In the Ottoman Empire the Muslim *umma* (community) provided a theological framework that formulated the relations between the ruler and the ruled. The ruler was to be obeyed if he maintained the laws of religion, even if he was a tyrant. The Ottoman sultans commanded full submission of their subjects. This

11 Roderic Davison, *Essays in Ottoman and Turkish History, 1774–1923: The Impact of the West* (Austin: University of Texas Press, 1990), 112–113; Moshe Maoz, *Ottoman Reform in Syria and Palestine, 1840–1861: The Impact of the Tanzimat on Politics and Society* (Oxford: Clarendon Press, 1968), 189–199.

12 'Abd al-Rahman al-Jabarti, *Maẓhar al-Taqdīs bi-Zawāl Dawlat al-Faransīs* (Cairo: Dār al-Kutub al-Miṣriyya, 1998), 27–28.

13 Haydar al-Shihabi, *Qiṣat Aḥmad Bāsha al-Jazzār Bayna Miṣr wal-Shām wa-Ḥawādithuhu Ma' Nābulyūn Būnābart* (Cairo: Maktabat Madbūlī, 2008), 144, 146.

14 For the response in Turkish, see Lewis, *The Emergence of Modern Turkey*, 64–72.

pattern of relations between ruler and ruled existed even in places that had, for periods of time, succeeded in revolting against the Ottomans and achieved autonomy.[15]

This context forms al-Jabarti's response and sheds some light on the marginality of using the word freedom. As part of his refutation, al-Jabarti presents three modes of seizing governance that were known to him: first, when it is acquired by inheritance from masters, as in Mamluk Egypt; second, when it is transferred from ancestors; and third, when it is obtained by suppression and subjugation (*al-ghalaba wal-qahrr*).[16] All these measures can be categorized as autocracy, in which the sovereignty is concentrated in the hands of one person. This definition was preserved in the temporal Arabic vocabulary, which used three common words that designate modes of governance: *sulṭān* (literally meaning sovereign), *malik* (king), and *amīr* (often used to designate army officers, though in places like Mount Lebanon it was used to refer to the local ruler). Arabic-speaking scholars who were familiar with this relatively simple order were challenged, in their encounter with the French, by different principles of governance. Republicanism, in relation to the familiar temporal models of governance, comprised more sophisticated and ambiguous political principles than the familiar temporal models of governance.[17]

The infrequent use of *ḥurriyya* in political discourse among Muslim scholars was emphasized in the illuminating account of ʿAbd Allah al-Sharqawi, the shaykh of al-Azhar at the time of the French expedition. Al-Sharqawi composed a chronicle around 1799 that recounts the history of Egypt. There he conveyed his perception of the French political and social norms:

> And the truth is that the French who arrived to Egypt are a group of permissive naturalist [*ṭabāʾiʿiyya*] philosophers [*falāsifa*], of whom it had been said that they are allegedly Christians who follow ʿIssa [Jesus] and reject the resurrection, heaven, and the prophecies of the prophets and the messengers. They believe in one God through logical explanation, and they employ reason to choose among them legislators to enact rules based upon reason,

[15] Ayalon, *Language and Change in the Arab Middle East: The Evolution of Modern Political Discourse*, 29–42.

[16] Al-Jabarti, *Maẓhar al-Taqdīs bi-Zawāl Dawlat al-Faransīs*, 28.

[17] Ami Ayalon extensively discussed the use of Arabic words referring to political authority. See Ayalon, *Language and Change in the Arab Middle East: The Evolution of Modern Political Discourse*, 29–42.

which they call laws [*sharā'i'*]. They believe that the prophets, Muhammad, 'Issa, and Musa [Moses], were a group of wise men [*'uqalā'*], and they established their [religious] laws by their reason to fit their own time. That is why [the French] use their reason to establish in Cairo and in Egypt's important villages councils that administrate that which suits the people's needs, and that was merciful on the Egyptian people.[18]

In his account he made a connection between religion, law, and political institutions that all have distinctive mechanisms among the French. To refer to French political principles, he switched from freedom and equality – the previously used signifiers of the French political principles – to *'aql* (reason). Furthermore, all Muslim chroniclers who wrote about the French presence in Egypt observed that French norms in politics and society were based on *'aql*.[19]

Reason, rather than freedom and equality, conveyed for contemporary Muslim scholars a familiar political meaning: On the one hand, reason indicated a stable content that was not necessarily ambiguous, and on the other hand, it had a rich history in the various Islamic traditions. Islamic history had been witness to many connotations of the concept of reason, which had been conceptualized according to particular traditions: as natural human knowledge in Islamic theology, as reason in philosophy, as God's first creation in Neoplatonism, and as a source for shari'a in jurisprudence.[20] The Arabic Muslim sources of the seventeenth and eighteenth centuries comprise all these notions.[21]

18 'Abd Allah al-Sharqawi, *Tuḥfat al-Nāẓirīn fī-man Waliya Miṣr min al-Mulūk wal-Salāṭīn* (Cairo: Maktabat Madbūlī, 1996), 122.

19 In al-Jabarti's words, the French are a "group that rule by reason and do not affiliate with any religion." The formal Ottoman response posits a similar approach, contending that the French creed is worldly (*dahr*) and does not affiliate with any religion. See al-Jabarti, *'Ajā'ib al-Āthār fī al-Tarājim wal-Akhbār*, 3:191; al-Jabarti, *Maẓhar al-Taqdīs bi-Zawāl Dawlat al-Faransīs*, 27–28; al-Shihabi, *Qiṣat Aḥmad Bāsha al-Jazzār Bayna Miṣr wal-Shām wa-Ḥawādithuhu Ma' Nābulyūn Būnābart*, 143, 146; al-Sharqawi, *Tuḥfat al-Nāẓirīn fī-man Waliya Miṣr min al-Mulūk wal-Salāṭīn*, 122.

20 For more details, see John L. Esposito, ed., "Aql," *The Oxford Dictionary of Islam* (Oxford: Oxford University Press, 2003), 22; Fazlur Rahman, "'Akl," *The Encyclopedia of Islam* (Leiden: E. J. Brill, 1986), 341.

21 The eighteenth-century Muslim Indian scholars Muhammad 'Ali al-Tahanawi and 'Abd al-Nabi bin 'Abd al-Rasul al-Ahmadnakri devoted an entry to *'aql* in their lexical works. Both indicated the hierarchy of separate intelligence (*'uqūl mufariqa*) as demonstrated in Neoplatonism (often divided into ten forms of *'aql*). Seventeenth-century scholar Abi al-Baqa' Ayub bin Musa al-Kafawi, who was born in Crimea and worked as a qadi in Istanbul and Jerusalem, also

The temporal meaning of reason in this context was interpreted by Muslim scholars in the beginning of the nineteenth century as innovation that is contrasted with transmission (*naql*) or religious prophecies.[22] The meaning of *'aql* was illuminated by ascribing it to *falsafa* (philosophy), which was perceived by Muslim contemporaries as a field of knowledge that was distinct from and competing with religious science. In this sense the word *'aql* is equivalent to *fiṭra* or *ṭabīʿa*, as a natural and independent way of knowing, distinct from the authority of religious revelation (hence depicting the French as naturalists, *ṭabāʾiʿiyya*).[23] *'Aql* signifies the epistemic realm, which exceeds the temporal horizons of Islamic legal theory. It is worth noting that in the French proclamation quoted above, *'aql* was used as a signifier for political legitimacy: The Mamluks lacked reason, science, and virtues (*'qal*, *'ilm*, *faḍāʾil*), and therefore they were not eligible to rule Egypt alone. In this sense reason was acknowledged by French and Muslims alike as a comprehensive leading principle that formulates norms of governance and society.

The reception of the sociopolitical use of freedom and equality among Christian scholars, as compared to that among Muslim scholars, had rather different implications and evoked much loaded content. From the perspective of the chronicler Niqula al-Turk (d. 1828), court

dedicated an entry to *'aql* in his philosophical lexicon. There he illuminates the different conceptions of *'aql* of Hanafi, Ashʿari, Muʿtazila, Sufi, and other perceptions derived from Greek philosophy and Neoplatonism. See Abi al-Baqa' Ayyub ibn Musa Kaffawi, "al-ʿAql," *al-Kulliyāt: Muʿjam fī al-Muṣṭalaḥāt wal-Furūq al-Lughawiyya* (Beirut: Muʾassasat al-Risāla, 1998), 617–619; Muhammad ʿAli al-Tahanawi, "ʿAql," *Kashshāf Iṣṭilāḥāt al-Funūn wal-ʿUlūm* (Beirut: Nāshirūn, 1996), 1194–1202; ʿAbd al-Nabi bin ʿAbd al-Rasul Ahmadnakri, "ʿAql," *Jāmiʿ al-ʿUlūm fī Iṣṭilāḥāt al-Funūn al-Mulaqqab bi-Dustūr al-ʿUlamāʾ* (Beirut: Muʾassasat al-Aʿlamī lil-Maṭbūʿāt, 1975), 327–332.

22 It is important to note that the construction of the two categories *'aql* and *naql* is not modern, and their political connotations are evident in medieval works. Ibn Khaldun (1332–1406) presents two patterns of governance in his work: administering the state by rational politics (*siyāsa 'aqliyya*) and managing the state by using religious law (*siyāsa sharʿiyya*). For temporal use of *'aql* as contrasted to *naql*, see al-Jabarti, *Maẓhar al-Taqdīs bi-Zawāl Dawlat al-Faransīs*, 28; ʿAbd al-Rahman Ibn Khaldun, *Muqaddimat al-ʿAllāma Ibn Khaldūn al-Musamma Dīwān al-Mubtadaʾ wal-Khabarr fī Taʾrīkh al-ʿArab wal-Barbar wa-man ʿĀṣarahum min Dhawī al-Shaʾn al-Akbarr* (Beirut: Dār al-Fikr, 2004), 203–204.

23 Rahman, "ʿAkl," 341.

poet of Bashir II of Lebanon,[24] freedom and equality have relevant functions. In his account of the French expedition,[25] he indicated that the French gave "freedom to the rest of the [non-Muslim] subjects,"[26] implying freedom of worship. This notion of freedom was evident among the Arabic-speaking Christians prior to the French expedition, especially among the followers of the Eastern churches that had united with Rome.[27] Al-Turk, who was Greek Catholic, belonged to a church that was not formally recognized as part of the millet system until the beginning of the nineteenth century. Compared to the Orthodox community, the Greek Catholic community that was established in the first half of the eighteenth century faced vast difficulties in practicing their faith and in building churches. In this context freedom implied collective emancipation from social and legal constraints.[28]

[24] Niqula al-Turk was dispatched by his master to Egypt to inform him about developments after the French invasion. Al-Turk spent most of his time in Damietta where he collected his stories and materials for his chronicle (the first Arabic edition was printed in Paris in 1839). He stayed in Egypt until the French withdrawal. For additional details about Niqula al-Turk's biography and his social and political influence in the court of Bashir II, see George M. Haddad, "The Historical Work of Niqula El-Turk 1763–1828," *Journal of the American Oriental Society* 81, no. 3 (1961): 247–251; Fruma Zachs, *The Making of a Syrian Identity: Intellectuals and Merchants in Nineteenth Century Beirut* (Leiden: Brill, 2005), 31–32.

[25] Al-Turk and Mikha'il al-Sabbagh (d. 1816), a Christian scholar who was born in Acre and left Egypt with the French evacuation, glorified Bonaparte in their poems. Additionally, al-Turk composed a special poem lamenting the assassination of Kleber. See Mikha'il al-Sabbagh, *Nashīd Qaṣīdat Tahāni li-Sa'ādat al-Qayṣar al-Mu'aẓam Nabūlyūn Sulṭān Faransā fī Mauwlid Bikrihi Sa'ādat Malik Rummiyya Nabūlyūn al-Thānī* (Paris: Dār al-Maṭba'a al-Ṣulṭāniyya, 1811); Niqula al-Turk, *Dhikr Tamalluk Jumhūr al-Faransāwiyya al-Aqṭār al-Miṣriyya wal-Bilād al-Shāmiyya, aw, al-Ḥamla al-Faransiyya 'ala Miṣr wal-Shām* (Beirut: Dār al-Fārābī, 1990), 167–169; Yusuf Ilyan Sarkis, *Mu'jam al-Maṭbū'āt al-'Arabiyya wal-Mu'arraba* (Cairo: Āyyāt Allah al-'Uẓma, 1928), 660–661.

[26] See al-Turk, *Dhikr Tamalluk Jumhūr al-Faransāwiyya al-Aqṭār al-Miṣriyya wal-Bilād al-Shāmiyya, aw, al-Ḥamla al-Faransiyya 'ala Miṣr wal-Shām*, 63.

[27] A few decades before the French expedition, the Damascene priest Mikha'il Burayk wrote about having the freedom to practice the Catholic faith in Greater Syria (*ḥurriyyat 'īmānina al-kāthūlīki*). See Mikha'il Burayk, *Wathā'iq Tārīkhiyya lil-Kursī al-Malakī al-Anṭākī* (Harisa: Maṭba'at al-Qiddīss Būluṣ, 1930), 133.

[28] The common phrase that was used in that sense was *iṭlāq al-ḥurriyya lil-naṣāra. See* the works of three Catholic chroniclers who composed their works between the end of the eighteenth century and the first half of the nineteenth century: ibid.; al-Turk, *Dhikr Tamalluk Jumhūr al-Faransāwiyya al-Aqṭār*

Despite this early connotation of freedom, al-Turk's employment of the term has an innovative layer: In his work the word is used in not only social or legal but also political contexts. In his account he elaborates the French request of the Egyptians: "According to [the principle of] freedom, the rule should be given to wise men from all [Egyptian] subjects, because in the eyes of God, all people are equal, and God only favored people by reason [*'aql*] and intention."[29] Freedom is closely associated with the ideals of the French Revolution; it is one of the consequences of equality and reason. Freedom in that sense broke the hierarchic balance of society and moved it toward a conception of equality between all subjects, with no regard to their religious identity. Although al-Turk presented his note as an explanation of French policy, his words marks an early sign of the evolvement of the modern political concept.

The reception of "freedom" reveals the differences its impact had on Ottoman socioreligious groups. In the political and social context of the Ottoman Empire, *ḥurriyya* generated different reactions: For the privileged Muslim scholars, equality attracted reaction because it was conceived as a quest to deprive the Muslim population of their social, political, and legal superiority, while for Christian scholars, freedom was conceived as a procedural method for social and normative change whose outcome should bear equal opportunities for all inhabitants. Among all Arabic-speaking scholars, the French political order was conceived of as a consequence of deist rationalism.

Among these political concepts, reason was the most dominant. This word underwent extreme semantic inflation by a variety of vocabularies that marked the scope of its practice in the spiritual, political, and social spheres. In the temporal context the concept of reason not only unearthed a transition toward the center of controversy, reimposed as a challenge to conventional faith, but also became extremely refined and appeared as distinct, comprehensive, and autonomous. The intensified shift toward antithetical interaction between *'aql* and *naql* by the

*al-Miṣriyya wal-Bilād al-Shāmiyya, aw, al-Ḥamla al-Faransiyya 'ala Miṣr wal-Shām*, 63; Tanus al-Shidyaq, *Kitāb Akhbār al-A'yān fī Jabal Lubnān*, vol. 1 (Beirut: Al-Maktaba al-Sharqiyya, 1970), 100; Tanus al-Shidyaq, *Kitāb Akhbār al-A'yān fī Jabal Lubnān*, vol. 2 (Beirut: Al-Maktaba al-Sharqiyya, 1970), 478.

29 See al-Turk, *Dhikr Tamalluk Jumhūr al-Faransāwiyya al-Aqṭār al-Miṣriyya wal-Bilād al-Shāmiyya, aw, al-Ḥamla al-Faransiyya 'ala Miṣr wal-Shām*, 29.

beginning of the nineteenth century was unprecedented and was manifested by the challenge to mark the borderline between the worldly and the spiritual spheres (this transition had a vast impact on the concept of politics, as detailed in the following chapters). The practice of reason that extensively conflated with *naql* was indicated in the temporal language by different signifiers that all indicate the nature and scope of its practice. The words used can be classified in two categories, the first of which indicates an antireligious attitude and includes the use of medieval words such as *ṭabāʾiʿiyya* (naturalists) and *dahriyya* or *dunyawiyya* (worldly). The temporal implied meanings of all these words indicate materialist sects that hold an actual creed or doctrine that was perceived as contrasting with Islam as a faith and a source of legislation.[30] In addition, in reference to the French creed, the practice of reason was often presented as attached to *ʿilm* (science), implying a shift from the medieval designations of *ṭabāʾiʿiyya*, *dahriyya*, or *dunyawiyya* to a new layer that marked the influence of modern natural sciences on the conception of reason.[31]

[30] As aforementioned, all the Arabic-speaking chroniclers used these words to refer to the French creed. In the eighteenth-century lexicon, *ṭabāʾiʿiyya* means a religious group that believes in the four elements of nature – heat, cold, wetness, and dryness – which are the origins of being (naturalism). *Dahrriyya* is equivalent to earthly and means "atheists" or "group of infidels that believe in the eternity of the world," as opposed to those who believe in the creation (see also *Tāj al-ʿArūs*). In the seventeenth-century lexicon *al-Kuliyyāt*, *duhrī* is the word equivalent to God (as in the *ḥadīth*: do not curse *dahr* because *dahr* is God), but this meaning does not apply to the current text. In his formal response, Sultan Selim III used, in his interpretation of the French creed, the words *ṭabīʿa* and *dahr/dahriyyūn* (nature or world) as contrasted to the monotheistic belief in a judgment day or life after death. See Muhammad ʿAli al-Tahanawi, "al-Tabiʿi," *Kashshāf Iṣṭilāḥāt al-Funūn wal-ʿUlūm* (Beirut: Nāshirūn, 1996), 1130; Muhammad ʿAli al-Tahanawi, "al-Dahriyya," *Kashshāf Iṣṭilāḥāt al-Funūn wal-ʿUlūm* (Beirut: Nāshirūn, 1996), 800; ʿAbd al-Nabi bin ʿAbd al-Rasul Ahmadnakri, "al-Dahrī," *Jāmiʿ al-ʿUlūm fī Iṣṭilāḥāt al-Funūn al-Mulaqqab bi-Dustūr al-ʿUlamāʾ* (Beirut: Muʾassasat al-Aʿlamī lil-Maṭbūʿāt, 1975), 118; Abi al-Baqaʾ Ayyub ibn Musa Kaffawi, "al-Duhri," *al-Kulliyāt: Muʿjam fī al-Muṣṭalaḥāt wal-Furūq al-Lughawiyya* (Beirut: Muʾassasat al-Risāla, 1998), 446; Muhammad Murtada al-Husayni al-Zubaydi, "D.h.r (al-Dahrī)," *Tāj al-ʿArūs min Jawāhir al-Qāmūs* (Kuwait: Maṭbaʿat Ḥukūmat al-Kūwayt, 1972), 349; al-Shihabi, *Qiṣat Aḥmad Bāsha al-Jazzār Bayna Miṣr wal-Shām wa-Ḥawādithuhu Maʿ Nābulyūn Būnābart*, 143–151.

[31] For further details on the variety of ways in which *dahriyya* was employed in the history of Arabic language, see Ignác Goldziher and Amélie Marie Goichon, "Dahriyya," *The Encyclopedia of Islam* (Leiden: E. J. Brill, 1965), 95–97.

The second category comprises words that were employed about a decade after the French evacuation of Egypt. The same political territory was indicated by the word *ʿalmānī* or *ʿalmāniyya* (secular, secularity). The word *ʿalmānī*, which was confined to Christian medieval sources, embeds a meaning that is synonymous with the Latin *saeculum*. Prior to nineteenth-century Arabic, the word derived from the word "world" (*ʿālam*, which is synonymous with *seculum* in Latin),[32] and it connoted common people or people who are not in a monastic order.[33] In the second decade of the nineteenth century, the French word *laïque* was rendered as *ʿalmānī*,[34] *sécularité* as *ʿalmāniyya*, and *sécularisation* as *tashlīḥ*.[35] Although the word *ʿalmānī* was not used in a political context, its rendition from French marked its transition

[32] In the seventeenth-century Latin-Arabic dictionaries, the Latin *seculum* is rendered as *ʿālam* (world). See Franciscus Raphelengius, "ʿAlam," *Lexicon Arabicum* (Leiden: Ex Officina Auctoris, 1613), 305; Jacobus Golius, "ʿAlam," *Lexicon Arabico-Latinum* (Lugduni Batavorum: typis Bonaventurae and Abrahami, Elseviriorum, prostant Amstelodami apud Johannem Ravesteynivm, 1653), 1639.

[33] For sources employing this word, see (listed below) the two tenth-century sources of the Coptic cleric Sawirus Ibn al-Muqaffaʿ; the thirteenth-century Coptic poet al-Asʿad Ibn ʿAsal (quoted in Lewis Shikhu's collection); the eighteenth-century cleric Mikhaʾil Burayk; and Francisco Cañes's eighteenth-century Latin-Arabic dictionary. In the ecclesiastical context, "secular ecclesiastical clerics" (*iklīriyūs ʿalmānī, al-iklīriyūs al-dunyawiyyīn*) means clerics who are not members of monastic orders (see the book on Martin Luther and the letter sent by the Greek Catholic patriarch Maksimus Mazlum in 1847 to his ecclesiastical community). The nonpolitical use of the word survived into the twentieth century in internal ecclesiastical writings. In the Coptic church, the word is frequently used to distinguish between married priests (*qissīs ʿalmānī*) and virgin or monastic priests. See Sawirus ibn al-Muqaffaʿ, *Tārīkh Baṭārikat al-Kanīsa al-Miṣriyya*, vol. 2 (Cairo: Jamʿiyyat al-Āthār al-Miṣriyya, 1943), 67–68; Sawirus ibn al-Muqaffaʿ, *The Lamp of the Intellect of Severus Ibn al-Muqaffaʿ* (Louvain: Secrétariat du CorpusSCO, 1975), 22; Louis Cheikho, *Kitāb Shuʿarāʾ al-Naṣrāniyya Baʿda al-Islām: Shuʿarāʾ al-Dawla al-ʿAbbāsiyya*, vol. 3 (Beirut: Maṭbaʿat al-Ābāʾ al-Yasūʿiyyīn, 1926), 362; Burayk, *Wathāʾiq Tārīkhiyya lil-Kursī al-Malakī al-Anṭākī*, 128–129; Francisco Cañes, "Secular," *Diccionario Español-Latino-Arabigo* (Madrid: Impr. de A. Sancha, 1787), 353; *Qiṣat Martin Luthir* (Falta, 1840), 10; Maksimus Mazlum, *Nabdha Tārīkhiyya: fīmā Jara li-Ṭāʾifat al-Rūm al-Kāthūlīk Mundhu Sant 1837 Famā Baʿdahā*, ed. Qustantin al-Basha (n.p.: 1907), 93, 137–142.

[34] Ellious Bocthor, "Laïque," *Dictionnaire Français-Arabe* (Paris: Chez Firmin Didot Freres, 1829), 3.

[35] Ellious Bocthor, "Sécularité and Sécularisation," *Dictionnaire Français-Arabe* (Paris: Chez Firmin Didot Freres, 1829), 310.

toward politicization. The word *tashlīḥ*, on the other hand, presented a rare use that aimed to capture a political and modern phenomenon. This word, which literally meant "takeover," presented a loose attempt to capture the process of secularization, which involves increasing state control of domains usually controlled by religious institutions. The first documented use of "secularization" in a European context took place in 1648 after the Thirty Years' War (ending with the peace of Westphalia) indicating the transferal of church lands to the state.[36] The Arabic word, on the other hand, was coined in the second decade of the nineteenth century, which witnessed policies of secularization in the Ottoman provinces. Muhammad ʿAli, who took control of Egypt in 1805, implemented policies between 1809 and 1814 aimed at weakening the social status of the ʿulama and seizing their economic power by levying taxes on their income from the charitable religious trusts' properties (*waqf*, *rizq*, *ahbasiyya*).[37] Similar policies were later executed in the field of education, where establishing the state schools broke the monopoly of al-Azhar and other religious establishments over education. As far as I can determine, the political connotations of *tashlīḥ* and *ʿalmani* appeared only in the lexicons. Additionally, though *tashlīh* did not survive, its coinage marked an attempt to capture new political meaning.

Although both of these categories put emphasis on matters of this world, rather than the next, both included distinctive aspects. Unlike *ṭabāʾiʿī* and *dahrī*, the meaning of *ʿalmānī* was not burdened with negative connotations regarding the conventional perception of religion;[38] the word indicated a category that was distinct from the cleric or monastic. The word, which was not frequently used during the nineteenth century, apparently continued to be confined to Christian

[36] R. Keddie Nikki, "Secularization and Secularism," *New Dictionary of the History of Ideas* (New York: Charles Scribner's Sons, 2005), 2194.

[37] Vatikiotis, *The Modern History of Egypt*, 57–58.

[38] In addition to the medieval social language of Eastern Christians, it is worth noting that the language of heterodox groups in Islam, such as the Druze and the ʿAlawites, conceptualized social reality in similar terms that make clear the distinction between two categories: those who engaged in religious truth and the common and ignorant people (*ʿuqāl/juhāl* and *khāṣa/ʿāma*). This distinction – which could be found also among Sufis – was not valid for the social language of the Orthodox Sunni Muslim, where *khaṣa/ʿāma* does not necessarily imply categories based on religious knowledge.

circles.[39] A comparison between the Arabic words employed by Muslim scholars to depict the phenomenon of secularity and their translation into Latin languages reveals this same difference of perception between the two categories; the seventeenth- and eighteenth-century dictionaries rendered the Arabic *ṭabīʿiyyīn* as humanist and naturalist (*humanista* and *naturalista*)[40] and *dahrī* as eternal (*aeternus*)[41] or impious (Latin *impius*).[42] Unlike "secular," all these renditions comprise negative connotations toward the monotheistic faiths. A few years after the French evacuation, additional signifiers, *siyāsa* and *madanī* – a temporary, rare word in contemporary sources – would be recruited from medieval philosophy to compete in marking this same territory, as will be detailed in the following chapters.[43]

The increasing authority of reason and the emphasis on the priority of worldly considerations had a deep impact on social norms during the French rule of Egypt. Niqula al-Turk's expression "according to [the

[39] The word appeared again in 1860s in the dictionary of the prominent Syrian Christian scholar Butrus al-Busani and was apparently frequent (as *ʿilmānī*) in the colloquial Arabic of Egypt. See Butrus al-Bustani, "ʿAlmānī," *Muḥīṭ al-Muḥīṭ* (Beirut: Maktabat Lubnān, 1998), 628; Socrates Spiro, "Secular," *An English Arabic Vocabulary of the Modern and Colloquial Arabic of Egypt* (Cairo: Al-Muqaṭṭam Printing Office, 1905), 465.

[40] Francisco Cañes, "Humanista, Naturalista," *Gramatica Arabigo-Española, Vulgar, Y Literal: Con Un Diccionario Arabigo-Español, En Que Se Ponen Las Voces Mas Usuales Para Una Conversacion Familiar, Con El Texto de La Doctrina Cristiana En El Idioma Arabigo* (Madrid: En la imprenta de don Antonio Perez de Soto, 1775), 218.

[41] Franciscus Raphelengius, "Dahrī," *Lexicon Arabicum* (Leiden: Ex Officina Auctoris, 1613), 165.

[42] Jacobus Golius, "Dahrī," *Lexicon Arabico-Latinum* (Lugduni Batavorum: typis Bonaventurae and Abrahami, Elseviriorum, prostant Amstelodami apud Johannem Ravesteynivm, 1653), 875.

[43] Ellious Bocthor, an Egyptian, uses *madanī* as equivalent to the French *citadin* (inhabitant of a city, bourgeois) but not *citoyen* (citizen), emphasizing the temporal, frequently nonpolitical use of the Arabic word. He renders *citoyen* as *baladī* (inhabitants of an actual city). Another contemporary, Rufa'il Zakhur, renders the Italian *civile* as equivalent to the inhabitants of a polity or city (*madanī, min ahl al-madanī wal-mudun*), and *madanī* as *cittadino* (urban, citizen), which implied usage that was close to the medieval political word. For further details about the medieval use of *madanī*, see footnote number 58 and chapter 2 in this volume. Ellious Bocthor, "Citadin, Citoyen," *Dictionnaire Français-Arabe* (Paris: Chez Firmin Didot Freres, 1828), 158; Rufa'il Zakhur, "Civile, Civile, Cittadino," *Dizionario Italiano E Arabo* (Bolacco: Dalla Stamperia Reale, 1822), 54.

principle of] freedom"[44] did not merely have an impact on the political conception of the term, but it also had profound repercussions forsocial norms.[45] Among the documented cases, contemporary accounts record the following: mixing of sexes in public in al-Azbakiyya Park, the involvement of women in public life, taking off the *ḥijāb* and dressing in French style, and Egyptian women imitating their French counterparts by seeking pleasures such as public drinking, dancing, and laughing. Furthermore, al-Jabarti indicates that Napoleon encouraged intermarriage between French soldiers and notable Egyptian women so as to present the French as being close to the Muslim population. Some of these women, he indicates, converted to Christianity. The most prominent exposure occurred through the governing of Muslims by a non-Muslim authority. Al-Jabarti, who referred to the French as *dahriyya*, ascribed their "infidel" and "obscene" acts to their corrupted morality.[46] He assesses the French hold over Egypt primarily from the moral and normative point of view, stating that they encourage neglecting Islamic norms by giving priority to worldly considerations.[47]

It was not a lack of information or state of ignorance that formulated the outlook of al-Jabarti, al-Sharqawi, and Isma'il al-Khashab

44 See al-Turk, *Dhikr Tamalluk Jumhūr al-Faransāwiyya al-Aqṭār al-Miṣriyya wal-Bilād al-Shāmiyya, aw, al-Ḥamla al-Faransiyya 'ala Miṣr wal-Shām*, 29.

45 As with *ṭabā'i'iyya* and *dahriyya*, the word *ḥurriyya* also displays aspects of infidelity to religion. These intertwined relations were indicated in sources prior to the nineteenth century. Al-Tahanawi's eighteenth-century entry on "freedom" indicates that one of the aspects of freedom was associated with atheism: "Atheists say that when the believer acquires freedom [*ḥurriyya*] he will no longer be obligated to God." See Muhammad 'Ali al-Tahanawi, "Ḥurr," *Kashshāf Iṣṭilāḥāt al-Funūn wal-'Ulūm* (Beirut: Nāshirūn, 1996), 641.

46 Al-Jabarti mentions that when the Ottomans restored their rule in Egypt, the women who were with the French company returned to wearing the *ḥijāb* and to behaving according to Islamic norms. See also Niqula al-Turk's account of public drinking and cases of marriage between French soldiers and Muslim women: Al-Jabarti, *'Ajā'ib al-Āthār fī al-Tarājim wal-Akhbār*, 1998, 3:132–133, 262–263, 310; al-Turk, *Dhikr Tamalluk Jumhūr al-Faransāwiyya al-Aqṭār al-Miṣriyya wal-Bilād al-Shāmiyya, aw, al-Ḥamla al-Faransiyya 'ala Miṣr wal-Shām*, 131–132, 161; Lewis Kalivaris, *Kitāb Sirat al-Mu'aẓam al-Murafa' al-Kabır Nabulyūn al-Awwal Imbaratūr al-Farānsawiyya* (Paris: 1855), 563; Vatikiotis, *The Modern History of Egypt*, 52.

47 See al-Jabarti's critical comments regarding French encouragement of celebrating the popular tradition of the *Mūlid* (celebration of saints) by Muslims in Egypt: Al-Jabarti, *'Ajā'ib al-Āthār fī al-Tarājim wal-Akhbār*, 1998, 3:138.

(d. 1815) – who filled the position of archivist in the administrative council (*dīwān*) that the French established in Egypt – on ideas such as "reason," "equality," and "secularity." During their service in the administrative council, all these prominent Muslim scholars were deeply engaged in intensive relations with the French, and they became acquainted with French political and social culture. Despite the interaction, their critical attitude was not much different from that of their other Muslim counterparts, such as Mustafa al-Safawi al-Qalawi (d. 1815) and 'Abd al-Salam al-Mardini (d. 1843), who wrote from relatively distant positions.[48]

In addition to the normative dissonance, there is room to question the universal statement of "freedom and equality" as presented by the French. In addition to French propaganda, their policies in governing Egypt did not present a substantive difference from other rulers; the French generally maintained the common political and social norms with no real attempt at implementing alternative or revolutionary models. This orientation was outlined by Napoleon himself before his soldiers set foot on Egyptian soil.[49] In one of his talks, he articulated his future policy in Egypt:

> My policy is to govern men as the majority wish to be governed. That is, I believe, the best way to recognize the sovereignty of the people. It was by making myself a Catholic that I ended the war in Vendee, by making myself a Muslim that I established myself in Egypt, and by making myself an Ultramontanist that I won the hearts of the Italians. If I had to govern a Jewish people, I would rebuild the temple of Solomon.[50]

[48] Mustafa al-Safawi al-Qalawi, *Ṣafwat al-Zamān fī man Tawalla 'ala Miṣr min Amīr wa-Sulṭān* (Alexandria: Dār al-Ma'rifa al-Jāmi'iyya, 2006); Muhammad Kafafi, "al-Ḥamla al-Faransiyya 'ala Miṣr fī Riwayat Aḥad al-Mu'āṣirīn," in *Ila Ṭaha Ḥusayn fī 'Īd Mīlādihi al-Sab'īn: Dirāsāt Muhdā min Aṣdiqā'ihi wa-Talāmīdhihi*, ed. 'Abd al-Rahman Badawi (Cairo: Dār al-Ma'ārif, 1962), 369–396; Isma'il al-Khashab, *Khulāṣat mā Yurād min Akhbār al-Amīr Murād* (Cairo: Dār al-'Arabī lil-Nashr wal-Tawzī', 1992), 42–45; Isma'il al-Khashab, *Akhbār Ahl al-Qarn al-Thāni 'Ashar: Ta'rīkh al-Mamālīk fī al-Qāhira* (Cairo: Al-Nāshir al-'Arabī, 1990).

[49] See Napoleon's proclamation during his voyageto Egypt in which he ordered his men to respect both Egypt's social traditions and Islam. Kalivaris, *Kitāb Sirat al-Mu'aẓam al-Murafa' al-Kabīr Nabulyūn al-Awwal Imbaratūr al-Farānsawiyya*, 106–107.

[50] Ian Coller, *Arab France: Islam and the Making of Modern Europe, 1798–1831* (Berkeley: University of California Press, 2011), 31.

France had captured Egypt after its revolution was over. During these years Napoleon began to fortify his despotic position, striving to establish an empire. In the beginning of the nineteenth century, France witnessed the Concordat with the Vatican (July 1801), which returned the church to its central function, the reestablishment of slavery (1802) in its colonies, and the establishment of a hereditary empire (1804). All these were signs of the restoration of the French "Ancien Régime" and the temporary retreat from the ideals of the revolution.[51]

In Egypt the French generally maintained the existing religious legal code with the addition that any legal issue between Muslims and the French would be subject to French rather than Muslim courts.[52] In the discussions of the administrative council between November 3, 1800, and July 6, 1801, the French did not make any effort to display their revolutionary ideas. Furthermore, the discourse dominating these discussions sustained the conventional norms; a request that was written by the members of the *dīwān* addressed Bonaparte as "chosen by God" to govern the French state and Egypt.[53] In subsequent translations of proclamations, the French concept of political equality between rich and poor was depicted as a part of Islamic justice (*'adl*, *inṣāf*, *murū'a*), while the state's discrimination was translated as *ẓulm* (unjustice). The *dīwān* was presented as a result of French mercy (*raḥma*) on the poor Egyptian population rather than a representative institution that is derived from the concept of sovereignty or civil rights.[54] In the same documents, the word *ḥurriyya* was used only twice as part of the formal French proclamations.[55] Correspondingly, the language of freedom was insignificant in the interior discussions of the council. Instead these discussions demonstrated Napoleon's policy and manifested how the French adapted their language to the conservative local norms.[56] Presenting Napoleon (or 'Ali, his adopted Egyptian name) Bonaparte as a Muslim leader, declaring his (supposed) attempt to adopt Islam (only in his proclamation in Arabic, not in French), dressing in Islamic style, and encouraging his officers to marry

[51] Ibid., 48, 65.

[52] For a translation of a French proclamation in this subject, see Isma'il al-Khashab, *al-Tārīkh al-Musalsal fī Ḥawādith al-Zamān wa-Waqāyi' al-Dīwān, 1800–1801* (Cairo: Al-Ma'had al-'Ilmī al-Faransī lil-Āthār al-Sharqiyya, 2003), 83–84.

[53] Ibid., 18. [54] Ibid., 29–31, 47, 50, 60, 65, 72. [55] See ibid., 29, 66.

[56] For the intensive Islamic rhetoric in the formal French proclamations, see two contemporary translations to Arabic: ibid., 27–32, 63–66.

Muslims, signified the inclusive orientation of France that initially aimed to gain legitimacy for its rule in Egypt.[57]

Despite the formal pragmatism, the cultural encounter generated new political words, offshoots of which evolved around the leading principle of freedom. The state of the individual in the polity, and the gap between the hierarchical medieval subordination and the politicized state of citizens, had strengthened after the French and American revolutions. The impact of the dissonance between the state of being a "subject" and that of being a "citizen" was marked during these years. The temporal Arabic word for denoting subjects was *raʿiyya*, designating subordination to political or religious authority.[58] This category, which was refined by the Enlightenment to emphasize increasing attempts to incorporate "the people" in the political domain, had ignited the struggle for civil rights (citizenship).[59] The archival documents of the council show that Arabic discussants often used the word *sitūyyān*, which was borrowed from the French *citoyen* to denote the distinctive status of the French members.[60] This word was used

57 French attempts to present themselves as close to Islam did yield some conversions, as in the case of General Jacques (later ʿAbdulla) Menou, who married Sitt Zobayda from Rosette. For further details about Menou's conversion to Islam, and on (ʿAli) Bonaparte's endeavor to present himself as a Muslim ruler, see al-Turk, *Dhikr Tamalluk Jumhūr al-Faransāwiyya al-Aqṭār al-Miṣriyya wal-Bilād al-Shāmiyya, aw, al-Ḥamla al-Faransiyya ʿala Miṣr wal-Shām*, 94, 131, 140–141; Cole, *Napoleon's Egypt: Invading the Middle East*, 123–142; Coller, *Arab France: Islam and the Making of Modern Europe, 1798–1831*, 31–32.

58 Under the influence of Greek philosophy, medieval Islamic philosophers used the word *madanī* as equivalent to "citizen," embracing the Aristotelian assumption that human beings are political animals by nature. *Madanī* emphasized the social and political function of the individual in the polity. Thus, for instance, al-Farabi (d. 950) distinguished between *ṣinaʿa madaniyya* (political art) and *ṣināʿat al-mulk* (royal art), contending that the first category concerns the citizen or the statesman (*madanī*) and the second concerns the king. See the Arabic source and its English translation in Abu Nasr Muhammad ibn Muhammad al-Farabi, *Fuṣūl al-Madanī: Aphorisms of the Statesman*, trans. D. M. Dunlop (Cambridge: Cambridge University Press, 1961), 28–29, 104–105. For more details regarding the modern use of the word, see Chapter 2 of this volume.

59 For more details about the differentiation between "subjects" and "citizens," see Ayalon, *Language and Change in the Arab Middle East: The Evolution of Modern Political Discourse*, 44–45.

60 The word was used few times in these documents, and it did not survive after the French withdrawal. See al-Khashab, *al-Tārīkh al-Musalsal fī Ḥawādith al-Zamān wa-Waqāyiʿ al-Dīwān, 1800–1801*, 1–6, 86, 99.

among the French as a designation for the republican isonomy that emphasized the equality of all individuals before the law.[61] In another case one of the Arabic speakers addressed Napoleon as "Citizen First Consul" soon after the French evacuation of Egypt.[62] The use of this word shows that some of the Arabic-speaking scholars acknowledged these political dissonances. However, the transition of Arabic political thought from discourse about the state of subjects to discourse about the state of citizens would take place only a few decades later.

Other signs of this political shift appeared with the advent of the idea of popular engagement in governance. One aspect of this change was expressed in the transition of the word *jumhūr* (public). This word, which in its eighteenth-century common usage meant simply "crowd" or "public," was increasingly politicized with the emergence of the popular masses as a force in politics.[63] From around the end of the eighteenth century the word *jumhūr*[64] began to be employed in Arabic sources as equivalent to "republic" (an archaic version of *jumhūriyya*)[65] and indicated increasing attempts to ascribe political

61 Coller, *Arab France: Islam and the Making of Modern Europe, 1798–1831*, 50.

62 See the letter sent by Nemir Effendi to Napoleon written in French and translated into English in George A. Haddad, "A Project for the Independence of Egypt, 1801," *Journal of the American Oriental Society* 90, no. 2 (1970): 182.

63 Prior to the nineteenth-century Arabic and Latin lexicons, *jumhūrī* ("belongs to the public" and later "republican") denoted a common wine (additionally, in *Tāj al-ʿArus*, to denote cooked juice) used by the public. For *jumhūrī* in the eighteenth-century lexicons, see Muhammad ʿAli al-Tahanawi, "Jumhūr," *Kashshāf Iṣṭilāḥāt al-Funūn wal-ʿUlūm* (Beirut: Nāshirūn, 1996), 582; Muhammad Murtada al-Husayni al-Zubaydi, "J.m.h.r," *Tāj al-ʿArūs min Jawāhir al-Qāmūs* (Kuwait: Maṭbaʿat Ḥukūmat al-Kūwayt, 1972), 474.

64 In addition to the contemporary chroniclers, see Francisci Meninski's dictionary (composed in the seventeenth century and republished in an updated version in 1780) and the second edition of Richardson's dictionary (republished in 1806), which both associate *jumhūr* with "republic": Francisci Meninski, "Jumhūr," *Lexicon Arabico-Persico-Trucicum: Adiecta Ad Singulas Voces et Phrases Significatione Latina, Ad Usitatiores Etiam Italica* (Viennae: Nunc secundis curis recognitum et auctum, 1780), 393–394; John Richardson, "Jamāhīr," *A Dictionary, Persian, Arabic, and English: with a Dissertation on the Languages, Literature, and Manners of Eastern Nations* (London: William Bulmer, 1806), 346; al-Jabarti, *ʿAjāʾib al-Āthār fī al-Tarājim wal-Akhbār*, 1998, 3:101; al-Turk, *Dhikr Tamalluk Jumhūr al-Faransāwiyya al-Aqṭār al-Miṣriyya wal-Bilād al-Shāmiyya, aw, al-Ḥamla al-Faransiyya ʿala Miṣr wal-Shām*, 20, 29, 46.

65 Medieval Muslim philosophers such as al-Farabi, who was familiar with the Greek political traditions, did not use *jumhūr* but rather *madīna* to denote city

traits to the common people by referring to them as a political category; *jumhūr* unified in one word the meaning of public and republic and stressed the role of people in establishing and defining the nature of polity. Contemporary Arabic witnessed the addition of many innovative phrases that underlie the principle of popular engagement in governance, such as the phrases *madhhab al-jumhūr* (laws of the republic/people), *māl al-jumhūr* (property of the republic/people), and *tābiʿ li-ḥukm al-jumhūr* (subject of the republic).[66] Furthermore, the word was used in the phrase *qiyām al-jumhūr* (popular uprising); it indicates an archaic signifier of the modern concept of revolution, which implies violent acts committed in the pursuit of political rights (later *thawra*).[67] In this sense the word embedded the revolutionary connotation that followed the republican experience of France.

Few manifestations of representation as a central aspect of the idea of popular engagement in governance can be found in changes that took place in governmental institutions. To a certain extent, the principle of elective representation was evident in the Ottoman Empire before the 1840s, but at the lower levels of local representative bodies, not in the central Ottoman government.[68] The administrative council to empower the ʿulama against the defeated Mamluk military elite was rather a distorted imitation of the French parliamentary model. In this institution the common people did not have any significant influence. The decisions of this council were subject to approval by the French military governor, who appointed its members by decree. Nevertheless,

or polity. The concept of *madīna* is discussed extensively in the next chapter. See Ami Ayalon, "Semantics and the Modern History of Non-European Societies: Arab 'Republics' as a Case Study," *The Historical Journal* 28, no. 4 (1985): 825; Lewis, *Political Words and Ideas in Islam*, 129–133.

66 For other phrases, see *khidmat al-jumhūr* (the service of the republic), *dukhūl al-jumhūr* (beginning the rule of the republic), *shajar al-jumhūr* (trees that belong to a republic), *takūn lil-jumhūr* (belongs to the republic). See al-Khashab, *al-Tārīkh al-Musalsal fī Ḥawādith al-Zamān wa-Waqāyiʿ al-Dīwān, 1800–1801*, 11–13, 16–17, 32, 34; Ellious Bocthor, "Républicain," *Dictionnaire Français-Arabe* (Paris: Chez Firmin Didot Freres, 1829), 269.

67 Al-Jabarti, *ʿAjāʾib al-Āthār fī al-Tarājim wal-Akhbār*, 3:27

68 Some of these bodies consisted of nonelected figures from the upper social strata, such as local *aʿyān* (magnates), *ashrāf* (notables), *ʾaʾimma* (Muslim clerics), and guild masters. In villages and hamlets there were local traditions of representation based on elections, such as the election of a council of elders or a headman (*mukhtār*). For more details, see Davison, *Essays in Ottoman and Turkish History, 1774–1923: The Impact of the West*, 98.

a limited notion of civil governance was expressed in the fact that the council members elected their president from among themselves.[69]

## Egyptians and Levantines in France, 1801–1820

Any search for systematic conceptions of Enlightenment or any schematic worldview that might stem from these ideas in Arabic during the French seizure of Egypt would be in vain; the sphere of ideas was burdened by a variety of scattered conceptions, confused notions, and pieces of information about the remote events of the great revolutions in Europe and North America. The implications of concepts such as freedom, equality, reason, secularity, and sovereignty were extremely politicized and significantly inflated, and they created a mutual flow of ideas that left their impact on the sociopolitical reality. Nevertheless, these transformations were far from being articulated in Arabic as consistent sociopolitical plans or worldviews. The interrelation between these concepts was not always understood, and their repercussions were qualified by deep skepticism and suspicion that mostly ascribed them to the foreign cultural realm or heterodox traditions.

The earliest documented evidence of systematic but also ambiguous implications of freedom employed by Arabic speakers was neither on Egyptian soil nor in Arabic. In August 1801, many Oriental refugees fled with the French evacuation to France. These refugees, who numbered a few hundred people, arrived from Egypt, Sudan, Greater Syria, and from non–Arabic-speaking regions such as Greece, Georgia, and the Caucasus. In France they established Oriental communities, first in Marseille and afterward in Paris.[70]

In August 1801 Yaʿqub Hanna, an Egyptian Copt and a general in the French army, died on a British frigate named the *Pallas* during the French evacuation of Egypt. Yaʿqub, who had formed the Coptic Legion within the French forces in Egypt, was the leader of the refugees.[71] The discovery of correspondence between Yaʿqub, the

[69] For the election process, see the documentation of the *dīwān* archivist: Al-Khashab, *al-Tārīkh al-Musalsal fī Ḥawādith al-Zamān wa-Waqāyiʿ al-Dīwān, 1800–1801*, 4, 38, 96; Vatikiotis, *The Modern History of Egypt*, 38.

[70] For more details on the composition of these communities, see Coller, *Arab France: Islam and the Making of Modern Europe, 1798–1831*, 21–46.

[71] For Yaʿqub's biography, see Aziz Suryal Atiya, ed., "Yaʿqub, General," *The Coptic Encyclopedia* (New York: Macmillan, 1991), 2349–2353; Coller, *Arab France: Islam and the Making of Modern Europe, 1798–1831*, 21, 38–39.

"secretary," and the agent of the "Egyptian delegation" on one side and the British and the French on the other revealed their ambition of outlining a political project for an independent Egypt. This project apparently constituted the main reason for the decision made by Yaʿqub and his men to leave Egypt for France.[72]

Yaʿqub's project involved the invasion of Egypt by a force led by him and backed by European naval forces. He also sought to enlist the Mamluk Mourad Bey and the Arab tribes of the desert against the Ottomans to defend his independent Egypt (Upper Egypt). After his death this grand plan was presented to the French and the British by Theodore Lascaris de Vintimille, a former Knight of Malta of Piedmontese origin who had joined the French administration in Egypt. Lascaris was presented in these letters as the secretary and interpreter of the Egyptian delegation. Their initial aim was to convince Napoleon to convene a peace conference in Paris to support their idea of independence. Their attempts were in vain and ended in disappointment, especially after the 1802 Treaty of Amiens between France and Britain, which restored Egypt to its original status as an Ottoman province.[73]

The plan that was drawn up in two languages, English and French, embeds an early modern political worldview that was presented, at least partly, by Arabic speakers. Ideas such as patriotism were displayed in a systematic way that associated the idea of political independence with the Enlightenment concepts of civilization and universal history. In these letters the motive beyond Yaʿqub's ambition for the independence of Egypt is denoted by the word "patriotic," and the new, suggested government presented by Nemir Effendi, the agent of the delegation, by the word "national." The argument around the act of seeking the independence of Egypt was presented as a patriotic endeavor against the foreign Ottoman rule and as a necessary act to "liberate" the Egyptians "from the yoke that weighs on their unfortunate homeland."[74]

[72] For more details about the correspondence with the British and the French and the political project of the Egyptian Delegation, see Haddad, "A Project for the Independence of Egypt, 1801," 169–178.

[73] Ibid., 172, 176–177; Coller, *Arab France: Islam and the Making of Modern Europe, 1798–1831*, 42–46.

[74] The correspondence was published in Haddad, "A Project for the Independence of Egypt, 1801," 179–183.

Freedom was conceived in this collective context as an equivalent word for civil independence. "Independent Egypt" was employed as a key word for the aspiration to economic prosperity and cultural revival; political independence was viewed as an act of restoration of Egypt to its natural course in history, the universal history of the Enlightenment. It was presented as an articulation of the will of a new political community that was referred to by the term "Egyptians." The unification of Egyptian and European history was demonstrated in Nemir Effendi's attempt to portray the visionary aspect of Egypt's independence:

> Nothing would be more glorious and magnanimous for them [for the European powers] than to dispel, by a simple stroke of politics, the darkness of ignorance and barbarism that covers these famous countries that were the birthplace of our enlightenment, of our sciences, of our arts, and in a word the ancient centre of civilization from which it spread to us through the Greeks. If Egypt, which was so prosperous in the past, cannot excite the gratitude, may it at least excite the pity of European powers so that it could, when restored to itself, be pleasing to all the governments that covet it and thus cause trouble to none of them.[75]

Nemir Effendi presented a sophisticated conception that associated politics with memory and a vision of the future that included the ideals of prosperity and cultural revival in the sciences and the arts. He placed Egypt at the core of the history of enlightenment by associating ancient Egypt with ancient Greece. The outcome was the complete interweaving of Egypt with France in a shared history and a common destiny. From Nemir Effendi's perspective, the Enlightenment was not sustained in remote cultural domains, but it was part of his history, a perception indicated by his repetition of the word "our." Contemporary Arabic documentation did not contain such a conception and would not do so for some three decades.

The plan of independence was presented as a condition for future change that was portrayed as necessarily better "because is not everything in the world preferable to Turkish despotism?"[76] An independent Egypt would march toward a much more civilized state. In Nemir's conception, the future is a better place; it is a positive category that is

[75] He uses the phrase "Arabs like us"; ibid., 180. [76] Ibid., 181.

conditioned by planned initiatives. Civilization was portrayed as comprising separate units that maintain different levels of development. The idea that Egypt had flourished in the past, given birth to Greek culture, and deteriorated on the same universal scale of civilization, was expressed in another letter that Nemir Effendi dispatched to Napoleon as part of his attempt to recruit him to embrace the delegation's plan: "In the past ages of the world, in those uncertain and distant epochs when France, hardly emerging from the hands of nature, presented perhaps nothing but ice and forests, Egypt! already flourishing and civilized gave lessons to the first Greek legislators."[77]

The subordinate state of non-European nations on the Enlightenment scale of civilization, and the state of universality of enlightenment, was articulated in Nemir Effendi's perception of the Egypt of his time. In his talk about the future regime that would be applied to an independent Egypt, he states that

> It should be sufficient to remark that it will not be in this case a revolution made by the spirit of enlightenment or by the fermentation of opposing philosophical principles, but a change occasioned by absolute necessity in a community of peaceful and ignorant men who at present almost know no more than two mental affections: interest and fear.[78]

Enlightenment discourse was presented as relevant to European plans, but not to the native. Enlightenment principles were not applicable in contemporary Egypt, where the inhabitants maintained a lower state on the Enlightenment universal scale of civilization. According to his perception, in the past Egypt had flourished, and in the future it would again, but in the present it needed to be governed in different ways than those employed by enlightened nations. Currently Egypt needed to be ruled merely by a native and just government.[79]

Although the word "progress" was not employed explicitly, and the word "liberty" had ambiguous implications, the previous analysis leaves no doubt that some Arabic speakers possessed a systematic, comprehensive conception of progress and enlightenment. This being the case, one should question the validity of these precursory ideas in Egypt itself. Not only can we not speak of the language of patriotism in the Arabic of that time, the political context apparently was the primary motive that formulated the language used in these letters.

[77] Ibid., 182. [78] Ibid., 181. [79] Ibid.

The content of patriotism was presented in an ambiguous way: Nemir Effendi spoke as an "Arab"[80] and in the name of "Egyptians, who commissioned it [the delegation]."[81] The ambiguity of the idea of patriotism was emphasized by the fact that another prominent member of the delegation, Lascaris, and many of the refugees were not of Arab origin, and their identification as "Egyptians" was a subject of profound doubt. Indeed, in no place in the correspondence did the delegation request the annexation of Egypt to the French colonies, but the ambiguity of their "national" demands and their use of Enlightenment argumentation only in relation to Europe put the originality of these ideas in question. In the larger context this discourse, which approached the European powers via their language, adopted these powers' own conventional rationalizations in order to obtain the delegation's political goal. Furthermore, there is substantial similarity between the delegation's discourse and that which the French used during their expedition. The attempt to approach "the Egyptians" (*al-umma al-Miṣriyya*) or "the Arabs" (*le patriotisme arabe*) as a united community that was politically separate from the Ottoman state had been made by the French a few years earlier.[82] Moreover, "civilization" had been the argument previously used by the French to justify their invasion of Egypt. Among the early published works that constructed the idea of strong spiritual and historical relations between Egypt and Greco-Roman history – the spiritual foundations of French Enlightenment – was the famous *Description de l'Égypte*, the major French scientific endeavor during their expedition.[83]

Given all this, the discourse employed by the delegation appeared to be an imitation of the French propaganda. These ideas, however, had less attraction in contemporary France, and their glow had been

[80] Ibid., 183. [81] Ibid., 180.

[82] See al-Jabarti, *ʿAjāʾib al-Āthār fī al-Tarājim wal-Akhbār*, 1998, 3:4–5; Henry Laurens, *L'expedition d'Egypte, 1798–1801* (Paris: A. Colin, 1989), 180.

[83] See the preface of this volume in: Joseph Fourier, "Priface Hisforique," in *Description de l'Égypte, Ou, Recueil de Observations et Des Recherches Qui Ont Été Faites En Égypte Pendant L'éxpédition de L'armée Française*, ed. Commission des monuments d'Égypte, 2nd ed. (Paris: Imprimerie de C. L. F. Panckoucke, 1826), a–clv. For the manifestation of this idea in the topographical maps in *Description de l'Égypte* and its utilization in the French invasion, see Anne Godlewska, "Map, Text and Image. The Mentality of Enlightened Conquerors: A New Look at the Description de l'Egypte," *Transactions of the Institute of British Geographers* 20, no. 1 (1995): 5–28.

remarkably reduced. In 1801 France was a militarized country that had gradually deserted its revolutionary policies in favor of practical politics.[84] It is important to stress that this early evidence of Enlightenment discourse was not articulated in the Arabic language.

These ideas flew with some of the eager refugees to France. There a few Arabic-speaking scholars integrated into the Parisian intellectual milieu, and by the beginning of the nineteenth century, some of them occupied distinguished positions: Rufa'il Zakhur, a Syrian Greek Catholic priest who was first an interpreter for Napoleon in Egypt and a member of the *Institut d'Égypte* and was appointed in 1803 to a personal chair in colloquial Arabic at the École des Langues Orientales (which he left in 1816 to go to work in Egypt under Muhammad 'Ali); Mikha'il al-Sabbagh, a descendant of a powerful Melkite family during the rule of Zahir al-'Umar, who occupied a position copying Arabic manuscripts in the *Bibliothèque Impériale;* and Ellious Bocthor (Ilyas Buqtur al-Asyuti), a Coptic scholar and teacher of Arabic at the École des Langues Orientales.[85]

These three prominent scholars filled key positions in the linguistic reformation of the Arabic language and its adjustment to the rapid changes that impacted the area with modernity. They reorganized the language according to a pragmatic view that intended to serve the practical requirements of the commerce and politics that were flourishing in the new spaces that emerged with the drifting imagined borders of civilization. Their contribution to the evolvement of Arabic took place in three major published works that integrate colloquial Arabic and foreign words in one lexical body of composition. Among their works are the first two Arabic-French and Arabic-Italian dictionaries written by Arabic speakers: *Dizionario Italiano e Arabo* by Rufa'il Zakhur (published in Egypt in 1822) and *Dictionnaire Français-Arabe* by Ellious Bocthor (published in 1828 after his death in Paris).[86] The third work is a treatise by Mikha'il al-Sabbagh that examines colloquial Arabic and includes a lexicon of foreign words that had penetrated the

[84] Coller, *Arab France: Islam and the Making of Modern Europe, 1798–1831*, 44, 50–51, 83.

[85] For more biographical details about these scholars, see ibid., 103–105, 112–113; Aziz Suryal Atiya, ed., "Ilyas Buqtur," *The Coptic Encyclopedia* (New York: Macmillan, 1991), 1284–1285.

[86] Bocthor composed the major part of his dictionary during the second decade of the nineteenth century and died in 1821. Ellious Bocthor, *Dictionnaire Français-Arabe* (Paris: Chez Firmin Didot Freres, 1828), i–vij; Rufa'il Zakhur, *Dizionario Italiano E Arabo* (Bolacco: Dalla Stamperia Reale, 1822).

Arabic language. It is worth mentioning that al-Sabbagh's composition was written with the assistance of Bocthor, who was the most eager supporter of Enlightenment ideas among the members of this group.[87]

With these precursory works, the evolving modern ideas acquired many sophisticated morphological forms in Arabic, including *ḥurriyya*. The significant semantic expansion in the use of *ḥurriyya* that took place in the second decade of the nineteenth century expressed various aspects of the characteristics of the polity. The evolution in its scope of reference penetrated two conceptual domains, the individual and the collective. The idea of political independence that constituted the major goal of general Yaʿqub and his delegation was articulated in Arabic by his nephew, Ellious Bocthor. In his dictionary he rendered the French *indépendant* as *khaliṣ ma huwa taḥta ḥukm* (free from political authority) and *pays libre* as *bilād ḥurriyya* (free areas or country) in an ambiguous and primary rendition of the concept of political freedom.[88]

In a corresponding development, and in one of the earliest translations of a European work into Arabic in the nineteenth century, Rufaʾil Zakhur translated Niccolò Machiavelli's *The Prince* in 1824–1825, by order of Muhammad ʿAli. In his translation Zakhur used the phrase "[*amīriyyāt*] *muḥarrara*" to render "free principalities" in Arabic.[89] In both cases the words *ḥurriyya* and *muḥarrara* were used to articulate an ambiguous political state that could refer to the collective domain, political independence, or the individual domain, thereby denoting the condition of the civil rights in a certain political entity. These coinages were articulated a few decades after there were significant developments in Ottoman foreign policy that emphasized the process of transformation from cosmopolitical empire to assimilation of nation-state norms in international relations, especially with the

[87] Mikhaʾil al-Sabbagh, *Al-Risāla al-Tāmma fī Kalām al-ʿĀmma: wal-Manāhij fī Aḥwāl al-Kalām al-Dārij* (Strassburg: Trübner, 1886).

[88] Ellious Bocthor, "Libre," *Dictionnaire Français-Arabe* (Paris: Chez Firmin Didot Freres, 1829), 14.

[89] Nineteenth-century Arabic often distinguished, in the European context, between *mamlaka* (kingdom), *dūqiyya* (duchy), *amīriyya* (principality or aristocracy), and *madīna ḥurra* (autonomous city). Part of Niccolò Machiavelli's Arabic text is quoted in Jamal al-Din al-Shayyal, *Tārīkh al-Tarjama wal-Ḥaraka al-Thaqāfiyya fī ʿAṣr Muḥammad ʿAli* (Cairo: Dār al-Fikr al-ʿArabī, 1951), 216; *Rawḍat al-Madāris*, February 11, 1876, 12–13; *al-Jinān* 7 (1883): 215–216.

inauguration of the first Ottoman embassies in Europe – first in London (1793), and afterward in Vienna (1794), Berlin (1795), and Paris (1796).[90] Shifts in the international arena had, already in the eighteenth century, affected the political concept of freedom in Turkish. With the political use of *serbestiyet*, Turkish articulated the concept of political independence – for example, where "free and entirely independent of any foreign power" refers to the new status of the Crimean Tatars in the Treaty of Küçük Kaynarca in 1774. Despite the fact that the Turkish preceded the Arabic in capturing the concept of political independence, *serbestiyet* would be replaced during the nineteenth century by the Arabic loanword *hürriyet* (and subsequently by *özgürlük*).[91]

The subject of civil rights gained additional morphological formations sometime around the second decade of the nineteenth century. Bocthor articulated the extension of freedom to the individual domain in Arabic with his rendition of the French *Liberté de conscience* as *ḥurriyyat al-adyān* (freedom of religion).[92] Although freedom of conscience includes, among many implied meanings, freedom of religion, for him this was the primary meaning taken from the French term.

Signs for an additional layer in the use of *ḥurriyya* were presented in Arabic by the orientalist Maximilian Habicht, who was originally from the town of Breslau (Wroclaw) and was employed in the Prussian embassy in Paris.[93] Habicht, who was connected to the Oriental intellectual milieu during his service in Paris, published a collection of correspondence in 1824 that he had received from his Arabic-speaking friends, including Rufa'il Zakhur and Micha'il Sabbagh. He translated his book's title into Arabic as *Kitāb janā' al-fawākih wal-athmār fī jam' ba'ḍ makātīb al-aḥbāb al-aḥrār min 'iddat amṣār* (The book of

[90] Lewis, *The Emergence of Modern Turkey*, 55–61; Daniel L. Newman, "Introduction," in *An Imam in Paris* (London: Saqi Books, 2011), 18.

[91] For further details on the history of this word in Turkish, see Lewis, *Political Words and Ideas in Islam*, 14–17.

[92] Other contemporary Western-Arabic dictionaries published between 1800 and 1820 did not indicate the semantic expansions of "freedom" and followed the medieval renditions. For comparison, see Bocthor, "Libre," 14; Johann Jahn, "Ḥurr," *Lexicon Arabico-Latinum* (Vindobonae: Apud C. F. Wappler et Beck, 1802), 170; Jacques Français Ruphy, "Libéral, Liberté," *Dictionnaire Abrégé Français-Arabe* (Paris: Impr. de la République, 1802), 120; David Hopkins, "Ḥurr," *A Vocabulary, Persian, Arabic, and English; Abridged from the Quarto Edition of Richardson's Dictionary* (London: Printed for F. and C. Rivingson, 1810), 224.

[93] Coller, *Arab France: Islam and the Making of Modern Europe, 1798–1831*, 76.

gathering fruits: a collection of letters from free friends from several regions).[94] The use of *aḥrār* (free) as an adjective could indicate two meanings: either the classical implication equivalent to "generous and noble," or "free" as a qualification that refers to the political position that his Arabic-speaking friends possessed. Despite the vast ambiguity in using the word, there is reason to believe that employing *aḥrār* had political connotations in the context of postrevolutionary France. There the public discourse was absorbed with the revolutionary ideals of universal liberty and the idea of constituting a "Grand Nation" that comprised sovereign national republics ("sister republics") under French aegis. Free friends, in that sense, is equivalent to "defenders of liberty," a most common designation in France during these years. The legal status of the Arabic-speaking community as refugees was apparently perceived by Habicht to be a result of their political position against Turkish (or Mamluk) despotism. The function of freedom as an adjective or as subject of identification with a concrete political position would take on clearer forms in Arabic a few years later.

Indeed, *ḥurriyya* gained many more sophisticated forms, but that did not at all mean that the course of evolvement of the word "freedom" in Arabic was rapid and smooth; *ḥurriyya* was still rarely used in political contexts, and it was absorbed by controversial notions that were indicated by a variety of vocabularies and concepts. Furthermore, the evolvement of the modern concept in Arabic was impeded by conceptual dissonances. Rifaʿa al-Tahtawi, who visited Paris for a few years between 1826 and 1831, observed that there the people were free to practice any religion they chose, without any constraints. In his articulation of the idea of freedom of religion, he did not use *ḥurr* but rather *yubāḥ* (permitted).[95]

The march of *ḥurriyya* through the political discourse in Arabic reveals profound differences, not only between ideas but also between traditions of thought. The difference between *ḥurr* and *yubāḥ* exposes a vast conceptual gap; on the one hand, al-Tahtawi's expression comprises an implication of authority that lies outside of the individual's will, usually possessed by the ruler or by clerics, while Bocthor's

[94] The letters are appended to the book: Maximilan Habicht, *Epistolae Quaedam Arabicae* (Wroclaw: Typis Universitatis Regis, 1824).

[95] In the phrase "*yubāḥ al-taʿabud bi-sāʾir al-adyān.*" Rifaʿa Rafiʿ al-Tahtawi, *Takhlīṣ al-Ibrīz fī Talkhīṣ Bārīz aw al-Dīwān al-Nafīs bi-Īwān Bārīs* (Bulaq: Dār al-Ṭibāʿa al-Khidīwiyya, 1834), 19.

articulation, on the other hand, embeds the concept of "right" that stemmed from the civil perception of the individual's status in a polity (citizenship). *Ḥurr* and *ḥurriyya* are associated with the secular tradition of the Enlightenment, while *yubāḥ* and *mubāḥ* have deep roots in shariʿa and denote one of the "five qualifications" (*al-aḥkām al-khamsa*) that regulate all actions in religious law.[96]

These modern ideas were distributed around the region during the second decade of the nineteenth century, and sophisticated modern worldviews began to take shape in Arabic texts in Egypt and the Levant. Mikhaʾil Mishaqa (1800–1888), who was born in Rushmayya and spent part of his life in Damascus,[97] wrote in a biographical note about the profound change that he had experienced around the end of the second decade of the nineteenth century (1814–1821):

> I was born a Christian in a respected and known family in the beginning of 1800 . . . I was enchanted by reading useful books, and when I turned 14 I studied mathematics, algebra, theology, geography, astronomy, and natural sciences [*ṭabīʿiyyat*]. I was lucky then to have a teacher who was one of my relatives, who learned these arts from the French who came to Egypt in 1799 [1798]. In a short period I learned a certain amount of knowledge that was fulfilling for one like me. The sciences that I've learned led me to realize the glory of God because through these sciences I became capable of seeing the greatness of his creation. But meanwhile, it drove me to condemn Christianity with the rest of the other religions, and I began to consider it as having been established by intelligent people [*ʿuqala*ʾ] in order to restrain the ignorant who do not know their boundaries . . . What makes me averse to Christianity and refute its preaching is what I consider in it to be a lack of correspondence with the truth, with justice, or that it contradicts the judgments of the senses.[98]

This testimony, published by a converted Protestant in the introduction to a polemic theological work that undermined the traditional faith of Christian churches, elucidated the powerful impact of the Enlightenment during the second decade of the nineteenth century in

[96] Which are as follows: *wājib* (mandatory), *mustaḥab* (preferred), *mubāḥ* (permitted), *makrūh* (disliked), and *harām* (forbidden).

[97] For further details about the social background and the intellectual biography of Mishaqa, see Fruma Zachs, "Mīkhāʾīl Mishāqa-The First Historian of Modern Syria," *British Journal of Middle Eastern Studies* 28, no. 1 (May 2001): 67–87.

[98] Mikhaʾil Mishaqa, *Al-Risālā al-Maūsūma bil-Dalīl ila Ṭāʿat al-Injīl* (Beirut: 1849), 3–4.

Greater Syria. The comprehensive connotations that these ideas gained by using concepts such as *ʿilm* (science) and *ʿaql* (reason) succeeded in establishing an epistemic base that considered secular human reason and experimentalism (derived from *ʿilm* that is based on senses) as the substantive references for truth and justice, including ethics and metaphysics. The theological emancipation of faith coincided with the transitions of concepts in the political domain. Modernity, in the Arabic language, began during this phase to be revealed as an all-embracing phenomenon that penetrated both the material and the spiritual life. The concept of freedom conjoined with these massive transitions, and its semantic connotations expanded substantially.

Before tracing the semantic evolution of "freedom" during the following decades in the collective and the individual political spheres, the next chapter examines the alteration that took place in perceptions of time and memory with the advancement of two modern concepts: progress and civilization. These two ideas, which are often employed in one phrase, gained extensive use after the 1820s; while the first indicated the way, the second marked the aim of the local intellectual movement. "Progress" purveyed the power of movement, and "civilization" provided the aspired-to, imagined future. "Progress" functioned as a comprehensive doctrine, a powerful force for change that would encompass the dynamics of political concepts, formulate their development, and integrate them into a schematic sociopolitical plan shaped by various interpretations of the concept "civilization." These two concepts would maintain the political and social aspect of motivation and would mark a transition in the development of freedom, from the theoretical aspects practiced in the realm of language to the social and political domains exercised by involvement and activism. To use Reinhart Koselleck's terminology, with the next conceptual evolvement, freedom would transform into a "struggle concept."[99]

[99] Koselleck uses the idiom "struggle concepts" to describe the "pragmatic function that a word has in political confrontation." Hans Erich Bödeker, "Concept – Meaning – Discourse. Begriffsgeschichte Reconsidered," in *History of Concepts: Comparative Perspectives*, ed. Iain Hampsher-Monk, Karin Tilmans, and Frank Van Vree (Amsterdam: Amsterdam University Press, 1998), 55–56.

# 2 *A Conceptual View of Arabic Modernity through Two Key Concepts, "Civilization" and "Progress" (*Tamaddun *and* Taqaddum*)*

## Politicizing "Progress" and "Civilization"

In an article written in the 1860s, (Ahmad) Faris al-Shidyaq, the most well-known journalist of his generation, observed a challenge facing the traditional customs regarding the treatment of women in Ottoman society:

Tradition [*'āda*] and civilization [*tamaddun*] often challenge each other in the arena of time, and one obtains victory over the other. [In our society], tradition defeated *tamaddun* in the custom that maintains that a man must join his wife if she is on the streets or in a stagecoach . . . but if you say that the custom of accompanying the wife is not related to *tamaddun*, I would answer that *tamaddun* has many meanings, as I previously mentioned, and it includes gentle treatment and behavior. It is evident that a man who keeps his wife distant and alienated, holding her in contempt, is [following a pattern of behavior] considered barbaric and not civilized.[1]

More than half a century passed between Nemir Effendi's early use of the word "civilization" in presenting his sociopolitical project and al-Shidyaq's observation.[2] During these years the concept became semantically inflated, from its initial, non-Arabic use in the context of French propaganda to its emergence as an integral concept in the sociopolitical language of modern Arabic. The transformation from "civilization" to "*tamaddun*" indicated, initially, the formation of a sociopolitical intellectual movement in Arabic that promoted ideas derived from perceptions of *tamaddun*. The Arabic discourse on "*tamaddun*," as was the case with the German concept "culture," was a historical moment

[1] Ahmad Faris al-Shidyaq, *Mukhtārāt min Āthār Aḥmad Fāris al-Shidyāq* (Beirut: Al-Mu'assasa al-Sharqiyya lil-Nashr, 2001), 163.
[2] Haddad, "A Project for the Independence of Egypt, 1801," 182.

of comprehensive cultural assessment that was launched against the background of the challenge the Enlightenment posed to local cultures. *Tamaddun*, in that sense, provides an internal perspective on the dialectics of modernity in Arabic.[3]

The powerful impact of *tamaddun* on the social discourse is portrayed by al-Shidyaq's observation of the contention he observed regarding *ʿāda*; while *ʿāda* denoted an inherited and consistent tradition, *tamaddun* implied the force of a movement that stimulated embracing new patterns of behavior. *Tamaddun* was presented by its adherents as an ideal that acquired its force from the future, in contrast with *ʿāda*, which derived its power from the past. *Tamaddun*, best temporally translated as "being civilized," reflects the perception of a process, an ongoing force and therefore integrates two ideas, civilization and progress; while the first word comprises the two notions, the second word was often used separately or with *tamaddun* in one phrase, for emphasis. Rizq Allah Hassun, a journalist who became famous as a result of his coverage of the Crimean War in the first private Arabic newspaper, which he founded in either 1854 or 1855 in Istanbul, articulated the intimate link between the two ideas with the phrase *al-taqaddum fī sabīl al-tamaddun* (progress toward civilization).[4]

The construction of the modern Arabic concepts of "civilization" (*tamaddun, taḥaḍḍur, tamaṣṣur*) and "progress" (*taraqqī, taqaddum*) took place in the beginning of the nineteenth century. Progress and civilization were constructed as comprehensive concepts denoting a paradigm that comprised all aspects of human life: ethical, religious, social, economic, political, and cultural. Political ideas such as freedom, equality, citizenship, patriotism, popular sovereignty, and reason were perceived as integral components of the paradigm of progress. Societies that implement or achieve advanced positions in the continuous, linear progression of civilization – often described by the phrase "ladder of civilization" (*sulam al-tamaddun*) – are conceived of as being more

[3] For comparison between the Arabic, French, German, and Turkish uses of the concept of "civilization" in the nineteenth century, see Birgit Schaebler, "Civilizing Others: Global Modernity and Local Boundaries (French/German/Ottoman and Arab) of Savagery," in *Globalization and the Muslim World: Culture Religion and Modernity*, ed. Birgit Schaebler and Leif Stenberg (New York: Syracuse University Press, 2004), 3–31.

[4] *Mirʾāt al-Aḥwāl*, March 22, 1877.

advanced in relation to others and are frequently categorized by the type of movement they practice, such as sustained regression (retreating toward the past) or traditional (static state). *Sulam al-tamaddun* is a universal parameter that reveals the comparative state of civilization and progress of every society in the world.

Half a century earlier, most of the Arabic-speaking scholars would have articulated al-Shidyaq's experience quite differently; neither the terminology nor the conception of progress and civilization played any significant role. Al-Jabarti, who wrote his history toward the beginning of the nineteenth century, was not acquainted with these concepts. Here, for instance, is how he articulates his observation of French advances in the sciences: "They [the French] have a larger amount of knowledge . . . and great diligence."[5] Neither *taqaddum* nor *tamaddun* were among the expressions he used.

By the 1860s, and even earlier, "civilization" and "progress" had already reached stable morphological forms, frequently indicated by *tamaddun* and *taqaddum*. The rivalry between the two worldviews, one relying on imagined ideals from the past and the other on idealization of an imagined future, emphasizes the profound impact of modern ideas that took place around the middle of the nineteenth century. The question that informed, to a large extent, the preoccupation of the Arabic-speaking proponents of progress was expressed by Mansur Carletti, a fellow at the Scientific Syrian Association and later the founder of the most important newspaper in Tunisia, *al-Rāʾid al-Tūnisī*.[6] In an article he composed in 1859 and published in *ʿUṭārid*, an early private newspaper in Arabic that was printed in Marseille and distributed in Egypt and Greater Syria, he posed the question: How did the Arabs fall into a state of negligence while the Europeans progressed?[7] By then both words, *tamaddun* and *taqaddum*, had become extremely thematized and were frequently used as cultural and political slogans. Many scholars designate the nineteenth century as "the age of civilization" (*ʿaṣr al-tamaddun*),[8] and in 1874 *al-Taqaddum* was the name of a

5 In Arabic, "*taṭaluʿ zāʾid . . . wa-ijtihād kabīr*." See al-Jabarti, *ʿAjāʾib al-Āthār fī al-Tarājim wal-Akhbār*, 1998, 3:58.
6 Filib Tarrazi, *Taʾrīkh al-Ṣiḥāfa al-ʿArabiyya*, vol. 1 (Beirut: Al-Maṭbaʿa al-Adabiyya, 1913), 60, 64–66.
7 "*Kayfa akhadhat al-ʿArab bil-taqāʿus wal-Ifaranj bil-taqaddum?*" in *ʿUṭārid*, July 13, 1859, 3.
8 *Al-Jawāʾib*, September 27, 1876, 5; *al-Ahrām*, July 10, 1879.

newspaper established by Yusif Shalfun, a prominent Syrian Lebanese journalist.

Among the political ideas being theorized within the intellectual preoccupation with progress and civilization was the idea of freedom. Progress and civilization served as the theoretical frame encompassing the construction of the discourse on freedom in Arabic. This aspect, or relation between ideas, was also indicated by one of al-Shidyaq's observations during the 1860s: "Many people, and especially those who lived with Europeans, contend that one of the requirements of civilization [*tamaddun*] is the need for freedom in every aspect and that society would not gain true civilization [*tamaddun*] without absolute freedom."[9] Other scholars, such as Salim al-Bustani, the son of Butrus al-Bustani, wrote during the second half of the nineteenth century about *al-ʿālam al-ḥurr al-mutamaddin* (the free civilized world) as a superior cultural model.[10] In a similar way, Yaʿqub Nawfal, a Christian biographer from a well-known family, wrote in *al-Ahrām* in February 1881, emphasizing the relation between *tamaddun* and freedom, that "freedom is the light of reason, reason is the father of science, science is a fruit of *tamaddun*, and *tamaddun* is a virtue of ethics."[11] The integration of freedom into the paradigm of progress and civilization paved the way for political theorization of the concept, as detailed in the coming chapters.

The temporal definition of "civilization" was given by a variety of prominent scholars during the nineteenth century, including al-Tahtawi, al-Shidyaq, and Butrus al-Bustani. In the most frequently repeated definition, *tamaddun* meant "acquiring the methods that are required for improving the conditions of sedentary people [*ahl al-ʿumrān*]. This means improving their ethics, their customs, and acquiring perfection in education [*kamāl al-tarbiyya*], and stimulating them to gain virtue, political perfection [*al-kamalāt al-madaniyya*], and elevation of their prosperity."[12] In another frequently used definition, the morphological relation between *tamaddun* and *madīna* (city) was

[9] Al-Shidyaq, *Mukhtārāt min Āthār Aḥmad Fāris al-Shidyāq*, 160.
[10] *Al-Jinān* 11 (1870): 321–22. [11] *Al-Ahrām*, February 9, 1881.
[12] This quotation is taken from al-Tahtawi, but its content is repeated in the works of many contemporary scholars. See Butrus al-Bustani, *Nafīr Sūriyya* (Beirut: Dār al-Fikr, 1990), 63–68; Ahmad Faris al-Shidyaq, *Kanz al-Raghā'ib fī Muntakhabāt al-Jawā'ib*, ed. Salim al-Shidyaq, vol. 1 (Istanbul: Maṭbaʿat al-Jawā'ib, 1871), 3; al-Tahtawi, "Kitāb al-Murshid al-Amīn lil-Banāt wal-Banīn," in *al-Aʿmāl al-Kāmila li-Rifāʿa Rāfiʿ al-Ṭahṭawī*, ed. Muammad

emphasized. In Butrus al-Bustani's dictionary, composed in 1860s, *tamaddan* is used as an adjective for mankind, and it means that people acquired the morals of the inhabitants of the city (those who have experienced urban life). Additionally, it indicates the transformation from the state of barbarism and ignorance to the state of civilization and knowledge.[13] These definitions, in their importance, do not map the temporal meaning and the semantic field of the concept. The coming subchapter highlights, in historical depth, the component of the modern concepts of civilization and progress.

## Time and the Structure of "Civilization" and "Progress"

In the diachronic line of inquiry, "civilization" and "progress" were composed of many layers that consisted of medieval and modern traditions. Despite the fact that the word *tamaddun* was rarely employed prior to the nineteenth century,[14] something close to the definition of civilization quoted earlier appears in Ibn Khaldun's *al-Muqaddima*. In his conception of civilization, which was known to Arabic-speaking scholars prior to the French expedition to Egypt, Ibn Khaldun typically used the word *'umrān* to signify the idea. In one of the many definitions that he gave for the word, he indicated that "civilization [*'umrān*] means that human beings have to dwell in common and settle together in cities and hamlets for the comforts of companionship and for the satisfaction of human needs, as a result of the natural

'Imara, vol. 2 (Cairo: Dār al-Shurūq, 2010), 351, 501; Rifa'a Rafi' al-Tahtawi, trans., *al-Ta'rībāt al-Shāfiya li-Murīd al-Jughrāfiyya* (Bulaq: Dār al-Ṭibā'a al-Khidīwiyya, 1834), app. 70; *al-Riyāḍ al-Miṣriyya*, September 21, 1888, 57–60.

[13] Interpretation of "civilization" in relation to the root *m.d.n.* also occurred frequently. For selected examples, see Butrus al-Bustani, "Tamaddan," *Muḥīṭ al-Muḥīṭ* (Beirut: Maktabat Lubnān, 1998), 843; *al-Jinān* 18 (1870): 600–602; *al-Ahrām*, March 1, 1881.

[14] The word *tamaddun* was not mentioned in the following medieval Arabic dictionaries (composed between the tenth and fifteenth centuries). Instead, the frequent forms used were *madīnī*, which indicated a person who belongs to the city of Medina, and *madana* and *tamdīn*, which meant simply "settled" and "settling." See Isma'il Ibn Hamad al-Juhari, "M.d.n.," *al-Ṣiḥāḥ fī al-Lugha: Tāj al-Lugha wa-Ṣiḥāh al-'Arabiyya* (Beirut: Dār al-'Ilm lil-Malāyīn, 1984), 2201; Ibn Sa'id al-Himyari Nashwan, "Tamdīn," *Shams al-'Ulūm wa-Dawā' Kalām al-'Arab min al-Kulūm* (Damascus: Dār al-Fikr al-Mu'āṣir, 1999), 6253; Muhammad Ibn Mukarram Ibn Manzur, "M.d.n.," *Lisān al-'Arab* (Beirut: Dār al-Ṣādir, 2004), 40; Muhammad Ibn Ya'qub Firuzabadi, "M.d.n.," *al-Qāmūs al-Muḥīṭ* (Beirut: Mu'assasat al-Risāla, 2005), 1233–1234.

disposition of human beings toward cooperation in order to be able to make a living."[15]

Ibn Khaldun, who identified the concept of human civilization as the object of his science,[16] elevated use of the term "civilization" to the level of a theory of history. He outlined his theory, stating that dynasties (*duwal*) have life spans, which he generally estimates as lasting for three generations and having three natural (*ṭabī'iyya*) stages of development. In the first stage the ruler relies on group feeling (*'aṣabiyya*), and this is regarded as the most basic level of development, which Ibn Khaldun identifies with the bedouin and "savage" (*tawaḥḥush*) state. In the second stage or generation, dynasties move to the stage of *ḥaḍāra* ("from desert attitude to sedentary culture"). The sedentary culture is followed by stabilization of the political regime, which involves a life of luxury and pleasures. In the third stage and generation, rulers forget their desert life and toughness (*khushūna*) and lose their group feeling – a state that eventually brings about the destruction of their dynasty.[17]

Preceding the modern concept, Ibn Khaldun portrays two pillars of the course of civilizations: *umam waḥshiyya*, which he identifies with the bedouin style of living, and *haḍar*, sedentary people. This high culture is presented as a consequence of historical circumstance: "For sedentary culture [*ḥaḍāra*] is the consequence of luxury; luxury is the consequence of wealth and prosperity; and wealth and prosperity are the consequences of royal authority [*mulk*] and related to the extent of territorial possessions which the people of a particular dynasty have gained."[18]

15 For an English translation and the Arabic sources, see 'Abd al-Rahman Ibn Khaldun, *The Muqaddimah: An Introduction to History*, trans. Franz Rosenthal, vol. 1 (Princeton, NJ: Princeton University Press, 1967), 84; Ibn Khaldun, *Muqaddimat al-'Allāma Ibn Khaldūn al-Musamma Dīwān al-Mubtada' wal-Khabarr fī Ta'rīkh al-'Arab wal-Barbar wa-man 'Āṣarahum min Dhawī al-Sha'n al-Akbarr*, 53.

16 Ibn Khaldun, *The Muqaddimah: An Introduction to History*, 1967, 1:77; Ibn Khaldun, *Muqaddimat al-'Allāma Ibn Khaldūn al-Musamma Dīwān al-Mubtada' wal-Khabarr fī Ta'rīkh al-'Arab wal-Barbar wa-man 'Āṣarahum min Dhawī al-Sha'n al-Akbarr*, 50.

17 Ibn Khaldun, *The Muqaddimah: An Introduction to History*, 1967, 1:343–347; Ibn Khaldun, *Muqaddimat al-'Allāma Ibn Khaldūn al-Musamma Dīwān al-Mubtada' wal-Khabarr fī Ta'rīkh al-'Arab wal-Barbar wa-man 'Āṣarahum min Dhawī al-Sha'n al-Akbarr*, 184–186.

18 Ibn Khaldun, *The Muqaddimah: An Introduction to History*, 1967, 1:351; Ibn Khaldun, *Muqaddimat al-'Allāma Ibn Khaldūn al-Musamma Dīwān*

He founds the application of his theory in the history of the Arabs, who built their kingdom using their group feeling (*'aṣabiyya*) and whose kingdom was destroyed during the 'Abbasid dynasty – especially during the reigns of al-Mu'tasim and his son al-Wathiq, because they both tried to strengthen their seizures of countries using Persians, Turks, and others. The destruction of their dynasty and civilization returned them to the first level, the level of the desert and savage life.[19]

No doubt the rediscovery of the relevance of Ibn Khaldun, who is designated in al-Tahtawi's account of his 1826–1831 journey in Paris (first published in 1834) as "Montesquieu of the Orient" or "Montesquieu of Islam,"[20] had a profound impact on the construction of the nineteenth-century concept of *tamaddun*. During the first half of the nineteenth century, Ibn Khaldun became a cultural icon; in France short, early portions of *al-Muqaddima* were published by Silvestre de Sacy, a prominent French orientalist who maintained strong relations with the Arabic-speaking scholars of Paris after 1801, especially Mikha'il al-Sabbagh[21] and later al-Tahtawi, who indicated that de Sacy was one of the commentators on an early draft of his book.[22] The first modern print edition of *al-Muqaddima* in Arabic was published in Bulaq in 1857. One year later the first European edition came out, followed by the first Turkish translation in 1859.[23] For the nineteenth-century Arabic-speaking scholars, Ibn Khaldun represented

*al-Mubtada' wal-Khabarr fī Ta'rīkh al-'Arab wal-Barbar wa-man 'Āṣarahum min Dhawī al-Sha'n al-Akbarr*, 188.

19 Ibn Khaldun, *The Muqaddimah: An Introduction to History*, 1967, 1:306–308, 314–317; Ibn Khaldun, *Muqaddimat al-'Allāma Ibn Khaldūn al-Musamma Dīwān al-Mubtada' wal-Khabarr fī Ta'rīkh al-'Arab wal-Barbar wa-man 'Āṣarahum min Dhawī al-Sha'n al-Akbarr*, 165–166, 169–170.

20 Al-Tahtawi, *Takhlīṣ al-Ibrīz fī Talkhīṣ Bārīz aw al-Dīwān al-Nafīs bi-Īwān Bārīs*, 150.

21 Silvestre de Sacy and Mikha'il Sabbagh were close friends. De Sacy translated two of Sabbagh's books into French. See Mikha'il al-Sabbagh, *Musābaqat al-Barq wal-Ghamām fī Su'āt al-Ḥamām* (Paris: Dār al-Maṭba'a al-Ṣulṭāniyya, 1805); al-Sabbagh, *Nashīd Qaṣīdat Tahāni li-Sa'ādat al-Qayṣar al-Mu'aẓam Nabūlyūn Sulṭān Faransā fī Mauwlid Bikrihi Sa'ādat Malik Rummiyya Nabūlyūn al-Thānī*.

22 Al-Tahtawi, *Takhlīṣ al-Ibrīz fī Talkhīṣ Bārīz aw al-Dīwān al-Nafīs bi-Īwān Bārīs*, 142–144.

23 For a survey of the early editions of *al-Muqaddima*, see Franz Rosenthal's introduction in: Ibn Khaldun, *The Muqaddimah: An Introduction to History*, 1967, 1:c–cix.

a Muslim attempt to explore society using scientific methods of thinking. It is worth noting that the famous political reformer Khayr al-Din al-Tunisi, who attained the post of grand vizier of the Ottoman Empire between 1878 and 1879, quoted Ibn Khaldun repeatedly in his 1867 book, *Aqwam al-masālik fī maʿrifat aḥwāl al-mamālik* (The surest path to know the conditions of the kingdoms), and was guided by many of his arguments regarding the rise and decline of civilizations. As with Ibn Khaldun's book, al-Tunisi's introduction (*al-Muqaddima*) was the most important part of his book, and it was translated separately under his supervision into French (1868) and Turkish (1878).[24] Something similar occurred with al-Tunisi's contemporary, Ahmad ibn Abi al-Diyaf (known as Bin Diyaf), a Tunisian bureaucrat who composed a voluminous history between 1862 and 1872 that begins with his own *Muqaddima*.[25] Under the inspiration of Ibn Khaldun, Bin al-Diyaf opens his work with an essay on political philosophy.[26] Despite the impact of Ibn Khaldun's comprehensive theory of history on the modern concept of civilization, *tamaddun* gained additional distinctive features that were acquired during the nineteenth century. The main difference between Ibn Khaldun's concept and the modern concept lay in the morphology and the political implications of "civilization." Ibn Khaldun signifies civilization using the words *ʿumrān*, *ḥaḍāra*, and *tamaddun*. Among these words he extensively uses *ʿumrān* and *ḥaḍāra*, which place strong emphasis on the material aspects of civilization. In this spirit he also employs *tamaddun* as a term referring predominantly to the concrete process of building cities as centers of social activity: "cities are used for security and protection."[27] Focusing on the theory

[24] See Maʿan Ziyada's introduction in Khyir al-Din al-Tunisi, *Aqwam al-Masālik fī Maʿrifat Aḥwāl al-Mamālik*, ed. Maʿan Ziyada (Beirut: Al-Muʾassasa al-Jāmiʿiyya lil-Dirāsāt wal-Nashr, 1985), 7–143.

[25] For Ibn al-Diyaf's introduction, see Ahmad Ibn Abi al-Diyaf, *Itḥāf Ahl al-Zamān bi-Akhbār Mulūk Tūnis wa-ʿAhd al-Amān*, vol. 1 (Tunis: Al-Dār al-Tūnisiyya lil-Nashr, 1989), 1–88.

[26] For a comparison of the three introductions, see Ahmad Ibn Abi al-Diyaf, *Consult Them in the Matter: A Nineteenth-Century Islamic Argument for Constitutional Government*, ed. Leon Carl Brown (Fayetteville: The University of Arkansas Press, 2005), 2–3, 21–29.

[27] "*Walmudun innamā ukhidhat lil-taḥaṣṣun.*" See the source and the English translation in Ibn Khaldun, *The Muqaddimah: An Introduction to History*, 1967, 1:75; Ibn Khaldun, *Muqaddimat al-ʿAllāma Ibn Khaldūn al-Musamma Dīwān al-Mubtadaʾ wal-Khabarr fī Taʾrīkh al-ʿArab wal-Barbar wa-man ʿĀṣarahum min Dhawī al-Shaʾn al-Akbarr*, 49.

of the history of civilization, Ibn Khaldun's concept scarcely placed any emphasis on the program that defines the "cultural" content of societies. In that sense comparisons between civilizations or between high sedentary cultures in different civilizations were not part of his preoccupation. He regarded civilization as a general phenomenon, and this is reflected in his concept of the transformation of civilizations: They are adopted by the nearby dynasties that inherit the rule of the declining dynasty. Thus, the Arab dynasties inherited the *ḥaḍāra* (civilization) of the Persian kingdom after it had been demolished.[28]

The dissonance between Ibn Khaldun's concept of civilization and the modern concept is revealed in the subject of politics. Compared to the modern concept, Ibn Khaldun's concept is burdened with less, if any, political content. This aspect is displayed in Ibn Khaldun's account of the political dimension of the word *madaniyya*. There he clearly makes a distinction between his conception and that which is frequent among philosophers. During his discussion of types of *siyāsa* (art of politics), he distinguishes his use of the word from *siyāsa madaniyya* (civil governance):

> We do not mean here [to discuss] that which is known as "*siyāsa madaniyya*." By that, the philosophers [*ḥukamā'*] mean the disposition of soul and character which each member of a social organization must have, if, eventually, people are completely to dispense with rulers. They call the social organization that fulfills these requirements the "ideal city" [*al-madīna al-fāḍila*]. The norms observed in this connection are called "*siyāsa madaniyya*." They do not mean the kind of politics [*siyāsa*] that the members of a social organization are led to adopt through laws for the common interest. That is something different. The "ideal city" [of the philosophers] is something rare and remote. They discuss it as a hypothesis.[29]

The words *ḥukamā'* and *falāsifa* (philosophers) are frequently identified with the medieval adherents of Greek philosophy in general,

[28] Ibn Khaldun, *The Muqaddimah: An Introduction to History*, 1967, 1:351; Ibn Khaldun, *Muqaddimat al-'Allāma Ibn Khaldūn al-Musamma Dīwān al-Mubtada' wal-Khabarr fī Ta'rīkh al-'Arab wal-Barbar wa-man 'Āṣarahum min Dhawī al-Sha'n al-Akbarr*, 188.

[29] 'Abd al-Rahman Ibn Khaldun, *The Muqaddimah: An Introduction to History*, trans. Franz Rosenthal, vol. 2 (Princeton, NJ: Princeton University Press, 1967), 137–138; Ibn Khaldun, *Muqaddimat al-'Allāma Ibn Khaldūn al-Musamma Dīwān al-Mubtada' wal-Khabarr fī Ta'rīkh al-'Arab wal-Barbar wa-man 'Āṣarahum min Dhawī al-Sha'n al-Akbarr*, 318.

especially advocators of Aristotelian metaphysics. There is reason to believe that it is this "rare and remote" use of the word that had the greatest impact on the choice, in the nineteenth century, of *tamaddun* rather than other signifiers of the concept. In medieval philosophical works, the word *madīna* (city) was a subject of politicization and theorization. Philosophers such as al-Farabi (d. 950) and Ibn Bajja (d. 1138) followed Greek philosophers by conceptualizing the state of man as being political by nature. From this perspective words derived from the root *m.d.n.* were most frequently used in a political context: *Madīna* was used as equivalent to the Greek *polis* and *politeia* (city-state and regime) and *madanī* (pl. *madaniyyīn*) as equivalent to *politēs* (citizen or statesman). Many other forms of the word indicate political aspects: *Al-madīna al-jamā'iyya wa madīnat al-aḥrār* (communal city and the city of free men, a denoted democratic polity),[30] *ṣinā'a madaniyya* (political art),[31] *jamā'a madaniyya* (political community),[32] *ta'aqul madanī* (practical political wisdom),[33] *al-sa'āda al-madīniyya* (happiness derived from the political state), and *tadbīr madīnī* (political management) – all these phrases and many others employ words derived from *m.d.n.* in a political context.[34]

In his political works, al-Farabi followed Greek philosophers, arguing that the political society *al-ijtimā' al-madanī* is the superior type of social organization. According to his sociopolitical theory, human organization (*jamā'āt insāniyya*) consists of many sorts of organizations – some are political (*mudun*), and some are not (*laysu madaniyyīn*) – and the highest form is his *al-madīna al-fāḍila* (the ideal or virtuous city). When referring to individuals who live in nonpolitical organizations, he uses the terms *bahā'im unsiyya* and *bahā'im waḥshiyya* (human beasts), and says that such people should be treated exactly as beasts. Al-Farabi's concept of human society presents two pillars of the theory of civilization, civilized people (*madaniyyīn*) and their opposite, savage people, both of which revolved around of the

30 Abu Nasr Muhammad ibn Muhammad al-Farabi, *Kitāb al-Siyāsa al-Madaniyya* (Beirut: Al-Maṭba'a al-Kāthūlīkiyya, 1998), 88.
31 For the Arabic text and its English translation, see al-Farabi, *Fuṣūl al-Madanī*, 28, 104–105.
32 Al-Farabi, *Kitāb al-Siyāsa al-Madaniyya*, 70.
33 Al-Farabi, *Fuṣūl al-Madanī*, 46, 130.
34 Abu Bakr Ibn Bajja, *Rasā'il Falsafiyya li-Abī Bakr Bin Bajja* (Beirut: Dār al-Thaqāfa, 1983), 197, 199.

value of the political state.[35] Furthermore, he elaborates that the aim of political life and human existence is to gain "happiness" (*sa'āda*), the greatest perfection of all (*al-kamāl al-aqṣa*).[36]

The correlation between medieval philosophy and the modern concept of *tamaddun* – which comprises ideas such as the assumption that human beings are by nature political and the ideals of perfection – did not end here. In a few philosophical compositions written in the Middle Ages, the relation between these philosophical principles was stressed. Thus, for instance, Ibn Rushd elaborates on the relation between political life and the importance of human cooperation:

> It is likewise seen to be impossible for one person to make [even] one of these virtues his own without the help of other persons; man is in need of others in acquiring his virtue. Therefore, he is a political being by nature.[37] This is something he needs, not for the human perfections[38] alone, but for the necessities of life as well. These are the things which men and animals have in common to some extent, [things] such as procuring food and obtaining shelter and clothing and, in general, everything man needs on account of the appetitive life forces in him.[39]

The relation between this philosophical background of *m.d.n.* and the morphological form of *tamaddun* appears in eighteenth-century works. One of the philosophical lexicons indicates that the "human being is political [*madanī*] by nature, and that means he needs to live in a political society [*tamaddun*] – that is, he needs to be part of a society that is composed of his kind, to cooperate and share in the effort of acquiring food, clothing, shelter, and other things."[40] These genealogies

[35] Al-Farabi, *Fuṣūl al-Madanī*, 37, 117; al-Farabi, *Kitāb al-Siyāsa al-Madaniyya*, 69, 87–101.

[36] Al-Farabi, *Kitāb al-Siyāsa al-Madaniyya*, 74.

[37] The Arabic origins of Ibn Rushd's *Commentary on Plato* were apparently lost. In the surviving medieval Hebrew translation, bin Yehuda here uses the word *midīnī* (political), which is equivalent to the Arabic *madanī*. The Arabic philosophical and medieval meaning of *madīna* and *madanī* continued to exist in Modern Hebrew, in which the word *midīna* means state, and *midīnī* means "political." For the Hebrew and English translations, see Averroes, *Averroes' Commentary on Plato's Republic*, trans. Erwin Isak Jakob Rosenthal and Samuel bin Yehuda (Cambridge: Cambridge University Press, 1956), 22, 113.

[38] *Ba-shlimuūt ha-inushiūt* in Hebrew, which is equivalent to the Arabic *al-kamālāt al-insāniyya*. Ibid.

[39] Ibid. Similar perceptions existed earlier in al-Farabi's works. See, for instance, al-Farabi, *Kitāb al-Siyāsa al-Madaniyya*, 88.

[40] See 'Abd al-Nabi bin 'Abd al-Rasul Ahmadnakri, "Madanī," *Jāmi' al-'Ulūm fī Iṣṭilāḥāt al-Funūn al-Mulaqqab bi-Dustūr al-'Ulamā'* (Beirut: Mu'assasat

leave, however, little doubt about the philosophical and morphological origins of *tamaddun*, illuminating the meaning of the modern concept as "being political" or "acquiring political life."[41] It goes without saying that the rest of the signifiers of civilization – *'umrān*, *taḥaḍḍur*, or *tamaṣṣur* – have less political emphasis, even in their modern usage.

These philosophical traditions were not commonly known among early nineteenth-century Arabic-speaking scholars, but some of their ideas and their relevance were rediscovered.[42] In the early 1830s al-Tahtawi defined the relation between his translation project and the Egyptian state as a necessity, especially for those involved in *al-siyāsa al-madaniyya* (civil governance), bureaucracy, the military, and mercantile activity.[43] His use of the term *siyāsa madaniyya* leaves no doubt about his acquaintance with these philosophical traditions. By using this concept al-Tahtawi followed ancient and medieval philosophical views that perceived the state as a political organism that consists of members who all act together in harmonic and hierarchic order.[44]

al-A'lamī lil-Maṭbū'āt, 1975), 233–234; 'Abd al-Nabi bin 'Abd al-Rasul Ahmadnakri, "Tamaddun," *Jāmi' al-'Ulūm fī Iṣṭilāḥāt al-Funūn al-Mulaqqab bi-Dustūr al-'Ulamā'* (Beirut: Mu'assasat al-A'lamī lil-Maṭbū'āt, 1975), 350.

41 For additional early modern usage of *m.d.n.*, see John Richardson, "Madanī," *A Dictionary, Persian, Arabic, and English: With a Dissertation on the Languages, Literature, and Manners of Eastern Nations* (London: William Bulmer, 1806), 898–890.

42 Al-Farabi's works were printed in Europe during the 1830s. One of his most important works about the subject of politics was printed in Cairo in 1874. See Abu Nasr Muhammad ibn Muhammad al-Farabi, *Rasāyil Falsafiyya* (Bonn, 1831); Abu Nasr Muhammad ibn Muhammad al-Farabi, *Hādhihi Sharḥ Fuṣūl al-Ḥikam lil-Mu'allim al-Thānī Abī Naṣr al-Fārābī* (Bulaq: Dār al-Ṭibā'a al-'Āmira, 1874). For sources printed or composed in the eighteenth and early nineteenth centuries that mention al-Farabi and discuss philosophical traditions, see 'Adad al-Din al-Ījī, *Kitāb al-Mawāqif* (Constantinople: Dār al-Ṭibā'a al-'Āmira, 1824), 471; Isma'il al-Kalanbawi, *al-Burhān* (Constantinople: Dār al-Ṭibā'a al-'Āmira, 1837), 122–123; Ahmadnakri, "Tamaddun," 350; Ahmadnakri, "Madanī," 165; 'Abd al-Nabi bin 'Abd al-Rasul Ahmadnakri, "al-Siyāsa al-Madaniyya," *Jāmi' al-'Ulūm fī Iṣṭilāḥāt al-Funūn al-Mulaqqab bi-Dustūr al-'Ulamā'* (Beirut: Mu'assasat al-A'lamī lil-Maṭbū'āt, 1975), 194; Muhammad 'Ali al-Tahanawi, "Siyāsa," *Kashshāf Iṣṭilāḥāt al-Funūn wal-'Ulūm* (Beirut: Nāshirūn, 1996), 993–994.

43 The following book is a condensed adaptation of different French books on geography: Al-Tahtawi, *al-Ta'rībāt al-Shāfiya li-Murīd al-Jughrāfiyya*, 3.

44 Al-Farabi defined his perception of the political function of individuals in a polity thus: "Just as the body is composed of different parts of a determinate number, some more, some less excellent, adjacent to each other and graded, each doing a certain work, and there is combined from all their action mutual

The use of this concept returned philosophy, and with it the political idea, to the fore in the Arabic Islamic discourse. In the same way that in al-Farabi's work *al-madīna* occupies the highest virtue of social human perfection (*awwal marātib al-kamālāt*), the progressive thought of the nineteenth century revived the concept of politics and political theory, as is discussed extensively in the coming chapters.[45] Rather than the political domain, *madanī* also occupied a socioreligious function in the nineteenth-century discourse. In the early translations of the French works of Georges-Bernard Depping and Voltaire, the word was used in the context of the contrast between reformed religion that harmonized with the nation-state (*tartīb al-qisīsīn al-madanī*) and reason, on the one hand, and unreformed, irrational, and thus corrupted religion (*bida*ʿ, *ʿaqāʾid fāsida*), on the other.[46] Furthermore, it was used to indicate the separation between religious marriage and civil marriage (*madanī*).[47]

It was against this politicized background of *m.d.n.* that the modern concept of *tamaddun* evolved. The meaning constructed by progressive thinkers of the nineteenth century was absorbed by political connotations; it was no longer ascribed to the city-state (*madīna*) but to the formative reality of the modern nation-state in the Middle East. In this context the political transition that the empire witnessed was perceived as a result of applying *tamaddun*. Reforms that took place in the fields of the military, education, law, finance, and infrastructure demonstrate an attempt to transform the empire from an organization

help towards the perfection of the aim in the man's body, so the city [*al-madīna*]." See al-Farabi, *Fuṣūl al-Madanī*, 37, 117.

45 Al-Farabi, *Kitāb al-Siyāsa al-Madaniyya*, 69.

46 In addition to translated works, the word *madanī* was used during this period among Christian Clerics to indicate realm that pertains from the state (civil), and not from the religious establishment. See for instance the Greek Catholic patriarch Maksimus Mazlum's use of the word in the thirties and forties of the nineteenth century. There, for instance, he used the phrase *baṭriyark madanī* (civil patriarch) to indicate a patriarch who is appointed by the state to fill a formal position. See Georges-Bernard Depping, *Kitāb Qalāʾid al-Mafākhir fī Gharīb ʿAwāʾid al-Awāʾil wal-Awākhir*, trans. Rifaʿa Rafiʿ al-Tahtawi (Bulaq: Dār al-Ṭibāʿa al-ʿĀmira, 1833), 85–94; Voltaire, *Maṭāliʿ Shumūs al-Siyar fī Waqāʾiʿ Karlūs al-Thānī ʿAshar*, trans. Muhammad Mustafa Bashjawish (Bulaq: Maṭbaʿat Sāḥib al-Saʿāda, 1841), 19, 22; Voltaire, *Rawḍ al-Azhar fī Tārīkh Buṭrus al-Akbar*, trans. Ahmad Muhammad ʿAubaid al-Tahtawi (Cairo: Dār al-Ṭibāʿa al-ʿĀmira, 1850), 60, 94, 287–293; Mazlum, *Nabdha Tārīkhiyya: fīmā Jara li-Ṭāʾifat al-Rūm al-Kāthūlīk Mundhu Sant 1837 Famā Baʿdahā*, 62–64, 232, 279–287.

47 Al-Shidyaq, *Mukhtārāt min Āthār Aḥmad Fāris al-Shidyāq*, 282–283.

that functioned mainly in a military and tax-gathering capacity into a pervasive central authority that had direct involvement in the individual's life – socially, economically, and culturally. The earliest steps were taken by Sultan Selim III. These led, in the almost two decades of his rule (1789–1807), to the policy of systematic reform called *Niẓām al-jadīd* ("New Order"), which aimed to renew the military systems of the empire.[48] The idea of reform was extended to include building infrastructure that would reinforce more efficient state control over various fields, including economics and education. These were the first steps toward the comprehensive reform movement (Tanzimat) that the empire underwent between 1839 and 1876.

Similar developments took place in the beginning of the nineteenth century in the semi-independent, Arabic-speaking entities Egypt and Tunisia. Egypt, for instance, the most advanced among the Arabic-speaking provinces, underwent structural alterations under Muhammad ʿAli and his successors. A bureaucratic apparatus controlled by the center was established; a governmental monopoly over agriculture was imposed during the 1820s (but gradually replaced after the 1840s);[49] direct taxation was extended; many Egyptian lands were annexed to the state by destroying the *iltizām* (tax farming) system and weakening the privileged classes; the involvement of native Egyptians in provincial and central councils was extended; after 1823 there was mass conscription of Egyptians, which gave the army an Egyptian character (though the introduction of uniform military service occurred only in the 1850s during Said's reign);[50] a new bureaucratic and educated elite that absorbed modern sciences was constituted; and

[48] For further details about Selim III's reforms, see Stanford J. Shaw, "The Nizam-I Cedid Army under Sultan Selim III 1789–1807," *Oriens* 18/19 (1965–1966): 168–184.

[49] For more details, see Ahmed Abdel-Rahim Mustafa, "The Breakdown of the Monopoly System in Egypt after 1840," in *Political and Social Change in Modern Egypt: Historical Studies from the Ottoman Conquest to the United Arab Republic*, ed. Peter M. Holt (London: Oxford University Press, 1968), 291–307.

[50] The first attempt at replacing Turkish officers with native Egyptians took place in 1840. By the 1870s all the lower ranks of administration had been Egyptianized. After the British occupation of Egypt, the Turks and Circassians had lost their monopoly over high command positions in the army and their position as the largest landowners. For more details about this transition, see Gabriel Baer, "Social Change in Egypt: 1800–1914," in *Political and Social Change in Modern Egypt: Historical Studies from the Ottoman Conquest to the United Arab Republic*, ed. Peter M. Holt (London: Oxford University Press, 1968), 147–150.

the pre-nineteenth-century subsistence economy was replaced by an export-oriented economy.

This reform movement was imagined by contemporary scholars to be an attempt to redefine the political state of the Ottoman subjects by turning them into a unified legal and political community. The transition from the state of subjectivity to the state of citizenship, from static nonpolitical to active political actors, and from conflicting religious groups to a harmonious Ottoman civil community (the ideology of Ottomanism) were the most important components of the idea of *tamaddun*. The philosophical views regarding organic society and social and political perfection would be used repeatedly by progressive scholars of the nineteenth century.

With no less emphasis, *tamaddun* acquired moral and scientific connotations: the belief in continuous improvement in ethics as a result of the distribution of knowledge and endless development in the sciences. The construction of *tamaddun* was conducted in the context of the extension of state education to the common people. In this field the extension of state authority manifested in the establishment of a state school system that functioned independently of the medieval *madrasa* (institution of religious education) and ultimately challenged the knowledge produced in the religious institutions. The earliest developments took place in Anatolia in the Ottoman Empire, beginning with the founding of the first European-style schools of geometry in Istanbul in 1734, followed by the Imperial Naval School in 1773, and the Military Engineering School in 1784. Similarly, Egypt's Muhammad ʿAli had, beginning in the second decade of the nineteenth century, established a series of schools. These schools were run by the state and derived from the needs of the military. Tunis under Ahmad Bey followed similar steps.

This duality of education systems, classical and state, spread all around the empire in the nineteenth century and established political and social tension between what was conceived as "traditional" and what stemmed from *tamaddun*. During Muhammad ʿAli's era social tension existed between the militarized bureaucratic strata, with its new education system, and its rival, the medieval strata of the ʿulama, with its inherited education system (*madrasa*).[51]

[51] John W. Livingston, "Western Science and Educational Reform in the Thought of Shaykh Rifaa al-Tahtawi," *International Journal of Middle East Studies* 28, no. 4 (1996): 543–544, 555.

Culturally, *tamaddun* denoted the extension of bourgeois culture and values from the capital city to the periphery – to the social organization of the town, the village, and the bedouin tribe. Fruma Zachs emphasizes the link between the construction of the idea in the Beirut Christian community and economic and class background. She argues that Christian scholars and merchants of Beirut conceptualized *tamaddun* in a variety of ways, creating their particular understanding of modernity. These middle-class scholars and merchants perceived themselves as "agents of modernization," reconstructing identity and ideals, not only for Beirut but also for Syrian society in general.[52]

The idea of progress constituted an additional layer in the modern concept of *tamaddun*. Historical time as outlined in Ibn Khaldun's theory is cyclic: Dynasties and civilizations rise, and there follows a stage of inevitable decline leading to inevitable demolition (*inqirāḍ*) and return to the primary state. The transition between the two pillars, the rise and the decline, is circular and natural. The future is associated with the past, and civilizations came back to their origin – from the barbaric to the civilized to the barbaric.[53] In the light of his theory, even the greatest kingdoms have to fall eventually. This circular conception of time has its roots in antiquity and in the monotheistic religions as revealed in the story of the creation that is followed by the fall, inevitable death, and redemption in the heavens. This conception of time is distinctly different from the modern idea of civilization. Unlike Ibn Khaldun's concept, the modern idea is intimately related to the idea of progress.

Primary notions of progress existed in Arabic medieval writings, as in Ibn Tufail's (d. 1185) composition *Ḥayy Ibn Yaqẓān*,[54] or in some of

[52] Zachs, *The Making of a Syrian Identity: Intellectuals and Merchants in Nineteenth Century Beirut*, 67–77; Fruma Zachs, "Cultural and Conceptual Contributions of Beiruti Merchants to the Nahḍa," *Journal of the Economic and Social History of the Orient* 55 (2012): 153–182.

[53] Ibn Khaldun, *The Muqaddimah: An Introduction to History*, 1967, 1:353–355; Ibn Khaldun, *Muqaddimat al-'Allāma Ibn Khaldūn al-Musamma Dīwān al-Mubtada' wal-Khabarr fī Ta'rīkh al-'Arab wal-Barbar wa-man 'Āṣarahum min Dhawī al-Sha'n al-Akbarr*, 189–190, 135–136.

[54] A story about using natural reason for improving knowledge and ethics. By following Neoplatonism, Ibn Tufail arrives at the idea of a creator and natural religion through reason and experiment. It is worth noting that according to Ibn Tufail, the idea of perfection lies in God, not in secular time. The major motivation for writing this composition was what he defines as being against

al-Farabi's texts.[55] The modern idea of progress is not merely a belief in the continuous improvement of reason; rather it comprises both a theory of time and a concept of perfection in the secular and earthly future.[56] It replaced the idea that the world is rushing toward its end with the idea of an open future.[57] This optimistic faith emphasizes the necessary connection between advances in knowledge and social betterment: The advancement of reason, the establishment of a rational state, and the improvement of secular sciences and human knowledge will lead to endless improvement and greater happiness and prosperity in this world.[58]

Given the historical circumstances of the French-Egyptian encounter in 1798–1801, *tamaddun* and *taqaddum* were deeply infused with the

"corrupted ideas of those who think that they are philosophers [*mutafalsifa*]." His primary objective in writing this composition was to reconcile philosophy and revelation. Muhammad ibn ʿAbd al-Malik Ibn Tufail, *Ḥayy Ibn Yaqẓān* (Cairo: Kalimāt, 2011).

55 See, for instance, al-Farabi, *Kitāb al-Siyāsa al-Madaniyya*, 82–83.

56 It is widely accepted to ascribe the idea of progress to Francis Bacon (d. 1626), the "grand architect" of the Enlightenment. Bacon, who apparently became known to Arabic journalists only in the second half of the nineteenth century (see *al-Laṭāʾif*), argued that classical philosophy had infected medieval Christian thought and retarded the progress of knowledge because of the confusion it had inherited (particularly from Plato and Aristotle) between natural science and theology. Implementing a theoretical rather than a practical approach in the study of nature left this field under the spell of philosophy, theology, and speculation. Bacon advocated conducting the study of nature using methods of experimentation and induction. He believed that when humanity succeeded in controlling nature and removing its constraints from the human body, the illusions that distort politics would also be revealed. For further details on the history of this idea in the West, see Jerry Weinberger, "Idea of Progress," *New Dictionary of the History of Ideas* (Detroit, MI: Charles Scribner's Sons, 2005), 1912–1916; Eric Robertson Dodds, "Progress in Classical Antiquity," *Dictionary of the History of Ideas: Studies of Selected Pivotal Ideas* (New York: Scribner, 1973–1974), 623–633; Morris Ginsberg, "Progress in the Modern Era," *Dictionary of the History of Ideas: Studies of Selected Pivotal Ideas* (New York: Scribner, 1974), 633–650; *al-Laṭāʾif* 2, no. 8 (1887): 337.

57 Reinhart Koselleck phrases the uniqueness of the new expectation of Western progress thus: "The experience of the past and the expectation of the future moved apart; they were progressively dismantled, and this difference was finally conceptualized by the common word progress." Reinhart Koselleck, *The Practice of Conceptual History: Timing History, Spacing Concepts* (Palo Alto, CA: Stanford University Press, 2002), 228–229.

58 In a comprehensive approach, Francis Bacon made the association between natural science, the foundation of a rational, secular state, and happiness. For more details, see Weinberger, "Idea of Progress," 1912–1913.

French conception of civilization and progress. Despite the fact that the French perceived themselves as culturally superior in early modernity, the word "civilization" entered the French language only in the middle of the eighteenth century, via Enlightenment scholars such as Mirabeau and Linguet, who employed it to denote a level of social perfection. The intellectual historian Stuart Woolf illustrated how after the French Revolution the French concept of civilization had acquired a quasi-scientific layer, and its political usage reached its peak during the Napoleonic Empire. Then, the word was instrumentalized to justify and legitimize French imperial policies.[59]

During the eighteenth century Voltaire divided the progress of civilizations, both inside and outside of Europe, according to levels of development.[60] European civilization occupied the highest level in the pyramid of civilized societies and contrasted with other societies in the external spheres that he depicted using the terms "barbaric" or "savage" (usually attributed to nations in Asia, Africa, and North and South America). In the internal European space, he designated elites by using "civilized" in contrast with the "ignorant" or "rural" common people who lived far from urban life and its economic patterns.[61] History, according to his periodization of progress, consists of three main periods that are characterized by their level of progress; unlike antiquity, the Middle Ages are perceived as a stage of backwardness, a regression or retreat from the advanced state of reason that was achieved in both antiquity and modernity.[62] In the Arabic-speaking provinces, the Voltairean view of progress and civilization was most influential. In fact Voltaire was for Arabic speakers one of the most prominent French philosophers of the Enlightenment. Al-Tahtawi and his disciples translated and published at least two of his works prior to the end of the first half of the nineteenth century: *History of Charles XII, King of Sweden*, published in 1841, was first, and *Russia under Peter the Great* was published in 1850.[63]

[59] Stuart Woolf, "French Civilization and Ethnicity in the Napoleonic Empire," *Past and Present* 124, no. 1 (August 1, 1989): 96–120.
[60] Ibid., 96. [61] Ibid., 97. [62] Ibid., 96.
[63] Voltaire, *Maṭāliʿ Shumūs al-Siyar fī Waqāʾiʿ Karlūs al-Thānī ʿAshar*; Voltaire, *Rawḍ al-Azhar fī Tārīkh Buṭrus al-Akbar*. Earlier unprinted Arabic translations of his works were produced from modern Greek versions. For more details, see Peter Hill, "The First Arabic Translations of Enlightenment Literature: The Damietta Circle of the 1800s and 1810s," *Intellectual History Review* (2015): 5–8.

The time of progress had a profound impact on the Arabic word *taqaddum*, which would eventually become the most frequently used signifier for this concept.[64] Seventeenth- and eighteenth-century philosophical lexicons categorize the use of the word *taqaddum* in five discursive categories: the field of time, in which *taqaddum* served as an adjective to denote a predecessor in time (as in Moses was *mutaqaddim* in relation to Jesus); the relation between absolute cause (*'illa tāma*) and effect, in which *mutaqaddim* is the activity that independently influences the incomplete cause (*'illa nāqiṣa*), as in the case of sunrise – *taqaddum al-shams* – in relation to day; level or place, in which *taqaddum* means to be closer to a certain principle or place (the relative principle); instinct or nature (*taqaddum bil-ṭab'*), such as the *taqaddum* of the number 1 in relation to the number 2; and in relation to honor, in which the predecessor has greater honor and reputation in relation to the successor (as in *taqaddum* Abu Bakr in relation to Umar Ibn al-Khatab).[65]

Among these five categories that cover the temporal eighteenth-century connotations of the use of *taqaddum*, the shift that took place during the 1820s and 1830s occurred predominantly in the first three categories. The frame of reference of *taqaddum* had transformed from past to future, in relation to the time, and with relation to the relative principle (see the third category). Prior to the nineteenth century, *taqaddum* was commonly used in relation to the past but not the future. In that sense, the word meant predecessor. Thus, yesterday precedes (*mutaqaddim*) today, and today succeeds (*muta'akhkhir*) the past. *Zamān mutaqaddim* meant "preceding time" while "*zamān*

64 This chapter does not attempt to explore the concept of time in Islam, but rather the emergence of the modern idea of progress and its impact on nineteenth-century Arabic thought. For research inquiring into the concept of time in the Qur'an, hadith, and the medieval theological and mystical Islamic traditions, see Gerhard Böwering, "The Concept of Time in Islam," *Proceedings of the American Philosophical Society* 141, no. 1 (1997): 55–66.

65 See these seventeenth- and eighteenth-century philosophical lexicons: Muhammad 'Ali al-Tahanawi, "Taqaddum," *Kashshāf Iṣṭilāḥāt al-Funūn wal-'Ulūm* (Beirut: Nāshirūn, 1996), 495; 'Abd al-Nabi bin 'Abd al-Rasul Ahmadnakri, "al-Taqaddum," *Jāmi' al-'Ulūm fī Iṣṭilāḥāt al-Funūn al-Mulaqqab bi-Dustūr al-'Ulamā'* (Beirut: Mu'assasat al-A'lamī lil-Maṭbū'āt, 1975), 334–338; Muhammad Murtada al-Husayni al-Zubaydi, "Q.d.m," *Tāj al-'Arūs min Jawāhir al-Qāmūs* (Kuwait: Maṭba'at Ḥukūmat al-Kūwayt, 2000), 235–250.

*muta'akhkhir*" denoted recent time.[66] Following the same logic, in Arabic dictionaries prior to the nineteenth century, the meaning of the word *mutaqaddimun* was presented as a synonym for *salaf* (predecessors),[67] and *taqaddum* was defined as "being first."[68] By the 1820s the time dimension of the word was infused with the concept of progress and frequently switched the frame of reference from past to future (a parallel shift took place in the meaning of *ta'akhur*, which came to denote regression). One aspect of this transition is expressed in the translation of the word into Western languages: In dictionaries composed prior to the nineteenth century, the word was translated as "precedence,"[69] while after the beginning of the nineteenth century the word was predominantly translated as "progress."[70] In modern Arabic, *mutaqaddim* means advanced in relation to others; advancement here has an imagined time reference and a connotation that is linked to the imagined space of the future.

[66] Thus, *mutaqaddim* is synonym to *sābiq* (which comes first) an in contrast with *muta'akhkhir* which denote *laḥiq* (which comes last). See: Al-Tahanawi, "Taqaddum," 496.

[67] For selected examples, see al-Juhari's tenth-century dictionary, al-Saghani's fifteenth-century dictionary, al-Kaffawis' and Ahmadnakri's seventeenth- and eighteenth-century dictionaries: Isma'il Ibn Hamad al-Juhari, "Salaf," *al-Ṣiḥāḥ fī al-Lugha: Tāj al-Lugha wa-Ṣiḥāh al-'Arabiyya* (Beirut: Dār al-'Ilm lil-Malāyīn, 1990), 1376–1377; al-Hassan bin Muhammad al-Hassan al-Saghani, "Salaf," *al-'Ibab al-Zakhir wal-Libab al-Fakhir* (Iraq: Dār al-Rashīd, 1981), 288–289; Abi al-Baqa' Ayyub ibn Musa Kaffawi, "al-Salaf," *al-Kulliyāt: Mu'jam fī al-Muṣṭalaḥāt wal-Furūq al-Lughawiyya* (Beirut: Mu'assasat al-Risāla, 1998), 511; Ahmadnakri, "al-Taqaddum," 335.

[68] Ahmadnakri, "al-Taqaddum," 334.

[69] None the following lexicons, which were composed prior to the first decade of the nineteenth century, use progress as a translation of *taqaddum*: Francisci Meninski, "Taqaddam," *Lexicon Arabico-Persico-Trucicum: Adiecta Ad Singulas Voces et Phrases Significatione Latina, Ad Usitatiores Etiam Italica* (Viennae: Nunc secundis curis recognitum et auctum, 1780), 103; William Kirkpatrick, "Qdm," *A Vocabulary, Persian, Arabic, and English* (London: Printed by Joseph Cooper, Drury-Lane, 1785), 115; John Richardson, "Taqaddam," *A Dictionary, Persian, Arabic, and English: with a Dissertation on the Languages, Literature, and Manners of Eastern Nations* (London: William Bulmer, 1806), 287; David Hopkins, "Taqaddam," *A Vocabulary, Persian, Arabic, and English; Abridged from the Quarto Edition of Richardson's Dictionary* (London: Printed for F. and C. Rivingson, 1810), 164.

[70] For selected example of early translations of "progress" as *taqaddum*, see Rufa'il Zakhur, "Progresso," *Dizionario Italiano E Arabo* (Bolacco: Dalla Stamperia Reale, 1822), 149.

The dimension that marked the relation between *taqaddum* and its relative principle[71] was defined by the word *tamaddun* (civilization): *taqaddum* underwent a change in tense and meaning, from "being first" in relation to the past (predecessor) to "being first" in relation to the future (most advanced) – wherein lies the idea of the perfect civilization (*tamaddun*). Using both words, *tamaddun* and *taqaddum*, as adjectives embeds the notion of "process" or "course of development," which moves in a metaphorical scale of time toward the future; while *taqaddum* possessed the idea of a metaphorical course of time, *tamaddun* conveyed the principle that switched the time reference from the past to the future, and more precisely, toward an imagined future that was significantly influenced by the Enlightenment.

This transformation in the use of *taqaddum* manifested in works composed in the second half of the nineteenth century. A well-known joke in Arabic that takes place in 1881 has the following dialogue between a Turk and a European:

E: I still see you these days as fanatics.
T: Why?
E: All your talk is related to love and romance. This does not fit the spirit of our century, the nineteenth century.
T: Excuse me, Sir, for this, but we still live in the thirteenth century, six centuries before your time, but when we reach your time, and become part of the nineteenth century, we will follow you and abandon these issues.[72]

The metaphorical time of the Turk, as someone who still lives in the past in relation to the "civilized" European, demonstrates the switch undergone by the word *taqaddum*.

In the larger context the evolution of *taqaddum* and *tamaddun* was widely influenced by local and global transitions in the concepts of time and distance. During the years when these modern concepts were evolving, revolutionary inventions in communication and transportation occurred. The inauguration of Arabic press and newspapers took place during the first two decades of the nineteenth century. The electric telegraph was adopted by the Ottoman government in the 1850s; in the

[71] The principle that defines the relational dimension and answers the question: *taqaddum* in relation to what?
[72] *Al-Jinān* 4 (1881): 160.

same decade the steam engine reached the Ottoman Empire, resulting in a change from the stagecoach to the steam locomotive. The first telegraph linked Europe to Istanbul in 1855, and the first telegraph line in Egypt linked Cairo with Alexandria in 1854 (though the first telegraph line in England began operating eighteen years earlier). The telegraph linking Istanbul to Baghdad began operating in 1861, while the first railway to operate in Egypt (between Cairo and Alexandria) opened in 1856. In that same year, a railway line was inaugurated in Anatolia from Izmir to Aydin (thirty-one years after the first railway line in England).[73]

The telegraph created a separation between transportation and communication: Messages no longer depended on horses, pigeons, or ships, and communication no longer depended on the constraints of geography and transportation on the power of an animal. These measures had an enormous impact on the spread of the press, journalism, and the spread of ideas.[74] Most of the nineteenth-century journals and newspapers had sections that focused on foreign news received by telegraph. These developments deeply influenced concepts of time and space and made contemporaries more aware of time than preceding generations had been.[75]

Texts composed during the 1820s and 1830s present, as a result of the encounter between language and new ideas, morphological instability and rare articulations and expressions. One of the illuminating texts that uniquely capture the dissonance between temporal language

[73] Davison, *Essays in Ottoman and Turkish History, 1774–1923: The Impact of the West*, 133; Ebubekir Ceylan, *The Ottoman Origins of Modern Iraq: Political Reform, Modernization and Development in the Nineteenth Century Middle East* (London: I. B. Tauris, 2011), 187–189.

[74] Some of these life-altering inventions were documented in Arabic by travelers who reached Europe. Faris al-Shidyaq described the telegraph as "the greatest miracle of our age" and the gas streetlights as "one of the greatest blessings." In addition to the steam engine, the modern press and hot air balloons attracted the attention of Eastern travelers. For the impression of all these inventions on al-Shidyaq and Salim Busturus, a merchant from Beirut who visited Europe in 1855, see Ahmad Faris al-Shidyaq, *al-Wāsiṭa ila Maʿrifat Aḥwāl Mālṭa wa-Kashf al-Mukhabbāʾ ʿan Funūn Ūrūbā* (Beirut: Kutub, 2002), 198, 205, 263, 306–307; al-Shidyaq, *Kanz al-Raghāʾib fī Muntakhabāt al-Jawāʾib*, 1871, 1:16–21, 21–22, 23, 49–51; Salim ibn Musa Bustrus, *al-Nuzha al-Shahiyya fī al-Riḥla al-Salīmiyya, 1855* (Beirut: Al-Muʾassasa al-ʿArabiyya lil-Dirāsāt wal-Nashr, 2003), 88–89.

[75] Davison, *Essays in Ottoman and Turkish History, 1774–1923: The Impact of the West*, 147, 155–156.

and the articulation of the time of progress is presented in al-Tahtawi's account of his journey to Paris:

As time rises [*fī al-ṣuʿūd*] toward the past [*taqādam*], you will observe people regressing [*taʾakhur al-nās*] in human skills and civil sciences [*al-ʿulūm al-madaniyya*], and the more you go downward and observe the descent of time [*fī al-hubūṭ*], you mostly will see their elevation and progress [in skills and sciences].[76]

In this articulation, al-Tahtawi employs the premodern concept of time that consists of a process of continuous falling. Thus he expresses the movement of time in terms of decline from a high position (the heavens) to one that is lower (the present). He combines this perception with the state of progress in skills and sciences, but without extending it to the perception of time as a linear course of progress. The dissonance is emphasized in the overall picture he portrays – a state of backwardness that is located in a higher position of time than the state of advancement in sciences and skills. It goes without saying that his expression might be vague for those alive at the end of the nineteenth century who had become acquainted with the idea of progress.[77]

## Theorization and Instrumentalization of "Civilization" and "Progress"

"Civilization" was already used as a theory of history by al-Tahtawi in his early account of his journey to Paris. He elaborated the three universal stages of the historical time of progress: savage nations (*mutawaḥḥishīn*), barbaric nations (*barābira*), and civilized nations (*ahl al-ʾadab wal-ẓarāfa wal-taḥaḍḍur wal-tamaddun wal-tamaṣṣur*). He classified the inhabitants of *bilād al-Sūdān* (the regions of the blacks) in the first category, the bedouin in the second, and the inhabitants of Egypt, Greater Syria, North Africa, eastern and western

[76] Al-Tahtawi, *Takhlīṣ al-Ibrīz fī Talkhīṣ Bārīz aw al-Dīwān al-Nafīs bi-Īwān Bārīs*, 6.

[77] The double meanings of the Arabic words *mutaqaddimīn* and *mutaʾakhkhirīn*, which imply both progressed or preceding and regressed or subsequent, were often used in nineteenth-century texts in the same sentence. For examples using these words with double meanings, see Karniliyus Fandik, "fī Faḍl al-Mutaʾakhkhirīn ʿala al-Mutaqaddimīn," in *al-Jamʿiyya al-Sūriyya lil-ʿUlūm wal-Funūn, 1847–1852*, ed. Butrus al-Bustani (Beirut: Dār al-Ḥamrāʾ, 1990), 79–82; *al-Muqtaṭaf* 8, no. 1 (1883): 479–483; *al-Laṭāʾif* 1, no. 12 (1886): 83–86.

Europe, and most of "the regions of America" (*bilād Amrīka*) in the third.[78] Al-Tahtawi believed that the highest "perfect civilized state" (*kamāl al-tamaddun, darajat al-kamāl*) and the perfectability of humanity are possible in the earthly state.[79]

In addition to his universal classification, parameters and principles that constitute the idea of progress acquired Islamic particularity.[80] Al-Tahtawi's parameters for the advancement of society pertain to the acquisition of scientific knowledge in both the religious sciences (*al-'ulūm shar'iyya*)[81] and the nonreligious sciences (*al-'ulūm al-ḥikmiyya*).[82] According to al-Tahtawi, in terms of the former, the Muslims were advanced, and according to the second they were backward. Based on this logic, he classified the world's five continents according to their "progress" in Islamic sciences and the distribution of Islam, making "the regions of America" the least advanced when compared with the other continents.[83]

In al-Tahtawi's works the idea of progress has a practical aspect. He legitimizes, in an apologetic way, the acceptance of European culture by arguing that the Muslims needed to learn the sciences that Europeans had taken from them in the past. He believed that progress in the sciences was necessary to close the development gap that existed between Muslim and European countries. He advocated the idea of acculturation by contending that "he [Muhammad 'Ali] does this because of their [the Europeans'] human qualities and knowledge, and not because they are Christians."[84]

Despite his esteem for the idea of progress, he distinguishes between his perception and that which he observed in France: The French

[78] Al-Tahtawi, *Takhlīṣ al-Ibrīz fī Talkhīṣ Bārīz aw al-Dīwān al-Nafīs bi-Īwān Bārīs*, 6–7.

[79] Al-Tahtawi, *al-Ta'rībāt al-Shāfiya li-Murīd al-Jughrāfiyya*, app. 67, 70.

[80] Ibid., 67.

[81] According to al-Tahtawi, *al-'ulūm al-shar'iyya* consists of law (*fiqh*), exegesis (*tafsīr*), and tradition (*ḥadīth*). See: Al-Tahtawi, "Kitāb al-Murshid al-Amīn lil-Banāt wal-Banīn," 806–807.

[82] According to al-Tahtawi, *al-'ulūm al-ḥikmiyya* consists of: literature (*'ulūm adabiyya*), mathematics (*'ulūm riyaḍiyya*), and rational sciences (*'ulūm 'aqliyya*). Mohammed Sawaie, "Rifa'a Rafi' al-Tahtawi and His Contribution to the Lexical Development of Modern Literary Arabic," *International Journal of Middle East Studies* 32, no. 3 (2000): 25–26; al-Tahtawi, "Kitāb al-Murshid al-Amīn lil-Banāt wal-Banīn," 806–807.

[83] Al-Tahtawi, *Takhlīṣ al-Ibrīz fī Talkhīṣ Bārīz aw al-Dīwān al-Nafīs bi-Īwān Bārīs*, 18.

[84] Ibid., 8.

believed that progress in different aspects of life and literature could constitute an alternative to religion. The French, whom he designates by the term *ibāḥiyyīn* (libertarians), did not believe in metaphysics; instead they regarded any human action verified by reason as legitimate.[85] This observation emphasizes al-Tahtawi's orthodox religious stance on the limits of progress and his early rejection of the naturalist Enlightenment idea of religious indifferentism: "that all religions are true, and their purpose is the creation of goodness."[86]

A few decades later another contemporary, Butrus al-Bustani, outlined different parameters of progress. He, like al-Tahtawi, presented two interpretations of the history of civilization: secular and religious. According to his secular interpretation, early civilizations maintained a primitive life (*tawaḥḥush, barbariyya*), acquired food by hunting, and developed language and societies only later. The next level of development was reached with agriculture, settlement, and the establishment of cities. At the highest level, science was invented and *taqaddum* was attained and spread.[87] Beside this secular interpretation, he presents his religious Christian perception: God created man and with him, human society. The revelation that accompanied the process of establishing religious laws instituted the primary civilizations, which had many offshoots that developed in different ways, filling different levels of progress. He agreed that civilizations should be categorized by their level of "perfection" (*kamāl*) in terms of progress, from the lowest to the highest.[88] He argues that the basic parameters for measuring a level of progress are justice and economic prosperity. Of these two universal elements, he stated, the idea of civil rights (*al-ḥuqūq al-jumhūriyya*), which constitutes a basic principle of justice, is the most important measurement for progress.[89]

[85] He presents French rationalism as a contradiction to metaphysics and as a conviction regarding religious truth. For examples of the nature of the relation between reason and religion, see al-Tahtawi, *Takhlīṣ al-Ibrīz fī Talkhīṣ Bārīz aw al-Dīwān al-Nafīs bi-Īwān Bārīs*, 19, 53.

[86] Ibid., 19, 35.

[87] Butrus al-Bustani, "Tamaddun," *Kitāb Dā'irat al-Ma'ārif* (Beirut: Dār al-Ma'ārif, 1882), 213.

[88] The above quotation from al-Bustani's essay aside (it had been published relatively late – in 1882), the idea of progress did appear in his early works. See ibid.; Butrus al-Bustani, *al-Jam'iyya al-Sūriyya lil-'Ulūm wal-Funūn, 1847–1852* (Beirut: Dāral-Ḥamrā', 1990), 47.

[89] Al-Bustani, "Tamaddun," 214.

Al-Bustani's universalism was also impacted by Protestant theological convictions. He argues that the origins of progress and civilization can be found in Christianity because Christianity brought and spread the idea that all men are born equal in nature, and they are part of one family, the human family.[90] Al-Bustani argued that this humanist equality is a fundamental principle of *tamaddun*, and its success is subject to the will of a political power to spread the idea of human solidarity from the church to the civil community of the state, and from religion to politics.[91] What al-Tahtawi (in the previous quotation) viewed as the French naturalist principle of religious indifferentism was exposed in al-Bustani's thought on the practical level as part of his theorization of the social and political ideal of *tamaddun*. Alongside his Christian faith, the idea of natural equality had evolved in al-Bustani's thought as part of the experience of the religious conflicts and the persecution of Christians in Greater Syria in 1860, as detailed in the coming chapters. He made the state of *tamaddun* conditional upon equality and tolerance, saying that the Syrian inhabitants (*ahālī Sūriyya*) would be able to reach the highest levels of civilization (*al-taqaddum fī al-ādāb wal-ṣanaʾiʿ wal-irtiqāʾ ila asma darajāt al-tamaddun*) if they were able to constitute a tolerant and equal society.[92]

From the perspective of the institutional scholar Faris al-Shidyaq, *tamaddun* is a pragmatic term. In a critical essay he wrote in 1861 on the Western aspects of *tamaddun*, he attacked the "barbarian" aspect of "civilized" societies of the West while stressing the powerful impact of this concept.[93] Against the background of the religious clashes in Syria, he argued that civilized nations nurture values such as religious tolerance, national solidarity, and cooperation: "The differences between various religions and their religious schools [*madhāhib*] should not be a reason for conflict between the inhabitants of a kingdom who share the same *waṭan* [homeland]." The social conflicts between subjects of the same kingdom, he argued, prevented the establishment of a completely civilized state (*tamadduntām*) and weakened the kingdom.[94] Following al-Bustani, al-Shidyaq argues

[90] Ibid., 215. [91] Ibid. [92] Al-Bustani, *Nafīr Sūriyya*, 48.
[93] Al-Shidyaq did not maintain a consistent attitude regarding *tamaddun*. For his pragmatic approach and inconsistent use of the term, see al-Shidyaq, *Mukhtārāt min Āthār Aḥmad Fāris al-Shidyāq*, 91–92, 108–124, 134, 154.
[94] Ibid., 155, 157.

that ignorance and fanaticism would lead to political weakness and backwardness.[95]

Faris al-Shidyaq, a scholar who converted from Maronite Christianity to Protestantism to Islam, identifies unity of language as a central reason for progress. In a distinction between the evolution of civilization as it occurred in the East and the West, he argued that in the West languages had evolved as part of the progress of civilization, while progress for "Arab" civilization (*tamaddun*) was based on developments in the language.[96] He claimed that what Europeans call *mutamaddin* (civilized) meant *muta'dib* (polite, having good manners) in Arabic.[97] The emphasis on language and ethics was stressed by Christian scholars such as the cleric and journalist Lewis al-Sabunji and Salim al-Bustani, who defined "uncivilized" (*ghayr mutamaddin*) as one who lacks good manners (*ādāb, akhlāq*) and knowledge (*ma'ārif*).[98]

The nineteenth century witnessed additional and more comprehensive conceptualizations of progress and civilization that go beyond the purposes of this chapter. The new conceptions of civilization and progress, in all their variety, undermined the social, religious, and political status quo by igniting the discussion about the paradox of modernity and tradition. This contention between the "old" and "new" was widely presented in the translated literature of the 1830s and 1840s. In an early translation of Depping by al-Tahtawi (published in 1833), "progress in sciences and arts" (*al-taqaddum fī al-'ulūm wal-funūn*) was presented in contrast with superstitions and corrupted beliefs (*al-'aqā'id al-fāsida, bida'*) and constituted an antonym of *taqlīd* (traditionalism).[99] This severe rivalry between the authority of reason and the authority of tradition was extensively perceived as a central theme in the quest for reform and progress. During the 1830s through the 1850s, Greek philosophical and Western Enlightenment works were translated into Arabic. One of the early translations (published in 1838) was a book by Khalifa Mahmud, an al-Tahtawi

95 Ibid., 154. 96 Ibid., 391.

97 Al-Shidyaq, *Kanz al-Raghā'ib fī Muntakhabāt al-Jawā'ib*, 1871, 1:3–4; *al-Jawā'ib*, July 12, 1876, 5.

98 *Al-Naḥla*, May 11, 1870, 5; *al-Jinān* 1 (1870): 22.

99 See al-Tahtawi's translation of Georges-Bernard Depping's *Aperçu historique sur les mœurs et coutumes des nations*: Depping, *Kitāb Qalā'id al-Mafākhir fī Gharīb 'Awā'id al-Awā'il wal-Awākhir*, 85.

student, that focuses on the idea of reason and logic, redefining the function of reason as a tool for understanding metaphysics.[100] A similar theme appeared in translations of history books that raised the subject of religious reformation.[101] Nevertheless, the contradiction between science and reason with irrational beliefs was most emphasized in translations of Voltaire into Arabic. Voltaire's raising of the subject of religious reforms stemmed from his belief in progress. As previously mentioned, in his works he contrasted reformed religion, reason, and science, on the one hand, with unreformed religion and superstitious beliefs, on the other. He conceptualized these contradictions by the terms "progress" and "tradition," which highlight the conflict between the interests of the enlightened state and the backward laws of the unreformed religious.[102] In his translated works the enemies of the Enlightenment were conceptualized in Arabic by the terms *taqlīd* (traditionalism) and *asra al-ʿawāʾid al-qadīma* (prisoners of the ancient traditions), which designate irrational, traditional, "ignorant" social forces.[103] These texts not only marked the social forces that

[100] This is a translation of the work of César Chesneau Dumarsais (d. 1756), one of the prominent figures of the French Enlightenment and a contributor to Diderot's famous *Encyclopédie*. César Chesneau Dumarsais, *Tanwīr al-Mashriq bi-ʿIlm al-Manṭiq*, trans. Khalifa Mahmud (Bulaq: Al-Maṭbaʿa al-ʿĀmira, 1838).

[101] See the early translated history of the Reformation in *Qiṣat Martin Luthir*. See also William Robertson, *Kitāb Itḥāf Mulūk al-Zamān bi-Tārīkh al-Imbirāṭūr Sharlakān Masbūqan bi-Muqaddimatihi al-Musammā Itḥāf al-Mulūk al-Alibbāʾ bi-Taqaddum al-Jamʿīyyāt fī Ūrūbā Mundhu Inqirāḍ al-Dawla al-Rūmāniyya*, trans. Khalifa Ibn Mahmud, vol. 1 (Bulaq: Al-Maṭbaʿa al-ʿĀmira, 1844), 87–123. See Voltaire's account of the religious reformation in Russia under Peter the Great in Voltaire, *Rawḍ al-Azhar fī Tārīkh Buṭrus al-Akbar*, 287–293.

[102] See the discussion on church reforms in Voltaire, *Maṭāliʿ Shumūs al-Siyar fī Waqāʾiʿ Karlūs al-Thānī ʿAshar*, 19, 22; Voltaire, *Rawḍ al-Azhar fī Tārīkh Buṭrus al-Akbar*, 60, 94, 287–293.

[103] In addition to the translations of Voltaire, see one of the published presentations of the Syrian Society for Sciences and Arts, 1847–1852, in which the author criticizes, in the name of enlightened reason (*al-ʿaql al-munawar*), the ancient traditions (*al-ʿawāʾid al-qadīma*) that he identifies with dark reason (*al-ʿaql al-muẓlim*) and ignorance. It is worth mentioning that Butrus al-Bustani published in 1882 an entry titled "tradition" (*taqlīd*). In this entry he gives a general definition of "tradition" as meaning following customs without rational evidence (*dalīl*). See Karniliyus Fandik, "fī Lidhat al-ʿIlm wa-Fawaʾiduhu," in *al-Jamʿiyya al-Sūriyya lil-ʿUlūm wal-Funūn, 1847–1852*, ed. Butrus al-Bustani (Beirut: Dār al-Ḥamrāʾ, 1990), 27–28; Voltaire, *Rawḍ*

hindered the movement of progress but also politicized the mental realm by establishing two groups, the opponents and the proponents of progress.

The intensive preoccupation with civilization and progress was not confined to theoretical debates. As in the French and British cases, some institutional and semi-institutional scholars instrumentalized the concept for the justification of state policies and military actions.[104] In an 1875 article about the Russian-British rivalry over India in his newspaper, *al-Jawā'ib*, al-Shidyaq surveys, in the semiformal Arabic voice of the empire, the failure of the diplomatic endeavor to keep Russia away from India. He comments that the Russian military advance in Central Asia and the spread of civilization (*tamaddun*) could be beneficial for the British by making these nations open to British commercial activity. He concludes that in the long run, making any place in the world become civilized (*tamaddun wal-'imrān*) would eventually attract British authority, as had happened in the Suez Canal – where initially its opening was opposed, but after its inauguration the British discovered its commercial importance and came close to controlling it. He explains *bilād mutamaddina* (civilized regions) as places safe from anarchy, making secure trade possible.[105]

Furthermore, al-Shidyaq uses the concepts of progress and civilization (*tamaddun*) to justify military actions and colonialism. In 1875 he commented on the news of the advance of the Egyptian army toward Ethiopia, contending that the Ethiopian king had attacked Egyptians and the British and had exploited his own "ignorant" people. Al-Shidyaq claims that because of the horrific and unprecedented actions committed by the king, the Egyptian state of the khedive should intervene "due to reasons of humanity and mercy" to establish peace and order and "to teach to its inhabitants arts, civilization [*tamaddun*], and good manners."[106] He argues that the Ethiopians are barbaric people (*qawm hamaj*), and their region is still underdeveloped – they have no factories, libraries, commerce, or agriculture. In his view, what

*al-Azhar fī Tārīkh Buṭrus al-Akbar*, 60, 94; Voltaire, *Maṭāli' Shumūs al-Siyar fī Waqā'i' Karlūs al-Thānī 'Ashar*, 19–20; Butrus al-Bustani, "Taqlīd," *Kitāb Dā'irat al-Ma'ārif* (Beirut: Maṭba'at al-Ma'ārif, 1882), 182–183.

104 For articles against "savage" or aggressive *tamaddun*, see *al-Jinān* 18 (1870): 633–634; *al-Muqtaṭaf* 9, no. 1 (1884): 393–397.

105 *Al-Jawā'ib*, July 28, 1875.

106 *Al-Jawā'ib*, December 15, 1875, 1.

made the situation worse was that the region had many unused natural resources, and he therefore urged Egypt to colonize Ethiopia (*istīṭān*) because of its close geographical position. Egyptian colonialism in Ethiopia could, in his view, be beneficial to Europe because it would allow European representatives (councils) to live in security. He found an additional benefit for the native "barbaric" inhabitants of Ethiopia in the fact that under Egyptian governance they would live under just Muslim rule that would prevent the slave trade. He suggests establishing Egyptian rule in Ethiopia without using violence by, for example, convincing the heads of the Ethiopian clans to accept "being saved" from anarchy by applying Egyptian rule, and "they would do it if they were human [*idhā kānū bashar*]." He argued that there was no similarity between the illegitimate case of the American invasion of Mexico and the attempted Egyptian step, because the government of Mexico was based on order and had laws, a parliament, and institutions, while Ethiopia did not – it was outside the circle of "civilization and justice" [*al-tamaddun wal-ʿadl*].[107] Instead he suggested that this case should be compared with the Russian invasions of Central Asia.[108] However, this was not the first time that al-Shidyaq used the argument of progress and civilization as part of a call to occupy Ethiopia. He urged action repeatedly for almost a decade and was criticized by some British authors.[109] However, aware of his non-Arab audience, he estimated that this time the British newspapers would support his idea.[110]

A similar approach was applied in other African regions, where a reporter from *al-Jawāʾib* in Khartoum portrayed the victory of the Egyptian khedive's armies in the region as a victory for those who "advocate the spread of civilization [*tamaddun*], the extension of the limits of trade, and the authority of the government and those who care for the benefits of the people of Darfur, for their assimilation into the state of humanity and their attainment of freedom, prosperity, and security."[111] *Al-Jawāʾib* transmitted to its readers the alleged joy of the people in gaining these benefits, and their statements that "they have exited from darkness to light [*min al-ẓalma ila al-nūr*] and regretted their former time when they were not under the rule of the khedive."

107 Ibid. 108 Ibid. 109 *Al-Jawāʾib*, June 10, 1868, 1.
110 *Al-Jawāʾib*, December 15, 1875, 1; *al-Jawāʾib*, December 14, 1875.
111 *Al-Jawāʾib*, July 12, 1876, 5.

They even hoped that the khedive would invade other territories in Africa and transform them from their state of barbarism.[112]

The same logic in using the concept of civilization applied in intra-Islamic spheres as well. Al-Shidyaq criticized Morocco, which maintained its independence under the Alaouite dynasty, separate from Ottoman influence. In an article he published in 1876, he criticized the diplomatic disconnection with the Ottomans in the name of *tamaddun*, contending that Morocco had no diplomatic representative in Istanbul, no commerce, no newspapers, no navy, and no schools for teaching the arts of war. He concluded that this state of affairs left any Muslim who loved civilization (*Muslim muḥib lil-tamaddun*) wondering about Morocco's miserable situation.[113]

Another intra-Islamic aspect of using *tamaddun* was related to the subject of minorities. There was a basic conviction in the empire that the Christian issue could be solved by progressive policies of reform, especially by establishing an Ottoman parliament. This argument was presented in defense against various internal and external critiques, especially the Russian claim that they were protecting Christian minorities in the Ottoman Empire.[114] The promised *tamaddun* filled, in that sense, a key function in allaying internal problems that faced the empire. The relation between *tamaddun* and reform was utilized in continuous debates. *Al-Jawā'ib*, for instance, quoted the criticism by the Tunisian government-controlled newspaper, *al-Rā'id al-Tūnisī*, of the Russian argument regarding the "barbarism" of the Turks. *Al-Rā'id* argued that the Turks had obtained a parliament and freedom while the Russians were the last country in Europe that still maintained absolute autocratic rule. The article concluded that these measures made the Ottomans more civilized, and therefore the Russians had no right to claim that they had the right to civilize (*al-ḥaq bi-tamdīn*) the Ottoman territories.[115]

It is worth noting that the ideas of progress and civilization were put to use during the first half of the nineteenth century by prominent European liberal bureaucrats and politicians as justifications of imperial policies. John Stuart Mill, an employee of the East India Company between 1823 and 1858, supported the imperial policies of Britain in

112 Ibid. 113 *Al-Jawā'ib*, March 9, 1876.

114 See al-Shidyaq's argument against the Russian claims: *Al-Jawā'ib*, November 23, 1876, 1.

115 *Al-Jawā'ib*, January 10, 1878, 8.

India using a justification derived from the idea of civilization. Similarly, his friend, French philosopher and politician Alexis de Tocqueville, who visited Algeria in 1841 and in 1846, used the concept of civilization in a report he wrote, in which he justified the French hold in the region. In this report he called for applying racial segregation to the native Algerians and taking aggressive military actions such as eliminating civilian housing.[116] Eventually civilization and progress were used politically in the Ottoman Empire and in western Europe. Many Occidentals who considered Europe to be the world's most superior culture used the concept of civilization to imbue the imperial policies of their countries with moral and cultural content. Meanwhile, many Orientals used the same arguments in relation to weaker and less developed countries.

The immense quest for *tamaddun* and *taqaddum* in Arabic marked the local emergence of modern discourse. The two ideas transformed into a single, central theme in both the scholarly and the formal language of the empire.[117] *Tamaddun*, in that sense, not only inaugurated the age of ideology but also imposed its own assessments on the history of the Arabic speakers by highlighting and reconstructing medieval philosophical legacies, conceiving them as most relevant to modernity. The discourse around *tamaddun* embedded ideas similar to those of the French Enlightenment: the spread of education coupled with a messianic expectation of a perfect kingdom on earth in which individuals became the subjects of a comprehensive project. The quest for *tamaddun* and *taqaddum* penetrated to the most intimate domains of the self by requiring continuous improvement, and it extended to the largest forms of human organization. In their internal political aspects, the ideas of *tamaddun* and *taqaddum* embedded a desire of the citizens to elevate their education and morality to higher levels, while in the external sphere the idea of *tamaddun* held a universal message of

[116] Michael Curtis, *Orientalism and Islam: European Thinkers on Oriental Despotism in the Middle East and India* (Cambridge: Cambridge University Press, 2009), 139–216.

[117] For selected examples of the use of the language of progress in formal decrees, see the *firman* given by the Sultan ʿAbd al-Aziz to the Egyptian ruler, Ismaʿil Pasha in 1867, in which the Sultan recognized him as khedive and changed the law of succession to direct decent. Additionally, see the response of Egypt's cabinet members to the speech of Khedive Ismaʿil in 1866: Ahmad Faris al-Shidyaq, *Kanz al-Raghāʾib fī Muntakhabāt al-Jawāʾib*, ed. Salim al-Shidyaq, vol. 5 (Istanbul: Maṭbaʿat al-Jawāʾib, 1877), 79–84, 101–104.

transformation of the world into a "rational," and thus better, place for living.

Nevertheless, the discourse around *tamaddun* embedded the particular experience of Arabic modernity, equipping it with special dynamics. As a concept that describes process, the use of *tamaddun* among the Arabic-speaking scholars created two separate spheres of expectation: The first refers to a present state, while the second refers to an ideal and future state. This duality constitutes a crucial component for understanding the acceptance and rejection of social and political values among the proponents of *tamaddun*. In many cases, advocating a certain political idea does not necessarily mean its acceptance in the present state, but as an ideal that could be relevant to the future. Its acceptance is contingent on the success of a process that is taking place in the present reality. These desired ideals could come into practice only after the elevation of society from the state of "being" to the state of "civilization" – in other words, after the success of the enlightenment of society. The duality of values that *tamaddun* creates characterizes the dynamics of the modern discourse in Arabic, also later in the twentieth century.

The quest for progress and civilization reassessed the principles underpinning social solidarity and the political system. The character of social relations between members of society became a theme and a subject for redefinition and polemics. Thinking about the progressive ideals of society raised new subjects: the informal (social) and formal (legal) status of non-Sunni Muslims; the rights of women in society;[118] the emancipation of slaves; the rights of the proletariat; the organization of society by political parties or organizations; and civil rights in general. All these ideas accompanied the massive semantic expansion of "progress" and "civilization."

Among the concepts significantly affected by the proliferation of the idea of progress was the subject of political identity. The primary intellectual implication of progress was articulated in the production of progressive historical narratives that revolve around the idea of acculturation, as illustrated in the early case of Nemir Effendi. The

[118] See the relation between the concept of *tamaddun* and the quest for women's education and status in society in the works of al-Tahtawi, al-Bustani, and al-Shidyaq during the 1860s: Al-Tahtawi, "Kitāb al-Murshid al-Amīn lil-Banāt wal-Banīn," 473–500, 517–540; al-Bustani, *Nafīr Sūriyya*, 65; al-Shidyaq, *Mukhtārāt min Āthār Aḥmad Fāris al-Shidyāq*, 135–148, 162–163, 265–281.

"Egyptian," the "Syrian," or the "Arabic" identity became a subject of theory and historicity. With al-Tahtawi's works the vision of history shared with Europe was revived, but this time it was in the context of Muhammad ʿAli's ambition to establish an independent Egypt. In 1833, in a glossary he appended to his translation of Depping, al-Tahtawi dedicated one entry to the Greeks. There he contends that most Greeks originated in tribes that emigrated from Egypt and Greater Syria. He stresses that the Greeks, who were famous for their philosophy, came to Egypt during its *jahiliyya* (the pre-Islamic era) to learn philosophy from Egyptian masters of the art.[119] The idea of the "seniority of Egypt in civilization and progress" later became a theme in a book he dedicated to the history of Egypt.[120] Being a patriot (*ḥubb al-waṭan*), or in this case Egyptian, was not merely a matter of political identity but rather part of a universal vision of *tamaddun* and *taqaddum* that embeds the implications of perceptions of the past, the present, and the future.

The paradigm of progress and civilization had particular impact on the political identity of Muslims. With the emergence of these modern concepts, the psychological boundaries that constituted the relation between the Orient and the Occident were profoundly shaken. There was no earlier historical phase in the encounter between *dār al-Islām* (abode of Islam) and Christendom that paved the way for massive cultural acculturation, as happened during the nineteenth century. The idea of progress and civilization, in that sense, filled an ontological function by constructing new imagined identities of political solidarity. Against the background of these massive transitions in perceptions of identity and ideas, the next chapter explores the evolvement of both the individual and the collective implications that freedom acquired mainly between 1820 and 1860.

[119] Depping, *Kitāb Qalāʾid al-Mafākhir fī Gharīb ʿAwāʾid al-Awāʾil wal-Awākhir*, app. 100–101; al-Tahtawi, *al-Taʿrībāt al-Shāfiya li-Murīd al-Jughrāfiyya*, app. 85.

[120] See the subchapter titled, "*aqdamiyyat miṣr fī al-taqaddum wal-tamaddun*" in Rifaʿa Rafiʿ al-Tahtawi, "Anwār Tawfīq al-Khalīl fī Akhbār Miṣr wa-Tawthīq Banī Ismaʿil," in *al-Aʿmāl al-Kāmila li-Rifāʿa Rāfiʿ al-Ṭahṭawī*, ed. Muammad ʿImara, vol. 3 (Cairo: Dār al-Shurūq, 2010), 32–34.

# 3 *Burdening the Political Aspects of Freedom: The Formative Period, 1820–1860*

## Texts, Politics, and Technological Developments

The years between 1820 and 1860 witnessed comprehensive conceptual transitions that were underpinned by structural changes in politics and society. The written word was heavily influenced by developments that took place in the field of technology, especially with the advancement of modern printing methods and journalism. The distribution of the written texts underwent two stages of development: The first was with the emergence of journalism that appeared as official circulars, beginning with *Jurnāl al-ʿIrāq*, published in Baghdad in 1816, and *Jurnāl Khidīwī* and afterward *al-Waqāʾiʿ al-Miṣriyya*, published in Cairo in 1821 and 1828, respectively. The second stage was the appearance of private nonofficial journalism in the 1850s.[1]

In conjunction with the growing economic and political ties, the cultural acculturation with Europe entered an accelerated phase that manifested in a variety of spheres; religiously, the institutional presence of Western Christianity, Catholicism and Protestantism, had grown significantly in the first half of the nineteenth century through widespread missionary activity in various social fields, including education. Politically, this period of time evidenced, in addition to the internal reforms (Tanzimat), a gradual European influence on the political entities of the region: Anatolia; Egypt and Tunisia, where Ottoman control was nominal; and Algeria, which became a French colony in 1830. During these years the cultural center had grown to include Beirut and Aleppo in Greater Syria, and Cairo and Tunis in North Africa. The intertwined interests of political power and cultural activity transformed Cairo into the most important center. Muhammad ʿAli, who in 1822 founded the official Egyptian printing press in Bulaq, made two decisions that had a

[1] Ami Ayalon, "'Sihafa': The Arab Experiment in Journalism," *Middle Eastern Studies* 28, no. 2 (1992): 259–261.

crucial impact on language transformation: The first was to send organized student missions to Europe, and the second was to establish a professional school for translation.

Many individual and religious scholars in Egypt and the Levant had made their way to Europe since the seventeenth century. Missionary and educational activity by Franciscans and Jesuits took place in the Ottoman territories,[2] but it was only with the student missions of the nineteenth century that the idea of cultural acculturation became formal policy in the Ottoman Empire, including in Egypt and Tunisia. The purpose of these formally organized missions was the promotion of professional training for civil servants and the military. ʿUthman Nur al-Din, the first student to be formally dispatched from Egypt to Europe in 1809, was followed by many others who were not native Egyptians: These were primarily of Turkish, Georgian, Albanian, and Syrian origins. The first organized group, which consisted of forty-four participants, left Egypt in 1826. In 1834 the Ottoman government sent a group for similar purposes.[3] The new atmosphere among those who retained political power and pursued the idea of gaining "Western sciences" turned Muhammad ʿAli's Egypt into the most important cultural center in the region for the construction of modern Arabic, at least during the period beginning in the 1820s and ending in the 1850s.[4]

Rifaʿa Rafiʿ al-Tahtawi's return to Egypt from Paris in 1831,[5] and his activities with his students in the field of translation marked a milestone in the transformation of Arabic from being a high classical to a practical language. The institutionalization of this process involved works

[2] For further details on cultural interrelations before the nineteenth century, see Bernard Lewis, "The Muslim Discovery of Europe," *Bulletin of the School of Oriental and African Studies* 20, no. 1/3 (1957): 409–416; Newman, "Introduction," 22–24; Alain Silvera, "The First Egyptian Student Mission to France under Muhammad Ali," *Middle Eastern Studies* 16, no. 2 (1980): 2–3.

[3] Newman, "Introduction," 19–24.

[4] Although the Egyptian press was the most influential, it is important to stress that Arabic books and translations were published in other places during the same period, for example, in Malta during the 1830s, as well as in Greater Syria, Istanbul, and other European capitals.

[5] For a contemporary biographical account, see the biography written by his student Majdi Salih, *Ḥilyat al-Zamān bi-Manāqib Khādim al-Waṭan* (Cairo: Al-Bāb al-Ḥalabī, 1958). For secondary sources, see: James Heyworth-Dunne, "Rifāʿah Badawī Rāfiʿ Aṭ-Ṭahṭāwī: The Egyptian Revivalist," *Bulletin of the School of Oriental Studies, University of London* 9, no. 4 (1939): 961–967; Newman, "Introduction," 31–56.

published by the students of the School of Translation (later named the School of Languages) established in 1835 under Muhammad ʿAli. (It was closed down by ʿAbbas I in 1850 and reopened by Ismaʿil.) In 1837 al-Tahtawi was appointed director of the school, after which he offered the only syllabus in Egypt's state schools that was not confined to military fields and included Islamic and modern sciences. The students of this institution were al-Azhar University's experts in the Arabic language as well as many professionals from different fields including medicine, engineering, and agriculture who strove to acquire foreign languages to assist them in their professions. The activity of these students in translation was most influential in other fields of study and institutions, both inside and outside of Egypt.[6]

From 1820 through the 1850s, Arabic underwent an unprecedented conceptual transformation, which manifested in coining neologisms and in borrowing words from European languages, predominantly from French. During these years France, as the center of cosmopolitan culture and French language, had the greatest effect on Arabic, replacing the formerly dominant position of Turkish. Books originally published in English, or in Latin and Greek, were in many cases translated into Arabic from their French editions. Furthermore, the institutionalization of the activity of translation had a profound impact on the production of knowledge in general. By breaking the monopoly of religious sciences (*al-ʿulūm al-sharʿiyya*) over knowledge, the semantic field of the concept of science (*ʿilm*) had expanded significantly by absorbing modern disciplines.[7] This period evidenced some of the first modern printed publications of translated works in natural and exact sciences,[8] in social sciences, including classical and modern philosophy, and in ancient and modern history and geography. Some of these translations were appended with glossaries and annotations for neologisms, which added to temporal Arabic a number of new ideas and vocabularies in a variety of fields.

[6] Vatikiotis, *The Modern History of Egypt*, 95.

[7] See al-Tahtawi's remarks in the beginning of the 1830s on the state of knowledge in the Islamic countries. He indicated critically that this part of the world focused on religious sciences and entirely neglected other sciences. Al-Tahtawi, *Takhlīṣ al-Ibrīz fī Talkhīṣ Bārīz aw al-Dīwān al-Nafīs bi-Īwān Bārīs*, 124–125.

[8] For the list of books translated during Muhammad ʿAli's reign, see al-Shayyal, *Tārīkh al-Tarjama wal-Ḥaraka al-Thaqāfiyya fī ʿAṣr Muḥammad ʿAli*, apps. 1 and 2.

The extensive process of borrowing words from European languages reflected the difficulties in finding appropriate terminology that expressed the modern experience in Arabic. During these years the transformation of Arabic was typified by instability; many of the new words were used temporarily, sometimes once only, and were replaced by many others until they reached a stage in which their use become conventional. In addition to the profound impact translation had on language, the realm of words prior to the inauguration of private journalism in Arabic (in either 1854 or 1855) was enriched by vocabularies used in journey descriptions, a genre that filled an important function in the cultural acculturation taking place during this period. Through their use of language, the works of travelers such as al-Tahtawi, Faris al-Shidyaq, and Salim Bustrus brought the political, legal, cultural, and spiritual experience of *bilād al-Ifranj* (Europe) to Arabic-speaking readers.[9]

In Egypt literary works were systematically distributed after 1822 by publishing them using modern printing processes and utilizing them in the curriculum of the state's new school system. A majority of the titles were selected for translation by al-Tahtawi and included in their introductory remarks a dedication to Muhammad ʿAli, who in turn rewarded al-Tahtawi in his endeavor by promoting him to the rank of amir alai in 1844, and two years later by granting him the title of bey.[10] The interrelation between state policies and strategies of knowledge production – especially in the selection of fields and titles for translation – is evident in many translated works.[11] History and

[9] The "traveling narratives" also filled an important function in the same period in western Europe and North America by informing readers about global events. In this regard it is worth mentioning that one year after al-Tahtawi published his journey description, the French politician Alexis de Tocqueville published the first volume of *Democracy in America*, one of the most influential works in the nineteenth century in Europe, after his visit to America. (He published additional observations during the 1840s after he traveled to England and Algeria.) For more details about the influence of the "traveling narratives" in Europe and North America in the same period, see Joanna Innes and Mark Philp, "Synergies," in *Re-imagining Democracy in the Age of Revolutions: America, France, Britain, Ireland, 1750–1850*, 193–210.

[10] Heyworth-Dunne, "Rifāʿah Badawī Rāfiʿ Aṭ-Ṭahṭāwī: The Egyptian Revivalist," 964–967.

[11] Al-Tahtawi and other translators such as Yuhanna Anhuri and Muhammad Mustafa Bashjawish outlined the benefit of their translations to the state and bureaucracy on many occasions. For selected examples, see al-Tahtawi,

geography especially attracted the attention of Muhammad ʿAli and his son Ibrahim Pasha.[12] The translations in the field of geography, for instance, acquired special importance precisely because that field overlapped with Muhammad ʿAli's imperial ambitions. In this respect al-Tahtawi's reward was due to his translation of one of the monumental works of geography.[13]

Through focusing on the intertwined relation between politics, knowledge production, and their impact on language transition, the following subchapters trace the construction of the concept of freedom in Arabic from 1820 through the 1850s. During subsequent years the ambiguous primary articulations that the political features of the term "freedom" had acquired by 1820 attained greater sophistication and stability. With policies of nation building that derived from great events such as the Tanzimat, in addition to external events such as the breakdown of the liberal revolutions of 1848 (Spring of Nations), freedom would gain a central function in both the informal and formal discourses in the territories of the Ottoman Empire. The next subchapters explore these changes, emphasizing the political semantic extension of freedom in two fields: the individual, which pertains to the idea of civil rights, and the collective, which was derived from the preoccupation with the function of larger frameworks such as institutions, social classes, and groups.

## The Emergence of the Language of Individual Freedom: Individual Principles, Constitutionalism, Sovereignty of the People, and Natural Rights

The idea of freedom of worship, which was rooted in early eighteenth-century Arabic and articulated by Ellious Bocthor as *ḥurriyyat al-adyān*, was presented during this period in association with a set of concepts that fell under the designation of "individual freedoms." The

*al-Taʿrībāt al-Shāfiya li-Murīd al-Jughrāfiyya*, 3; Nicolas Perron, *al-Azhar al-Badīʿa fī ʿilm al-Ṭabīʿa: Kitāb al-Ṭabīʿa*, trans. Yuhanna Anhuri (Bulaq: Maṭbaʿat Ṣāḥib al-Saʿāda al-Khidīwiyya, 1838), 3–4; Voltaire, *Maṭāliʿ Shumūs al-Siyar fī Waqāʾiʿ Karlūs al-Thānī ʿAshar*, 3–4.

12 See correspondence between Muhammad ʿAli and Ibrahim Pasha in 1833 regarding the publication of two books, *The History of Napoleon Bonaparte* and *Testament of Frederick II*: Asad Rustum, *al-Maḥfūẓāt al-Malakiyya al-Miṣriyya*, vol. 2 (Beirut: Al-Maṭbaʿa al-Amrīkiyya, 1941), 268, 352.

13 See Ibrahim Pasha's 1833 order to translate geography books: ibid., 2:295.

temporal Arabic articulation of this idiom acquired many morphological forms – *ḥurriyya shakhṣiyya, ḥuqūq shakhṣiyya*, and *dhātiyya* – and frequently appeared in translated works, journey literature, and formal documents.[14] By the 1850s the semantic field of "individual freedoms" had expanded rapidly and acquired stable content; texts from the same period of time presented components of the idea of "individual freedoms" that extended beyond "freedom of worship" and comprised "property rights,"[15] "freedom of expression" and "freedom of the press,"[16] "freedom of conscience,"[17] and "freedom of movement."[18]

The overlap between coining some of these idioms in translated works in Arabic and their use for articulating local experience was almost immediate. Early use of this terminology was displayed in

[14] In the translation of Voltaire, it appears as *ḥurriyyat nafsihi* and *al-ḥurriyya al-shakhṣiyya al-kāmila*. In other translations from French, the idea was articulated as *ḥuqūq shakhṣiyya* or *dhātiyya* and *dhat kul waḥid minhum yastaqill bihā wa-yaḍman ḥurriyyatahā*. For early sources that express this idea in Arabic, see al-Tahtawi, *Takhlīṣ al-Ibrīz fī Talkhīṣ Bārīz aw al-Dīwān al-Nafīs bi-Īwān Bārīs*, 67, 75; Voltaire, *Maṭāliʿ Shumūs al-Siyar fī Waqāʾiʿ Karlūs al-Thānī ʿAshar*, 22, 271; Robertson, *Kitāb Itḥāf Mulūk al-Zamān bi-Tārīkh al-Imbirāṭūr Sharlakān Masbūqan bi-Muqaddimatihi al-Musammā Itḥāf al-Mulūk al-Alibbāʾ bi-Taqaddum al-Jamʿīyyāt fī Ūrūbā Mundhu Inqirāḍ al-Dawla al-Rūmāniyya*, 1:23, 106.

[15] Voltaire, *Maṭāliʿ Shumūs al-Siyar fī Waqāʾiʿ Karlūs al-Thānī ʿAshar*, 271.

[16] In addition to the description of al-Tahtawi's journey, see that of Faris al-Shidyaq, who visited the island of Malta in 1834 (he stayed there for fourteen years) and afterward London and Paris. See al-Tahtawi, *Takhlīṣ al-Ibrīz fī Talkhīṣ Bārīz aw al-Dīwān al-Nafīs bi-Īwān Bārīs*, 76, 67, 135, 159; al-Shidyaq, *al-Wāsiṭa ila Maʿrifat Aḥwāl Mālṭa wa-Kashf al-Mukhabbāʾ ʿan Funūn Ūrūbā*, 327.

[17] In addition to "freedom of religion," "freedom of conscience" includes "freedom from religion." See al-Tahtawi's description of his journey and Khalifa ibn Mahmud's early translation of William Robertson's history of Emperor Charles V, which employs *ḥurriyya* in the context of emancipation from the authority of the Catholic Church (*ṭalab al-ḥurriyya wal-khulūṣ min asr al-kanīsa; al-ḥurriyya al-dīniyya*). See al-Tahtawi, *Takhlīṣ al-Ibrīz fī Talkhīṣ Bārīz aw al-Dīwān al-Nafīs bi-Īwān Bārīs*, 67, 76; Robertson, *Kitāb Itḥāf Mulūk al-Zamān bi-Tārīkh al-Imbirāṭūr Sharlakān Masbūqan bi-Muqaddimatihi al-Musammā Itḥāf al-Mulūk al-Alibbāʾ bi-Taqaddum al-Jamʿīyyāt fī Ūrūbā Mundhu Inqirāḍ al-Dawla al-Rūmāniyya*, 1:104, 241; William Robertson, *Kitāb Itḥāf Mulūk al-Zamān bi-Tārīkh al-Imbirāṭūr Sharlakān Masbūqan bi-Muqaddimatihi al-Musammā Itḥāf al-Mulūk al-Alibbāʾ bi-Taqaddum al-Jamʿīyyāt fī Ūrūbā*, trans. Khalifa Ibn Mahmud, vol. 3 (Bulaq: Al-Maṭbaʿa al-ʿĀmira, 1850), 169.

[18] Al-Shidyaq, *Kanz al-Raghāʾib fī Muntakhabāt al-Jawāʾib*, 1877, 5:12–14.

the 1830s during the Egyptian seizure of Greater Syria. A Christian-Orthodox eyewitness to the Egyptian invasion depicts the state of *ḥurriyya* in Syria under Egyptian rule as "unprecedented, since the beginning of the Islamic conquest [*futūḥ*]."[19] The use of *ḥurriyya* in this context referred to the freedom Christians had to practice their daily life without constraints, and it included the security of life and property. Additionally, contemporary textual evidence conveys further implications regarding individual freedom: A local Christian chronicler, who described the increasing influence of the Druze community in Mount Lebanon during these years, complains that Druze dominance was a reason that Christians did not have the freedom (*wa ʿadimū ḥurriyyatahum*) to express themselves and to live in security, freely and without intervention.[20] In these texts the meaning of *ḥurriyya* was extended not only semantically but also practically, gaining a variety of meanings in the local domain of Arabic speakers.

In the sociopolitical context of the Ottoman Empire, the notion of freedom of worship of *ahl al-kitāb* (people of the book), gained its highest significance during this era. External pressures, especially from the Russian tsars, who saw themselves as the protectors of the Orthodox Christians, and the French kings, who perceived themselves as the protectors of the Catholics, invigorated the relevance of this idea in the international politics of the empire. Furthermore, internal events, such as the persecution of subjects affiliated with the new Catholic churches – the Armenian and the Greek Catholic – and their formal recognition in 1831 by the Ottoman authorities as millets independent of the Orthodox, gave this idea greater political and social actuality.[21]

Profound changes in this regard began to take place during and after the Egyptian invasion (1831–1841). Under the Egyptian seizure, the

[19] The anonymous author served as *kātib* (secretary) in Damascus under Egyptian, and later, Ottoman rule. Aḥad Kutāb al-Ḥukūma al-Dīmashqiyyīn, *Mudhakarāt Taʾrīkhiyya*, ed. Qustantin al-Basha (Harisa: Maṭbaʿat al-Qiddīss Būluṣ, 1926), 96.

[20] The following source was composed during the 1840s: Mikhail al-Dimashqi, *Taʾrīkh Ḥawādith al-Shām wa-Lubnān* (Beirut: Maṭbaʿat al-Kāthūlīk lil-Ābāʾ al-Yasuʿiyyīn, 1912), 88.

[21] Formal recognition was given first to the Armenian Patriarch, who became responsible for all Catholic churches in 1831. For the Ottoman edicts that address this subject in the 1830s and the temporal employment of *ḥurriyya*, see Mazlum, *Nabdha Tārīkhiyya: fīmā Jara li-Ṭāʾifat al-Rūm al-Kāthūlīk Mundhu Sant 1837 Famā Baʿdahā*, 147–162, 193–211, 330–331.

Christians of Greater Syria enjoyed considerable improvement in all fields, including security of life, greater justice, and a more equal system of taxation. Christians were used as soldiers, and they were allowed to express their religious feelings in public by, for example, carrying crosses.[22] On the formal level it was only under Egyptian rule that the question of inequality between Muslims and non-Muslims in Greater Syria was approached. This subject was not substantially challenged under Sultan Mahmud II, and it had to wait for the Egyptians and the subsequent era of ʿAbdal-Majid.[23]

A significant landmark in the history of individual freedoms during these years was their assimilation in the formal language, which thus made them a central theme in the internal political and legal discourse. An early signifier for freedom in formal documents was derived from the Turkish word *serbestiyet*. In an edict promulgated in October 1834 that formally recognized the right of the Greek Catholics in Egypt to practice their religion independently, the phrase *bikāmil al-sirbistiyya* (in complete freedom) stressed the independent state of this church. In later translated edicts this phrase was rapidly replaced by the Arabic *ḥurriyya* (as in *al-ḥurriyya al-tāma*).[24] The frequency of the use of "freedom" in formal discourse gradually increased, and its semantic meaning expanded significantly. The first Tanzimat edict, Hatti Serif of Gulhane, was promulgated in November 1839 by ʿAbd al-Majid. The edict promised to improve the condition of the empire's inhabitants by securing honor, life, and prosperity in addition to reregulating the tax system (abolishing *iltizām*) and changing the guidelines for recruiting soldiers (thereby making entry to the military available to non-Muslims). The edict followed ideas presented earlier in the informal language and explicitly used the word "freedom" in two phrases: "Each one shall possess his property of every kind and shall dispose of it in all freedom [*kemal-iserbestiyette, kamāl ḥurriyyatihi*]" and "each one of these assemblies shall freely [*serbestce, bi-ḥurriyya*] express his ideas and give his advice."[25] Furthermore, although the

22 Maoz, *Ottoman Reform in Syria and Palestine, 1840–1861: The Impact of the Tanzimat on Politics and Society*, 15–18.
23 Ibid., 20.
24 The edicts are appended to: Mazlum, *Nabdha Tārīkhiyya: fīmā Jara li-Ṭāʾifat al-Rūm al-Kāthūlīk Mundhu Sant 1837 Famā Baʿdahā*, 147–153, 193–203.
25 For English and Arabic translations, see Jacob Coleman Hurewitz, *Diplomacy in the Near and Middle East: A Documentary Record* (New York: Octagon

text did not use the word "equality," it addressed all subjects "without exceptions," including in ʿAbd al-Majid's statement about the "the duty of all the inhabitants to furnish soldiers" – referring to a political and legal reality in which non-Muslims were not allowed to carry weapons. Ignoring the word "equality" and using ambiguous phrasing manifested the author's desire not to emphasize the radical break with the Islamic tradition.[26] Nevertheless, "equality" and nondiscrimination were clearly conceived among the Christians: A letter sent by the Greek Catholic notables of Damascus to the sultan, about two years after the declaration of the edict, left no doubt that the ambiguous formulation of the edict addressed "freedom and equality." In this letter the author explicitly used these words (*ḥurriyya*, *musāwā*) to emphasize the values that arose earlier from the Hatti Serif of Gulhane.[27]

The gradual intensification of these two ideas and their central function in the reforms undertaken by the Ottoman authorities were expressed in international agreements and in edicts that addressed internal affairs, such as the edict of Hatti Humayun of February 1856. The great need of the Ottomans for the Western powers and the Ottoman attempt to present goodwill were to a large extent what lay behind this courageous proclamation. The edict reaffirmed principles indicated previously – freedom of property and expression, and, ambiguously, equality before the law – and extended the recognition of freedom and equality. The author of the edict addressed united and equal community members rather than Muslims and non-Muslims: "all my subjects who in my sight are all equal, and equally dear to me and who are united to each other by the cordial ties of patriotism." Equality meant "without distinction of classes or of religion."[28] The extension of the edict's application, as stated, was to include the

Books, 1972), 113–116; Naʿm Allah Nawfal, trans., *al-Dustūr* (Beirut: Naẓārat al-Maʿārif al-Jalīla, 1883), 1–4.

26 Hurewitz, *Diplomacy in the Near and Middle East: A Documentary Record*, 113–116; Nawfal, *al-Dustūr*, 1–4.

27 See the appended letter sent in June 1841: Mazlum, *Nabdha Tārīkhiyya: fīmā Jara li-Ṭāʾifat al-Rūm al-Kāthūlīk Mundhu Sant 1837 Famā Baʿdahā*, 242–251.

28 In the Treaty of Paris (March 30, 1856), which ended the Crimean War and preceded Hatti Humayun, the Ottoman Sultan promised, in Article 9, to treat all subjects "without distinction of religion and ethnicity [*jins*]." See the Arabic translation of the agreement in: Al-Shidyaq, *Kanz al-Raghāʾib fī Muntakhabāt al-Jawāʾib*, 1877, 5:6–15.

state's institutions and civil and military schools. Furthermore, equality was to be applied in the judicial system. Commercial, correctional, and criminal suits between Muslims and non-Muslims were referred to mixed tribunals. These tribunals received testimonies from all subjects without taking their religion into account, as was previously the accepted practice. In addition the edict ordered equal taxation and an equal sharing of burdens. The formal use of "freedom" was rooted in and significantly defined by this edict. In addition to freedom of expression and property, the edict stressed the principle of freedom of worship: "My sublime Porte will take energetic measures to insure to each sect, whatever be the number of its adherents, entire freedom [*bikul ḥurriyya*] in exercise of its religion."[29] It was the first time that equal status between subjects (including complete freedom of worship) was explicitly mentioned.[30] The edict declared that all designations describing any group as inferior to another "on account of their religion, language or race" should be removed from any formal documents. Hatti Humayun went so far as to promise popular representation on the provincial and the state high councils.[31] The most significant contribution of this edict to the formal discourse was the association it formally made between *ḥurriyya*, equality, and "civil community" (Ottomanism), a theorization that marked a formal attempt to establish a civil foundation for the Ottoman community.

The changes in the Arabic language preceded these edicts in articulating political words that outline more sophisticated conceptions. In addition to the ideas concerning individual freedoms, the earliest and the most rooted historically, the language of the 1830s and 1840s developed political terminology that associated these ideas with the political realm that maintained competition between ideological rivals. The previously common words used to describe this sphere at the beginning of the century were metaphysical: *ṭabāʾiʿiyya*

[29] Hurewitz, *Diplomacy in the Near and Middle East: A Documentary Record*, 149–153; Nawfal, *al-Dustūr*, 5–11; Ahmet Mithat, *Uss-I Inkılap* (Istanbul: 1877), 277–282.

[30] Additionally, in the agreement of 1856, Articles 20, 23, and 28 indicated the idea of "freedom of movement" (*ḥurriyya fī safar*), and Articles 23 and 28 stressed the principle of "freedom of religion" (*al-ḥurriyya fī al-tadayyun*): Al-Shidyaq, *Kanz al-Raghāʾib fī Muntakhabāt al-Jawāʾib*, 1877, 5:14.

[31] Hurewitz, *Diplomacy in the Near and Middle East: A Documentary Record*, 149–153; Nawfal, *al-Dustūr*, 5–11; Maoz, *Ottoman Reform in Syria and Palestine, 1840–1861: The Impact of the Tanzimat on Politics and Society*, 27.

(naturalists), *dahriyya*, and *dunyawiyya* (worldly). In the 1830s additional signifiers indicating the emergence of modern politics and emphasizing the secular aspects of political activity came into play. For describing the realm of politics, early nineteenth-century scholars used the borrowed word *bulītīqa* (from politics) to indicate the sphere of ideological contestation. Thus, for instance, al-Tahtawi used *madhhab fī al-bulītīqa* to denote a political party or school of political thought.[32] In an entry he published in 1834, al-Tahtawi defined *bulītīqa* as a "word used for discussing state affairs, its situation, and its management [*siyāsa*] in relation to its internal affairs with its inhabitants, or in relation to its foreign policies with other states [*siyāsat dawla maʿ man jāwarahā*] . . . Politician [*bulītīqī*] denotes one who speaks in managing and conducting [*mutakalim fī al-siyāsāt wal-tadābīr*] state affairs."[33] *Bulītīqa*, according to al-Tahtawi, is a wide concept that includes *siyāsa*. *Siyāsa*, which in its common medieval use denoted "statecraft" or simply "management," only partially outlines the modern concept of politics, which redefined international relations according to secular-national interests and established the basic political relationship as being between "citizens" rather than religious groups. The borrowed term in Arabic was loaded with indications of the competition between interests. During these years the adjective "political" (*bulītīqī*) had negative connotations and a meaning equivalent to "creating plots."[34] By the 1850s the term *siyāsa* had gradually replaced the borrowed *bulītīqa*,[35] indicating a shift toward the secular in which

[32] See al-Tahtawi, and other contemporary sources that use the borrowed word *bulītīqa* or *bulītīka*: Al-Tahtawi, *Takhlīṣ al-Ibrīz fī Talkhīṣ Bārīz aw al-Dīwān al-Nafīs bi-Īwān Bārīs*, 163; Rifaʿa Rafiʿ al-Tahtawi and Mustafa al-Zarabi, trans., *Bidāyat al-Qudamāʾ wa-Hidāyat al-Ḥukamāʾ* (Bulaq: Dār al-Ṭibāʿa al-ʿĀmira, 1838), 90–91; Nassif Mallouf, "Politique," *Dictionnaire Français-Turc* (Paris: Maisonneuve et Cie, 1856), 610; Kalivaris, *Kitāb Sirat al-Muʿaẓam al-Murafaʿ al-Kabīr Nabulyūn al-Awwal Imbaratūr al-Farānsawiyya*, 6, 9–10.

[33] Al-Tahtawi, *al-Taʿrībāt al-Shāfiya li-Murīd al-Jughrāfiyya*, app. 69.

[34] For examples of using the word to mean "plot," see: ibid.; Antun Dahir ʿAqiqi, *Thawra wa-Fitna fī Lubnān: Ṣafḥa Majhūla min Tārīkh al-Jabal min 1841 ila 1873* (Beirut: Al-Ittiḥād, 1939), 153.

[35] In the glossary appended to Napoleon's biography, *bulītika* was rendered as *ʿilm al-siyāsa*. In a similar way *astrātijiyyā* (strategy) was rendered as *ʿilm al-ḥarb*. Faris al-Shidyaq used the phrase *al-umūr al-duwaliyya* to denote international affairs (politics). See Kalivaris, *Kitāb Sirat al-Muʿaẓam al-Murafaʿ al-Kabīr Nabulyūn al-Awwal Imbaratūr al-Farānsawiyya*, ي, ز; al-Shidyaq, *Mukhtārāt min Āthār Aḥmad Fāris al-Shidyāq*, 156.

political rivalry was portrayed in terms that replaced the medieval theological perceptions of *dār al-Islām* and *dār al-ḥarb* (these two terms are discussed extensively in the next subchapters). The emphasis on the irreligious realm apparently played a major role in the choice of *siyāsa* for replacing *bulītīqa*; in the Middle Ages, the word *siyāsa* was frequently used to denote the discretionary authority of the ruler exercised outside the framework of the shariʿa. In that sense the word was often conflated with *fiqh* (jurisprudence) and it implied actions that are beyond the norms prescribed by shariʿa. Thus, for instance, the word indicated a punishment that exceeds the penalties (*ḥadd*) stated in the shariʿa.[36] Some medieval Muslim philosophers, such as al-Farabi, elevated *siyāsa* above shariʿa and viewed it as a separate branch of philosophy, while other scholars, such as Ghazali and Ibn Taymiyya, subordinated *siyāsa* to *fiqh* (jurisprudence).[37]

This heritage of the word *siyāsa* was enlisted by the nineteenth-century scholars who strove to find Arabic words that expressed the new irreligious realm that grew with the foundation of nation-states. Thus, the new regulations that the Ottomans enacted along with the reforms were perceived by some of these scholars as part of the realm of *siyāsa*.[38] Corresponding with these morphological changes, *madhhab fī al-bulītīqa* was replaced during this period by *madhhab siyāsī* as a significant sign for the construction of the concept in Arabic.[39] The transformation of *siyāsa* in that sense revealed one of the aspects of the evolvement of secularism in which political disputes were described

36 Clifford Edmund Bosworth, "Siyāsa: In the Sense of Statecraft," *The Encyclopedia of Islam* (Leiden: E. J. Brill, 1997), 693–694; Lewis, *Political Words and Ideas in Islam*, 31–46.

37 The gap between shariʿa and *siyāsa* was the background for the emergence of the late medieval concept of *siyāsa sharʿiyya* (governance in accordance with the shariʿa), which conveys the meaning of a legal doctrine that harmonizes between the law and *fiqh*. For further details, see Frank E. Vogel, "Siyāsa: In the Sense of Siyasa Sharʿiyya," *The Encyclopedia of Islam* (Leiden: E. J. Brill, 1997), 695–696; Ian Richard Netton, "Siyāsa: In the Context of Political Philosophy," *The Encyclopedia of Islam* (Leiden: E. J. Brill, 1997), 694.

38 See Ibn al-Diyaf's defense of Ottoman reforms (Tanzimat). In his work he argues that these reforms are a result of *qānūn* (civil law) and *siyāsa*, and they do not contradict the divine laws of Islam. Ibn Abi al-Diyaf, *Itḥāf Ahl al-Zamān bi-Akhbār Mulūk Tūnis wa-ʿAhd al-Amān*, 1:52–77.

39 See early use of the phrase *madhhab siyāsī* in: Robertson, *Kitāb Itḥāf Mulūk al-Zamān bi-Tārīkh al-Imbirāṭūr Sharlakān Masbūqan bi-Muqaddimatihi al-Musammā Itḥāf al-Mulūk al-Alibbāʾ bi-Taqaddum al-Jamʿīyyāt fī Ūrūbā Mundhu Inqirāḍ al-Dawla al-Rūmāniyya*, 1:51.

using worldly terminology. Discussing political matters in Arabic was further manifested in the emergence of modern political thought in the second half of the nineteenth century. The medieval *siyāsāt madaniyya* (civil governance) was presented in the nineteenth century as an appellation for a type of regime that was contrasted with *siyāsāt ʿaskarriyya* (military regime) and, correspondingly, *ḥukm madanī* was contrasted with *ḥukm ʿaskarī* (civil governance versus military governance). Late nineteenth-century lexicographer Yuhanna Abkariyus follows these early definitions and interprets *madanī* as equivalent to "political" and *siyāsī*, or "civil," as pertaining to society in contrast to the military.[40]

The conflict created by the extension of state authority to institutions that were previously considered part of the religious domain of influence, such as the educational system and the judicial system, reached an unprecedented point, first with the Egyptian invasion of Greater Syria and after it with the Tanzimat.[41] One of the early statements relating to the domination of the state's impact on legal status and political affiliation appears in Ibrahim Pasha's argument that Christians and Muslims are both subjects of the state and that religious affiliation has no relation to civil governance (*ma lahu madkhal fī al-siyāsa*). He stressed that religious belief is a personal matter and that no one should interfere with it.[42] The Tanzimat edicts, whose primary aim was to strengthen

[40] In a similar way, *al-Jawāʾib* explained the French term *civil* as the laws and decrees legislated by the king, in contrast to laws imposed by a military regime. *Al-Jawāʾib*, September 26, 1878, 2; Yuhanna Abkariyus, "Civil," *Qāmūs Inklīzī wa-ʿArabī* (Beirut, 1887), 105.

[41] In Syria under Muhammad ʿAli, the Egyptians made vast changes in the judicial system as part of their effort to use state officials as the sole authority. Under the Egyptians, the judicial authority of the traditional *maḥkama* (religious court) was limited to matters of personal status, while criminal or commercial cases were turned over to the local state administrations. See the request in the 1833 appeal submitted by a Christian who asked not to be judged in *maḥkama* and to be transferred to the *shūra* council in Aleppo: Rustum, *al-Maḥfūẓāt al-Malakiyya al-Miṣriyya*, 2:340. For further details about the transition in the judicial system and in secularization of Ottoman law during this period, see Maoz, *Ottoman Reform in Syria and Palestine, 1840–1861: The Impact of the Tanzimat on Politics and Society*, 14–15; Dora Glidewell Nadolski, "Ottoman and Secular Civil Law," *International Journal of Middle East Studies* 8, no. 4 (1977): 517–543.

[42] Furthermore, Ibrahim Pasha maintained signs of an irreligious lifestyle as, for instance, in his controversial stay at a Catholic monastery in Jaffa in 1834. See his remarks on this issue in a discussion between him and his father, Muhammad ʿAli, in: Rustum, *al-Maḥfūẓāt al-Malakiyya al-Miṣriyya*, 2:117, 403.

the empire by creating regulations that subjected major fields to state inspection, made the empire more involved in the lives of its subjects. The transition of the Ottoman state from an empire to an entity that assimilated nation-state norms was observed by al-Shidyaq, who wrote in 1861 in the context of his discussion of the Tanzimat that these edicts were established to redefine the norms of relations between the Muslim empire and the Western countries. He assumed that the aim of the Tanzimat was to base the empire's international relations on an earthly (*dunyawī*), political foundation and not on religious belief.[43] He added that the practical manifestation of this orientation was the establishment of civil laws (*qawanīn*) that constitute a separate legal body from the shariʿa.[44] With the changes introduced by the Tanzimat, secularism had rather comprehensive implications, not only for the concept of politics but also for the foundations of the legal system of the empire. This transition was accompanied by the march of the philosophy of natural rights. The 1830s and 1840s witnessed the coinage of many phrases showing the content of this idea as a legal philosophy: Phrases such as *ḥuqūq ṭabīʾiyya*, *sharīʿa ṭabīʿiyya*, *ḥuqūq bashariyya*, *ḥuqūq kul insān*, *al-ḥuqūq al-insāniyya*, and *ḥuqūq al-ʾādamiyya* (natural rights, human rights) either were recruited from medieval philosophy or were coined in the nineteenth century.[45] Despite the clear reference of the Arabic coinage to all human beings, early nineteenth-century Muslim scholars such as Abu al-Suʿud[46] and al-Tahtawi did not perceive the idea of "natural rights" necessarily as a universal value but rather as particular to the French philosophical tradition, as something that underpinned their theory of law.[47] Al-Tahtawi and his Muslim predecessors

[43] Al-Shidyaq, *Mukhtārāt min Āthār Aḥmad Fāris al-Shidyāq*, 187.

[44] Ibid., 187–188.

[45] Al-Tahtawi, *Takhlīṣ al-Ibrīz fī Talkhīṣ Bārīz aw al-Dīwān al-Nafīs bi-Īwān Bārīs*, 10, 150, 154; Abu al-Suʿud ʿAbd Allah, *Kitāb naẓm al-Laʾālīʾ fī al-Sulūk fī man Ḥakama Faransā wa-man Qābalahum ʿAla Miṣr min al-Mulūk* (Cairo: Maṭbaʿat Ṣāḥib al-Saʿāda, 1841), 183–188; Robertson, *Kitāb Itḥāf Mulūk al-Zamān bi-Tārīkh al-Imbirāṭūr Sharlakān Masbūqan bi-Muqaddimatihi al-Musammā Itḥāf al-Mulūk al-Alibbāʾ bi-Taqaddum al-Jamʿiyyāt fī Ūrūbā Mundhu Inqirāḍ al-Dawla al-Rūmāniyya*, 1:107; ʿAqiqi, *Thawra wa-Fitna fī Lubnān: Ṣafḥa Majhūla min Tārīkh al-Jabal min 1841 ila 1873*, 259–260; Mazlum, *Nahdha Tārīkhiyya: fīmā Jara li-Ṭāʾifat al-Rūm al-Kāthūlīk Mundhu Sant 1837 Famā Baʿdahā*, 233.

[46] ʿAbd Allah Abu al-Suʿud, *Kitāb naẓm al-Laʾālīʾ fī al-Sulūk fī man Ḥakama Faransā wa-man Qābalahum ʿAla Miṣr min al-Mulūk*, 183–188.

[47] There is a minor difference between the two editions of al-Tahtawi's journey to Paris regarding his statement about natural rights (the first edition was

articulated the epistemic difference between the foundations of the French and Islamic systems of law by engaging with the concept of secularism: Whereas Islamic law was seen as based on the interpretation of divine scriptures, French law was viewed as a result of political secular needs (*siyāsiyya*).[48] Different approaches were articulated among early Christian scholars. The Greek Catholic patriarch, Maksimus Mazlum, wrote in October 1841 to the government in Istanbul stressing his loyalty to the sultan and elaborating that the Catholic belief obliged its followers to be loyal to rulers, all of whom are chosen by God. He emphasized his belief in the principle of the freedom of individuals to move from one religious doctrine to another within the same religion because "God gave human beings free will naturally," implying the integration of the secular concept of natural rights (*sharīʿa ṭabīʿiyya*) with his religious creed. In an earlier letter to the Russian council, he expressed his belief in the separation of religious belief and civil governance (*siyāsa madaniyya*) as a principle that underpins equality between inhabitants who are not members of the same religion.[49] During this early era the philosophy of natural rights was not necessarily accepted among Muslim scholars as a principle on which to base laws and rights.

In the discourse on politics that emerged, the idea of freedom in general evolved in a defined political camp. Following *ḥurriyya*, "individual freedom" was presented with the political orientation that perceived freedom as a right and not merely as a mercy vouchsafed by a ruler, by attaching it to two political principles: constitutionalism and sovereignty of the people. The literature from the 1830s and onward developed a special morphology that articulated these political camps; the significant event that marked the emergence of these political expressions in Arabic was the 1830 "July Revolution" in France, the second wave of the French Revolution. Eyewitness Rifaʿa al-Tahtawi portrayed, for the first time in nineteenth-century Arabic,

published in 1834 and the second in 1849). Part of the phrase "natural rights that the French consider the origin of their laws" was not completed in the first edition. For comparison, see al-Tahtawi, *Takhlīṣ al-Ibrīz fī Talkhīṣ Bārīz aw al-Dīwān al-Nafīs bi-Īwān Bārīs*, 10, 150, 154; al-Tahtawi, *al-Dīwān al-Nafīs fī Īwān Bārīs aw, Takhlīṣ al-Ibrīz fī Talkhīṣ Bārīz*, 215.

48 Al-Tahtawi, *Takhlīṣ al-Ibrīz fī Talkhīṣ Bārīz aw al-Dīwān al-Nafīs bi-Īwān Bārīs*, 77.

49 The two letters were appended to: Mazlum, *Nabdha Tārīkhiyya: fīmā Jara li-Ṭāʾifat al-Rūm al-Kāthūlīk Mundhu Sant 1837 Famā Baʿdahā*, 229–235, 256–269.

the conflict between two schools of political thought: the proponents of absolutism and the proponents of freedom. This event, which witnessed the overthrow of Bourbon King Charles X and his replacement by Louis Philippe of the Orleanist dynasty, marked the substitution of the principle of popular sovereignty ("King of the French") for that of heredity right ("King of France"). This constitutional and liberal statement, which had provided a powerful stimulus to constitutional reforms in other countries, including Great Britain,[50] was covered extensively by al-Tahtawi. In his published observation he uses words that demarcate political orientations, coining the word *malakiyya* for the royalist camp, and using *ḥurriyya* to indicate their rivals, "the proponents of freedom." This transformation in political language extended from the 1830s into the 1850s and gained new coinages that rooted the attempt to construct these political perceptions in Arabic. While al-Tahtawi's *malakiyya* captured almost literally the meaning of "royalists," other contemporary translations articulated this political orientation as *rabbjiyyīn*, from the word *rabb* (patron), indicating proponents of the monarchic-absolutist regime.[51] In the second camp there were more attempts to express the political orientation of its adherents, and many terms were coined; al-Tahtawi used *madhhab al-ḥurriyya* (school of freedom) and *arbāb al-ḥurriyya* or *ḥurriyyūn* (proponents of freedom),[52] while other contemporary sources used *ahl al-sarāḥ* (supporters of freedom), employing *sarāḥ* (release) as a signifier for freedom.[53] These coinages illustrate, for the first time in Arabic, the ideological dimension of freedom by giving speakers the opportunity to locate themselves in a political space. Furthermore, the expression of this political orientation was dominated by the use of *ḥurriyya*, which gained considerable stability in Arabic during this period as the

[50] Robert John Weston Evans, "Liberalism, Nationalism, and the Coming of the Revolution," in *The Revolutions in Europe 1848–1849: From Reform to Reaction*, ed. Robert John Weston Evans and Hartmut Pogge von Strandmann (Oxford: Oxford University Press, 2002), 14.

[51] Kalivaris, *Kitāb Sirat al-Muʿaẓam al-Murafaʿ al-Kabīr Nabulyūn al-Awwal Imbaratūr al-Farānsawiyya*, 247.

[52] Al-Tahtawi, *Takhlīṣ al-Ibrīz fī Talkhīṣ Bārīz aw al-Dīwān al-Nafīs bi-Īwān Bārīs*, 157–158, 161, 165–166.

[53] Correspondingly, *sarāḥ biladihi* means "freedom of his country," *maḥabatuhum lil-sarāḥ wal-istiwāʾ* means "their love of freedom and equality," and *tasarraḥ* means "liberated." See Kalivaris, *Kitāb Sirat al-Muʿaẓam al-Murafaʿ al-Kabīr Nabulyūn al-Awwal Imbaratūr al-Farānsawiyya*, 94, 334.

sole indicator for a particular political camp that maintained a more or less consistent set of political principles. The transition in the use of *ḥurriyya* – from being a political principle prior to the 1830s to meaning a particular political orientation from the 1830s onward – marked a significant development in the concept of freedom in Arabic.

The scholarly engagement in portraying the political arena elaborated the features and nature of these two models of governance. The first model presented by al-Tahtawi is absolute monarchy (*muṭlaq al-ḥukm*), in which the king has absolute freedom and control over his subjects. The second model, identified with *ḥurriyya*, consisted of two camps: proponents of constitutional monarchy (*mamlaka muqayada, malik yaḥfaẓ al-ḥurriyya*) and proponents of a republican regime. The first model is "constitutional governance" (*ghayr muṭlaq al-taṣarruf, ḥukm al-kunstītūsyuwn*), in which the ruler governs within the frame of the law, and his rule is based on the satisfaction of his subjects.[54] The second model strives to revoke the institution of the monarchy entirely and to replace it with a republic (*jumhūriyya, ribūblikā*) that is ruled by representatives (*mashāyikh, wukalā', jumhūr, nuwwāb*).[55] Other contemporary authors used the neologism *ribūblikān, ribūblikāniyyīn* (republicans) to indicate the same political camp.[56]

[54] In the biography of Napoleon, *ḥukm al-kunstītūsyuwn* (constitutional regime) is interpreted as *ḥukm yaḥid qudrat al-rā'ī biwasiṭat al-dīwān* (regime that limits the king's authority by parliament). Al-Tahtawi's term, *muṭlaq al-taṣarruf* or *al-taṣarruf al-muṭlaq* becomes the conventional expression for absolutism. See Depping, *Kitāb Qalā'id al-Mafākhir fī Gharīb 'Awā'id al-Awā'il wal-Awākhir*, 104–106; al-Tahtawi, *Takhlīṣ al-Ibrīz fī Talkhīṣ Bārīz aw al-Dīwān al-Nafīs bi-Īwān Bārīs*, 67; Kalivaris, *Kitāb Sirat al-Mu'aẓam al-Murafa' al-Kabīr Nabulyūn al-Awwal Imbaratūr al-Farānsawiyya*, 9; Robertson, *Kitāb Itḥāf Mulūk al-Zamān bi-Tārīkh al-Imbirāṭūr Sharlakān Masbūqan bi-Muqaddimatihi al-Musammā Itḥāf al-Mulūk al-Alibbā' bi-Taqaddum al-Jam'īyyāt fī Ūrūbā Mundhu Inqirāḍ al-Dawla al-Rūmāniyya*, 1:149; William Robertson, *Kitāb Itḥāf Mulūk al-Zamān bi-Tārīkh al-Imbirāṭūr Sharlakān*, trans. Khalifa Ibn Mahmud, vol. 2 (Bulaq: Al-Maṭba'a al-'Āmira, 1846), 135.

[55] Contemporary authors used these words to mean representatives. See al-Shidyaq, *al-Wāsiṭa ila Ma'rifat Aḥwāl Mālṭa wa-Kashf al-Mukhabbā' 'an Funūn Ūrūbā*, 151; al-Shidyaq, *Kanz al-Raghā'ib fī Muntakhabāt al-Jawā'ib*, 1877, 5:60; Kalivaris, *Kitāb Sirat al-Mu'aẓam al-Murafa' al-Kabīr Nabulyūn al-Awwal Imbaratūr al-Farānsawiyya*, 223; 'Aqiqi, *Thawra wa-Fitna fī Lubnān: Ṣafḥa Majhūla min Tārīkh al-Jabal min 1841 ila 1873*, 84–86.

[56] Kalivaris, *Kitāb Sirat al-Mu'aẓam al-Murafa' al-Kabīr Nabulyūn al-Awwal Imbaratūr al-Farānsawiyya*, 248.

Al-Tahtawi's observation in the 1830s provides further elaboration of the nature of relations between ruler and ruled in both models of governance. The first model, which is absolute, consists of the subordination of the ruled by the ruler, has no citizens' rights, and is based on divine theory and supported by the church. In the second model the king merely functions as an executive power, and he is subordinate to the law and the sovereignty of his people. The first was supported by clerics, who were perceived as enemies of enlightenment (*al-anwār wal-ma'ārif*), while the second model was supported by philosophers, scientists, and most of the subjects.[57] Although these models of governance became prominent in the translations of the 1840s and 1850s, Arabic during these years did not have consistent terms for them.[58] Furthermore, these details were not always perceived by contemporaries. Another traveler, who visited a few cities in Europe in 1855, referred to the force that resulted in Louis Philippe's abdication during the 1848 revolutions as "'*uṣbat al-ḥurriyya*" (faction of freedom), comprising all the revolutionary forces in one phrase, without emphasizing any difference between them.[59]

These words, coined extensively during this period in the translated French books and journey literature, were used to portray the politics in Europe, not in the Ottoman Empire. In Europe massive political events took place from the 1830s through the 1850s. In addition to the July events, revolutionary waves, unprecedented in the history of Europe, reached their peak in the 1848 Spring of Nations. These revolutions constituted an international force, and no part of the continent was immune from their effect. Their repercussions expanded until the 1860s and reached Mexico and the Ottoman lands, as detailed in the next chapter. During this wave of revolutions, ideology had a

[57] Al-Tahtawi, *Takhlīṣ al-Ibrīz fī Talkhīṣ Bārīz aw al-Dīwān al-Nafīs bi-Īwān Bārīs*, 119, 157, 160.

[58] Khalifa Mahmud, translator in the School of Language, renders constitutional limitations on the executive authority as *ḥurriyyat al-qawānīn*. Al-Tahtawi uses *qānūn muqayyīd*. The author of the biography of Napoleon uses the neologism *kunstītūsyuwn*. For further details, see ibid., 66; Voltaire, *Maṭāli' Shumūs al-Siyar fī Waqā'i' Karlūs al-Thānī 'Ashar*, 6; Robertson, *Kitāb Itḥāf Mulūk al-Zamān bi-Tārīkh al-Imbirāṭūr Sharlakān Masbūqan bi-Muqaddimatihi al-Musammā Itḥāf al-Mulūk al-Alibbā' bi-Taqaddum al-Jam'īyyāt fī Ūrūbā Mundhu Inqirāḍ al-Dawla al-Rūmāniyya*, 1:45; Kalivaris, *Kitāb Sirat al-Mu'aẓam al-Murafa' al-Kabīr Nabulyūn al-Awwal Imbaratūr al-Farānsawiyya*, 9.

[59] Bustrus, *al-Nuzha al-Shahiyya fī al-Riḥla al-Salīmiyya, 1855*, 82.

larger impact on European politics, especially after the establishment of the party system in some of the European states. These revolutionary forces across Europe consisted of liberals, democratic radicals, and socialists (the Communist Manifesto was issued by Karl Marx and Friedrich Engels on the eve of the 1848 revolutions), but the political programs were dominated by national and liberal agendas. The two ideologies, nationalism and liberalism, interacted continuously: liberalism stemmed from the idea of progress for individuals and groups, and nationalism stood for the claim of political recognition of national communities. Furthermore, adding republicanism, all these ideologies were frequently conflated because all of them evolved in contrast to absolutism and provided an alternative to its divine legitimacy. In light of the temporal perception of nationalism, the force of the public embedded liberal content: Bringing the power to the people contrasted with the authority of a single ruler, and establishing representative institutions was equivalent to politics derived from the idea of freedom that was defined in contrast to absolutism.

Contemporary Arabic captured the comprehensive distinction made between countries under autocracy and "free countries" that maintained the principles of sovereignty of the people and constitutionalism. The interrelation between the "common good" and the necessity of limiting political power was outlined in the 1830s journey literature and translations with the minting of phrases such as "freedom of homeland," "free country," and "free nation." In one of the earliest nineteenth-century printed renditions of the Greek philosophical heritage, Husain ʿAbd Allah al-Misri, a translator in the School of Language, loosely uses *ḥurriyyat al-waṭan* (freedom of homeland) in depicting the failure of Solon's reforms against the background of Pisistratus's autocracy in ancient Athens. The content of this freedom is summed up in Solon's words by his ambition to protect the laws of Athens that were threatened by the attempt of his rival, Pisistratus, to institute an autocracy.[60] Solon used the phrase "governance based on freedom" (*siyāsa mabniyya ʿala al-ḥurriyya*) to distinguish his political orientation from Pisistratus's autocracy. In his opinion those who followed the autocracy destroyed "sovereignty of the people and freedom" (*al-jumhūriyya wal-ḥurriyya*).[61] In this context "free country"

[60] Diogenes Laertius, *Mukhtaṣar Tarjamāt Mashāhīr Qudamāʾ al-Falāsifa*, trans. Husain ʿAbd Allah al-Misri (Bulaq: Dār al-Ṭibāʿa al-ʿĀmira, 1836), 21.

[61] The French source did not use the word "freedom." Apparently, the translator used this word to stress the relation between a democratic (republican) regime

was interpreted not only as sustaining a constitution and the rule of law (in contrast to autocracy) but also as a place that maintained equality between people (*yastawī fihi jamī' al-nāss*) and preserved their freedoms.[62] The political employment of *ḥurriyya* in this context emphasizes the comprehensiveness of freedom, which is associated with sovereignty of the people and constitutionalism as a substantive principle that protects individuals from autocracy.

The intertwined dynamics between these concepts also appear in later translations. In parallel with the concept of *ḥurriyyat al-waṭan*, Muhammad Mustafa Bashjawish transmitted Voltaire's definition of "free nation" (*al-milla al-ḥurra*) to Arabic in his translation of Voltaire's book *History of Charles XII, King of Sweden*, which was published in Arabic in 1841. Voltaire defined "free nation" as a group of people who are responsible for their fate and who acknowledge their collective interests, including when these interests place them in opposition to their king. Voltaire argues that the king should submit to the will of his people according to the "virtue of freedom" (*shahāmat al-ḥurriyya*).[63]

Nineteenth-century Arabic underwent substantial changes in relation to the state of the language prior to the nineteenth century. Phrases such as *ḥurriyyat al-qawm* that had previously denoted "notables of the community,"[64] became, in the 1830s and 1840s, heavily infused with political connotations. Phrases such as *milla ḥurra* (free nation), *waṭan ḥurr* (free homeland), and *mamlaka ḥurra* (free kingdom) explicitly indicated a nation or country governed by a constitution and a parliament.[65]

The temporal meaning of the phrase "free nations," as indicated, imported two sorts of regimes, either republican or constitutional monarchy. The republican regime was signified by a variety of newly

and freedom. For comparison, see ibid., 22; Diogenes Laertius, *Les Vies Des plus Illustres Philosophes de L'antiquité* (Paris: Richard, 1769), 34.

62 Laertius, *Mukhtaṣar Tarjamāt Mashāhīr Qudamā' al-Falāsifa*, 23.

63 Voltaire, *Maṭāli' Shumūs al-Siyar fī Waqā'i' Karlūs al-Thānī 'Ashar*, 52.

64 For the meaning of this phrase, see the eighteenth-century dictionary: Muhammad Murtada al-Husayni al-Zubaydi, "H.r.r," *Tāj al-'Arūs min Jawāhir al-Qāmūs* (Kuwait: Maṭba'at Ḥukūmat al-Kūwayt, 1972), 587.

65 For additional examples using *mamlaka ḥurra*, see Voltaire's translation. Voltaire distinguished between constitutional monarchy, which is limited by the parliamentary representative system, as in Sweden and England, and absolute monarchy, as existed in France and Spain in his time. Voltaire, *Maṭāli' Shumūs al-Siyar fī Waqā'i' Karlūs al-Thānī 'Ashar*, 6.

coined words. The most common was *jumhūr* (public, republic) which, as previously mentioned, was significantly politicized by the end of the eighteenth century. This word, which marked the march of the principle "sovereignty of the people" to Arabic, indicated the political power of the common people and was frequently used in contrast to the notables (aristocracy) and the monarchy.[66] Sources in the first half of the nineteenth century used the word to indicate a republic, empowered by connotations of a political community consisting of the solidarity of the common people, as in "*ma tasaraḥa al-jumhūr al-faransāwī illā ba'd muḥāraba*" ("the French people liberated only by war").[67] Al-Tahtawi used *jumhūr* in a broader sense to denote representatives of the public (parliament members),[68] and he used *jumhūriyya* (borrowing from Turkish) to indicate "republic," coining the common modern term for the concept.[69] Furthermore, the word was used as a synonym for "free nation," as in al-Tahtawi's depiction of the Druze as *umma jumhūriyya*, emphasizing their tendency toward sovereignty and independence in contrast to submission to the sultan.[70] In 1834 al-Tahtawi defined *jumhūriyya* as an entity that is "ruled by a number of natives," emphasizing the self-governance of communities through the application of their particular

[66] *Jumhūr al-ra'āyyā* (common people) was frequently used in clear distinction to notables. For example, see Nasif al-Yaziji, *Risāla Tārīkhiya fī Aḥwāl Jabal Lubnān fī 'Ahdihi al-Iqṭā'ī* (Beirut: Dār Ma'n, 2002), 43; al-Shidyaq, *al-Wāsiṭa ila Ma'rifat Aḥwāl Mālṭa wa-Kashf al-Mukhabbā' 'an Funūn Ūrūbā*, 37.

[67] In some sources *jumhūr* indicated the sovereignty and solidarity of the people, while "republic" was signified by different appellations. See, for instance, the biography of Napoleon, where the author used *ribūblikā* (republic) and *jumhūr* in the same paragraph. See also Butrus al-Bustani's political use of this word in 1860–1861: Kalivaris, *Kitāb Sirat al-Mu'azam al-Murafa' al-Kabīr Nabulyūn al-Awwal Imbaratūr al-Farānsawiyya*, 93–94; al-Bustani, *Nafīr Sūriyya*, 37, 42–43.

[68] In addition to al-Tahtawi, see the translated letter published in 1861 in *al-Jawā'ib* from the "Italian People" to the French parliament representatives. The author requested, in the name of the Italian people, "permission of the parliament's representatives" (*taṣrīḥ ra'ī al-jumhūr*) to recognize Italian independence and to evacuate the French army from Rome: Al-Tahtawi, *Takhlīṣ al-Ibrīz fī Talkhīṣ Bārīz aw al-Dīwān al-Nafīs bi-Īwān Bārīs*, 68; al-Shidyaq, *Kanz al-Raghā'ib fī Muntakhabāt al-Jawā'ib*, 1877, 5:20–23.

[69] Al-Tahtawi, *Takhlīṣ al-Ibrīz fī Talkhīṣ Bārīz aw al-Dīwān al-Nafīs bi-Īwān Bārīs*, 157; Ayalon, "Semantics and the Modern History of Non-European Societies: Arab 'Republics' as a Case Study," 829.

[70] Conrad Malte-Brun, *al-Jughrāfiyya al-'Umūmiyya*, trans. Rifa'a Rafi' al-Tahtawi, vol. 3 (Bulaq: 184–?), 20, 66, 70.

laws.[71] "Republican regime" (*jumhūr, jumhūriyya*) was used during these years as a general term that indicated all the models of governance that apply the principles of sovereignty of the people and representation, without distinguishing between democracy and aristocracy or between confederation and city-state.[72] Contemporary sources rarely used a special term for democracy;[73] instead they extensively employed the general term of *jumhūr*. Nevertheless, there were some early attempts to coin special words for democracy, especially in translated works. The idea of the "rule of the people [*ra'iyya, jumhūr, khalq*]"[74] was indicated during this period by a variety of coinages; *maḥkūma bil-'āmma* (governed by public);[75] *d[i]muqrāṭiyya* and *ḥukm d[i]muqrāṭī*;[76] *dāmūkrātī* and *dāmūkrāsiyyā*.[77] Despite the intertwined meaning, some sources made rare use of distinctions

[71] In Arabic, "*ḥukum 'idda min uṣūl ahl bilād wilāyya*": see the glossary al-Tahtawi appended to one of his early works. He illustrates this concept by using the example of the federal republic of Switzerland, or the medieval Italian independent city-states of Genoa and Venice: Al-Tahtawi, *al-Ta'rībāt al-Shāfiya li-Murīd al-Jughrāfiyya*, app. 72–73.

[72] Following Montesquieu, al-Tahtawi conceived democracy and aristocracy in the 1830s as types of republics. In a similar way, and about fifty years later, Butrus al-Bustani defined "republic" (he published his entry in 1882) as a way of governance ruled directly by the public or by representatives. He distinguished between four variants of republics: those ruled by aristocracy (*aristuqrāṭiyya*) or by shaykhs (*mashyakhiyya, mashyakha*); those ruled by distinguished people from the public, notables (*khawāṣ*), or by some of the people; a democracy that is ruled by the majority of the people (*dimuqrāṭiyya*); and united political entities ruled by one regime (confederation, *ittiḥādiyya*). See ibid., 62, 72–73; Butrus al-Bustani, "Jumhūriyya," *Kitāb Dā'irat al-Ma'ārif* (Beirut: Dār al-Ma'arif, 1882), 534; Montesquieu, *The Spirit of the Laws*, 10–15, 21–25.

[73] The medieval Muslim philosopher al-Farabi denoted classical Greek democracy by using the phrase *madīna jamā'iyya* (collective polity). See al-Farabi, *Kitāb al-Siyāsa al-Madaniyya*, 99–101.

[74] Al-Tahtawi defines it as the rule of people, directly or by representatives. He used the model of the French republic after the revolution to exemplify the concept. In the biography of Napoleon I, the translator follows Ellious Bocthor and translates "democracy" as "*tābi' ḥukm al-jumhūr*" (which refers to public governance). He renders "republic" as "the rule of the people" (*ḥukm al-khalq*). See Ellious Bocthor, "Démocrate," *Dictionnaire Français-Arabe* (Paris: Chez Firmin Didot Freres, 1828), 248; al-Tahtawi, *al-Ta'rībāt al-Shāfiya li-Murīd al-Jughrāfiyya*, app. 76; Kalivaris, *Kitāb Sirat al-Mu'aẓam al-Murafa' al-Kabīr Nabulyūn al-Awwal Imbaratūr al-Faransawiyya*, 9, 224, 550.

[75] Laertius, *Mukhtaṣar Tarjamāt Mashāhīr Qudamā' al-Falāsifa*, 24.

[76] Al-Tahtawi, *al-Ta'rībāt al-Shāfiya li-Murīd al-Jughrāfiyya*, app. 76.

[77] *Dāmūkrāsiyyā* and *dāmūkrātī* (an archaic version of the term democracy) is listed in a glossary appended to the biography of Napoleon I under the title of "foreign words." See Laertius, *Mukhtaṣar Tarjamāt Mashāhīr Qudamā'*

between the two concepts, democracy and republic. Whereas *jumhūr* was used to imply the principle of sovereignty in general, *dāmūkrāsiyyā* was used to stress particularly the principle of equality. Napoleon was presented in his biography in Arabic as the greatest *dāmūkrātū* (democrat) in Europe because he demolished the privilege system (*ikhtiṣāṣāt al-mabghūḍa*) of the Ancien Régime (*al-ḥukm al-qadīm*).[78] In the same composition the word *rib[v]ūblikānī* was also employed to mean republican rather than democrat, as a separate political designation.[79]

Although the temporal language neglected the concept of the direct "rule of the people," it emphasized, in many frequently used words, the representative aspect of their rule. The most common word used for indicating rule by representatives was *mashyakha* (from *shaykh*, which could refer to an elder, a Muslim cleric, a head of a tribe, or a notable). This word, which was often used to indicate high positions and seniority (such as chief clerics)[80] or a tribal system of collective governance, was politicized during the French invasion and used as one of the signifiers of "republic." The word emphasized a state of governance that derives from the principle of representation by council or parliament, with no regard to the procedure of selection.[81] The use of *jumhūr* or *mashyakha* to mean a republican regime was

*al-Falāsifa*, 21; Kalivaris, *Kitāb Sirat al-Mu'aẓam al-Murafa' al-Kabīr Nabulyūn al-Awwal Imbaratūr al-Farānsawiyya*, 224, 550.

78 Kalivaris, *Kitāb Sirat al-Mu'aẓam al-Murafa' al-Kabīr Nabulyūn al-Awwal Imbaratūr al-Farānsawiyya*, 27, 224–225.

79 Ibid., 88.

80 As in *mashyakhat al-Azhar* (al-Azhar that is directed by the chief cleric), *mashyakha lil-'ulūm fī bārīs* (higher institution for sciences in Paris), *mashyakhat madīnat bārīs* (city council of Paris), *kursī al-mashyakha* (director of the institution), and so forth. See John Richardson, "Mashyakha," *A Dictionary, Persian, Arabic, and English: with a Dissertation on the Languages, Literature, and Manners of Eastern Nations* (London: William Bulmer, 1806), 939; *Kitāb Majmū' Ḥawādith al-Ḥarb al-Wāqi' Bayna al-Faransāwiyya wal-Namsāwiyya fī Awākhir Sant 1802 al-Masīḥiyya* (Paris, 1807), 2–3; Reinhart Pieter Anne Dozy, "Mashyakha," *Takmilat al-Ma'ājim al-'Arabiyya* (Baghdad: Dār al-Shu'ūn al-Thaqāfiyya al-'Āmma, 1997), 395; al-Shidyaq, *al-Wāsiṭa ila Ma'rifat Aḥwāl Mālṭa wa-Kashf al-Mukhabbā' 'an Funūn Ūrūbā*, 247; *al-Naẓẓārāt al-Miṣriyya*, September 16, 1879, 16.

81 Rafa'il Zakhur also used *mashyakha* to indicate "republic" (see the quote in al-Shayal): Al-Jabarti, *'Ajā'ib al-Āthār fī al-Tarājim wal-Akhbār*, 1998, 3:101; al-Turk, *Dhikr Tamalluk Jumhūr al-Faransāwiyya al-Aqṭār al-Miṣriyya wal-Bilād al-Shāmiyya, aw, al-Ḥamla al-Faransiyya 'ala Miṣr wal-Shām*, 21; al-Shayal, *Tārīkh al-Tarjama wal-Ḥaraka al-Thaqāfiyya fī 'Aṣr Muḥammad 'Ali*, 216; Kalivaris, *Kitāb Sirat al-Mu'aẓam al-Murafa' al-Kabīr Nabulyūn al-Awwal Imbaratūr al-Farānsawiyya*, 141.

common during the nineteenth century, and it was gradually replaced by *jumhūriyya*.[82]

The use of *jumhūr* and *mashyakha* reflected the perception of the contemporary Arabic-speaking scholars with regard to the idea of the political involvement of ordinary people in politics: Although the temporal Arabic emphasized the general idea of popular sovereignty (*jumhūr*) and the idea of representation (*mashyakha*), it neglected the democratic procedure involved.[83] In that sense the idea of elections, and with it the sovereignty of the people as manifested in the idea of indirect representation, gained less relevance than different methods of popular representation that are not necessarily democratic. This perception nurtured the idea of representation with less emphasis on the idea of political freedom (political rights).[84]

Muhammad ʿAli executed this concept in Egypt through the founding of a Council of State and a Private Council that he appointed from among his high military and public officials, marginalizing the

[82] For selected examples of using the word in journey literature and translated books in the first half of the nineteenth century, see al-Tahtawi, *Takhlīṣ al-Ibrīz fī Talkhīṣ Bārīz aw al-Dīwān al-Nafīs bi-Īwān Bārīs*, 157; Robertson, *Kitāb Itḥāf Mulūk al-Zamān bi-Tārīkh al-Imbirāṭūr Sharlakān Masbūqan bi-Muqaddimatihi al-Musammā Itḥāf al-Mulūk al-Alibbāʾ bi-Taqaddum al-Jamʿīyyāt fī Ūrūbā Mundhu Inqirāḍ al-Dawla al-Rūmāniyya*, 1:36, 38, 52; Henry Markham, *Hadhā Kitāb Siyāḥat Amrīqa*, trans. Saʿd Naʿam (Bulaq: Dār al-Ṭibāʿa, 1846), 64. In addition to these words, Arabic only occasionally indicated "republic" at the end of the eighteenth century and the beginning of the nineteenth century by using borrowed forms such as *ribūblik* and *būblika*. See Besim Korkut, *al-Wathāʾiq al-ʿArabiyya fī Dār al-Maḥfūẓāt bi-Madīnat Dubrūnik* (Sarajevo: Orijentalni Institu u Sarajevu, 1960), 50, 58, 72, 74, 84.

[83] The use of the word "democracy" in this context should be taken carefully, especially because this concept was still ambiguous. During the early decades of the nineteenth century, "democracy" was a concept in transition, and it would receive clear modern content comprising both the principle of elections and the principle of indirect representation as a manifestation of popular sovereignty around the time of the 1848 revolutions. Democracy then became a political slogan and was employed extensively in the political discourse in western Europe and North America. For more details, see Joanna Innes and Mark Philp, "Introduction," in *Re-imagining Democracy in the Age of Revolutions: America, France, Britain, Ireland, 1750–1850*, 1–10.

[84] This concept was common in Europe prior to the French Revolution. Many bodies in monarchic France presented themselves as "representative" of the nation or people when not all of them were elective. Malcolm Crook shows how in eighteenth-century France, "representation did not traditionally connote election." For more details, see Malcolm Crook, "Elections and Democracy in France, 1789–1848," in *Re-imagining Democracy in the Age of Revolutions: America, France, Britain, Ireland, 1750–1850*, 83–97.

representation of notables, clerics, and common people.[85] In the 1830s the idea of representative councils gained central importance in the Egyptian rule of Greater Syria and in the reforms that followed. Although the reform edict of 1839 did not address the idea of representative government, it opened the door for wider changes in laws and institutions. The edict of January 1840 to provincial officials – which required the establishment of administrative councils in the provinces – began a tradition of representation at higher levels but not in the central government. Although the purpose of these councils was first of all to help in collecting taxes, and they did not represent the common people and to a large extent maintained the old dominant strata, they established the principle of elections as one of the elements of political legitimacy. The imperial edict of 1856 emphasized the representative principle in the lower administrative levels, including the provinces[86] and the millet system (completed in 1864). In that sense, by the 1860s the idea of nondemocratic representation preserved its dominance in both formal and informal language. In 1868 the Council of State – the main law-drafting body of the empire – started to meet delegates from provincial general assemblies, and the first formal connection between the central government and the representative councils was made.[87]

These developments disclose the perception of representation as it was manifested in language. The application of these ideas took place as a result of decrees and acts initiated by the rulers. In addition to what took place in Istanbul, in Tunisia there was an experiment with representation between 1861 and 1864, and in Egypt the khedive had constituted the first Assembly of Delegates in 1866.[88] The political language was, by 1860, less developed with regard to principles of

[85] Vatikiotis, *The Modern History of Egypt*, 67.

[86] This created the *vilayet* system that incorporated the representation principle in administrative councils in each *vilayet*, *sancak*, and *kaza*; in local courts; and in the general assembly for each *vilayet*. For more details, see Davison, *Essays in Ottoman and Turkish History, 1774–1923: The Impact of the West*, 102–103; Ceylan, *The Ottoman Origins of Modern Iraq*, 109–110.

[87] Davison, *Essays in Ottoman and Turkish History, 1774–1923: The Impact of the West*, 96–108.

[88] The word *jumhūr* was frequently attached to the formal language of constituting these councils. See the khedive's speech in November 1866. At the opening of the *majlis shūra al-nuwwāb* in Egypt, he frequently used phrases such as *manfa'a lil-jumhūr* (beneficial for the public) to depict the benefits of the council. For more details about Tunisia and Egypt, see al-Shidyaq, *Kanz al-Raghā'ib fī Muntakhabāt al-Jawā'ib*, 1877, 5:205–206; *Dustūr: A Survey of*

democracy (political freedom and elected representation) than it was with regard to constitutional language, which was driven by idea of individual freedoms and which demonstrated more consistency and acquired increasing relevance in both formal and informal discourse.

The development of the constitutional idea in the Ottoman Islamic context had special implications for its particular relation with ideas derived from democratic principles that act as limitations on autocratic executive power: "sovereignty of the people" and "political freedom." On an illuminating note, al-Tahtawi translated Depping's two models of governance, the absolutists and the constitutional, into Arabic. Depping classified the first model with the Asian political traditions, including in his account the Ottoman regime of the "Sultan of Islam." In his translation al-Tahtawi decided to omit this part because it was not "appropriate" for his readers.[89] Although the classification of "free countries" versus "autocratic countries" was received with deep skepticism when it referred to the internal affairs of "*dar al-Islām*" (abode of Islam), some early books that combine translations from French and compositions by local authors embedded this critical outlook. During the 1830s, in a statement that pointedly contrasts between the concepts of political freedom and autocracy, al-Tahtawi gave the loss of justice (*ʿadl*) among Greeks and their natural tendency toward "freedom and independence" (*al-ḥurriyya wal-istiqlāl*) as reasons for their revolution against monarchies and their replacing them with democracies (*jumhūriyyāt*).[90] This logic rapidly penetrated al-Tahtawi's assessment of contemporary internal events. Writing in the same decade, he described the Greek revolt against the Ottoman sultan by using the word *ḥurriyya* in explaining the Greek reason for revolution. He further elaborated that the sultan's regime sustained absolutism (*muṭlaq al-taṣarruf*), emphasizing the conceptual association between freedom, revolution, and sovereignty, in contrast with absolutism.[91]

*the Constitutions of the Arab and Muslim States* (Leiden: Brill, 1966), 1–5, 24–32.

89 Depping, *Kitāb Qalāʾid al-Mafākhir fī Gharīb ʿAwāʾid al-Awāʾil wal-Awākhir*, 105–106.

90 This source combines composition with additions of translated and edited texts from various sources by al-Tahtawi and colleagues from the School of Languages. See al-Tahtawi and al-Zarabi, *Bidāyat al-Qudamāʾ wa-Hidāyat al-Ḥukamāʾ*, 71.

91 In other phrases he elaborates the sultan's absolute authority, as it was executed without any limits over the life of his subjects and their property

Against this background al-Tahtawi defined the comprehensive appellation *bilād ḥurriyya* (an archaic version of *bilād ḥurra*, free areas or country) from an internal Islamic perspective: "And what they [the French] desire and call freedom [*al-ḥurriyya*] is precisely what we [the Muslims] designate as justice [*'adl wal-inṣāf*], and that is because the meaning of freedom is equality before the law in which the rulers do not discriminate between human beings but apply the state of law [as the highest value]."[92] This concept of freedom is therefore a synonym for the principle of the rule of law, and hence it is a state of executing *'adl* by complying with the legal and moral rules of religion. This starting point illuminates the route taken in the construction of the particular Islamic concept of individual freedom and constitutionalism. Some Muslim scholars approached the idea of constitutionalism from this perspective, assuming that constitutionalism is a synonym for the principle of the rule of law. According to this orientation, freedom was defined not against absolutism but in contrast to the lack of order. The idea of constitutionalism thus did not necessarily evolve in contrast with autocracy but rather with anarchy and absence of the execution of religions laws. This interpretation of freedom emerged within the epistemic conception of religion, and it became a cornerstone in the evolving constitutional thought in Arabic, as detailed later.

The temporal meaning of *'adl* was presented in an entry written by al-Tahtawi during the 1830s in which he defined the word *ẓālim* (literally "unjust [ruler]").[93] There he elaborated the meaning of injustice in a political context. The word *ẓālim*, he states, was occasionally applied

(*yataṣarraf kamā yurīd fī anfusihim wa-amwālihim*). The following reference is compiled from various sources: Al-Tahtawi, *al-Ta'rībāt al-Shāfiya li-Murīd al-Jughrāfiyya*, 125–126. For additional sources from the same decade that use the word *ḥurriyya* to depict the same event, see *Kitāb al-Kanz al-Mukhtār fī Kashf al-Arāḍī wal-Biḥār* (Malta, 1836), 59.

92 Al-Tahtawi, *Takhlīṣ al-Ibrīz fī Talkhīṣ Bārīz aw al-Dīwān al-Nafīs bi-Īwān Bārīs*, 73.

93 The adjective *'ādil* has many implied meanings in religion, theology, philosophy, and law. As a judicial conception, *'adl* denotes a state of moral and religious perfection. A "just" man means a person who obeys the rules of his religion, morally and legally. In that sense this principle applies also to non-Muslims. It is worth mentioning that a codification implemented in the Ottoman Empire around the middle of the nineteenth century defined a "just" person as "one in whom good impulses prevail over bad." The closest translation in English therefore would be "person of good morals." For further details, see Emile Tyan, "'Adl," *The Encyclopedia of Islam* (Leiden: E. J. Brill, 1986), 209; Muhammad 'Ali al-Tahanawi, "'Adala," *Kashshāf Iṣṭilāḥāt al-Funūn wal-'Ulūm* (Beirut: Nāshirūn, 1996), 1166–1167.

to Roman rulers when they ruled independently, without constraints and without obeying the laws. Additionally, this word was used to describe a king who rules without legitimacy. Obviously, al-Tahtawi's definition ascribes the notion of justice that is contrasted with autocracy to a non-Islamic foreign tradition.[94] Echoes of al-Tahtawi's particular interpretation of constitutionalism in Arabic – merely as rule of law – appear in the works of other prominent scholars, such as Faris al-Shidyaq, who use "free country" (*bilād al-ḥurriyya*) to indicate a state that is ruled by law.[95]

Interpreting freedom against the background of autocracy, not in contrast with it, resulted in a concept of freedom that was not necessarily perceived as a political "right" stemming from the principle of the sovereignty of the people (citizenship) but as a "privilege" or "permission" that is given by the ruler – the absolute sovereign.[96] Contemporary lexicons published during this era documented this concept in their translation of *liberté* into Arabic as *rukhṣa* (permission), *rukhṣat ikhtiyyār* (permission to choose), and *rukhṣat irādah* (permission to have a free will). Following the same logic, *liberté de conscience* was rendered as *rukhṣa fī al-'aqayyid* (permission for belief).[97] Similarly, al-Tahtawi had earlier written about the idea of freedom that was

[94] Al-Tahtawi, *al-Ta'rībāt al-Shāfiya li-Murīd al-Jughrāfiyya*, app. 82. For extensive discussion on the "circle of justice" in the nineteenth century Ottoman Empire, see Linda T. Darling, *A History of Social Justice and Political Power in the Middle East: The Circle of Justice from Mesopotamia to Globalization* (London: Routledge, 2013), 157–182.

[95] In addition al-Shidyaq uses the same phrase *bilād al-ḥurriyya* to indicate states (such as Britain) that do not apply taxes to visitors entering or departing the country. See al-Shidyaq, *al-Wāsiṭa ila Ma'rifat Aḥwāl Mālṭa wa-Kashf al-Mukhabbā' 'an Funūn Ūrūbā*, 63, 120, 212.

[96] The early use of freedom as part of the idea of civil rights was in journey and translated literature that recounted different political events in the history of Europe. There, Arabic-speaking scholars coined many phrases – *ḥuqūq al-ra'iyya*, *ḥuqūq al-ahāli*, *ḥurriyya 'umūmiyya* – that aimed to express the integration of the ideas of freedom and civil rights. For selected examples see al-Tahtawi, *Takhlīṣ al-Ibrīz fī Talkhīṣ Bārīz aw al-Dīwān al-Nafīs bi-Īwān Bārīs*, 67; Robertson, *Kitāb Itḥāf Mulūk al-Zamān bi-Tārīkh al-Imbirāṭūr Sharlakān Masbūqan bi-Muqaddimatihi al-Musammā Itḥāf al-Mulūk al-Alibbā' bi-Taqaddum al-Jam'iyyāt fī Ūrūbā Mundhu Inqirāḍ al-Dawla al-Rūmāniyya*, 1:155; Robertson, *Kitāb Itḥāf Mulūk al-Zamān bi-Tārīkh al-Imbirāṭūr Sharlakān Masbūqan bi-Muqaddimatihi al-Musammā Itḥāf al-Mulūk al-Alibbā' bi-Taqaddum al-Jam'iyyāt fī Ūrūbā*, 3:30.

[97] Alexandre Handjéri, "Libéral, Libérateur, Libération, Liberté, Indépendance," *Dictionnaire Français-Arabe-Persan et Turc: Enrichi D'examples En Langue Turque Avec Des Variantes, et de Beaucoup de Mots D'arts et Des Sciences* (Moscow: Impr. de l'Université impériale, 1841), 397–399; Nassif Mallouf,

bestowed by kings: "If he [the French king] gave freedom to people [*i'ṭā' al-ḥurriyya*] that desire this characteristic."[98] Another contemporary, historian Tanus al-Shidyaq, brother of Faris al-Shidayq, who published his work about the history of Mount Lebanon in 1859, used the word *ḥurriyya* to mean "permission," stating that "the state permitted the Christians to choose a ruler."[99] In another chronicle the people of Mount Lebanon were depicted as having gained *ḥurriyya* when the sultan chose, in 1840, a popular ruler from the Chehab dynasty (Bashir III) to govern after the withdrawal of the Egyptian forces. The same chronicler, who stated that "the people gained freedom [from the state] and the unjust and bad habits were removed,"[100] followed earlier arguments by associating the granting of freedom with executing *'adl* (just policies). Further indications of freedom and justice can be found in the same period in texts that give this combination a sociopolitical implication. A letter from June 1840, on the eve of the Christian and Druze revolt in Mount Lebanon against the Egyptian authorities, recounted their unjust experiences under Muhammad 'Ali's rule. They asserted that they lost their freedom and any just treatment, referring to corvée labor and high taxes implemented by the authorities. Freedom, with regard to the Druze and Christian communities, was used in contrast to the social (high taxes) and political (loss of free will) meanings that are identified with *ẓulm*.[101]

These shifts in the use of "freedom" and "justice" were early apostles of the modern meaning of *'adl*, which overlaps with the idea of political equality (later coined as *al-'adl bil-sawiyya*, justice based on

"Libéral, Libre," *Dictionnaire Français-Turc* (Paris: Maisonneuve et Cie, 1856), 414–415.

[98] In the first edition of his book (published in 1834), al-Tahtawi used *firqa* (group), and in the second (published in 1849) he used *umma* (people). See al-Tahtawi, *Takhlīṣ al-Ibrīz fī Talkhīṣ Bārīz aw al-Dīwān al-Nafīs bi-Īwān Bārīs*, 162, 165; Rifa'a Rafi' al-Tahtawi, *al-Dīwān al-Nafīs fī Īwān Bārīs aw, Takhlīṣ al-Ibrīz fī Talkhīṣ Bārīz* (Beirut: Dār al-Suwaydī lil-Nashr wal-Tawzī', 2002), 227, 231.

[99] In Arabic: "*aṭlaqat al-dawla al-ḥurriyya lil-naṣāra bi'an yakhtārū wāliyan.*" See al-Shidyaq, *Kitāb Akhbār al-A'yān fī Jabal Lubnān*, 1970, 1:100; al-Shidyaq, *Kitāb Akhbār al-A'yān fī Jabal Lubnān*, 1970, 2:478.

[100] In Arabic, "*wahaṣala il-nās fī ḥurriyya, wairtafa'at tilk al-maẓālim wal-'awā'id al-radiy['']a.*" See: Al-Dimashqi, *Ta'rīkh Ḥawādith al-Shām wa-Lubnān*, 104–105.

[101] For additional temporal use of *ḥurr* (*muḥararīn*) in contrast with the burden of taxes, see: Kalivaris, *Kitāb Sirat al-Mu'aẓam al-Murafa' al-Kabīr Nabulyūn al-Awwal Imbaratūr al-Farānsawiyya*, 6.

equality between all subjects)[102] and social equality (later coined as *'adl ijtimā'ī*). In this regard it is worth emphasizing that the temporal meaning of material justice hardly plays any role in the theory of Islamic law.[103] Such social aspects of freedom were employed broadly in a few of the 1830s translations. In al-Tahtawi's translation of Depping, and in a chapter titled "Slavery and Servitude," Depping associates the abolition of slavery and servitude and the destruction of the feudal system with the rise of modern sciences. The peasants, he contended, were treated like animals, and they were not aware that they had a "right to freedom" (*istiḥqāqahum lil-ḥurriyya*) in reference to their right to social emancipation. This social freedom was obtained, Depping asserted, after the abolition of the feudal system, following the French Revolution.[104]

In a state where the subject of sovereignty was attached to autocratic rule, the language of freedom developed a concept that acknowledged the substantial place of authority as lying outside the individual and that regarded freedom as a royal grant. The idea of freedom acquired a different meaning in contexts where the concept of "sovereignty of the people" developed in contrast with political or social order. A marginal and perhaps exceptional case was presented in the political language of Mount Lebanon during the 1840s and 1850s. There, where society maintained semipolitical communities and the influence of the central government was nominal, the word *jumhūr* proliferated and became much more frequent, especially during the revolt against Egyptian rule.[105] Phrases such as "we, the Druze public" (*naḥnu jumhūr al-Durūz*) or "we, the Christian public" (*naḥnu jumhūr al-Naṣāra*) appeared often. Presenting the demands of a group of people in the

[102] See a letter sent by one of the anonymous Ottoman subjects from Bulgaria: Al-*Jawā'ib*, November 24, 1875, 2.

[103] Tyan, "'Adl," 209; Asad Rustum, *al-Uṣūl al-'Arabiyya li-Tārīkh Sūriyya fī 'Ahd Muhammad 'Ali Bāshā*, vol. 5 (Beirut: Manshurāt al-Maktaba al-Bulisiyya, 1988), 108–110.

[104] See this entry in al-Tahtawi's translation of Georges-Bernard Depping; for lexical interpretations of the terms employed in this work, see Jalal's book: Depping, *Kitāb Qalā'id al-Mafākhir fī Gharīb 'Awā'id al-Awā'il wal-Awākhir*, 84; Iman al-Sa'id Jalal, *Alfāẓ al-Ḥaḍāra fī Miṣr bil-Qarn al-Tāsi' 'Ashar: Ruṣidat min Kitāb Rifā'a al-Ṭahṭawī Qalā'id al-Mafākhir fī Gharīb 'Awā'id al-Awā'il wal-Awākhir, Ma'a al-Naṣṣ al-Kāmil lil-Kitāb* (Cairo: Maktabat al-Ādāb, 2008), 52–248.

[105] See the use of the word in two documents dated June 1840. Rustum, *al-Uṣūl al-'Arabiyya li-Tārīkh Sūriyya fī 'Ahd Muhammad 'Ali Bāshā*, 5:112–114, 117–118.

first person was a significant transformation in the political language of subjectivity, moving toward a much more politicized community that acknowledged the principle of sovereignty. This combination of the idea of freedom with the idea of sovereignty crystallized the modern concept of revolution and is an illustration of popular demand replacing political authority with popular rule.[106] By the first half of the nineteenth century, the temporal signifiers in Arabic of the concept of revolution were negative or neutral. Words such as *fitna*, *qiyām*, *nuhūḍ*, *hiyāj*, *khurūj*,[107] *taghyīr*,[108] and *inqilāb*,[109] in addition to particular words used mostly in Mount Lebanon such as *ḥaraka*, *ʿiṣāwa*, and *iṣyān*,[110] were used to indicate different kinds of revolt, while the most frequently used term during Muhammad ʿAli's invasion

[106] See the Christian-Druze pact in Mount Lebanon in 1840: ibid., 5:100. See also the Mount Lebanon rebels' reference to the French "heroic" fight against their enemies: ibid., 5:101–103.

[107] As in "*qiyām al-jumhūr*," used by al-Jabarti and al-Turk to refer to the French Revolution. Al-Turk also uses the words "*nuhūḍ*" and "*hiyāj*" (uprising). Al-Tahtawi employed "*fitna ʿẓīma wa-naṣrat al-fransāwiyya fī ṭalab al-ḥurriyya*" or "*qiyāmat al-franāwiyya wa-ṭalabuhum lil-ḥurriyya wal-musāwā.*" Faris al-Shidyaq uses the same word in his description of Paris, which he published in 1855, in addition to *ʿisyān* and *khurūj* (rebellion). See: Al-Turk, *Dhikr Tamalluk Jumhūr al-Faransāwiyya al-Aqṭār al-Miṣriyya wal-Bilād al-Shāmiyya, aw, al-Ḥamla al-Faransiyya ʿala Miṣr wal-Shām*, 18–19; al-Jabarti, *ʿAjāʾib al-Āthār fī al-Tarājim wal-Akhbār*, 1998, 3:27; al-Tahtawi, *Takhlīṣ al-Ibrīz fī Talkhīṣ Bārīz aw al-Dīwān al-Nafīs bi-Īwān Bārīs*, 72, 147, 163–164; Ahmad Faris al-Shidyaq, *al-Sāq ʿala al-Sāq fī Mā Huwa al-Fāryāq* (Beirut: Dār Maktabat al-Ḥayā, 1966), 631; al-Shidyaq, *al-Wāsiṭa ila Maʿrifat Aḥwāl Mālṭa wa-Kashf al-Mukhabbāʾ ʿan Funūn Ūrūbā*, 261; Robertson, *Kitāb Ithḥāf Mulūk al-Zamān bi-Tārīkh al-Imbirāṭūr Sharlakān Masbūqan bi-Muqaddimatihi al-Musammā Ithḥāf al-Mulūk al-Alibbāʾ bi-Taqaddum al-Jamʿiyyāt fī Ūrūbā Mundhu Inqirāḍ al-Dawla al-Rūmāniyya*, 1:10, 65; Voltaire, *Rawḍ al-Azhar fī Tārīkh Buṭrus al-Akbar*, 94–95; Rustum, *al-Uṣūl al-ʿArabiyya li-Tārīkh Sūriyya fī ʿAhd Muhammad ʿAli Bāshā*, 5:243; Asad Rustum, *al-Uṣūl al-ʿArabiyya li-Tārīkh Sūriyya fī ʿAhd Muḥammad ʿAli Bāshā*, vol. 1 (Beirut: Al-Maṭbaʿa al-Amīrikāniyya, 1987), 65.

[108] This word was employed in the Arabic translation of William Robenson's history of Emperor Charles V. For comparison between the English text and the Arabic translation, see: Al-Shayyal, *Tārīkh al-Tarjama wal-Ḥaraka al-Thaqāfiyya fī ʿAṣr Muḥammad ʿAli*, 221.

[109] See an early historical account of the French Revolution in: Kalivaris, *Kitāb Sirat al-Muʿaẓam al-Murafaʿ al-Kabīr Nabulyūn al-Awwal Imbaratūr al-Farānsawiyya*, 8.

[110] As in *ḥarakat al-Durūz* (Druze revolt during the Egyptian rule of Syria) or *ḥaraka mughāyira; iẓhār al-ʿiṣāwa*. See local correspondence from the 1840s and a chronicle composed in 1869 by Iskandar Abkariyus, an eyewitness to

of Greater Syria was *khurūj*, "revolt," against the sultan or against the will of God (*khurūj 'ala al-sultan, khurūj 'ala amr Allah*).[111] Similar to the traditional concept, the modern concept of revolution was perceived by some early nineteenth-century Arab chroniclers, Christian and Muslim alike, in metaphysical terms, as an act of heresy or misleading innovation.[112]

A formal approach toward the concept of modern revolution appears in an early text composed and collected by 'Abd Allah Abu al-Su'ud, an Arabic teacher in the School of Languages (published in 1841). His book was designed to be taught in the Egyptian state schools. Abu al-Su'ud, who composed his work in the form of questions and answers, interprets the breakdown of the French Revolution. In a question addressing the reasons for the "revolution and failure in the kingdom of France" (*al-fitna wal-fashal fī mamlakat faransā*), he focuses on the taxation imposed by the regime, the crisis between the king and the national assembly that brought about the violent reaction of the people that was referred to as a "strong fanatic and instinctive tendency."[113] Although Abu al-Su'ud mentions that the inhabitants composed their requests in terms of "what they called human rights," he does not indicate that the ambition for freedom was a reason for the revolution.[114]

An additional layer in the construction of "revolution" was added during the 1850s, with its association with freedom, sovereignty, equality, and human rights. The revolt of Mount Lebanon against

the war that erupted after the Egyptian retreat from Lebanon: Iskandar Abkariyus, *Nawādir al-Zamān fī Waqā'i' Jabal Lubnān* (London: Riyāḍ al-Rayyis lil-Kutub wal-Nashr, 1987), 209; Rustum, *al-Uṣūl al-'Arabiyya li-Tārīkh Sūriyya fī 'Ahd Muhammad 'Ali Bāshā*, 5:80, 97–98, 108; Asad Rustum, *al-Uṣūl al-'Arabiyya li-Tārīkh Sūriyya fī 'Ahd Muhammad 'Ali Bāshā*, vol. 3–4 (Beirut: Manshurāt al-Maktaba al-Bulisiyya, 1988), 228.

111 Rustum, *al-Uṣūl al-'Arabiyya li-Tārīkh Sūriyya fī 'Ahd Muḥammad 'Ali Bāshā*, 1987, 1:71, 76.

112 Al-Jabarti interpreted the revolutionary act against the French monarchy as a misleading innovation (*bid'a*), while the Catholic monk Hananiya al-Munayyir, who wrote from the area of Lebanon in the first decade of the nineteenth century, interpreted it as a result of "heresy" (*harṭaqa*). See al-Jabarti, *Maẓhar al-Taqdīs bi-Zawāl Dawlat al-Faransīs*, 52; Hananiya al-Munayyir, *al-Durr al-Marṣūf fī Tārīkh al-Shūf* (Lebanon: Jrus press, n.d.), 96.

113 'Abd Allah, *Kitāb naẓm al-La'ālī' fī al-Sulūk fī man Ḥakama Faransā wa-man Qābalahum 'Ala Miṣr min al-Mulūk*, 183.

114 Ibid., 183–188.

the Egyptians under Ibrahim Pasha was articulated by the new, temporary word *'āmmiyya*, which is derived from *'āmma/'awām* and denotes "common people."[115] After the Egyptians retreated from Mount Lebanon, they left behind social and religious tensions between the Druze minority, which comprised the majority of the feudal notables, and a Christian majority that constituted the majority of the peasants. In 1843 this tension took on a formal aspect with the division of Mount Lebanon into two territories: one in the south ruled by Druze and the other in the north ruled by Christians.

The use of *'āmmiyya* signified a shift in the concept of revolution from the common negative or neutral signifiers to a conception that emphasized the political function of the common people. The association of modern political concepts with revolution was manifested in Tanyus Shahin's revolt and seizure of Keserwan that started in 1858. The uprising against the local feudal notables was described by an eyewitness as a popular revolt that demanded a share of the feudalist property. He indicated that Tanyus Shahin, the leader of this popular revolt, acquired some of these properties via the "power of the people" (*biquwat al-jumhūr*) and by the power of the public authority or republican government (*ḥukūma jumhūriyya*).[116] This brief experience witnessed a rather significant change in the language and in politics: The government of this political entity not only spoke in the name of the interests of the public (*maṣāliḥ al-jumhūr*) but also established a system that was managed by representatives of the public.[117]

[115] The word *'āmmiyya* was used in a letter from 1845 to denote the common people who are not clerics in the Druze community (synonymous with *juhāl*, in contrast with *mashāyikh* or *'uqāl*, Druze clerics). Additionally, *al-qawma al-'āmmiyya* (revolution) was used in 1859 to refer to the revolutions of 1848, and in particular the revolt of the Italian states against the Austrian seizure of parts of Italy. See *'Uṭārid*, July 2, 1859, 1; Salim Hassan Hashi, *al-Murāsalāt al-Ijtimā'iyya wal-Iqtiṣādiyya li-Zu'amā' Jabal Lubnān Khilāl Thalāthat Qurūn (1600–1900)*, vol. 3 (Beirut: Dār al-Bāḥith, 1985), 92–94; 'Aqiqi, *Thawra wa-Fitna fī Lubnān: Ṣafḥa Majhūla min Tārīkh al-Jabal min 1841 ila 1873*, 40.

[116] 'Aqiqi, *Thawra wa-Fitna fī Lubnān: Ṣafḥa Majhūla min Tārīkh al-Jabal min 1841 ila 1873*, 86–87. For extensive historical discussion of this revolt, see Elizabeth Thompson, *Justice Interrupted: The Struggle for Constitutional Government in the Middle East* (Cambridge, MA: Harvard University Press, 2013), 37–60.

[117] For language used during this revolt, see 'Aqiqi. Published translated and primary sources from the nineteenth century show that modern concepts were

Furthermore, a concept such as "social equality" was highly emphasized in contemporary letters that referred to the principles of equal distribution of public wealth, equality, freedom, the revocation of discrimination, and human rights.[118] It is important to stress that this revolt came less than two years after of the edict of 1856 that promised to secure equality among all Ottoman subjects.[119] "Revolution" would acquire stable morphological form a few decades after this event by recruiting the medieval word *thawra*[120] and infusing it with the modern conception.[121]

The idea of freedom expanded significantly during this period, generating many political implications that changed with the context and with the dynamics created with other political principles. In the mainstream of these changes, "individual freedoms" crystallized as an

already evident in Lebanon's political language of the 1840s. The late translation of these documents from Western languages to Arabic makes the study of their language and terminology difficult. For selected translated primary sources, see Philippe al-Khazin and Farid al-Khazin, eds., "Nashrat al-Thuwār al-Lubnāniyyīn ila Muwāṭinihim Bita'rīkh 8 Ḥuzairān Sant 1840," in *Majmū'at al-Muḥarrarāt al-Siyāsiyya wal-Mufāwaḍāt al-Duwaliyya 'an Sūriyya wa-Lubnān min Sanat 1840 ila Sanat 1910*, vol. 1(Beirut: Dār al-Rā'id al-Lubnānī, 1983), 3–5; 'Aqiqi, *Thawra wa-Fitna fī Lubnān: Ṣafḥa Majhūla min Tārīkh al-Jabal min 1841 ila 1873*, 40, 159–160, 164, 168, 181, 200.

118 See the letter from 1858 in: 'Aqiqi, *Thawra wa-Fitna fī Lubnān: Ṣafḥa Majhūla min Tārīkh al-Jabal min 1841 ila 1873*, 259–260.

119 The edict and its content were referenced in contemporary letters from Mount Lebanon. See ibid., 161–163.

120 The root of the word was used in the Qur'an, and *thawra* was employed in medieval sources denoting revolt or uprising. See, for instance, Ibn Khaldun, *Muqaddimat al-'Allāma Ibn Khaldūn al-Musamma Dīwān al-Mubtada' wal-Khabarr fī Ta'rīkh al-'Arab wal-Barbar wa-man 'Āṣarahum min Dhawī al-Sha'n al-Akbarr*, 178. An account of Tanyus Shahin's revolt uses *'āmmiyya* and *thawra* in the same composition: see Mansur Tanus al-Hatuni, *Nabdha Tārīkhiyya fī al-Muqāṭa'a al-Kisrwāniyya* (Beirut, 1884), 242, 323, 338, 341, 343, 347, 353, 363.

121 See al-Marrash and Nakhla, two early journey accounts from the 1860s and 1870s that use *thawra* to mean revolution. See also the use of the term in the early newspaper *Birjīs Barīs*. Salim al-Bustani later interpreted the French Revolution as a violent act for restoring civil rights that had been confiscated by the tyrant. The concept became part of a controversy in the 1870s between the progressive *al-Jinān* and the conservative *al-Bashīr*. See Fransis Fathalah Marrash, *Riḥlat Bārīs 1867* (Beirut: Al-Mu'assasa al-'Arabiyya lil-Dirāsāt wal-Nashr, 2004), 48; Salih Nakhlah, *al-Kanz al-Mukhabbā lil-Siyāḥa fī Ūrūbā* (Cairo: 1876), 98; *Birjīs Barīs*, November 9, 1859; *Birjīs Barīs*, November 23, 1859; *Birjīs Barīs*, April 25, 1860; *al-Jinān* 2, no. 11 (1871): 566, 573–575; *al-Bashīr*, May 13, 1871, 416–417.

idea that developed implications ranging from being a mercy vouchsafed to being a right. The interrelations between "individual freedom," with its principles of constitutionalism, and "sovereignty of the people" exhibit, to a large extent, the particular content that these dynamics generated during this formative phase. The next subchapter underscores an additional aspect of freedom concerned with social and political organizations that exceeded the interpretations generated by individual principles and moved toward concepts derived from collective social organizations such as nationalism, social institutions, and classes.

## Collective Aspects of the Language of Freedom: Freedom of Dynasties, Political Entities, and Institutions

During the period between the 1820 and 1860, the word "freedom" not only integrated the expressions that articulate the individual's relation to state and society but also penetrated to the larger realm that concerns political entities and social organizations. The earliest signs of these expansions of the concept refer to the subject of the ruling dynasties. A Christian from Damascus who witnessed the Egyptian invasion of Syria indicated in his chronicle that Syrian towns under Muhammad ʿAli enjoyed complete freedom (*bikul ḥurriyyatihim*), implying that Muhammad ʿAli's dynasty had the freedom to rule without intervention from the Ottoman sultan.[122] Similar connotations were articulated in correspondence between Muhammad ʿAli and Ibrahim Pasha in 1832, in which the former stated that his family's ambition to be free and independent in ruling Egypt was becoming real.[123] In the political reality of Egypt and Syria during the first half of the nineteenth century – in which most of the territories were ruled by autonomous governors, mountain and bedouin chieftains, and dynasties[124] – freedom, therefore, referred to the freedom of local rulers to govern and to gain nominal independence from the power of the central authorities in Istanbul.[125] Against the background of central authority

[122] Al-Dimashqi, *Taʾrīkh Ḥawādith al-Shām wa-Lubnān*, 53.
[123] Rustum, *al-Maḥfūẓāt al-Malakiyya al-Miṣriyya*, 2:86.
[124] For further details about the political situation in Greater Syria during these years, see Maoz, *Ottoman Reform in Syria and Palestine, 1840–1861: The Impact of the Tanzimat on Politics and Society*, 5.
[125] For similar implications derived from the use of *ḥurriyya* in the 1830s, see al-Dimashqi, *Taʾrīkh Ḥawādith al-Shām wa-Lubnān*, 92.

intervention, this implied meaning of freedom was not confined to relations with the Ottomans but was also used in relation to the authority of the local rulers themselves. A description of the visit of the ruler of Mount Lebanon to Acre, which had been seized by Muhammad ʿAli, used the phrase "in complete freedom," denoting freedom of the ruler of Mount Lebanon to move without the interference of the Egyptian authorities.[126]

While *ḥurriyya* was frequently used in reference to internal state affairs, the concept of the freedom of states from foreign rule rapidly acquired new words. The Egyptian French Coptic lexicographer Ellious Bocthor used the same ambiguous Arabic phrase – *bilād ḥurriyya* (free areas or country) – as a translation of the French *indépendant*.[127] This ambiguity was clarified with the semantic inflation of *ḥurriyya* in the 1830s: With the rise of new notions of collective political identification, including nationalism, and with the proliferation of international nation-state norms requiring that formally recognized states define their borders, the word *istiqlāl* became dominant for denoting state sovereignty. The Treaty of Paris (signed on March 30, 1856), which formally ended the Crimean War (1853–1856), stressed the independence of the Ottoman Empire. The word used in Arabic translations of the treaty was *istiqlāl al-salṭana* (the independence of the sultanate) rather than *ḥurriyya*. Correspondingly, the autonomous status of Wallachia and Moldavia (Article 23) and Serbia (Article 28) was indicated by the same word (*idāra ahliyya mustaqilla*, *istiqlāl*). *Ḥurriyya* was used in the same document in relation to internal affairs such as the constitutional rights of the inhabitants of these entities, which were summed up by "freedom of religion, freedom of legislation, economic freedom,[128] and freedom of movement in rivers and seas."[129] This distinction between the concept of state independence (*istiqlāl*) and the republican or constitutional

[126] For further examples of the use of the word in similar contexts, see ibid., 98; Rustum, *al-Maḥfūẓāt al-Malakiyya al-Miṣriyya*, 2:70.

[127] Similar use was made in the 1830s by al-Tahtawi. In his account of the French imperial power after the fall of Napoleon, he elaborated that under the French there were only small territories that demanded freedom (*turīd al-ḥurriyya*) in reference to political independence. See Bocthor, "Libre," 14; al-Tahtawi, *Takhlīṣ al-Ibrīz fī Talkhīṣ Bārīz aw al-Dīwān al-Nafīs bi-Īwān Bārīs*, 176.

[128] It is worth adding that al-Shidyaq translated "economic freedom" as *ḥurriyyat al-matjar* in earlier accounts. See al-Shidyaq, *al-Wāsiṭa ila Maʿrifat Aḥwāl Mālṭa wa-Kashf al-Mukhabbāʾ ʿan Funūn Ūrūbā*, 142.

[129] In Arabic, "*al-ḥurriyya fī al-tadayyun, wal-aḥkam al-sharʿiyya, wal-matjar wa-safar al-baḥr wal-anhār*." For additional use of *ḥurriyya* and *istiqlāl* with

concepts (*ḥurriyya*) was not always clear. Muhammad Mustafa Bashjawish, who translated Voltaire into Arabic, used both words to indicate independence. For example, he uses the word *ḥurriyya* to refer to the threat of losing political independence when he describes the danger of a Danish invasion of Danzig, the autonomous and "free" city-state (*madīna ḥurra*).[130] Similarly, in one of the earliest translations from the nineteenth century, the word *istiqlāl* in the phrase *ḥurriyya wa-istiqlāl* is used to indicate a meaning synonymous with *ḥurriyya*, as contrasted with living under an autocratic regime.[131]

The extension of the meaning of freedom to denote the defined political position of entities had deeply influenced the common terminology used for political liberation. By the 1830s the dominant words used to signify military seizure and occupation were *fatḥ*, *istīlā'*, *akhdh*, and *iḥtilāl*. While the last three words meant simply capturing and occupying, with no special reference to ideological content, the frequent use of *fatḥ* had an embedded theological implication. The word was frequently employed in the Qur'an to indicate the victory of the true faith.[132] During the Middle Ages this word was commonly used to denote occupation derived from the religious doctrine of *jihād* (holy war) as in *iftitāḥ dār al-ḥarb*,[133] or *fataḥa al-Muslimūn dār al-kufr* (conquering the abode of war or infidelity).[134] This theological

distinctive meanings, see al-Shidyaq, *Kanz al-Raghā'ib fī Muntakhabāt al-Jawā'ib*, 1877, 5:12–14; Robertson, *Kitāb Itḥāf Mulūk al-Zamān bi-Tārīkh al-Imbirāṭūr Sharlakān Masbūqan bi-Muqaddimatihi al-Musammā Itḥāf al-Mulūk al-Alibbā' bi-Taqaddum al-Jam'iyyāt fī Ūrūbā Mundhu Inqirāḍ al-Dawla al-Rūmāniyya*, 1:65; *Birjīs Barīs*, October 26, 1859.

130 Voltaire, *Maṭāli' Shumūs al-Siyar fī Waqā'i' Karlūs al-Thānī 'Ashar*, 67.

131 For a comparison between the original French edition and the Arabic translation see: Laertius, *Mukhtaṣar Tarjamāt Mashāhīr Qudamā' al-Falāsifa*, 55; Laertius, *Les Vies Des plus Illustres Philosophes de L'antiquité*, 79–80. For an additional early example, see *Kitāb al-Kanz al-Mukhtār fī Kashf al-Arāḍī wal-Biḥār*, 106.

132 For example, "If you [disbelievers] seek the victory – the defeat has come to you [*fatḥ*]. And if you desist [from hostilities], it is best for you; but if you return [to war], We will return, and never will be availed by your [large] company at all, even if it should increase; and [that is] because Allah is with the believers." Qur'an, al-'Anfāl 8:19.

133 See this thirteenth-century dictionary: Muhammad Ibn Mukarram Ibn Manzur, "F.t.ḥ," *Lisān al-'Arab* (Beirut: Dār al-Ṣādir, 2004), 119–121.

134 For selected examples, see: Muhammad Murtada al-Husayni al-Zubaydi, "F.t.ḥ," *Tāj al-'Arūs min Jawāhir al-Qāmūs* (Kuwait: Maṭba'at Ḥukūmat al-Kūwayt, 1994), 5–10.

conception of *fatḥ* embeds the notion of an enlightened conquest stemming from the idea of spreading the true faith of Islam.

All these words, however, including *fatḥ*, were used during the Egyptian invasion of Greater Syria to refer to capturing different cities: In a speech on the eve of the invasion of Acre, Ibrahim Pasha urged his soldiers to occupy Acre (*fatḥ*) as they had occupied cities in their previous battles in Greece.[135] In other correspondence with the governor of Tripoli, Ibrahim used the phrase "*akhdh ʿAkkā ʿunwatan*" (capturing Acre by force),[136] and in correspondence between Ibrahim Pasha and Druze religious leaders, he used the synonymous phrase "*akhdh ʿAkkā wal-istīlāʾ ʿalayhā ʿunwa bil-saiyff*" (taking Acre and capturing it by force).[137] These articulations sustained the traditional perceptions of occupation and maintained its pre-nineteenth-century terminology.

The penetration of freedom into the realm of collective political liberation was indicated by the word *taḥrīr*. By the beginning of the nineteenth century, the common use of *taḥrīr* had nonpolitical implications, such as the process of editing (in literature), liberating from slavery, or devotion to God.[138] The word underwent a significant shift with the domination of nation-state norms, and conjointly with the emergence of "independence," *taḥarur* was used in translated literature to indicate political liberation.[139]

The use of freedom in collective contexts was not limited to dynasties and foreign seizure of political entities. The word *ḥurryya* was used equivalently to indicate independence of ecclesiastical institutions within the Ottoman millet system. In the context of Mount Lebanon,

[135] Rustum, *al-Uṣūl al-ʿArabiyya li-Tārīkh Sūriyya fī ʿAhd Muḥammad ʿAli Bāshā*, 1987, 1:113–114.
[136] Ibid., 1:138.
[137] Asad Rustum, *al-Uṣūl al-ʿArabiyya li-Tārīkh Sūriyya fī ʿAhd Muḥammad ʿAli Bāshā*, vol. 2 (Beirut: Manshurāt al-Maktaba al-Bulisiyya, 1987), 5–9; Rustum, *al-Maḥfūẓāt al-Malakiyya al-Miṣriyya*, 2:70.
[138] For selected examples of *taḥrīr*, see two sources: the first was composed in the 1830s and the second in the eighteenth century. Rustum, *al-Maḥfūẓāt al-Malakiyya al-Miṣriyya*, 2:53; al-Zubaydi, "H.r.r," 587–593.
[139] See, for instance, in the phrase "*yataḥararūn min ḥukm al-inqlātirra*" (American liberation from the English seizure). For selected examples, see use of *taḥarur/taḥrīr/aḥrār*, and see translated sources and speech in: Kalivaris, *Kitāb Sirat al-Muʿaẓam al-Murafaʿ al-Kabīr Nabulyūn al-Awwal Imbaratūr al-Farānsawiyya*, 76; *Birjīs Barīs*, June 24, 1859, 48; *Birjīs Barīs*, August 18, 1859, 2.

the word indicated the autonomous state of the Christian clergy; in a letter from the Maronite community to the sultan, the words "*bikāmil al-ḥurriyya*" and "*aḥrār*" (in complete freedom, free) were employed in a request to preserve the freedom of the Maronite clergy to maintain their religious authority freely in every aspect related to "their religion, their ecclesiastical positions, and their traditions." In other contemporary and similar requests that proliferated after the inauguration of the reforms, the authors used the phrase "free patriarch" (*baṭriyarkan ḥurran, iklīriyūs ḥurr*) to indicate the formal recognition of the Eastern Catholic churches as a separate millet, and the right to maintain its internal affairs.[140]

## Language of Nationalism, Transitions in Group Appellations, and Concepts of Belonging

The most comprehensive shift in the collective political meanings of *ḥurriyya*, and the latest chronologically, took place in relation to freedom of groups. The overlap of the transition of the language of identity, which had been deeply influenced by the rise of nationalism, with shifts in perceptions of the borders of civilizations, peaked to a large extent with the expansion of freedom into the collective domain. Concepts of civilization and concepts of identity had been deeply altered; until the beginning of the nineteenth century, Arabic usually designated Europeans by the single word *Ifranj*. This word, which reached the Muslims via the Byzantines during the ninth century, at that time denoted the inhabitants of Charlemagne's empire. During the Middle Ages the semantics of the word extended to include European ethnicities in general.[141] In addition to its cultural and geographical implications, the word was used to distinguish between religious categories in Christianity, as in *ruhbān al-Ifranj* (Latin monks), *ruhbān al-Rūm* (Greek

[140] See the October 1840 letter from the Maronite clergy and community to Sultan ʿAbd al-Majid. Additionally, see the account of the civil separation between the Armenian Catholic and the Greek Catholic churches (dated 1846): Rustum, *al-Uṣūl al-ʿArabiyya li-Tārīkh Sūriyya fī ʿAhd Muhammad ʿAli Bāshā*, 5:208–211; Mazlum, *Nabdha Tārīkhiyya: fīmā Jara li-Ṭāʾifat al-Rūm al-Kāthūlīk Mundhu Sant 1837 Famā Baʿdahā*, 279–287.

[141] For the evolvement of the word during the Middle Ages, see: Bernard Lewis, "Ifrandj," *The Encyclopedia of Islam* (Leiden: E. J. Brill, 1986), 1044–1046; Lewis, "The Muslim Discovery of Europe," 410–412.

Orthodox monks), and *ruhbān al-Arman* (Armenian monks).[142] At the end of the eighteenth century, *Ifranj* was not normally applied to ethnicities such as Russians, Slavs, and Greeks, and it loosely comprised all communities living in western Europe.[143]

Beyond all these implications, *Ifranj* was intensively laden with Islamic theological perceptions: from the view of an eighteenth-century Muslim, Europe – the "land of *Ifranj*" – was synonymous with Christendom, which is part of the "abode of war" (*dār al-ḥarb*). In contrast to the "abode of Islam" (*dār al-Islām*), where true faith was related to practices, the "abode of war" was conceived of as an unattractive, remote place that was drowning in infidelity. On the one hand, this perspective melted the differentiation between ethnicities and made it less relevant to the Muslim observer, and on the other, this outlook reflected the self-perception of a Muslim community that conceived itself as a unified body of believers in contrast to unbelievers. This theological perception, however, formulated the Muslim concept of political identity (political loyalty) and made distinctions between *Ifranj* less interesting. This conclusion manifested in the state of the language: By the beginning of the nineteenth century, Arabic scarcely had words that characterized specific and distinguishable single European nations.[144]

The Islamic theological outlook regarding communities was extremely challenged by the beginning of the nineteenth century, which marked, at least in Europe, a seedtime for nationalism. The language of nationalism that emerged after the French Revolution left a deep impact on political language in the Middle East through various channels, including direct military invasion and local transformations. By the end of the nineteenth century the use of the medieval and general term *Ifranj* decreased gradually in favor of nationally oriented terminology.

[142] See a formal request to repair the church of al-Ṭūrr Mountain in Palestine. The letter is dated October 1834: Rustum, *al-Uṣūl al-ʿArabiyya li-Tārīkh Sūriyya fī ʿAhd Muḥammad ʿAli Bāshā*, 1987, 2:141–145.

[143] Thus, for instance, it was acceptable to say "European Jewish" (*Ifranjī Yahūdī*). See the documented investigation of the Damascus blood libel. The document is dated March 1840: Rustum, *al-Uṣūl al-ʿArabiyya li-Tārīkh Sūriyya fī ʿAhd Muhammad ʿAli Bāshā*, 5:39.

[144] Ayalon, *Language and Change in the Arab Middle East: The Evolution of Modern Political Discourse*, 16–17.

The exposure to new conceptions of nationalism was initially manifested in the fluctuation of words that were chosen to capture the phenomenon; afterward a relative stability in terminology for modern nations set in. The beginning of the nineteenth century was characterized by a lack of consistency in using specific labels for distinctive features of groups, and the contemporary chronicles presented less sophisticated language for characterizing national traits. Muslim and Christian chroniclers referred to Europeans by using words that emphasized the theological, prenational outlook: *al-Ifranj*, *al-kuffār* (unbelievers), and *jumū' al-shirk*, *al-mushrikīn* (polytheists).[145] Discussing intra-European affairs had often imposed terminology that addressed single nations as *al-Frinsīs*, *al-Fransāwiyya*, *al-Inklīz* (French and English) and *al-Maskūb* (Russians)[146] and referred frequently to their geographical entities by using national appellations such as *Iṭālya* (Italy), *Isbānya* (Spain), *bilād al-Nimsā* (Austria), *bilād al-Inklīz* or *Injlīz* (England).[147]

The translation of works in the field of geography in general, and especially al-Tahtawi's translation of the monumental work of Conrad Malte-Brun (d. 1826), *Précis de la géographie universelle*, into Arabic at the end of the 1830s and during the 1840s, marked a milestone in its contribution to the stabilization of morphological national appellations.[148] In his introduction al-Tahtawi stresses the importance of this work, which contains accounts of the history of nations around

[145] It is worth mentioning that the Christian chronicler Niqula al-Turk infrequently depicted the French as infidels. For selected examples of temporal use of these words, see: Niqula al-Turk, *Dhikr Tamalluk Jumhūr al-Faransāwiyya al-Aqṭār al-Miṣriyya wal-Bilād al-Shāmiyya, aw, al-Ḥamla al-Faransiyya 'ala Miṣr wal-Shām*, 28; Muhammad Kafafi, "al-Ḥamla al-Faransiyya 'ala Miṣr fī Riwayat Aḥad al-Mu'aṣirīn," 377.

[146] Al-Khashab, *al-Tārīkh al-Musalsal fī Ḥawādith al-Zamān wa-Waqāyi' al-Dīwān, 1800–1801*, 3, 19; al-Munayyir, *al-Durr al-Marṣūf fī Tārīkh al-Shūf*, 13; al-Turk, *Dhikr Tamalluk Jumhūr al-Faransāwiyya al-Aqṭār al-Miṣriyya wal-Bilād al-Shāmiyya, aw, al-Ḥamla al-Faransiyya 'ala Miṣr wal-Shām*, 42; al-Jabarti, *'Ajā'ib al-Āthār fī al-Tarājim wal-Akhbār*, 1998, 3:14–15, 310.

[147] Ami Ayalon has extensively discussed the evolvement of Arabic words that designate communities and groups during the nineteenth century. See Ayalon, *Language and Change in the Arab Middle East: The Evolution of Modern Political Discourse*, 16–28.

[148] For details about al-Tahtawi's strategy of translation, see Sawaie, "Rifa'a Rafi' al-Tahtawi and His Contribution to the Lexical Development of Modern Literary Arabic," 395–410.

the globe. Through recounting the history of geography in the first volume, medieval words such as *bilād al-Ifranj* were redefined and rediscovered historically, ethnically, and geographically. During the first half of the nineteenth century, the general designation *bilād al-Ifranj* or *al-bilād al-Ifranjiyya* (European countries) was gradually replaced by *Ūrbā* or *Ūrūbā* (Europe) or *bilād al-Gharb* (Western countries),[149] usage of which eventually stabilized enough to become the conventional words for designating Europe in modern Arabic.[150]

The transition from the pre-nineteenth-century language to the modern was reflected in the fluctuation of country names. Some of the names that had been coined during the end of the1820s and the beginning of the 1830s fell out of use by the end of the nineteenth century. Initial attempts at word coinage such as, for example, *Ibrīzīla* (Brazil); *Asqīmū* (Eskimo); *Sakandināwa* (Scandinavia); *Shīlī* (Chile); *Gurwāland, Gurwānland, Gurnuladyā* (Greenland); *Asūj* (Sweden); *Inqlātīrrā* (England); *Nurmanda* (Normandy); *Biljum, Bilj* (Belgium); *Brutūkāl, Burtūqalū* (Portugal); and *Swīsa* (Switzerland) were replaced after a few decades.[151] Most of these renditions were presented as

149 Al-Munayyir, *al-Durr al-Marṣūf fī Tārīkh al-Shūf*, 113; al-Turk, *Dhikr Tamalluk Jumhūr al-Faransāwiyya al-Aqṭār al-Miṣriyya wal-Bilād al-Shāmiyya, aw, al-Ḥamla al-Faransiyya ʿala Miṣr wal-Shām*, 25; al-Shihabi, *Qiṣat Aḥmad Bāsha al-Jazzār Bayna Miṣr wal-Shām wa-Ḥawādithuhu Maʿ Nābulyūn Būnābart*, 141; al-Sharqawi, *Tuḥfat al-Nāẓirīn fī-man Waliya Miṣr min al-Mulūk wal-Salāṭīn*, 123.

150 Conrad Malte-Brun, *al-Jughrāfiyya al-ʿUmūmiyya*, trans. Rifaʿa Rafiʿ al-Tahtawi, vol. 1 (Bulaq, 1838), 22; Malte-Brun, *al-Jughrāfiyya al-ʿUmūmiyya*, n.d., 3:10. In addition see the collection of summaries in al-Tahtawi's *Geography*: Al-Tahtawi, *al-Taʿrībāt al-Shāfiya li-Murīd al-Jughrāfiyya*, 8–28, 35–136; see also one of the early translations of the same subject, which was published in Malta: *Kitāb al-Kanz al-Mukhtār fī Kashf al-Arāḍī wal-Biḥār*, 10–14.

151 This transition in the meaning of words was comprehensive, and it was not confined to the field of geography. Similar transformations occurred in the field of culture with the use of newly coined words such as: *biyān* (piano); *bāl* (ballet); *karnawāl* (carnival); *tiyātr* (theater); *sbaktākil* (spectacle); *qīṭār* (guitar); *kūmīk* (comedy); *waraqāt al-yawmiyya, awrāq al-waqāʾiʿ, al-waqāʾiʿ al-yawmiyya, jurnālāt, kāziṭāt* (newspaper, journal, gazette); and *akadimiya, akadama,* or *aqadama* (academia), which were replaced later by others. See al-Tahtawi, *Takhlīṣ al-Ibrīz fī Talkhīṣ Bārīz aw al-Dīwān al-Nafīs bi-Īwān Bārīs*, 33, 74, 79, 87–91, 97, 117, 128–129; Depping, *Kitāb Qalāʾid al-Mafākhir fī Gharīb ʿAwāʾid al-Awāʾil wal-Awākhir*, 49, 72, 74, app. 2, 4–5, 51, 57, 62, 95; al-Tahtawi and al-Zarabi, *Bidāyat al-Qudamāʾ wa-Hidāyat al-Ḥukamāʾ*, 155; Kalivaris, *Kitāb Sirat al-Muʿaẓam al-Murafaʿ al-Kabīr Nabulyūn al-Awwal Imbaratūr al-Farānsawiyya*, 3–4.

entries dedicated to each country in a special section that address the "foreign words" (*kalimāt gharība*) that al-Tahtawi appended to his translation into Arabic of Georges-Bernard Depping's *Aperçu historique sur les moeurs et coutumes des nations*.[152]

Translating the countries' national appellations had multiple impacts: the transmission of European national perceptions regarding collective identity that incorporated historical narratives of the past, and the adaptation of Arabic to the new terminology and conceptions. During the 1830s nationalism become a prominent factor in conceptualizing history in Arabic. The most frequent use of terminology related to nationalism during this decade is displayed in books translated from French. These books not only transmitted national imaginative perceptions of history but also applied their national discourse to the history of the Arab Muslim region. The gradual transformation of *bilād al-Ifranj* to national designations conjoined with an alteration in the concept of *bilād al-Islām*, which was frequently replaced by the use of particular civil or ethnic designations. The Islamic or Ottoman Empire was frequently designated as Turkish, and the ethnicities were more commonly referred to as Arab, Hindu, and correspondingly *bilād al-ʿArab*, *bilād al-Afghanistān*, *bilād al-Atrāk*.[153] Among the Arabic-speaking provinces, the area of the Levant (*bilād al-Shām*), which was religiously less homogenized, was heavily influenced by identity transitions. It was only from 1831 that *bilād al-Shām* or *bar al-Shām* was unified for the first time as one central administrative unit under Egyptian rule. During the 1830s a variety of names were employed to designate this region: *bar al-Shām*, *bilād al-ʿArab*, *ʿArab*

[152] Al-Tahtawi finished his Depping translation in November 1829 and published it in 1833. Al-Tahtawi uses the phrase "foreign words" in many of his translated works, which usually had detailed glossaries. Some of the medieval versions of country names were changed in favor of new variants that were influenced by their common name in European languages. That is, for instance, how the medieval Arabic *Siqilya* become *Sisiliya* (Sicily) and *Iqrtish* become *Krid* and later *Krit* (Crete). See also the biography of Napoleon I, which contains a glossary of "foreign words" (*kitāba gharība*): Depping, *Kitāb Qalāʾid al-Mafākhir fī Gharīb ʿAwāʾid al-Awāʾil wal-Awākhir*, 111–112, app. 1–105; al-Tahtawi and al-Zarabi, *Bidāyat al-Qudamāʾ wa-Hidāyat al-Ḥukamāʾ*; al-Shayyal, *Tārīkh al-Tarjama wal-Ḥaraka al-Thaqāfiyya fī ʿAṣr Muḥammad ʿAli*, 213; Kalivaris, *Kitāb Sirat al-Muʿaẓam al-Murafaʿ al-Kabīr Nabulyūn al-Awwal Imbaratūr al-Faransawiyya*, 5, 533–563.

[153] For selected examples, see Depping, *Kitāb Qalāʾid al-Mafākhir fī Gharīb ʿAwāʾid al-Awāʾil wal-Awākhir*, 95, 98, 100–101.

*istān*,[154] *bilād Sūriyya*,[155] *'Arabistān*,[156] and *'Arab-bustān*.[157] In 1865, with the expansion of Damascus's jurisdiction, the area was designated for the first time as the "vilayet of Syria," and the transition from the medieval and geographical concept of *bilād al-Shām* to the modern concept of Syria stabilized – largely owing to its theorization by Syrian Lebanese patriots who attributed to "Syria" a cultural unification and shared history.[158]

Another aspect of interaction between transitions of provinces names and construction of political identity in the region was the growing frequency in the use of territory names to label communal belonging: Beginning in the second half of the nineteenth century, texts increasingly used labels such as "Syrian" and "Egyptian" to indicate identity and belonging. This transformation had a reciprocal impact: The growing intralanguage of patriotism (*waṭaniyya*) formulated a new vocabulary regarding the perception of the outside imagined borders of civilization, especially the "West."

The rise of nationalism had a great impact on the meaning of Arabic words used to designate communities and groups and on terms used to express collective belonging: *milla*, *umma*, *ṭā'ifa*, *qabīla*, *jins*, *sha'b*, *jumhūr*, *qawm*, and *waṭan*. The advent of the language of nationalism in Arabic during the first half of the nineteenth century produced frequent fluctuations in the morphology of these words, extending the semantic field of some and dismissing the use of others. In the first

154 Rustum, *al-Uṣūl al-'Arabiyya li-Tārīkh Sūriyya fī 'Ahd Muḥammad 'Ali Bāshā*, 1987, 1:99–102, 108; Rustum, *al-Uṣūl al-'Arabiyya li-Tārīkh Sūriyya fī 'Ahd Muḥammad 'Ali Bāshā*, 1987, 2:6.

155 Ibid., 2:98–99.

156 See the title in the Arabic manuscript (number 369) in the Cambridge University Library. This manuscript is an 1849 abbreviation, made by Antun Ibn Jabur Khayat, of Haydar al-Shihabi's history. Haydar al-Shihabi, "Kitāb Nuzhat al-Zamān fī Ḥawādith 'Arabistān" (Cambridge: 1849).

157 Al-Dimashqi, *Ta'rīkh Ḥawādith al-Shām wa-Lubnān*, 53.

158 For further details about the Christian roots of the modern concept of Syria, see Fruma Zachs, "Toward a Proto-Nationalist Concept of Syria? Revisiting the American Presbyterian Missionaries in the Nineteenth-Century Levant," *Die Welt Des Islams* 41, no. 2 (2001): 145–173. For the impact of political and institutional developments, see: Moshe Maoz, "Attempts at Creating a Political Community in Modern Syria," *Middle East Journal* 26, no. 4 (1972): 391–392; Thomas Philipp, "Identities and Loyalties in Bilad al-Sham at the Beginning of the Early Modem Period," in *From The Syrian Land to the States of Syria and Lebanon*, ed. Thomas Philipp and Christoph Schumann (Würzburg: Ergon in Kommission, 2004), 17–25.

half of the nineteenth century, the use of these inherited words did not always capture the content of the original meaning (this frequently occurred in translated texts), and thus it failed to convey the national content.

The word *umma* had been used extensively since the emergence of Islam. The word, which basically implies the unification of a group of people, was transformed in the Qur'an in conjunction with the conceptual evolution of the religious community established by the Prophet Muhammad.[159] The medieval use of the word embeds many notions that indicate groups that had racial,[160] ethnic, religious, generational, or civil components.[161] By the eighteenth century the word was in frequent use and designated a pious community, as in *al-umma al-Islāmiyya* and *al-umma al-Naṣrāniyya* (Islamic community and Christian community), and the word was already being translated to Western languages as synonymous with nation, people, sects, or religions.[162]

Infrequent use of the word is displayed in the first French Proclamation (1798) that addressed *al-umma al-Miṣriyya*, the Egyptian nation. The transition in the use of the word from its medieval associations with a religious community to indicating a political community was made by Arabic-speaking scholars primarily during the 1830s and afterward. The translators of French books, mainly al-Tahtawi and

159 For more details on the use of *umma* in the Qur'an, see Frederick Mathewson Denny, "Umma," *The Encyclopedia of Islam* (Leiden: E. J. Brill, 2000), 859–863.

160 *Umma* does not necessarily indicate a group consisting of human beings, as in the Qur'anic verse: "And there is no creature on [or within] the earth or bird that flies with its wings except [that they are] communities [*umam*] like you." Qur'an, al-An'ām, 6:38.

161 The civil components of *umma* were expressed in medieval philosophy. Al-Farabi assumed that human societies consist of nations (*ummam*), and nations comprise cities that maintain civil communities (*ijtimā'āt madaniyya*). See al-Farabi, *Kitāb al-Siyāsa al-Madaniyya*, 69–70.

162 *Umam* was translated at the end of the eighteenth century into Latin as "*coetus*" (group, crowd) or "*populus*" (people). The Spanish *nacion* was translated at the end of the eighteenth century as *ṭā'ifa*, *umma*, *milla*, and *qabīla*. For further renditions during the eighteenth century and before 1820, see Johann Jahn, "Umam," *Lexicon Arabico-Latinum* (Vindobonae: Apud C. F. Wappler et Beck, 1802), 16; Francisco Cañes, "Nacion," *Diccionario Español-Latino-Arabigo* (Madrid: Impr. de A. Sancha, 1787), 489; John Richardson, "Umam," *A Dictionary, Persian, Arabic, and English: with a Dissertation on the Languages, Literature, and Manners of Eastern Nations* (London: William Bulmer, 1806), 111.

his disciples, employed the word to indicate groups that maintained an imagined common history with a political essence, as in *al-umma al-Yūnāniyya* (the Greek nation) and *al-umma al-Fransāwiyya*.[163] This usage gradually became more frequent in the second half of the nineteenth century.

Among the most common terms employed at the turn of the century for designating a nation were the words *milla* and *ṭā'ifa*. The first word was identified with religious social organizations, and it implied a community of believers such as a Christian community (*al-milla al-Naṣrāniyya, al-milla al-'Īsawiyya*), regardless of ethnic or linguistic differences existing within that community. In the Ottoman Empire the word was used to identify religious communities that maintained semiautonomous units that were dominated by the normative aspect of Sunni Islam, which was often designated as *al-milla* (the community). Different religious communities within the same religion were also called *milla* – for example, the Latin Christian community (*Naṣāra al-milla al-Lāṭiniyya*).[164] However, at the beginning of the nineteenth century the word was also used in reference to nonreligious nations, as in *al-milla al-Fransāwiyya* (the French nation). At the same time, *ṭā'ifa*, which often indicated a group of people that constituted one part of a group, was used in similar combinations, such as *ṭawā'if al-Ifranj* (European communities).[165] The word indicated any kind of group, including those divided according to religion or ancestry. That, for instance, is how Nasif al-Yaziji, a prominent language scholar from Lebanon, used this word: to indicate sectarian groups of people (*ṭawā'if... al-Naṣāra wal-Durūz* – Druze and Christian sects) and to mean a group that maintains family ties (*al-ṭā'ifa al-shihābiyya* – the dynasty of the house of Shihab). In much the same way, al-Tahtawi used

163 Depping, *Kitāb Qalā'id al-Mafākhir fī Gharīb 'Awā'id al-Awā'il wal-Awākhir*, app. 100; al-Tahtawi, *Takhlīṣ al-Ibrīz fī Talkhīṣ Bārīz aw al-Dīwān al-Nafīs bi-Īwān Bārīs*, 12.

164 Voltaire, *Rawḍ al-Azhar fī Tārīkh Buṭrus al-Akbar*, 61.

165 See three selected sources that employ *ṭawā'if al-Ifranj*. The first is Haydar al-Shihabi; the second is correspondence in Acre under Egyptian rule, dated 1833; and the third is a published description of a journey written by Salim Bustrus who visited a few cities in Italy and France in 1855: Al-Shihabi, *Qiṣat Aḥmad Bāsha al-Jazzār Bayna Miṣr wal-Shām wa-Ḥawādithuhu Ma' Nābulyūn Būnābart*, 144–145; Rustum, *al-Uṣūl al-'Arabiyya li-Tārīkh Sūriyya fī 'Ahd Muḥammad 'Ali Bāshā*, 1987, 2:77–78; Bustrus, *al-Nuzha al-Shahiyya fī al-Riḥla al-Salīmiyya, 1855*, 70.

the word to indicate ethnic groups such as Kurds and Turkmen.[166] This word was often used during the first half of the nineteenth century as equivalent to *milla*,[167] and it was extensively politicized around the time of the establishment of the Mutasarrifate in 1860 and came to indicate a sectarian community.[168]

In many cases the word *umma* was replaced or used as synonymous with *qawm*.[169] This last word implied, prior to the nineteenth century, a "group of people" (often men, without the women), and it was commonly used to denote a faction or clan.[170] Despite the word's emphasis on kinship relations, it was employed during the first half of the nineteenth century to denote religious nations, as in *qawm ʿĪsa* (people of Jesus). In addition it was used to indicate a civil nation – for example, *qawm al-Amīrkā* (the American nation), and in that last sense it often replaced *jumhūr*.[171] *Qawm* was used infrequently in the mid-1800s to

166 Malte-Brun, *al-Jughrāfiyya al-ʿUmūmiyya*, n.d., 3:66; al-Yaziji, *Risāla Tārīkhiya fī Aḥwāl Jabal Lubnān fī ʿAhdihi al-Iqṭāʿī*, 45. 54.

167 ʿAqiqi, *Thawra wa-Fitna fī Lubnān: Ṣafḥa Majhūla min Tārīkh al-Jabal min 1841 ila 1873*, 199–200.

168 For extensive discussion of *milla* and *ṭaiʾifa*, see Ayalon, *Language and Change in the Arab Middle East: The Evolution of Modern Political Discourse*, 19–22.

169 As in "*al-umma (min al-rajul qawmuhu)*" (when *umma* refers to a man, it indicates his *qawm*). See the seventeenth- and the eighteenth-century lexicons. Additionally, nation was rendered in Arabic as *umma* or *qawm* (see Alexandre Handjéri): Muhammad Murtada al-Husayni al-Zubaydi, "U.m.a," *Tāj al-ʿArūs min Jawāhir al-Qāmūs* (Kuwait: Maṭbaʿat Ḥukūmat al-Kūwayt, 2000), 230; Abi al-Baqaʾ Ayyub ibn Musa Kaffawi, "Umma," *al-Kulliyāt: Muʿjam fī al-Muṣṭalaḥāt wal-Furūq al-Lughawiya* (Beirut: Mu'assasat al-Risāla, 1998), 176; Alexandre Handjéri, "Nation," *Dictionnaire Français-Arabe-Persan et Turc: Enrichi D'examples En Langue Turque Avec Des Variantes, et de Beaucoup de Mots D'arts et Des Sciences* (Moscow: Impr. de l'Université impériale, 1841 1840), 567.

170 *Qawm*, prior to the nineteenth century, was rendered in Latin as *populus* (people, members of the society), *viri* (men). Muhammad Murtada al-Husayni al-Zubaydi, "Q.w.m," *Tāj al-ʿArūs min Jawāhir al-Qāmūs* (Kuwait: Maṭbaʿat Ḥukūmat al-Kūwayt, 2000), 305–321; Abi al-Baqaʾ Ayyub ibn Musa Kaffawi, "Qawm," *al-Kulliyāt: Muʿjam fī al-Muṣṭalaḥāt wal-Furūq al-Lughawiyya* (Beirut: Muʾassasat al-Risāla, 1998), 728; ʿAbd al-Nabi bin ʿAbd al-Rasul Ahmadnakri, "Qawm," *Jāmiʿ al-ʿUlūm fī Iṣṭilāḥāt al-Funūn al-Mulaqqab bi-Dustūr al-ʿUlamāʾ* (Beirut: Muʾassasat al-Aʿlamī lil-Maṭbūʿāt, 1975), 98; Jacobus Golius, "Qawm," *Lexicon Arabico-Latinum* (Lugduni Batavorum: typis Bonaventurae and Abrahami, Elseviriorum, prostant Amstelodami apud Johannem Ravesteynivm, 1653), 1982.

171 As, for instance, in the two phrases from *The Biography of Napoleon* in Arabic, "*qawm al-firinsīs aḥibāʾ al-aqwām kuluhum*" and "*jumhūr al-firinsīs*

denote the ethnic characteristics of modern nations (*aqwām*):[172] In a translated speech from 1867, the ruler of Serbia began his speech with "*ya qawmī*" (my people).[173] In addition to religious and ethnic characteristics, the word was employed to indicate clan relations in single-religion or sectarian groups.[174] The rendering of "nation" as *qawm* was still quite infrequent, but unlike *umma*, only in the twentieth century did it become the conventional Arabic word for cultural-ethnic nationalism.

Another common word used to designate groups of people was *sha'b*. Prior to the nineteenth century it meant a group having a common ancestry. During the Middle Ages the most frequently used terms for designating groups having common kinship were *sha'b*, *qabīla*, *'amāra*, *baṭn*, *fakhdh*, *'ashīra*, and *ḥayy*. One of the eighteenth-century sources defines the word as "large *qabīla* [agnatic group]."[175] At the beginning of the 1800s, the word denoted, in both English and Latin, people or nation.[176] Niqula al-Turk wrote, in describing the revolutionary turmoil in France, that the "people [*sha'b*] of this kingdom

*aḥbāb al-jamāhīr kuluhum*" (the French nation loved by all nations): Kalivaris, *Kitāb Sirat al-Mu'aẓam al-Murafa' al-Kabīr Nabulyūn al-Awwal Imbaratūr al-Farānsawiyya*, 7, 32, 76; Thomas Xavier Bianchi and Jean Daniel Kieffer, "Qawm," *Dictionnaire Turc-Français: À L'usage Des Agents Diplomatiques et Consulaires, Des Commerçants, Des Navigateurs, et Autres Voyageurs Dans Le Levant* (Paris: Impr. royale, 1837), 529.

172 See the lexicons published during the first three decades of the nineteenth century. All of them emphasize the equivalence between *qawm* and nation: John Richardson, "Qawm," *A Dictionary, Persian, Arabic, and English: with a Dissertation on the Languages, Literature, and Manners of Eastern Nations* (London: William Bulmer, 1806), 742; David Hopkins, "Qawm," *A Vocabulary, Persian, Arabic, and English; Abridged from the Quarto Edition of Richardson's Dictionary* (London: Printed for F. and C. Rivingson, 1810), 444; Ellious Bocthor, "Peuple," *Dictionnaire Français-Arabe* (Paris: Chez Firmin Didot Freres, 1829), 157.

173 Al-Shidyaq, *Kanz al-Raghā'ib fī Muntakhabāt al-Jawā'ib*, 1877, 5:111.

174 See the historical work of al-Yaziji (d. 1871): Al-Yaziji, *Risāla Tārīkhiya fī Aḥwāl Jabal Lubnān fī 'Ahdihi al-Iqṭā'ī*, 45.

175 The order and the number of these kinship categories might change from one source to another. See these eighteenth-century lexicons: Abi al-Baqa' Ayyub ibn Musa Kaffawi, "Sha'b," *al-Kulliyāt: Mu'jam fī al-Muṣṭalaḥāt wal-Furūq al-Lughawiyya* (Beirut: Mu'assasat al-Risāla, 1998), 524; Muhammad Murtada al-Husayni al-Zubaydi, "Sh.'a.b," *Tāj al-'Arūs min Jawāhir al-Qāmūs* (Kuwait: Maṭba'at Ḥukūmat al-Kūwayt, 2000), 133–146.

176 John Richardson, "Sha'b," *A Dictionary, Persian, Arabic, and English: with a Dissertation on the Languages, Literature, and Manners of Eastern Nations* (London: William Bulmer, 1806), 567–568; Bocthor, "Peuple," 157.

rose up in great rebellion."[177] Although the word was frequently used to denote ethnic groups, it was also used during the beginning of the nineteenth century to indicate groups that maintain religious ties, as in *al-shaʿb al-Mārūnī* (Maronite people).[178]

Other words that at the turn of the century were also used to mean "nation" were *qabīla* and *ʿashīra*.[179] These words had different levels of association with "clan" and were also used to indicate modern nations. The Catholic monk Hananiya al-Munayyir wrote – in the first decade of the nineteenth century, referring to European opposition to the spread of the "heresy" of the French Revolution – that many "kings, kingdoms, peoples [*shuʿūb*] and tribes [*qabāʾil*]" opposed the distribution of these ideas.[180] The word *ʿashīra* was often used to refer to a religious community, as in *al-milla al-Masīḥiyya wal-ʿashīra al-ʿĪsawiyya* (the Christian community).[181] Although the words *qabīla* and *ʿashīra* were commonly used as a subcategory of *shaʿb*, they were employed to indicate European nations.

Another rarely used word for designating European nations was *jins*. This word was translated in the beginning of the nineteenth century as genus, species, or kind,[182] with no reference to a specific category. It refers to anything, including human beings, as in *al-nās ajnās* (human

177 Al-Turk, *Dhikr Tamalluk Jumhūr al-Faransāwiyya al-Aqṭār al-Miṣriyya wal-Bilād al-Shāmiyya, aw, al-Ḥamla al-Faransiyya ʿala Miṣr wal-Shām*, 18.

178 See the letter dated October 1840: Rustum, *al-Uṣūl al-ʿArabiyya li-Tārīkh Sūriyya fī ʿAhd Muhammad ʿAli Bāshā*, 5:208–211; Ayalon, *Language and Change in the Arab Middle East: The Evolution of Modern Political Discourse*, 26.

179 For the translation of nation to *qabīla*, see: Jacob Berggren, "Nation," *Guide Français-Arabe Vulgaire Des Voyageurs et Des Francs En Syrie et En Égypte: Avec Carte Physique et Géographique de La Syrie et Plan Géométrique de Jérusalem Ancien et Moderne, Comme Supplément Aux Voyages En Oreint* (Upsal: Leffler et Sebell, 1844), 580.

180 Al-Munayyir, *al-Durr al-Marṣūf fī Tārīkh al-Shūf*, 96.

181 See a letter from 1834 in Rustum, *al-Uṣūl al-ʿArabiyya li-Tārīkh Sūriyya fī ʿAhd Muḥammad ʿAli Bāshā*, 1987, 2:141–145.

182 Jacobus Golius, "Jins, Jinsiyya," *Lexicon Arabico-Latinum* (Lugduni Batavorum: typis Bonaventurae & Abrahami, Elseviriorum, prostant Amstelodami apud Johannem Ravesteynivm, 1653), 543; William Kirkpatrick, "Jins," *A Vocabulary, Persian, Arabic, and English* (London: Printed by Joseph Cooper, Drury-Lane, 1785), 37; David Hopkins, "Jins," *A Vocabulary, Persian, Arabic, and English; Abridged from the Quarto Edition of Richardson's Dictionary* (London: Printed for F. and C. Rivingson, 1810), 209; Johann Jahn, "Jins," *Lexicon Arabico-Latinum* (Vindobonae: Apud C. F. Wappler et Beck, 1802), 63.

beings are many kinds).[183] *Jinsiyya*, which later came to designate "citizenship," was translated in the beginning of the nineteenth century into English as "the correspondence of a kind."[184] ʿAbd al-Rahman al-Jabarti used *ajnās al-Ifranj* to refer to European "kinds," with the implied meaning of race.[185] This word was also loaded with more general implied meanings during the 1830s,[186] and it was in many cases synonymous with "nation."[187] In correspondence between Ibrahim Pasha and Syrian notables regarding the confirmation of Jasper Chasseaud's appointment as the American consul in Syria in 1833, Ibrahim expresses his wishes for Chasseaud's success in conducting the matters of his compatriots, "*abnāʾ jinsihi*" (literally, those who belong to his kind).[188]

A modern layer of meaning was added to the word during the 1830s and 1840s, and *jins* was employed as equivalent to the English "race" or "ethnicity."[189] Al-Tahtawi wrote during the 1830s: "These tribes are

183 This word has different connotations that correspond to the various traditions in language, theology, philosophy, and jurisprudence. In these disciplines the use of the word could change from denoting a general category to a subcategory. Thus, for instance, the common meaning in Muslim jurisprudence denotes a much more general category than *nawʿa* (kind); an animal is *jins*, while a human being is *nawʿa* – a subcategory of *jins*. In contrast, philosophers usually switched between the two categories. For more details, see these eighteenth-century Arabic lexicons: Muhammad Murtada al-Husayni al-Zubaydi, "J.n.s," *Tāj al-ʿArūs min Jawāhir al-Qāmūs* (Kuwait: Maṭbaʿat Ḥukūmat al-Kūwayt, 1975); Abi al-Baqaʾ Ayyub ibn Musa Kaffawi, "al-Jins," *al-Kulliyāt: Muʿjam fī al-Muṣṭalaḥāt wal-Furūq al-Lughawiyya* (Beirut: Muʾassasat al-Risāla, 1998), 338–339; Muhammad ʿAli al-Tahanawi, "al-Jins," *Kashshāf Iṣṭilāḥāt al-Funūn wal-ʿUlūm* (Beirut: Nāshirūn, 1996), 594–595.

184 John Richardson, "Jins," *A Dictionary, Persian, Arabic, and English: with a Dissertation on the Languages, Literature, and Manners of Eastern Nations* (London: William Bulmer, 1806), 348.

185 Al-Jabarti, *ʿAjāʾib al-Āthār fī al-Tarājim wal-Akhbār*, 1998, 3:273.

186 See, for instance, local correspondence in 1831 between two governors in Syria, where the word *jins/ajnās* is employed to denote "merchants, any kind of subject, or soldiers from any military, small or big, private or public, subjects or others." Rustum, *al-Uṣūl al-ʿArabiyya li-Tārīkh Sūriyya fī ʿAhd Muḥammad ʿAli Bāshā*, 1987, 1:30–31.

187 See, for instance, the use of *jins* in: Kalivaris, *Kitāb Sirat al-Muʿaẓam al-Murafaʿ al-Kabīr Nabulyūn al-Awwal Imbaratūr al-Farānsawiyya*, 94, 575.

188 Rustum, *al-Uṣūl al-ʿArabiyya li-Tārīkh Sūriyya fī ʿAhd Muḥammad ʿAli Bāshā*, 1987, 2:97–98.

189 Race was translated around the end of the eighteenth century into Arabic as *sulala, nasl* (decent). Jacques Français Ruphy, "Race," *Dictionnaire Abrégé*

a particular race (*ha'ūlā' al-umam jins makhṣūṣ*)," assuming that ethnicities embed naturally inherited racial features.[190] Al-Tahtawi rendered the racial-anthropological features of nations as "natural characteristics" (*awṣāf ṭabī'iyya*), and these included their rapidity of movement, their ethics, and their toughness.[191] In the same spirit he indicated that the Egyptians are not a race (*jins min ajnās al-umam*) but a group (*ṭā'ifa*) that gathered together from different places.[192] Al-Tahtawi ascribed sociopolitical features to the French nation (*jins*), contending that its natural tendency toward freedom made it closer to the Arabs than to the Turks.[193] The politicization of *jins* and its use as equivalent to the modern concept of "nation" became evident around the mid-1800s; thus, for instance, the Italian quest for national unity was rendered in the newspaper *al-Jawā'ib* in 1861 as *wiḥda jinsiyya*.[194]

Much explicit use of race was made under the influence of modern anthropology. In the second half of the nineteenth century, the periodical *al-Jinān* published an article arguing that human society consists of five races divided according to color: white, yellow, copper, red, and black.[195] The article describes the natural features of these races. In the case of Persians, the article argued, the white Persian race was the primary component of the nation ("*al-umma al-Fārisiyya*," the Persian nation). In addition to the Persian, Syrian, and Iraqi ancient nations, the article says that the Syriacs and the Chaldeans belong to the white race that contributed more than any other to building human civilization.[196]

*Français-Arabe* (Paris: Impr. de la République, 1802), 173; Ellious Bocthor, "Race," *Dictionnaire Français-Arabe* (Paris: Chez Firmin Didot Freres, 1829), 224.

190 His contemporary, Faris al-Shidyaq, also made equivalent use of the word. See Malte-Brun, *al-Jughrāfiyya al-'Umūmiyya*, 1838, 1:100; al-Shidyaq, *Mukhtārāt min Āthār Aḥmad Fāris al-Shidyāq*, 157; al-Shidyaq, *al-Wāsiṭa ila Ma'rifat Aḥwāl Mālṭa wa-Kashf al-Mukhabbā' 'an Funūn Ūrūbā*, 34.

191 Malte-Brun, *al-Jughrāfiyya al-'Umūmiyya*, n.d., 3:20–21.

192 Al-Tahtawi, *Takhlīṣ al-Ibrīz fī Talkhīṣ Bārīz aw al-Dīwān al-Nafīs bi-Īwān Bārīs*, 195.

193 Ibid., 199–204.

194 Al-Shidyaq, *Kanz al-Raghā'ib fī Muntakhabāt al-Jawā'ib*, 1877, 5:20–23.

195 *Al-Jinān* 4 (1880): 108–112.

196 An earlier version of racial division appears in al-Tahtawi's work published in 1873. Al-Tahtawi, "Kitāb al-Murshid al-Amīn lil-Banāt wal-Banīn," 350; Ibid. For early anthropological theories, see Cornelius Van Dyck, *Kitāb al-Mir'ā al-Waḍ'iyya fī al-Kura al-Arḍiyya* (Beirut, 1852), 7–20.

An additional modern layer of meaning of this word was also displayed with the rise of civic nationalism: in the context where national identity was civic (liberal or constitutional), the word *jins* had legal rather than racial implications, and it indicated the legal status of a civil community. Faris al-Shidyaq, who went to England in 1848 and stayed there and in Paris for few years,[197] used the phrase *ḥimāya jinsiyya* (legal protection) to denote citizenship that guaranteed civil rights.[198] By then the common meaning of the form *jinsiyya* denoted gender relations.[199] Formal Ottoman documents denoted legal affiliation by using the words *tabaʿat* or *tabaʿiyyat al-dawla* (state affiliates, subjects of the state) rather than *jinsiyya*.[200]

In addition to transitions in the communal appellations, significant shifts took place in the concept of belonging, which is derived from the word *waṭan* (homeland). This word, which was equivalent to the Latin word *patria* and prior to the nineteenth century indicated "the place of one's residence" or the "place where one was born" (which could refer to a village, town, or country),[201] underwent extreme

[197] For the biography of al-Shidyaq, see Mohammed Alwan, "The History and Publications of al-Jawāʾib Press," *MELA Notes*, no. 11 (1977): 4–5; Geoffrey Roper, "Aḥmad Fāris al-Shidyāq and the Libraries of Europe and the Ottoman Empire," *Libraries & Culture* 33, no. 3 (1998): 233–235.

[198] His journey account was published for the first time in 1867. See also a later article he published in *al-Jawāʾib*: Al-Shidyaq, *al-Wāsiṭa ila Maʿrifat Aḥwāl Mālṭa wa-Kashf al-Mukhabbāʾ ʿan Funūn Ūrūbā*, 264; *al-Jawāʾib*, June 22, 1875, 2.

[199] See lexicons published between the 1830s and 1850s: Thomas Xavier Bianchi and Jean Daniel Kieffer, "Jins, Jinsiyya," *Dictionnaire Turc-Français: À L'usage Des Agents Diplomatiques et Consulaires, Des Commerçants, Des Navigateurs, et Autres Voyageurs Dans Le Levant* (Paris: Impr. royale, 1835, 1837), 395; Jacob Berggren, "Race," *Guide Français-Arabe Vulgaire Des Voyageurs et Des Francs En Syrie et En Égypte: Avec Carte Physique et Géographique de La Syrie et Plan Géométrique de Jérusalem Ancien et Moderne, Comme Supplément Aux Voyages En Oreint* (Upsal: Leffler et Sebell, 1844), 665; Francis Johnson, "Jins, Jinsiyya," *A Dictionary, Persian, Arabic, and English* (London: Wm. H. Allen and Co., 1852), 440.

[200] See the Arabic translation of the Ottoman "Law of Subjectivity": Nawfal, *al-Dustūr*, 13–14; al-Shidyaq, *Kanz al-Raghāʾib fī Muntakhabāt al-Jawāʾib*, 1877, 5:152.

[201] For the meaning of *waṭan* (plural *awṭān*, *mawāṭin*) in Arabic and its translation into Latin languages prior to the nineteenth century, see Jacobus Golius, "Waṭan, Mauṭin," *Lexicon Arabico-Latinum* (Lugduni Batavorum: typis Bonaventurae and Abrahami, Elseviriorum, prostant Amstelodami apud Johannem Ravesteynivm, 1653), 1694; Abi al-Baqaʾ Ayyub ibn Musa Kaffawi, "al-Waṭan," *al-Kulliyāt: Muʿjam fī al-Muṣṭalaḥāt wal-Furūq al-Lughawiyya*

politicization during the nineteenth century that extended its semantic field.[202] The inflation of this concept and its modern form appeared in the early translations of French works into Arabic. In the second decade of the nineteenth century, Ellious Bocthor rendered the French ideology of *patriotisme* to *ma'azat al-waṭan* (love of homeland) and *patriot* to *kathīr al-ma'aza li-waṭanihi* (one who loves his homeland).[203] The use of *waṭan* in a political context became more frequent in translations from the 1830s and 1840s. In a book that includes biographies of prominent figures from ancient Greece, Husain 'Abd Allah al-Misri translates the episode in which Solon departed Athens after his political failure. Pisistratus, Solon's rival, sends him a letter using the words *ḥubb al-waṭan* to refer to his leaving Athens, implying his appreciation of Solon's patriotism, which was displayed in his decision to give priority to the common interest of the Athenians.[204] After the 1830s *ḥubb al-waṭan* was presented as a concept that defined political identity and as a force of unity and power. Its theorization in Arabic took place in the works of Rifa'a al-Tahtawi and Butrus al-Bustani. Both scholars composed works that redefine the imagined

(Beirut: Mu'assasat al-Risāla, 1998), 940; William Kirkpatrick, "Waṭan," *A Vocabulary, Persian, Arabic, and English* (London: Printed by Joseph Cooper, Drury-Lane, 1785), 189; Francisco Cañes, "Tierra, Pais, O Patria," *Gramatica Arabigo-Española, Vulgar, Y Literal: Con Un Diccionario Arabigo-Español, En Que Se Ponen Las Voces Mas Usuales Para Una Conversacion Familiar, Con El Texto de La Doctrina Cristiana En El Idioma Arabigo* (Madrid: En la imprenta de don Antonio Perez de Soto, 1775); 'Abd al-Nabi bin 'Abd al-Rasul Ahmadnakri, "al-Waṭan," *Jāmi' al-'Ulūm fī Iṣṭilāḥāt al-Funūn al-Mulaqqab bi-Dustūr al-'Ulamā'* (Beirut: Mu'assasat al-A'lamī lil-Maṭbū'āt, 1975), 459; Muhammad 'Ali al-Tahanawi, "al-Waṭan," *Kashshāf Iṣṭilāḥāt al-Funūn wal-'Ulūm* (Beirut: Nāshirūn, 1996), 1800.

202 For further details about the use of *waṭan* prior to the nineteenth century, see Ulrich Haarmann, "Waṭan," *The Encyclopedia of Islam* (Leiden: Brill, 2002), 175.

203 Ellious Bocthor, "Patriot, Patriotisme," *Dictionnaire Français-Arabe* (Paris: Chez Firmin Didot Freres, 1829), 138.

204 For further examples of the early use of *waṭan* as equivalent to *patria*, see: Laertius, *Mukhtaṣar Tarjamāt Mashāhīr Qudamā' al-Falāsifa*, 10, 15, 20–21; Robertson, *Kitāb Itḥāf Mulūk al-Zamān bi-Tārīkh al-Imbirāṭūr Sharlakān Masbūqan bi-Muqaddimatihi al-Musammā Itḥāf al-Mulūk al-Alibbā' bi-Taqaddum al-Jam'iyyāt fī Ūrūbā Mundhu Inqirāḍ al-Dawla al-Rūmāniyya*, 1:106, 130; Voltaire, *Maṭāli' Shumūs al-Siyar fī Waqā'i' Karlūs al-Thānī 'Ashar*, 17, 44, 70; -, "Patriotisme," *Dictionnaire Français-Arabe* (Beirut: Imprimerie Catholique, 1857), 503; Albert de Biberstein-Kazimirski, "Waṭan," *Dictionnaire Arabe-Français* (Paris: Barrois, 1850), 1563.

past: The first wrote about Egyptian and the second about Syrian patriotism.[205]

During the first half of the nineteenth century, the use of communal designations lacked consistency, and words were employed interchangeably: The word *jins*, for instance, in the phrase "these are Christians from your kind" (*hum Naṣāra min jinsikum* or *ajnās al-Naṣrāniyya*)[206] was replaced by the words *milla*, *umma*, *ṭā'ifa*, *sha'b*, *jumhūr*, or *qawm*.[207] Often the two words *jinsiyya* and *umma* were used together as *jinsiyyat al-umam* in an ambiguous meaning of nationality or citizenship (nationality or citizenship of people).[208] This inconsistency was also reflected in the choice of words to capture the phenomenon of nationalism: Al-Tahtawi, for instance, rendered the French *peuple* as *umma*,[209] and he translated *nations* as *shu'ūb wa-qabā'il*.[210] Correspondingly, Khalifa Mahmud, another translator in the School of Languages, translated European nations and residents during the same phase as *al-milal al-Ifranjiyya*.[211] Furthermore, these

[205] This section focuses on the morphological evolution of *waṭan* and *waṭaniyya* and on the background of the emergence of new forms of sociopolitical organization, with less emphasis on intellectual history. Many published works have dealt extensively with the intellectual aspects of al-Tahtawi's and al-Bustani's work. For further details, see Hourani, *Arabic Thought in the Liberal Age, 1798–1939*, 1970, 67–102; Jacques Couland, "Waṭaniyya," *The Encyclopedia of Islam* (Leiden: Brill, 2002), 175–176; Butrus Abu-Manneh, "The Christians between Ottomanism and Syrian Nationalism: The Ideas of Butrus al-Bustani," *International Journal of Middle East Studies* 11, no. 3 (1980): 287–304; Livingston, "Western Science and Educational Reform in the Thought of Shaykh Rifaa al-Tahtawi," 543–564.

[206] Kalivaris, *Kitāb Sirat al-Mu'aẓam al-Murafa' al-Kabīr Nabulyūn al-Awwal Imbaratūr al-Farānsawiyya*, 26.

[207] See, for instance, the use of *jins* and *milla* in: Al-Dimashqi, *Ta'rīkh Ḥawādith al-Shām wa-Lubnān*, 3; Voltaire, *Rawḍ al-Azhar fī Tārīkh Buṭrus al-Akbar*, 63.

[208] Al-Shidyaq, *Kanz al-Raghā'ib fī Muntakhabāt al-Jawā'ib*, 1877, 5:84.

[209] For a comparison between the original French edition and al-Tahtawi's translation, see Depping, *Kitāb Qalā'id al-Mafākhir fī Gharīb 'Awā'id al-Awā'il wal-Awākhir*, 85; Georges-Bernard Depping, *Aperçu Historique Sur Les Mœurs et Coutumes Des Nation* (Paris: Mairet et fournier, 1842), 184.

[210] For comparison, see Depping, *Kitāb Qalā'id al-Mafākhir fī Gharīb 'Awā'id al-Awā'il wal-Awākhir*, 104; Depping, *Aperçu Historique Sur Les Mœurs et Coutumes Des Nation*, 323.

[211] For a comparison between the English and the Arabic texts of William Robenson's history of Emperor Charles V, see al-Shayyal, *Tārīkh al-Tarjama wal-Ḥaraka al-Thaqāfiyya fī 'Aṣr Muḥammad 'Ali*, 221.

inconsistencies are displayed in the same text by the same translator: The use of *umma* in al-Tahtawi's translations did not always conform to the common prenational use. Thus, for instance, the common combination of *al-umma al-Islāmiyya* became, in al-Tahtawi's translation of Conrad Malte-Brun, *umam al-Islam* (Islamic peoples or nations), emphasizing the diversity of peoples within the allegedly unified body of the Islamic nation.[212] In the same translation, and in his discussion of the ethnic and religious diversity of Greater Syria, he mentioned that this region has many kinds of groups (*umam*) that differ ethnically (*jins*) and religiously (*dīn*). Living there, he indicates, are many *umam*, including Druze, ʿAlawites, Arabs, Maronites, Shiʿa, and so on. The word *umma* had a loose meaning, and it denoted a unified body of people of any kind.[213] Along with this inconsistency, the adjective "national" was rendered into Arabic prior to the mid-nineteenth century as "what concerns the group (*ṭāʾifa* and not *umma*)."[214] The ambiguous attempts to construct ethnic or civil political language in Arabic generated a variety of concepts of liberation.

## Language of National Liberation, 1798–1882

Despite the fluctuating language of the first half of the nineteenth century, there were a few attempts, made mainly by invaders, to approach groups by using the language of nationalism. Early signs of the political use of this terminology were evident in dissonances that arose in the 1798 debate between the French and the Ottomans, immediately following the French seizure of Egypt. Addressing *al-umma al-Miṣriyya* (the Egyptian nation), rather than *al-umma al-Islāmiyya*, in Napoleon's first proclamation in Egypt was neither accidental nor rare.[215] This articulation was part of the French attempt to distribute the idea of republican revolutionary nationalism, which they had also done in the

212 Malte-Brun, *al-Jughrāfiyya al-ʿUmūmiyya*, n.d., 3:88. 213 Ibid., 3:66.

214 For the quotation, see the Cañes entry in his eighteenth-century lexicon. Similarly, see the second reference, which indicatesthat the French *nationalité* was rendered, around the middle of the nineteenth century, in Turkish as *milletlik* (your religious people, or simply, your people). See Cañes, "Nacion," 489; Nassif Mallouf, "Nationalité," *Dictionnaire Français-Turc* (Paris: Maisonneuve et Cie, 1856), 500.

215 Al-Jabarti, *ʿAjāʾib al-Āthār fī al-Tarājim wal-Akhbār*, 1998, 3:6.

territories they conquered in Europe.[216] The idea of nationalism that came to prominence during the late eighteenth century evolved during the French Revolution and, against the background of absolutism, proliferated as a theory of legitimacy. The revolutionaries, the proponents of a republic, sought to replace the absolutism of the king and the heritage of a hierarchical society of privileges with the idea of the nation as a source of political legitimacy. The ideas of a constitutional legal regime and a popular assembly dedicated to representing the citizens of the nation were a manifestation of this endeavor: to shift the concept of "right" from the theory of the divine right of kings to the political rights of the people (nation, people, citizens). The temporal call for nationalism was articulated in practice in two ways: by the establishment of nation-states through the unification of smaller entities, thus creating civil identities, and by the overthrow of multiethnic empires, resulting in the construction of new nation-states.[217]

The French invaders of Egypt sought to utilize these ideas in their propaganda against the Mamluks by attempting to recruit the native Egyptian elite – the notables and the ʿulama – to their side. Sultan Selim III's formal reaction to the ideas displayed in the French proclamation reflected deep awareness of the danger embedded in the French ideas; in their response the Ottomans stated that Napoleon was plotting to destroy the unity of the Islamic nation ("*al-umma al-Muḥammadiyya wal-milla al-Muḥammadiyya*").[218] The French, it was indicated, deserted their religion, their belief in Judgment Day, and their loyalty to their rulers: they "provoked the public [*jamāhīr*] against the rival groups [*ṭawāʾif*] aiming to destroy the foundations of their religions."[219] The use of the word *jumhūr*, the same temporal signifier of republic, is in this respect loaded with implied content corresponding to the republican revolutionary idea of popular legitimacy. The revolt of the public (*jamāhīr*) against the social components of the Ancien

216 David Thomson, *Europe since Napoleon* (New York: Knopf, 1957), 29–34.

217 Timothy Baycroft, "Nationalism," *New Dictionary of the History of Ideas* (Detroit, MI: Charles Scribner's Sons, 2005), 1578–1579; Evans, "Liberalism, Nationalism, and the Coming of the Revolution," 5.

218 Al-Shihabi, *Qiṣat Aḥmad Bāsha al-Jazzār Bayna Miṣr wal-Shām wa-Ḥawādithuhu Maʿ Nābulyūn Būnābart*, 145.

219 Ibid.

Régime – the clerics and the aristocracy – was denoted in the Ottoman response by the loosely defined word *ṭawāʾif*.

This was an early encounter with the modern idea of nationalism. Indeed, the new layers of the concept *jumhūr* had acquired some collective aspects of secular sovereignty ("will of the people"), but the nature of this community and its sentimental association with the idea of defined territory and shared history was not yet relevant. This language had a stronger impact on the group gathered around General Yaʿqub, which strove for an "independent Egypt." But in this case too the impact these ideas had on the Arabic of the first decade of the nineteenth century left no sign of their proliferation beyond some few texts written in foreign languages.

Much like the failed French experience, the Egyptian invasion of Greater Syria evidenced an attempt to utilize the language of nationalism for political purposes and propaganda. The conflict between Muhammad ʿAli and Sultan Mahmud II, which came to the fore after the Battle of Navarino in 1827, was allegedly one of many common patterns of conflicts involving a weakened central authority and a rising semiautonomous and ambitious ruler. Muhammad ʿAli's ambition to establish an independent dynasty in Egypt, particularly against the background of the conflict with the sultan, created a suitable climate for utilizing terminology emphasizing the particularity of groups under his rule. Ibrahim Pasha, Muhammad ʿAli's son and the leader of the Egyptian expedition to Greater Syria, embraced unclear protonational concepts. In an 1832 letter to his father, he indicated that the war with the sultan was a war between nations, emphasizing the racial conception of nationalism.[220] In many letters from the same year, he expressed his admiration of the idea of national martyrdom – as, for example, in

[220] The sentence is "*ḥarb al-qawmiyya wal-ʿunṣuriyya.*" It is not clear if these letters were originally written in Arabic or in Turkish and translated later to Arabic. However, the Turkish neologism *kavim* is derived from the Arabic word *qawm*, and by the first half of the nineteenth century, the word constituted one of the terms to denote "nation" or "people." By then its Arabic abstraction *qawmiyya* had nonpolitical meanings and denoted physical build or pleasant appearance (*qāma*, *qawam*) or *qumiyya*, responsibility. In the Biberstein-Kazimirski lexicon, published in 1850, and in Butrus al-Bustani's *Muḥīṭ al-Muḥīṭ*, the word appears as *qawmiyya* and means height and size. Rustum, *al-Maḥfūẓāt al-Malakiyya al-Miṣriyya*, 2:48; Bianchi and Kieffer, "Qawm," 529; Nassif Mallouf, "Nation," *Dictionnaire Français-Turc* (Paris: Maisonneuve et Cie, 1856), 500; al-Zubaydi, "Q.w.m," 305–321; Albert de Biberstein-Kazimirski, "Qawmiyya," *Dictionnaire Arabe-Français*

the statement that a man "should sacrifice his life for his nation." The desire to die for the sake of Egypt constituted a significant secularization of the discourse on martyrdom, replacing the previous religious perceptions of martyrdom (*shahāda*, death for sake of Islam) with death for an ethnic nation or homeland.[221] It is not evident, however, to which group Ibrahim Pasha referred when using these concepts. In another letter from the same year, he mentioned that one of the purposes of invading Greater Syria was "capturing Arab and other nearby lands to rescue the poor nation from the disasters that afflicted it."[222] In this statement it is also not entirely clear if he was referring to the Arabs as a unified group in contrast to the Turks (although ethnically, he was not an Arab). Nevertheless, these ideas embedded a potential threat to the Ottoman seizure of Greater Syria, which was frequently referred to in the 1830s as "Arab Lands" (*ʿArabistān*). Ibrahim might have thought to utilize these ideas to provoke the Arab population against the Ottomans. It was no accident that George Antonius, who searched for the origins of Arab nationalism about a century later, contended that the seeds of this idea emerged with Ibrahim Pasha's rule in Greater Syria.[223]

An ethnic appellation that undermined the imagined unity of the then-dominant identities of pious nations was common among early Arabic linguistics by the end of the eighteenth century. In one of his early works, Mikhaʿil al-Sabbagh, who referred to the Ottomans by their ethnic designation (*al-Turk*), contends that natural sciences proved that this group was naturally barbaric, anticultural, and responsible for the deterioration of "our region." Using pseudosciences to

(Paris: Barrois, 1850), 840; Butrus al-Bustani, "Qam," *Muḥīṭ al-Muḥīṭ* (Beirut: Maktabat Lubnān, 1998), 763–764; Reinhart Pieter Anne Dozy, "Qawm," *Takmilat al-Maʿājim al-ʿArabiyya* (Baghdad: Dār al-Shuʾūn al-Thaqāfiyya al-ʿĀma, 1997), 416–428.

221 The concept of secular-national martyrdom appeared in translated literature of the 1840s and 1850s. See the translation of a phrase from Voltaire: *shahīd ḥurriyyat baldatihi* (martyr for his country's freedom). For further examples of death in the name of freedom, see the decree published in *al-Jawāʾib* in 1865 that relates the assassination of the king of Prussia in the name of national unity and freedom: Voltaire, *Maṭāliʿ Shumūs al-Siyar fī Waqāʾiʿ Karlūs al-Thānī ʿAshar*, 93; al-Shidyaq, *Kanz al-Raghāʾib fī Muntakhabāt al-Jawāʾib*, 1877, 5:63–67.

222 Rustum, *al-Maḥfūẓāt al-Malakiyya al-Miṣriyya*, 2:48.

223 George Antonius, *The Arab Awakening: The Story of the Arab National Movement* (London: Hamish Hamilton, 1938), 4–30.

define ethnic traits, however, characterized the national discourse of the time. It is noteworthy that al-Sabbagh worked in Paris with the well-known orientalist Silvestre de Sacy and was one of the pioneers of the modern study of Arabic.[224]

The idea of nationalism had a more obvious influence on the language used in the second half of the nineteenth century.[225] The conceptual transformation and the mental gap between the first two decades of that century and the end of the 1850s are reflected in words used in an article published by Faris al-Shidyaq in *al-Jawāʾib* during the 1860s. Al-Shidyaq, the editor of the newspaper writing from Istanbul, presents his observation regarding the Vienna Settlement of 1815, which had been signed between the European powers and dealt with the subject of restoration after the defeat of Napoleon I at Waterloo. Al-Shidyaq writes that the 1815 treaty addressed the subject of restoration assuming that the countries conquered by Napoleon should be returned to their owners, the dynasties that ruled before the Napoleonic invasions, without regard to the residents' national identity. That, however, was before the spread of the idea of nationalism that flourished later. "Then [when the treaty was written in 1815], the idea of the interests of the nation (*maṣlaḥat al-umma*) was not kept in mind at all."[226]

This observation emphasizes the conceptual transformation that took place during the second half of the nineteenth century from the perspective of an Arabic-speaking scholar in Istanbul. Prior to these events a few European states – such as France, Great Britain, Sweden, and Spain – had already become nation-states, but the 1848 revolutions marked a milestone in the emergence of nationalism as a popular force in Europe. Although these revolutions have been assessed by modern historians as a defeat of the revolutionary forces – "the

224 Al-Sabbagh contends that the "Turk's nature was typified by the natural scientists [*al-ʿulamāʾ al-ṭabīʿiyyīn*] as barbaric, cruel and oppressive." It is worth mentioning that the Ottomans persecuted the al-Sabbagh family due to its relations with Zahir al-Umar in Palestine. In much the same way, Niqula al-Turk contends that the Turks (*ibn al-Turk*) were patronizing toward the Arabs (*ibn al-ʿArab*). See al-Sabbagh, *Musābaqat al-Barq wal-Ghamām fī Suʿāt al-Ḥamām*, 9, 47; al-Sabbagh, *al-Risāla al-Tāmma fī Kalām al-ʿĀmma: wal-Manāhij fī Aḥwāl al-Kalām al-Dārij*, 8; al-Turk, *Dhikr Tamalluk Jumhūr al-Faransāwiyya al-Aqṭār al-Miṣriyya wal-Bilād al-Shāmiyya, aw, al-Ḥamla al-Faransiyya ʿala Miṣr wal-Shām*, 163.

225 For discussion about the emergence of the idea of Pan-Arabism, see Suleiman, *The Arabic Language and National Identity: A Study in Ideology*, 69–112.

226 Al-Shidyaq, *Kanz al-Raghāʾib fī Muntakhabāt al-Jawāʾib*, 1877, 5:84–85.

turning-point when Europe failed to turn" – they stimulated long-term political transformation. As a result a number of national communities enjoyed international recognition of their independence a few decades after these events – for example, the unification of Italy and later of Germany.[227]

The second half of the nineteenth century witnessed much more consistency and compatibility in using words for portraying national experience. Although words such as *milla*, *qabīla*, *ṭā'ifa*, *sha'b*, and *qawm* stayed in use, they were less frequently used for designating political communities.[228] Correspondingly, words such as *umma*, and with it *jins* and to a lesser extent *jumhūr*, were intensively used in a political context. A comparison between lexicons published before and during the 1880s reveals the vast semantic inflation of these words. Prior to the 1880s these words, especially *umma*, frequently appeared as the noun "nation" and its adjective "national." During the 1880s they acquired many additional meanings related to nationalism; nation (*umma*, *qawm*, *jins*) rose to a central ideological level with combinations such as *waṭanī*, *mukhtaṣṣ bil-umma*, *mukhtaṣṣ bil-jinsiyya* (national); *ḥubb al-umma* (love of one's nation); *anghām al-umma* (anthem); *munāfarat al-umma* (national antipathies); *bank al-umma* (national bank); *bayraq al-dawla* (national flag); *ghayrat al-umma* (national spirit); *taba'iyya*, *jinsiyya*, *ummiyya* (nationality); and *'ammama al-umma bihi* (nationalize, to make general among a people).[229]

Unlike the Turkish *kavim*, early Arabic terminology for ethnic political affinity very rarely made political use of *qawm*, instead using *jins* and *jinsiyya*. *Qawmiyya* would return to dominate the politics of identity in Arabic later, but only after World War II. *Jins*, however, stabilized in the second half of the nineteenth century, denoting national content, frequently ethnocultural and racial nationalism.[230]

227 Evans, "Liberalism, Nationalism, and the Coming of the Revolution," 4–24.
228 Thus, for instance, *a'yyād ṭā'ifiyya* indicates national holidays. See *al-Bashīr*, May 27, 1871, 341; *al-Jawā'ib*, October 18, 1876, 7; *al Baṣṣīr*, July 28, 1881.
229 See lexicons published in the 1880s: George Percy Badger, "Nation," *An English-Arabic Lexicon* (London: C. K. Paul & Co., 1881), 658; Yuhanna Abkariyus, "Nation," *English-Arabic Reader's Dictionary* (Beirut: Librairie du Liban, 1974), 440; Yuhanna Abkariyus, "Nation," *Qāmūs Inklīzī wa-'Arabī* (Beirut, 1887), 414.
230 As, for instance, in *al-jins al-ṭilyānī* (Italian nation or ethnicity) and in a more explicit use in a national-political context: *wiḥda jinsiyya* (national unity).

Despite the intensified political use of the word in the 1850s to indicate features of nationalism, as in *ḥamāsa jinsiyya* (national enthusiasm),[231] *jins* was rarely used solely in its racial meaning. In the context of reforms, the racial differences between communities of the Ottoman Empire (*ikhtilāf al-jinsiyya fī al-ʿUthmāniyya*) were perceived as one of the reasons for the empire's political weakness, and thus the racial content of the word underwent very little theorization.[232] The positivist periodical *al-Muqtaṭaf* argued in 1885 that those among the Syrians who could prove the purity of their Arab racial origins (*al-jinsiyya al-ʿArabiyya*) were very rare.[233] Prominent scholars believed that the imagined communities in the Arabic-speaking regions (Syrian, Egyptian, and Ottoman) did not consist of pure "races" (*ajnās*), and therefore the idea of racial nationalism was not very relevant to the politics of their time.[234]

Instead, during the 1860s and 1870s, *jins* absorbed ethnocultural content. One prominent scholar who contributed to this theorization was Butrus al-Bustani, who through his historical publications on the Arabic language presented the imaginary dimension of Syrian Arab identity. He contributed significantly to the construction of the Arab past as a unified, continuous, coherent narrative, both before and after the advent of Islam.[235] As part of a broad approach toward Arabs and Syrians, he – and after him his son Salim – theorized the two

Texts of that time distinguished between two categories of affiliation: *jinsiyya* (ethnic, national, or racial) and *madhhabī* or *dīnī* (religious). See: *Birjīs Barīs*, August 18, 1859, 2; Ahmad Faris al-Shidyaq, *Kanz al-Raghāʾib fī Muntakhabāt al-Jawāʾib*, ed. Salim al-Shidyaq, vol. 2 (Istanbul: Maṭbaʿat al-Jawāʾib, 1873), 89; *Mirʾāt al-Aḥwāl*, May 24, 1877, 9; *al-Jawāʾib*, September 27, 1876, 12; *al-Ahrām*, December 20, 1876; *al-Ahrām*, March 29, 1882.

231 *Birjīs Barīs*, April 25, 1860.

232 *Al-Ahrām*, September 5, 1878; *al-Ahrām*, August 12, 1880.

233 *Al-Muqtaṭaf* 3, no. 11 (1886): 441.

234 *Al-Jawāʾib*, September 27, 1876, 1.

235 Much of his writing focuses on Arabic literature. For selected works, see Butrus al-Bustani, *Udabāʾ al-ʿArab fī al-Jāhiliyya wa-Ṣadr al-Islām* (Beirut: Maktabat Ṣādir, 1953); Butrus al-Bustani, *Maʿārik al-ʿArab fī al-Sharq wal-Gharb* (Beirut: Dār al-Makshūf, 1944). The middle of the nineteenth century witnessed vast interest in Arab history, and there were authors writing earlier than al-Bustani who composed historical works about this subject. See, for instance, the Armenian author who in 1851 wrote in his composition "owing to the large interest of the people in Greater Syria in Arab history of the pre-Islamic era": Iskandar Abkariyus, *Kitāb Nihayat al-Irab fī Akhbār al-ʿArab* (Marseille: Maṭbaʿat al-Faʿla, 1852), 2.

concepts *jins* and *waṭan* and associated them with one another. The background for Butrus al-Bustani's preoccupation with these ideas was the 1860 massacres of Christians in Greater Syria. During these events al-Bustani published eleven articles – between September 19, 1860 and April 22, 1861 – in *Nafīr Sūriyya*, suggesting utilizing the idea of *ḥubb al-waṭan* (love of homeland) as the sole political identity for Syrians and as a constructive solution for ending the religious conflict in Syria. He spoke about *al-jins al-ʿArabī* (Arab community), which was equivalent to *abnāʾ al-waṭan* (compatriots), and sought to use these ideas as a fundamental basis for coexistence between communities that were affiliated with a variety of religions (*madhāhib*). In his articles he associated patriotism with a vision of progress, tolerance, freedom, equality, prosperity, and civilization for the inhabitants of Syria (*Sūriyya, bar al-Shām, ʿArabistān*).[236]

Al-Bustani's son Salim continued this effort of theorization by emphasizing the idea of Arab solidarity. In his works "civilized" and "advanced" (*tamaddun, mutamaddin*) society is connected to the idea of solidarity (*ḥamiyya*), elevating this concept to its most politicized state in the Arabic discourse of the nineteenth century. Following Ibn Khaldun's argument regarding *ʿaṣabiyya* (group feeling), he contends that Arabs reached political and cultural dominance in the past when they cultivated their Arab ties. He suggests that the Arab ethnocultural identity (*al-ʿuṣba al-jinsiyya, al-ḥamiyya al-ʿArabiyya*) should be the main element around which social solidarity revolves, and that without *al-ʿuṣba al-jinsiyya*, the Arabs will deteriorate to the lowest cultural levels, which involves splitting into smaller and weaker groups.[237]

Both Butrus and his son Salim, Protestant scholars affiliated with a small religious community within a larger Ottoman society consisting of organized millets, advocated the idea of solidarity based on *jins*. By wielding their skills as journalists, they hoped to achieve their goal of "killing the religious collective bonds [*ʿuṣba*]" and replacing them with ethnocultural Arab ties. They argued that the situation of the inhabitants of the region would remain hopeless with *al-ʿuṣba al-dīniyya* (religious bonds), which they identified as a source of regression and intolerance.[238]

[236] Al-Bustani, *Nafīr Sūriyya*, 9–70. [237] *Al-Jinān* 24 (1874): 845–846.
[238] *Al-Jinān* 2 (1870): 52–53; *al-Jinān* 22 (1870): 673–677.

The al-Bustanis' theorization for secularizing sociocultural bonds took place in the context of the constitutional process undergone by the empire before 1878, under the tent of Ottomanism. Politicizing the idea of Arab identity (*al-ʿusba al-umma al-ʿArabiyya*) was therefore strictly associated with the idea of *waṭan* (*al-ʿusba al-waṭaniyya*) – the smaller "homeland" of Syria and the greater homeland, the Ottoman Empire. Salim al-Bustani articulated this relationship by stressing the correlation between ethnicity and patriotism: "the ethnic ties that fit the patriotic ties" (*al-ʿuṣba al-jinsiyya al-muwāfiqa lil-ʿuṣba al-waṭaniyya*).[239]

Salim al-Bustani was convinced of the independent identity of Arabs. By the 1870s he had ascribed ethnic features to the Arabs and to the Turks, acknowledging what he defined as the spirit of the age. Influenced by the model of the United States of America, he compared the Arab nation with nations, such as the Irish, that had lost their political independence but maintained their ethnic solidarity. Aware of the opposition that these ideas might evoke in the multicultural empire, he estimated that the Ottomans would not reject his vision of ethnic Arab unity. He assumed that the relationship between Arab ethnicity and Ottoman authority was like the relationship between the different ethnicities in the United States, where differences in religion and *jinsiyya* (ethnicity) were minimized and unity promoted. He contended that developing Arabism would be important for the Ottomans and would lead to progress, especially given the cooperation between the Arabs and the Turks. If the Ottoman state did not support these ideas, he argued, the weakness of the Arabs would lead to weakness of the state.[240] Al-Bustani's articles in his periodical, *al-Jinān*, emphasized the subject of demolishing religious "fanaticism" more than any other value, calling for following the experience of Enlightenment.[241]

These theoretical seeds of Arab nationalism were common among some Arab scholars of the time. The construction of Arab *jinsiyya* was made by Christians, inside and outside the borders of the Ottoman Empire. The national Arab narrative that was underpinned by the assumption that Arab civilization reached its peak during Arab rule of the Islamic Empire and later deteriorated (with an implied meaning

[239] Ibid. [240] *Al-Jinān* 22 (1870): 673–677. [241] Ibid.

for the rule of non-Arabs), was spread by journalists such as Butrus al-Bustani and Rashid al-Dahdah, who was originally from the Keserwan district in Lebanon. Al-Dahdah, like al-Bustani, made extensive use of the term "the Arab nation" in his articles.[242] With the journalistic activity of the 1860s and 1870s, the early general appellation *abnāʾ al-ʿArab* (Arabs) was gradually replaced by newly coined words. Phrases such as *al-umma al-ʿArabiyya* (Arab nations), *abnāʾnā al-ʿArabiyyīn* (our Arab compatriots), *al-jāmiʿa al-ʿArabiyya* (Arab solidarity), and *al-bilād al-ʿArabiyya* and *aqṭār ʿArabiyya* (Arab regions) became much more common.[243]

The dissolution of the Ottoman constitution in 1878 by Sultan ʿAbd al-Hamid II and the decline of Ottomanism marked a turning point in the internal use of the concept of national liberation in Arabic. At that point the political role of Arab ethnicity became relevant, and calls for Arab independence spread throughout the region.[244] These sentiments were supported by European newspapers such *as al-Ittiḥād al-ʿArabī*, which was published in England in 1881 (established by Lewis Sabunji), and by Arabic-French newspapers that followed French foreign policy and advocated Arab separation from the Ottomans, especially *al-Baṣṣir* (1881–1882) and its successor *Kawkab al-Mashriq* (1882–1883).[245]

The quest of Arabs for national independence was advocated by *al-Baṣṣir*, a pro-French newspaper that defended the French seizure of Algeria. "The Arabs we know are the Arabs who tend toward freedom [*yamīlūn ila al-ḥurriyya*]," wrote Khalil Ghanim Afandi, a Maronite

[242] *Birjīs Barīs*, November 23, 1859.
[243] For selected articles, see: ibid.; *al-Jinān* 23 (1873): 793; *al-Ahrām*, February 2, 1877; *al-Ahrām*, May 11, 1877; *al-Muqtaṭaf* 3, no. 6 (1881): 551–556; *al-Baṣṣīr*, February 2, 1882; *al-Baṣṣīr*, September 21, 1882; *al-Iʿlām*, January 28, 1885, 2.
[244] See the report in *al-Ahrām* about the distribution of proclamations in Damascus demanding independence and the revival of the Arab state. See also the report in the French *al-Baṣṣir* about the spread of revolutionary proclamations issued in Mecca calling for an Arab revolt against the "Turks." See also correspondence between Yusuf Karam, a notable from Mount Lebanon, with ʿAbd al-Qadir al-Jazaʾiri: Al-*Ahrām*, June 22, 1880; *al-Baṣṣīr*, July 7, 1881; *al-Baṣṣīr*, August 25, 1881; *al-Baṣṣīr*, December 15, 1881; ʿAdil Salih, *Suṭūr min al-Risāla: Tārīkh Ḥaraka Istiqlāliyya Qāmat fī al-Mashriq al-ʿArabī Sant 1877* (Beirut: 1966), 106–113.
[245] See *Kawkab al-Mashriq*, June 29, 1882.

and a former member of the disbanded Ottoman parliament, who was deeply disappointed by the failure of the Ottoman reforms.[246] In his publication he systematically supported the idea of Arab separatism in North Africa.[247]

The idea of Arab independence ignited in 1881 debate between Khalil Ghanim and Faris al-Shidyaq. At the center of this debate stood Ghanim's argument that Ahmad ʿUrabi's movement in Egypt was a separatist Arab movement that attempted to establish an independent Arab kingdom. He contended that the crisis emphasized the hatred of "Arab Egyptians" toward the "Turks." Ghanim continued by implying that the Ottoman attempt to send troops to Egypt predominantly aimed at returning Egypt to their control. In his counterargument al-Shidyaq refuted these claims, arguing that Ghanim strove to spread the seeds of dispute between the khedive and the sultan. Al-Shidyaq attacked the idea of the separation of the Arab nation, justifying his argument that these ideas were aimed at weakening the Ottoman Empire and establishing feeble entities that would eventually be subject to European control. He contended that Ghanim's calls served the French cause, which strove to extend French domination beyond Algeria. Ghanim in turn argued that the Arabs should be independent (using the word *aḥrār*) from the weak Ottoman Empire and that the sultan was not recognized as caliph by the major part of the Muslim community. The idea of constitutionalism, which was in the background of this debate, was pointed out by Ghanim, who criticized the dissolution of the Ottoman constitution, attacking al-Shidyaq for defending the authoritarian regime. Ghanim claimed that his newspaper was a "free newspaper" (*jarīda ḥurra*) that defended the idea of freedom and was fundamentally different from *al-Jawāʾib*, which served the sultan and his autocratic policies.[248] Ghanim ended the debate with personal insults attacking Faris al-Shidyaq, "who sold his religion and his honor in the streets of Malta, London, and Paris,"[249] thus

246 *Al-Baṣṣīr*, July 7, 1881; *al-Baṣṣīr*, August 25, 1881; *al-Baṣṣīr*, December 15, 1881.

247 Ibid.

248 For the debate see *al-Baṣṣīr*, October 20, 1881; *al-Jawāʾib*, November 29, 1881; *al-Baṣṣīr*, December 1, 1881; *al-Jawāʾib*, December 13, 1881; *al-Baṣṣīr*, December 15, 1881; *al-Baṣṣīr*, December 29, 1881; *al-Jawāʾib*, January 10, 1882.

249 *Al-Baṣṣīr*, January 12, 1882.

closing one of the earliest debates on the subject of national liberation in Arabic.

The discourse that evolved around *jins* had less impact among Muslim scholars than among their Christian compatriots. In his later works of the 1860s and the beginning of the 1870s, al-Tahtawi attributed equivalent meanings to *jins*, *milla*, and *abnāʾ al-waṭan* (compatriots), assuming that all these appellations referred to groups that "live in the same country, use the same language, have the same ethical values and traditions, and mostly follow the same law and affiliate with the same state."[250] In his works he theorizes the idea of a civil community living under a monarchy, without any attempt to emphasize the ethnic or religious differences within this community. The "nation" that he addresses is a collection of people who are organized in a state and who therefore have a common interest in prosperity, progress, and power. In that sense al-Tahtawi's use of *jins* emphasizes the different contexts in which the word evolved: In monarchic Egypt this word evolved within the context of central authority, while in Syria the idea was theorized where there was no autonomous central government. With al-Tahtawi the ethnocultural notion of *jins*, therefore, did not reach an independent political level, and it remained as a subordinate principle to the idea of the civil-state community.

In this early stage not only did *jins* not play a significant role in the construction of an independent Arab national community, it was strongly rejected by conservatives such as Jamal al-Din al-Afghani and Muhammad ʿAbdu. In an 1884 article dedicated to *jins*, they completely refute it as an option for achieving political solidarity among Muslims. They argue that *jins* is an unnatural variant of loyalty. The Muslim believer, they continue, cannot adopt these bonds – *jins* and *shaʿb* – because according to the Islamic faith a true Muslim should regard religion as the natural social bond. Both argue that the uniqueness of Islam lies in the fact that it is not limited to spiritual belief but also shapes morals, the laws of society, and rights; Islamic law is a comprehensive system that answers all, including political, challenges. It is enough for Muslim rulers to follow shariʿa to reach glory: they do not need to utilize any values outside of Islam, including those of the "proponents of civilization and freedom" (*aʿwān al-tamaddun*

[250] Al-Tahtawi, "Kitāb al-Murshid al-Amīn lil-Banāt wal-Banīn," 457–461.

*wal-ḥurriyya*). Rejecting any political bond outside the bond of religion, which they saw as the highest and most holy type of solidarity, was the most significant aspect of their work during these years.[251] These political controversies, however, contributed to the refutation of both Arab national liberation and Arab separatism.

Toward the end of the nineteenth century, nationalism (*jins*) as a sole subject of identification was barely accepted. Instead Arabic ethnicity was politicized under the tent of Islam. An early manifestation of this idea also appears in the works of Khalil Ghanim. In his articles from the 1880s, he advocates the restoration of Arab rule over Islam, which would replace the then-current Turkish domination. In one of the articles, he contends that the Hashemites, the rulers of Hejaz who had begun to fill a major role in the opposition to Turkish dominance, were the most adequate and well-known family among the Arabs able to take on this mission. Ghanim makes the association between the Ottoman reclamation of the idea of a caliphate and their retreat from reforms. He criticizes the utilization of the ʿulama in discharging and convicting the famous constitutionalist Midhat Pasha. Furthermore, he argues that the reason for reviving the idea of a caliphate was to create a counterweight to the Arab separatist tendency, "the Arab rights." Arab criticism of the Turkish caliphate, especially in *al-Ittiḥād*, which was published by the Egyptian journalist Ibrahim al-Muwaylihi,[252]

[251] Jamal al-Din al-Afghani and Muhammad ʿAbdu, "al-ʿUrwa al-Wuthqa," in *al-Āthār al-Kāmila: Al-Sayyid Jamāl al-Dīn al-Ḥusainī al-Afghānī*, ed. Sayyid Hadi Khusru Shahi, vol. 1 (Cairo: Maktabat al-Shurūq al-Duwaliyya, 2002), 103–106.

[252] He was a famous Egyptian journalist who fled in 1879 to Italy with the exiled Khedive Ismaʿil. There he established *al-Khilāfa*, and after it *al-Ittiḥād* in Paris, in which he criticized Sultan ʿAbd al-Hamid II, who supported the idea of dethroning Ismaʿil. In his newspaper he attacked the sultan's attempt to declare himself caliph, contending that "this autocrat" [*hadhā al-mustabid*] had no right to do so, and his caliphate was not legitimate. The "Christian countries" [*al-mamālik al-ʿĪsawiyya*], he argued, demanded for years that the pope be deprived of his political power. The Western Christians did not accept treating him as a holy leader, despite the fact that he was the head of their religion, implying that religion and politics should be separated. Al-Muwaylihi assumed that the reason for the deterioration of the empire and the Muslims' current state was the autocratic regime. He wondered how it could be that the Muslim sultan was placed under Western non-Muslim pressure to apply justice to his Muslim subjects: "This makes the foreigner laugh and the Muslim cry." For al-Muwaylihi's biography and criticism of ʿAbd al-Hamid II's caliphate, see Ibrahim al-Muwaylihi, *Ibrāhīm al-Mūwaylihī: Al-Aʿmāl*

was from Ghanim's point of view no less than a mark of the beginning of an Arab revolt against the Turks. This discourse, however, was employed by *al-Baṣṣir* as a counterargument to the Islamic solidarity – "*al-ta'aṣṣub al-Islamī*" (Islamic fanaticism) – that Istanbul promoted, including in Algeria, after the failure of the Tanzimat.[253]

Compared to the national variant of *jins*, the revival of Arabs as a leading group in the Islamic nation (*umma*) was an idea that Muslim scholars received more enthusiastically. Prominent Muslim scholars such as Muhammad 'Abdu and 'Abd al-Rahman al-Kawakibi frequently used the term "Arab nation" (*al-umma al-'Arabiyya*) when referring to an Islamic state.[254] One prominent publication that theorized this idea was al-Kawakibi's *Umm al-Qura*, which he wrote around the end of the nineteenth century. In his publication al-Kawakibi stressed the special position of the Arabs in Islam by arguing that the problem of Islam could be solved if the caliphate were to be transferred from the hands of the Ottomans and restored to the Quraysh: Then an Arab caliph would sit in Mecca and he rule with the help of the Islamic principle of consultation (*shūra*), and his political authority would be limited to Hejaz. The Arab caliph will be the highest spiritual authority for all Muslims around the world and symbol of their unity. Al-Kawakibi argues that reviving an Arab caliphate would return the Muslim spirit to its glorious past.[255]

The impact of nationalism was not confined to words denoting communities and groups. More than *jins*, the word that captured the imagination of these generations was *waṭan*. The idea of "patriotism" played an important role in the works of contemporary progressive Ottoman scholars, both Arabic and Turkish speakers. Patriotism was presented as a key concept for resolving the weakness of the Ottoman state through strengthening the idea of Ottoman solidarity. Ottomanism, which was based on the logic of the reforms, embedded the idea that all citizens are equal, based on their legal affiliation with the state (that is, their citizenship), irrespective of their religious, racial, or social

*al-Kāmila*, ed. Roger M. A. Allen (Cairo: Al-Majlis al-A'la lil-Thaqāfa, 2007), 7–20; *al-Ittiḥād*, October 7, 1880; *al-Ittiḥād*, December 25, 1880.

253 *Al-Baṣṣīr*, December, 1881; *al-Baṣṣīr*, January 26, 1882.

254 *Al-Ahrām*, November 5, 1877.

255 'Abd al-Rahman al-Kawakibi, *Umm al-Qura: aī Ḍabṭṭ Mufāwaḍāt wa-Muqararāt Mu'tamar al-Nahḍa al-Islāmiyya al-Mun'aqid fī Makka Sant 1316* (Egypt: Al-Sayyid al-Furātī, n.d.), 158–176.

background. Progress, al-Bustani and al-Tahtawi assumed, could be achieved through collective cooperation between all compatriots of a diverse society (*abnāʾ al-waṭan*). Al-Tahtawi, following medieval Platonists, equated *al-waṭan* with a body that needs the collective action of all of its organs, without which there would be no progress: Patriotism, he claimed, was the only way to achieve collective prosperity and progress.[256]

The theorization of the word during the 1860s underlined its morphological extension, and new forms stemming from the same root were coined. The first was the noun-adjective *waṭanī*, which at first meant someone who is rooted in a particular homeland, usually used as "native/citizen" as opposed to "foreign." This word suggests an alternative to the common *raʿiyya* (subjects) when referring to the status of individuals in a polity. In the theoretical engagement with redefining communal borders, state, identity, and ruler-ruled relations, *waṭanī* was coined to express the aspect of rights that is derived from the legal affiliation to a certain territory (*waṭan*), as detailed in the next chapter.[257] The word was used in a political context, as in the phrase "rights of a local inhabitant" (*al-ḥuqūq al-latī lil-waṭanī*).[258]

An additional newly coined form was the abstraction *waṭaniyya*. This word entered the political lexicon with two meanings. The earliest was derived from "native country." In his article from 1860, Butrus al-Bustani scarcely uses *waṭaniyya* in his depiction of the "charity that is dedicated for the country" (*al-iḥsānāt al-waṭaniyya*), which refers to the financial support aimed at helping Syria during an economic crisis.[259] The use of *waṭaniyya* in this sense refers to the civil community of the native country. Thus, *waṭaniyyīn* (natives, those who are affiliated with the civil community) is used in the phrases *mutawaẓifūn waṭaniyyūn* (native employers)[260] and *ʿuqalāʾ*

256 Al-Tahtawi, "Kitāb al-Murshid al-Amīn lil-Banāt wal-Banīn," 458.

257 The next chapter extends the discussion of the temporal concept of rights that this word conveyed. See also the discussion that explores the transition of words from denoting the concept of "subject" to that of "citizen" in Arabic: Ayalon, *Language and Change in the Arab Middle East: The Evolution of Modern Political Discourse*, 43–53.

258 For further use of the word *waṭanī*, see al-Tahtawi, "Kitāb al-Murshid al-Amīn lil-Banāt wal-Banīn," 457; *al-Jawāʾib*, June 22, 1875; *al-Ahrām*, October 18, 1878; al-Bustani, "Rusu," *Kitāb Dāʾirat al-Maʿārif* (Beirut: Al-Adabiyya, 1887), 2.

259 Al-Bustani, *Nafīr Sūriyya*, 32.

260 *Al-Ahrām*, September 26, 1878.

*al-waṭaniyyīn* (notable natives),[261] in contrast to *mutawaṭinīn* (settlers) or *ajnabiyyīn* (foreigners).[262]

Under the influence of the state ideology of Ottomanism and the Arabic theorization of patriotism (*ḥamiyya waṭaniyya*,[263] *ghayra waṭaniyya*, *ʾilfa waṭaniyya*),[264] the word acquired an additional layer. The new usage gradually replaced the phrase *ḥubb al-waṭan* with *waṭaniyya*. In a translated 1867 document in *al-Jawāʾib*, al-Shidyaq uses the phrase "*ḥukūma ahliyya ḥasab al-qawāʾid al-waṭaniyya al-jumhūriyya*" to indicate French government run by the inhabitants of France, with a national democratic orientation.[265] The transition in meaning from "native" to "the civil community" (national) overlapped the civic concept of nation. Butrus al-Bustani called the school he established in 1863 "*al-Madrasa al-Waṭaniyya*," the "National School." This was followed by similar phrases such as *ḥukūma waṭaniyya* or *wazāra waṭaniyya* (national government), *maḥākim waṭaniyya* (national courts), *ʿasākir waṭaniyya* (national soldiers), *al-shūra al-waṭaniyya* (national council), *manāfiʿ waṭaniyya* (national benefits), and *ḥuqūq waṭaniyya* (national rights).[266] The components of the new community gained appellations that indicated national solidarity, such as *abnāʾ al-waṭan* or *ahl al-waṭan* (compatriots),[267] and phrases that indicated a new aspect of collective memory derived from national solidarity, such as *ʿīd waṭanī* (national holiday).[268]

The collective solidarity of *waṭaniyya* (patriotism) prior to 1882 developed particular implications; in most cases this concept did not

261 Al-Shidyaq, *Kanz al-Raghāʾib fī Muntakhabāt al-Jawāʾib*, 1877, 5:104.
262 For selected examples, see *al-Ahrām*, October 18, 1878; *al-Baṣṣīr*, October 6, 1881; *al-Baṣṣīr*, December 28, 1882.
263 The phrase used in one of the translated sultanate's declarations of 1874. See al-Shidyaq, *Kanz al-Raghāʾib fī Muntakhabāt al-Jawāʾib*, 1877, 5:265; *al-Ahrām*, December 20, 1876.
264 *Al-Baṣṣīr*, October 27, 1881; *al-Jawāʾib*, August 29, 1882, 1.
265 Al-Shidyaq, *Kanz al-Raghāʾib fī Muntakhabāt al-Jawāʾib*, 1877, 5:108.
266 For selected examples of the use of these phrases, see works published from the 1860s through the 1880s: Rifaʿa Rafiʿ al-Tahtawi, *Muqaddima Waṭaniyya Miṣriyya* (Bulaq: Maṭbaʿat Bulaq, 1866), 2; *Rawḍat al-Madāris* 7, no. 2 (July 1871): 3; al-Shidyaq, *Kanz al-Raghāʾib fī Muntakhabāt al-Jawāʾib*, 1871, 1:176; *al-Ahrām*, December 20, 1876; *Mirʾāt al-Aḥwāl*, March 22, 1877, 2; *al-Jawāʾib*, January 1, 1879, 4; al-Shidyaq, *Kanz al-Raghāʾib fī Muntakhabāt al-Jawāʾib*, 1877, 5:101, 107, 265; *al-Naẓẓārāt al-Miṣriyya*, April 1, 1880; *al-Jawāʾib*, November 29, 1881; *al-Jawāʾib*, August 29, 1882, 1.
267 *Birjīs Barīs*, November 23, 1859; *al-Naḥla*, May 11, 1870, 11.
268 *Al-Baṣṣīr*, July 28, 1881.

include the idea of national sovereignty, which made it distinctly different from and less political than the ideology of nationalism that spread across Europe during that era. Egyptian and Syrian patriotism evolved in correlation with larger circles of identification such as Ottoman (indicated by Ottomanism, *al-ghayra al-waṭaniyya al-ʿUthmāniyya, umma ʿUthmāniyya*),[269] and "Levantine" or "Eastern" identities (*al-umma al-Sharqiyya, Sharqiyyīn, ahāli al-mashriq*),[270] which evolved during and after the 1850s in the context of the intensified influence of the West.

A variety of forms of solidarity evolved by 1882. Most of these ideas were constructed against the background of the Ottoman Empire's weakness and as a quest to strengthen the solidarity and unity of its social components. In the Arabic-speaking provinces, nationalism – in its Western variants that ascribe political sovereignty to civic or ethno-cultural communities – gained very few equivalent words. Instead, the idea of patriotism that addresses social solidarity, shared memory, and legal affiliation had a greater impact on the realm of words. In these transitions of ideas, freedom of national groups within the empire was very rarely articulated. Because of the frequent inconsistency in the use of *waṭaniyya* and *jinsiyya* for the idea of sovereignty, the use of freedom with these words did not necessarily indicate national independence or liberation. The demand for freedom of geographical entities or groups in Arabic primarily implied a demand for autonomy under the central authority of the Ottomans. That is what phrases like "make Lebanon free" (*yakūn Lubnān ḥurran*), used in the 1870s, meant: the opportunity to manage Mount Lebanon as an autonomous area and not as an independent political entity.[271] The political discourse rarely employed the word *ḥurriyya* in the internal national context of the Ottoman Empire.

[269] Al-Shidyaq, *Kanz al-Raghāʾib fī Muntakhabāt al-Jawāʾib*, 1877, 5:291; *al-Ahrām*, March 4, 1880.

[270] In an article Muhammad ʿAbdu published in 1877, he wrote: "You Easterners (*yā maʿshar al-sharqiyyīn*). You are the sons of one homeland . . . brothers that were born from the same mother." For other forms of Easterners or Levantines, see July 2, 1859; *Birjīs Barīs*, February 27, 1861; *al-Naḥla*, November 5, 1870, 10; *al-Jawāʾib*, November 23, 1876, 4; *al-Ahrām*, February 2, 1877; *al-Jinān* 2 (1881): 33–35.

[271] ʿAqiqi, *Thawra wa-Fitna fī Lubnān: Ṣafḥa Majhūla min Tārīkh al-Jabal min 1841 ila 1873*, 153.

With the sophistication in both the collective and the individual language, the concept of freedom underwent, during and after the 1860s, a transition from being a political idea to becoming stabilized as a main principle or signifier for a comprehensive ideology. The next chapter probes the ideological meaning of freedom in the context of the political thought that systematically developed between 1860 and 1882.

# 4 *The Construction of Modern Ideologies in Arabic, 1860–1882*

## From the Ideas of Freedom to the Ideologies of Freedom

During the second half of the nineteenth century, Arabic-speaking scholars continued to employ al-Tahtawi's general translation of the "proponents of freedom" to refer to political streams in western Europe. With the launch of the private Arabic press, the semantic field of "the proponents of freedom" extended to include additional ideological orientations, going beyond al-Tahtawi's constitutional and republican meanings. The private press played a major role in transferring ideas from more distant spheres – those outside of the Ottoman Empire – to within the Ottoman territories. This medium provided a more efficient alternative to the genre of journey literature for exposing the region to European political traditions. Utilization of modern methods of communication such as the telegraph and the postal system made the private press most effective in connecting Arabic-speaking provinces with the historical events taking place outside the borders of the empire. The telegraph connected the Ottoman territories with western Europe and transmitted news on a nearly real-time basis, while the postal system was highly utilized for distributing newspapers throughout the vast territories of the empire.

The "proponents of freedom" – signified by *ahl al-ḥurriyya* (supporters of freedom), *ahl ḥurriyyat al-afkār* (free thinkers), *madhhab al-ḥurriyya* (school of freedom), and *ḥizb al-ḥurriyya* (group of the proponents of freedom)[1] – expanded to signify all libertarian political streams, including socialists, anarchists, liberals, republicans, radicals, and revolutionists. It loosely comprised all the proponents of the idea of progress. This semantic extension took place against the

[1] For selected examples of the use of these phrases as equivalent to "libertarians," see *al-Bashīr*, March 4, 1871, 220; *al-Bashīr*, May 13, 1871, 318; *al-Bashīr*, November 2, 1872; *al-Bashīr*, November 28, 1873; *al-Bashīr*, June 28, 1878; *al-Baṣṣīr*, July 7, 1881; *al-Bashīr*, February 8, 1889.

background of the deep interest Arabic newspapers had in political events that went beyond the borders of France and western Europe to other countries and continents, such as Russia and North America. Besides the general appellation "proponents of freedom," Arabic formulated, from the end of the 1850s onward, the coinage of new idioms denoting specific ideologies.

The transition from "proponents of freedom" to words signifying ideologies derived from problematizing, criticizing, and theorizing freedom took place against the background of a series of events that occurred in the 1860s and the beginning of the 1870s. During these two decades political words that had emerged or were reshaped in Arabic between 1820 and 1860 acquired much more stabilized structures. The employment of "freedom" in a context that went beyond intellectual activity and integrated other concepts such as "reason," "equality," "progress," and "patriotism" with political activity increased in frequency. The vague neologism *bulītīqa* or *bulītīka* remained in use along with *siyāsa* during the 1870s, but its ambiguous meaning was gradually replaced by more comprehensible phrases.[2] The increasing use and the inflation in meaning of "politics" were followed by the emergence of systematic modern political thought in Arabic from the 1860s onward.

"Politics" became widely recognized as a key concept for progress, and the relation between *ʿaql*, *tamaddun*, *taqaddum*, *ḥurriyya*, *musāwā*, *waṭaniyya*, and *siyāsa* became subject to theoretical construction. Owing to this interaction, the temporal meaning of "politics" implied a strong emphasis on constant change. Inspired by the idea of progress, Salim al-Bustani wrote in 1873 that "the best politics is the politics that suits the state of the subjects because moods of nations change constantly: what fits today might not be relevant tomorrow."[3] The gap between the medieval use of *siyāsa* (as management or statecraft) and the modern concept became much more significant because of its association with the vision of progress, civilization, and prosperity. *Siyāsa* was perceived as a method for reorganizing the relations between

[2] For selected examples, see "political interests," which was translated to incomprehensible phrases such as "*ṣawaliḥ al-bulitīkiyya*." Additionally, see al-Shidyaq's translation of "political treaty of the state" as *muʿāhadāt al-dawla al-ʿuliyya al-bulitīqiyya*: *Birjīs Barīs*, February 3, 1863; *al-Jawāʾib*, February 20, 1878, 7; al-Shidyaq, *Kanz al-Raghāʾib fī Muntakhabāt al-Jawāʾib*, 1877, 5:207.

[3] *Al-Jinān* 18 (1873): 613.

societies on the basis of tolerance, both inside and outside the Ottoman Empire. That is how the French Arabic-language newspaper *al-Baṣṣir* defined the concept: It is a method for conducting the interests of various communities having different traditions and norms. This conception, the newspaper states, is fundamentally different from the common negative meaning of *siyāsa*: "plots that intend to harm."[4] True politics aims to facilitate the promotion of common interests that improve the common good. This value is necessarily based on reason and experience because it serves to benefit all individuals in a society, and it is necessarily subject to change all the time. True politics is a fundamental cornerstone for progress in all fields, including building civilization.[5]

During these decades the concept of politics was integrated into the paradigm of progress and conceived of as a rational method for solving national conflicts, planning the future of societies, and achieving tolerance, prosperity, and international peace. Salim Bakhus, a contemporary Syrian Lebanese scholar who lived in Egypt, captured the uniqueness of the temporal meaning of politics: "[States nowadays, in a way that differs from the past] maintain identical policies that have similar aims, which are to bring the uncivilized nations into the circle of civilization and to intensify the [values] of civilization among the civilized nations. Politics aims to qualify the people [*jamāhīr*] for freedom, demonstrating that they are humanists, and not savages, and that their acts are motivated by reason and recognition, and not by natural instincts."[6] This comprehensive outlook comprises to a large extent the function of "politics" during this period: "Politics" was a method for rationalizing human relations based on an optimistic vision of progress.[7]

The practical meaning of politics, which was previously limited only to those who possessed political authority, extended to include the public. Needless to say, the evolving discourse on politics was associated mainly with men, not women.[8] With politics the theme of governance becomes a thinkable subject that is exposed to controversy and

[4] *Al-Baṣṣīr*, May 26, 1881. [5] Ibid.
[6] *Al-I'lām*, January 28, 1885, 1. [7] Ibid.
[8] For more details about the discourse on women's rights in Greater Syria in the second half of the nineteenth century, see Fruma Zachs and Sharon Halevi, *Gendering Culture in Greater Syria: Intellectuals and Ideology in the Late Ottoman Period* (London: I. B. Tauris, 2015), 16–41.

criticism. In the Ottoman Empire "politics" emerged against the background of the Young Turks' activity and the inauguration of reform-oriented state policies that yielded the first Ottoman constitution and parliament. In addition to the social function that religious scholars filled, the emergence of this space was accompanied socially by the creation of two new professionals: the journalist and the politician. Al-Shidyaq, who was an eyewitness in Istanbul during the announcement of the constitution of 1876, elaborates the emergence of two camps that were defined politically:

> When the news about the state's attempt to constitute a parliament erupted, many [scholars and civil servants] in Istanbul expressed their opinions on this important issue. There were those who said that establishing parliament contradicts the pure shariʿa, and there were those who said that shariʿa imposes a government based on consultation [*ḥukūma shūriyya*] and not on autocratic rule [*ḥukūma istibdādiyya*]. That is why the people of Istanbul divided into two opposing camps, and it is not a secret that this division embedded a harmful situation for the state. While one camp consisted of [religious] students [*ṭalabat al-ʿilm*] opposed to the establishment of the council, the other requested that we publish in *al-Jawāʾib* the introduction of *aqwam al-masālik* [Khayr al-Din al-Tunisi's book].[9]

This description conveys the temporal political controversy at the center of the empire: On one side were conservative religious scholars and on the other were progressive and institutional scholars such as Khayr al-Din al-Tunisi and al-Shidyaq. Against this background, and as part of the state's attempt to recruit supporters for the constitution, al-Shidyaq serialized the introduction to al-Tunisi's book in his *al-Jawāʾib*,[10] later distributing it among his readers in pamphlet form for free.[11] The political nature of the division between the two camps, however, was not convincing to all scholars. Another contemporary, Rizq Allah Hassun, the most prominent journalist to oppose the Ottomans during the 1870s, interpreted the new political sphere by indicating the conflict was between two groups: supporters of the constitution (*ḥizb yaqūm bi-nuṣrat al-dustūr*) and those who opposed it and argued that it was against religion. Hassun contended that the

[9] *Al-Jawāʾib*, July 12, 1876, 4.
[10] The first part was published in *al-Jawāʾib*, July 19, 1876, 6.
[11] *Al-Jawāʾib*, July 12, 1876, 4.

difference between the two groups was not political and was not concerned with any kind of political opposition. According to him it was related to competition between those who had government positions and those who did not.[12]

The morphological stabilization and dissemination of *siyāsa* in the public discourse conjoined with the invention of temporal words portraying the inflated political sphere: Leftist politicians in Europe were referred to as *aṣḥāb al-shamāl* and *ahl al-yasār* (proponents of the left) or, in less political terms, *ḥizb muḍād lil-dawla* (group that opposes the state). Additional political appellations coined to distinguish between the two political orientations were *siyāsa muḥāfiẓa* and *siyāsa ḥurra* (conservative and liberal politics).[13] These developments in the political terminology gradually drew the demarcation of political ideas by using ideological terms, a development that was accompanied by the redefinition of "proponents of freedom," using terms that made a clear distinction between liberals and radicals, socialists and nihilists. These changes came to the fore in journalism during the 1870s. *Al-Bashīr*, the conservative Jesuit organ, published an article in 1871 that differentiates between the "proponents of freedom" and *ahl al-ishtirāk* (an archaic term for "socialists").[14] In much the same way, *al-Jinān* distinguished between the "proponents of freedom" in France – which included the republicans "that request freedom in stages" – and the revolutionary leftist radicals (*al-ḥizb al-aḥmar*).[15]

Beginning in the 1860s the word "freedom" became an attractive slogan, and different publications, both conservative and progressive newspapers and periodicals, used "*ḥurriyya*" in their mottos in an attempt to domesticate its meaning. The conservative *al-Bashīr* used the word in the motto on its opening page: "Then you will know the truth, and the truth will set you free (John 8:32)." *Al-Naẓẓarat al-Miṣriyya* (1879–1880), published in Paris by Abu Nazzara (Yaʿqub Sannuʿ) – a journalist supportive of Prince Halim Pasha and opposed to Khedive Ismaʾil (who ruled between 1863 and 1879) and his successor Tawfiq (1879–1892) – chose, as the motto appearing on its first

[12] *Mirʾāt al-Aḥwāl*, March 22, 1877; *Mirʾāt al-Aḥwāl*, June 4, 1877.
[13] For selected examples, see *al-Jawāʾib*, June 15, 1875; *al-Bashīr*, October 26, 1872; *al-Jawāʾib*, November 8, 1881, 3.
[14] For selected examples, see *al-Bashīr*, September 2, 1871, 478–480; *al-Bashīr*, April 20, 1872.
[15] *Al-Jinān* 2 (1871): 35.

page, words close to those of the French Revolution: "Viva Equality, Fraternity, and Liberty." Adib Ishaq's newspaper, *Miṣr al-Qāhira*, published in Paris in 1879, also adopted the slogan of the French Revolution.[16] The Arabic-speaking Freemasons followed the trend of using the French revolutionary slogan and inserted *ḥurriyya* into their formal name in Arabic (*madhhab al-bināyya al-ḥurra*), using the word as a subject of identification (*al-massūni al-ḥurr*).[17] The identification with freedom as a political slogan evolved further with its use as a subject of journalistic political identification. Khalil Ghanim portrayed his newspaper *al-Baṣṣir* as a "free newspaper" (*ṣaḥīfa ḥurra*),[18] promoting ideas such as constitutionalism and striving to spread the political values of the "free countries" (*bilād ḥurra*) in the territories of the Ottoman Empire.[19] *Al-Ittiḥād*, a weekly newspaper, located itself politically as "*jarīida ḥurra*" (free newspaper). Published in Paris, it called on the Muslims to revolt against the "Turkish king" who reigned as an autocrat and took Muslims as his slaves.[20] The transition from the general designation of "proponents of freedom" to denoting particular, systematic ideologies during the 1860s and 1870s was accompanied by acquaintance with modern politics and with local attempts to produce interpretations of freedom that corresponded with the particular needs of the Ottoman societies.

## From "Proponents of Freedom" to Socialism, Communism, and Anarchism

The terms "socialist" and "socialism" apparently first appeared in Italian in 1803, but it was not until 1827 that they came to designate a cooperative doctrine. The terms were widely distributed after the French Saint-Simonians adopted *socialisme* to refer to their philosophy during the 1830s.[21] Arabic was not far behind in adopting these

[16] Filib Tarrazi, *Ta'rīkh al-Ṣiḥāfa al-'Arabiyya*, vol. 2 (Beirut: Al-Maṭba'a al-Adabiyya, 1914), 257–258.
[17] For the use of these words, see one of the Freemasons' formal publications in Egypt: *Al-Laṭā'if* 1, no. 6 (1891): 3, 9.
[18] *Al-Baṣṣīr*, December 15, 1881.
[19] *Al-Baṣṣīr*, August 25, 1881; *al-Baṣṣīr*, December 22, 1881; *al-Baṣṣīr*, February 9, 1882.
[20] *Al-Ittiḥād*, December 25, 1880; *al-Ittiḥād*, October 7, 1880.
[21] George Esenwein, "Socialism," *New Dictionary of the History of Ideas* (Detroit, MI: Charles Scribner's Sons, 2005), 2227–2228.

changes, and during the same decade al-Tahtawi, in one of his early translations from French, used the phrase *ashghāluhum mushtaraka* to mean the cooperative, social, and economic lifestyle of a Christian sect in North America.[22]

The 1830s saw the idea of commonly held property appearing in translations,[23] and early Saint-Simonian socialists reached prominent positions in Muhammad ʿAli's administration during the same decade.[24] Despite this direct encounter, a special term for socialism was coined in Arabic only few decades later, apparently by borrowing from Turkish, which had a word for socialism by the 1840s. In 1845, the Governor of Izmir showed one of his visitors a document about a "socialist proclamation" published in Paris, and the term later coined in Turkish was *ishtirāk-i emwāl* (sharing property).[25]

Intensified leftist political activity following the institution of the International Workingmen's Association (often referred to as the First International) in London in 1864 attracted limited interest from Arabic-speaking journalists, but the most significant events that drew their attention to the term were the activities of the Paris Commune that ruled Paris from March 18 until May 28, 1871. After the Paris Commune, use of the terms *madhhab al-ḥurriyya* (school of freedom) and *ahl al-ḥurriyya* (supporters of freedom) underwent fundamental change. The enormous interest of Arabic-speaking journalists in the activity of leftist groups in Europe and Russia, primarily socialists, communists, and anarchists, revealed the complexity of the political use to which the general appellation *madhhab al-ḥurriyya* was put. This term, which signified all the proponents of freedom, started to appear less frequently: specific ideological idioms came into favor, and new words were coined. Words such as *sūsiālizm*, *jamʿiyyat al-ṣūsiālist*, *al-ṣūshiālist*, *al-sūsiālist*, *al-qāʾilīn bil-ishtirāk*, *ahl al-ishtirāk*, *al-ishtirākiyyīn* (socialists); *kumūn*, *kumūnist*, *madhhab al-musāwā*, *fawḍa* (commune, communists); and *nīhilist*, *ʿadamiyyūn*, *fawḍa*

22 Depping, *Kitāb Qalāʾid al-Mafākhir fī Gharīb ʿAwāʾid al-Awāʾil wal-Awākhir*, 110.

23 See also Laertius, *Mukhtaṣar Tarjamāt Mashāhīr Qudamāʾ al-Falāsifa*, 14–15.

24 For the Saint-Simonian impact on Egypt, see Pamela Pilbeam, *Saint-Simonians in Nineteenth-Century France* (New York: Palgrave Macmillan, 2014), 104–130.

25 Hence *ishtirakji* (socialist) and *ishtiraki* (socialistic). The term was replaced later by *sosyalist*. Wahba, "The Meaning of Ishtirakiyah," 44; Lewis, *Political Words and Ideas in Islam*, 141.

(nihilists and anarchists) were in widespread use in newspapers during the 1870s.[26]

In 1871 the Catholic *al-Bashīr* distinguished between *madhhab al-ḥurriyya*, which had transformed into a term more identified with liberalism, and *ahl al-ishtirāk*. The newspaper explained that the first concept focuses on the subject of freedom, which included freedom of the press, the right to vote, freedom from religion, and freedom of education (secular education), while the second indicated materialism or deism (*māddiyya, dahriyya*), which advocated radical republicanism.[27] This insight by *al-Bashīr* was relatively early compared to famous newspapers that emphasized the ambiguity of these words and presented their content in confused terms. *Al-Jawāʾib* reported on the Parisian events warily and promised its readers to investigate the political ideas of the Commune: "We are making great effort to trace the Commune's situation in Paris and to reveal its aims, its ideas, structure, and the consequences of its strange actions and forbidden modes."[28] The newspaper reported that this group, which attempted to take advantage of the French crisis during the German invasion of France, succeeded in convincing Parisians that the Commune was the true representative of the republic.[29] Use of the signifiers of socialism was in vogue at the beginning of the 1870s, but it was not always accurate, and the difference between the various leftist ideologies was not consistently recognized. Thus, for instance, al-Shidyaq contends in one of his articles in 1875 that "I consider nihilists all those who can work and instead choose to beg. These groups are known in Europe as communists."[30] In the same spirit he argues, about two years later, that the Russian nihilists, who were presented as radicals in French,

[26] *Fawḍa* (anarchy, disorder) was used to refer to communists and anarchists. For selected examples, see *al-Bashīr*, April 22, 1871; *al-Bashīr*, June 10, 1871; *al-Bashīr*, September 2, 1871, 478–480; *al-Bashīr*, April 20, 1872; *al-Ahrām*, February 10, 1877; *al-Ahrām*, September 26, 1878; *al-Ahrām*, October 18, 1878; *al-Jawāʾib*, January 1, 1879, 4; *al-Ahrām*, May 15, 1879; *al-Ahrām*, February 26, 1880.

[27] *Al-Bashīr*, September 2, 1871, 478–480; *al-Bashīr*, April, 20, 1872.

[28] In Arabic: "*afʿāl gharība wal-aṭwār al-munkara*." The article was published in *al-Jawāʾib* in May 1871. See al-Shidyaq, *Kanz al-Raghāʾib fī Muntakhabāt al-Jawāʾib*, 1873, 2:221.

[29] Ibid.

[30] In Arabic: "*Ibaḥiyyīn al-maʿrufīn ʿind al-ifranj bil-kumūnist*." See *al-Jawāʾib*, August 12, 1875, 1.

rebelled against Russian absolutism and demanded freedom.[31] These political words were frequently used interchangeably to refer to the same ideology. In 1878 al-Shidyaq wrote an article in which he argues, commenting on internal Russian politics, that the adjective "socialist" is synonymous with nihilist (*ishtirākiyyūn hum al-nīhlist*).[32] He goes on to say that this same group is termed "socialist" (*sūsiālist*) in Germany and "communist" (*kumūnist*) in France, without outlining any differences.[33] In subsequent articles he replaces his previous use of the word *ishtirākiyya* with *nīhlist*, explaining to his readers that "one of my friends told me that nihilists are not like the communists [*kumūnist*], which indicates socialists who call for the poor to share in the property of the rich [*ishtirāk al-fuqarā' fī amwāl al-aghniyyā'*], but they [the nihilists] demand an elected government [*ḥukūma shūriyya*] that is not authoritarian [*istibdādiyya*]."[34] In light of this distinction, the author concludes that as opposed to the misled socialists who view wealthy people as their enemies, the anarchist's demands are reasonable.[35] The interchangeable use of terms that captured ideas in very general ways without preserving the nuances between them occurred frequently during the 1870s in the Arabic discourse on socialism.[36]

The difficulties in comprehending the content of these neologisms and translated terms reflect not only the state of Arab scholarship, which viewed socialist activity from afar, but also the protean state of socialist doctrine during that time. Indeed, all organizations identified as socialist stressed the significance of the economic system in human behavior and considered material circumstances to be the key for understanding human society. Meanwhile, however, mid-nineteenth-century European socialism existed in many variations. Socialist groups such as the "utopian socialists" (which consisted of three main groups – Saint-Simonians and Fourierists in France and Owenites in Great Britain) and the later revolutionary communists, followers of Karl Marx, had different ideological orientations. While the first group evolved through the concept of reform, the Marxists

31 *Al-Jawā'ib*, January 10, 1877, 1.
32 Al-Shidyaq probably referred in his comments to the nihilist-socialist movement inspired by Nikolai Chernyshevsky, who incorporated nihilism with socialism after the early breakdown of anarchist actions in Russia during and after the 1860s.
33 *Al-Jawā'ib*, August 26, 1878. 34 *Al-Jawā'ib*, October 24, 1878, 4.
35 Ibid. 36 *Al-Jawā'ib*, August 26, 1878; *al-Jawā'ib*, April 17, 1883.

rejected the idea of reform and adopted a revolutionary stance that strove for the complete destruction of the capitalist order and the constitution of a socialist state.[37]

Morphologically, in Europe of the 1830s, the term "socialism" had strong connotations of economic and social rights. It was used to distinguish between those groups emphasizing the promotion of social and collective rights and those stressing the subject of an individualist order (especially liberals, the proponents of laissez faire). In the political arena socialism referred to collective regulation of public affairs on a cooperative basis, stressing the quest for the equitable distribution of wealth. This theoretical position put socialists in conflict with liberals and liberalism, the predominant ideology of Europe in the nineteenth century. Marxism attained another significant level in its evolution with the 1848 revolutions, when Karl Marx and Friedrich Engels published their Communist Manifesto using the term "communism" and not "socialism." "Communism," which came into more frequent use during the 1870s and embedded a militant connotation that "socialism" did not have, was used to distinguish Marx's "scientific socialism" from the previous socialist theories.[38]

In the Arabic of the 1870s, socialism (*sūsiālizm*, *sūsiālism*, *ishtirākiyya*) was interpreted as "sharing of property."[39] The failure of the Commune of Paris, the escape of some of its leaders to London, and the involvement of Karl Marx in their activity were known to Arabic readers.[40] News about the socialists in Italy, their attempt to assassinate the king, and their violent acts in Russia, Germany, Austria, Spain, Britain, and Denmark routinely appeared in Arabic newspapers.[41] During this decade the leftist parties started to emerge throughout Europe at a time when the most dominant socialist groups were Marxist. In France, Germany, Belgium, and other places where large communities

[37] Esenwein, "Socialism," 2228. [38] Ibid.

[39] In Arabic "*ishtirāk fī al-amwāl*," and less frequently *ishtirākiyya*, means common or collective, as in *ḥurriyya ishtirākiyya* (collective freedom). See *al-Bashīr*, April 22, 1871, 304; *al-Jinān* 8 (1871): 222; *al-Ahrām*, February 12, 1881.

[40] See an article in *al-Jawāʾib* that reported about Karl Marx's impact on the Commune's decisions to assassinate one of the sons of Emperor Napoleon III. The article was published in 1873: Al-Shidyaq, *Kanz al-Raghāʾib fī Muntakhabāt al-Jawāʾib*, 1877, 5:198–199.

[41] For selected reports covering all these countries, see *al-Jawāʾib*, December 11, 1878, 4, 81; *al-Jawāʾib*, January 1, 1879, 4.

of industrial workers existed, communism flourished.[42] The political terminology that formulated the leftist discourse in Europe, which revolved around the values of social justice and the interests of the working class, evolved in Arabic during the same decade. Words such as *intirnāsyunāl* were borrowed to show the influence of the International Workingmen's Association.[43] Additional leftist terms such as *al-thawra al-kuzmbulīṭ* (cosmopolitan revolution), indicating the socialist utopia of universalism,[44] *jam'iyya mutashārika fī al-'amal wal-naf'*, indicating labor unions,[45] and *burjwāzī* (bourgeoisie), which referred to the class struggle between the bourgeoisie and the proletariat, were also borrowed from French.[46]

Reports translated into Arabic in the mid-1870s contained a great deal of information about the political and social ideas of these groups – ideas that went beyond the call for the poor to have a share in the property of the rich (*al-qa'ilīn bil-ishtirāk*). In a summarized report covering the convention of the German followers of Ferdinand Lassalle and Karl Marx, *al-Jawā'ib* transmits their demands regarding the following: their opposition to the workers' low salaries, the need to cancel privileged political rights, the need to institute labor unions with the assistance of the state and under the leadership of the democratic workers, the establishment of a law for equal voting rights, and free and equal education for all citizens, as well as other demands related to social justice. Al-Shidyaq comments that their demands are vague to him, especially the demand for opposition to the low wages that workers received. He concludes with the criticism that their demands have no real content.[47]

42 Esenwein, "Socialism," 2230.

43 *Al-Bashīr* elaborated that the aim of the First International was to spread revolution all over the world and to establish an international republic that fused all nations (*qabā'il*) under one regime. *Al-Jinān* concluded that this organization consisted of workers in manufacturing and agriculture, and its main goal was to obtain social rights from the wealthy, who were often not equitable managers. See *al-Bashīr*, April 22,1871, 301; *al-Bashīr*, July 10, 1871, 361; *al-Jinān* 16 (1871): 541–543.

44 *Al-Bashīr*, May 13, 1871; *al-Bashīr*, May 27, 1871.

45 *Al-Jawā'ib*, June 23, 1875, 3–4.

46 "Bourgeois" was interpreted as "those who are not aristocrats and not from the riff raff, which means they are the middle class [*ahl al-rutba al-wusṭa* and *ahl al-ḥāla al-wusṭa*]." See *al-Bashīr*, June 3, 1871; *al-Bashīr*, June 10, 1871; *al-Bashīr*, November 28, 1873.

47 *Al-Jawā'ib*, July 23, 1875, 3–4.

At the end of the 1870s, translated articles from European newspapers elaborated the demands of the socialist movements, especially those related to Russia, the Ottomans' greatest opponent. Anarchists had greater influence in Russia and Spain than did the communists, and their activities attracted much attention in the Arabic-language press. Anarchism was one of the most significant political movements within nineteenth-century socialism, and its followers sustained prolific debates with Marxists that resulted in continuous divisions within the First (1864–1876) and Second Internationals (1889–1914). Despite the differences between the variants of anarchism, these groups were united in their opposition to Marxism. The intellectual controversy between anarchists and Marxists revolved around the role of the state: The Marxists considered it to be a most vital vehicle for leading society toward full communism, while anarchists rejected this idea, arguing that the state is oppressive, and therefore it should not fill any function. The anarchists believed that society should overturn capitalism by developing working-class institutions and by continuous struggle against the oppression by the middle classes. Above all Marxism was opposed to their concept of liberty. Russian anarchist Mikhail Bakunin elaborated this in his famous declaration that communism "is the negation of liberty."[48]

Some of these ideological controversies were known in Arabic. Translated articles in *al-Jawāʾib* elaborated the history of anarchism, conveying anarchist proclamations to its readers. A quotation from one of the Russian anarchists emphasized their particular demands in a comparison with the other "supporters of freedom" (*ahl al-ḥurriyya*): "We don't seek any more constitutional regulations. They are not relevant to our current situation. What we need now is justice and equality for all. As long as we cannot achieve this aim, we will turn our powers to kill the tsar and his close circle."[49] By the end of the 1870s, the activity of the socialists was extensively covered, including their ideas, strikes, and their revolutionary actions and violent activities.[50]

The 1880s witnessed further concern regarding the revolutionary activity that gained so much power across Europe. The assassination of Russian Tsar Alexander II in 1881 by radical leftists drew a great

48 Esenwein, "Socialism," 2230. 49 *Al-Jawāʾib*, May 22, 1879, 4.
50 For selected reports and criticism, see ibid.; *al-Jawāʾib*, May 21, 1879, 3; *al-Jawāʾib*, June 26, 1879, 41; *al-Bashīr*, January 31, 1879.

deal of interest in the Arab press. About a year later, *al-Ahrām* translated the demands the anarchists made of the Russian government and presented Bakunin's anarchist principles, transmitting modern revolutionary methods of activism into Arabic. After the assassination the newspaper published a translated socialist proclamation, presenting to its readers the "hostility" of this group.[51]

The most up-to-date reports about the ideological orientations and differences between these groups were published in Arabic by the positivist periodical *al-Muqtaṭaf*. The socialists and the communists, on the one hand, strove for liberty through equality and cooperation between human beings. The anarchists, on the other hand, were the most popular and the most violent in their actions. They, unlike the socialists and the communists, did not have any political aims, and they did not present any plans for their postrevolutionary future. They wished to destroy the unjust system, not merely reform it, including religion, law, state, and values. *Al-Muqtaṭaf* elaborates their ideology based on their idioms: Because of their dissatisfaction with the current situation and because they do not propose an alternative, they are called nihilists (*ʿadamiyyūn*). They believe in absolute freedom for individuals, a principle that explains their endless attempts to destroy, with no further concern for the construction of any alternative. They leave this question to the "enlightened ages" that will be liberated from the chains of tradition (*taqlīd*). The article has quotations from a famous speech made by Bakunin in which he attacked the idea of God ("the first lie"), contending that it contradicts freedom, the idea of rights ("the second lie"), which was created by the powerful to protect their power, and the socialists, arguing that they are a danger to individual freedom because they believe that the state should control all the capital.[52]

The philosophical ideas of communism and anarchism had a very marginal impact on prominent Arabic-speaking journalists, who hardly engaged in any controversies related to these political streams.[53] Most of the famous scholars condemned and rejected the revolutionary

[51] In addition to the indicated newspaper articles, see Adib Ishaq's 1881 publications, which were collected in: Adib Ishaq, *Adīb Isḥāq: Al-Kitābāt al-Siyāsiyya wal-Ijtimāʿiyya*, ed. Naji ʿAlush (Beirut: Dār al-Ṭalīʿa, 1978), 147–152; *al-Jawāʾib*, April 20, 1881, 45; *al-Ahrām*, April 29, 1880; *al-Ahrām*, May 13, 1881; *al-Ahrām*, April 8, 1880.

[52] *Al-Muqtaṭaf* 10, no. 4 (1879): 289–292.

[53] There was marked early controversy between *al-Bashīr* and *al-Jinān* on the subject of the Communes of 1789 and 1871. *Al-Jinān* argued that the first

quests of the radical left, criticizing their social and metaphysical materialist and libertarian philosophies. Salim al-Bustani attacked the ideas of the Paris Commune, referring to its members as "riffraff" (*awbāsh al-kumūn*). He condemned their revolutionary acts and argued that they struggled against legitimate government that represented the people.[54] Faris al-Shidyaq portrayed them as "a collection of evil and corrupted people,"[55] and Bishara and Salim Taqla, the founders and editors of *al-Ahrām*, wrote expressing similar hostility.[56] Adib Ishaq also criticized their radicalism and their distorted conception of ethics and liberty, arguing that they were the leftist version of despotism.[57] Even positivists such as Yaʿqub Saruf and Faris Nimir, *al-Muqtaṭaf*'s editors, dedicated an article titled "The Corruption of Socialists" to refuting their principle of social equality. In this article they contend that the differences between human beings are part of their nature, and they suggest adopting policies that would reduce the economic gap between classes.[58] These reforms, they argue, guarantee stability and refutation of the socialist claims.[59] Adherents of socialism appeared

Commune and the French Revolution were the reason that France transitioned from being a weak monarchy to becoming a powerful state. *Al-Jinān* compares the two Communes and concludes that the last one is a failure and that there is no relation between the two events except in name. On the other hand, *al-Bashīr* argues that both Communes are the outcome of revolution, and both caused destruction. *Al-Bashīr* claims that the Commune is an outcome of Masonic ideas and calls for secularizing education, marriage, and social services. For further details, see *al-Bashīr*, May 27, 1871, 337–341; *al-Bashīr*, July 3, 1871, 347–350; *al-Jinān* 10 (1871); *al-Bashīr*, June 10, 1871, 360; *al-Bashīr*, June 23, 1871, 378.

54 *Al-Jinān* 10 (1871); *al-Jinān* 13 (1871): 429–431. See his negative representation of the character of the socialist in some episodes of his novel *Samiyya*, published serially in *al-Jinān* 13 (1882): 410–415; *al-Jinān* 14 (1882): 442–447; *al-Jinān* 15 (1882): 474–479; *al-Jinān* 16 (1882): 506–511.

55 *Al-Jawāʾib*, May 22, 1879, 4; *al-Jawāʾib*, May 21, 1879, 3; *al-Jawāʾib*, June 26, 1879, 4; al-Shidyaq, *Kanz al-Raghāʾib fī Muntakhabāt al-Jawāʾib*, 1873, 2:224.

56 *Al-Ahrām*, May 13, 1881.

57 Ishaq, *Adīb Ishāq: Al-Kitābāt al-Siyāsiyya wal-Ijtimāʿiyya*, 147–152.

58 Despite the broad criticism of leftist ideas, social and political values that were generally identified with leftist discourse, such as social justice, workers' rights, international solidarity, mass education, and anticlericalism, took a central place in late nineteenth-century thought. For extensive discussion on the establishment of global networks that fostered the distribution of radical ideas, see Khuri-Makdisi, *The Eastern Mediterranean and the Making of Global Radicalism, 1860–1914*, 15–34.

59 The Tunisian newspaper *al-Rāʾid* also referred to the actions of socialists using the word *ifsād* – "corrupting" (see the quotation in *al-Jawāʾib*). In addition to

in the 1880s – among them Shibli Shumail, who was attracted to the ideas of socialism from the standpoint of his interest in positivist and scientific social theories. His most influential work during the 1880s was his translation of Ludwig Buchner's *Kraft und Stoff* in 1884,[60] which was followed a few years later by his public advocacy of social Darwinism.[61]

The attacks of communists and anarchists on the Catholic Church and on the idea of religion in general had the greatest impact on Arabic-speaking scholars. These political organizations were perceived as *ibāḥiyya* (libertinism), referring to their revolutionary positions against tradition and religion.[62] Manifestations of scorning religion and its rules had reached the public space in Syria, and an intellectual trend of anticlericalism became evident among Catholic intellectuals.[63] In 1878 *al-Jawā'ib* reported that "defamation of religion" and drinking alcohol in public had become very prominent in Syria, and local government enacted special regulations to prevent these actions in public.[64]

The prominent voices against positivist and materialist political and social philosophies came from conservative religious scholars, first from Catholics and afterward from Muslims. The most crucial attack on socialist ideas in general came from the editors of *al-Bashīr* during the 1870s. The clerics Yuhanna Blu, Yusif Ruz, Filibus Kush, Lewis Abuji, and Jirmanus Drubrtulah had consistently attacked the materialism of these groups. *Al-ishtirākiyūn* (the socialists), *al-Bashīr* stated, are the absolute contradiction of the creed of the church. They are

the editorial articles attacking socialism in general, *al-Ahrām* published articles by other writers criticizing the "barbarism" of the anarchists. See *al-Jawā'ib*, September 27, 1876; *al-Muqtaṭaf* 10, no. 4 (1879): 289–292; *al-Ahrām*, April 9, 1881; *al-Muqtaṭaf* 6, no. 14 (1890): 361–364.

60 Shibli Shumail, *Kitāb Falsafat al-Nushū' wal-Irtiqā'* (Cairo: Maṭba'at al-Muqtaṭaf, 1910), 63–224.

61 For more details about the thought of Shumail, see Reid, "The Syrian Christians and Early Socialism in the Arab World," 183–185.

62 For selected reports about their violence against churches, see al-Shidyaq, *Kanz al-Raghā'ib fī Muntakhabāt al-Jawā'ib*, 1873, 2:222–224; *al-Jawā'ib*, August 23, 1876, 2.

63 In addition to the rise of anticlerical secularism among journalists such as Adib Ishaq, attacks on the idea of clericalism were prominent among Protestants, especially through their organs *al-Nashra al-Shahriyya* and its successor *al-Nashra al-Usbū'iyya*. For selected examples of Ishaq's anticlerical criticism at the end of the 1870s, see Ishaq, *Adīb Ishāq: Al-Kitābāt al-Siyāsiyya wal-Ijtimā'iyya*, 143–147.

64 *Al-Jawā'ib*, September 19, 1878, 7.

anti-Christian and defaming God's will, the newspaper argues, referring to socialist doctrines as libertinism (*ibāḥiyyīn*) and infidelity (*kufr*). *Al-Bashīr* defined libertarians (*madhhab al-ibāḥiyya*) as those who believe in absolute freedom for human beings, including the cancellation of every authority over humans, both religious and political. The consistent attempt of these groups to detach religious norms from state and society attracted particular criticism from conservatives. As guardians of the "Ancien Régime," *al-Bashīr* attacked these groups for their republican perception, arguing that they strive to replace the sovereignty of God with the sovereignty of the people. Socially, the newspaper attacked their defamation of religious norms and laws, their undermining of the authority of social religious and political leaders, their quest for equality, and their demand to detach the laws of "personal status" from religious laws and norms (those that relate to marriage, inheritance, and death).[65]

The Jesuit newspaper associated Protestantism with materialism: the seed of the philosophy of materialism, *al-Bashīr* argues, originated in the Protestant movement of the sixteenth century and in its antiestablishment orientation, which undermined the authority of the Catholic Church, replacing it with individualization of religious belief. This last principle eventually led to complete freedom and the cancellation of the rule of revelation over human life in favor of the rule of nature. Modern materialism, or nihilism, surpassed this early state by undermining every authority. Nihilism believes in freedom in every area, including freedom of religion, conscience, and the freedom of individuals not only in relation to the church but also to Jesus and God. *Al-Bashīr* even associated liberalism (*madhhab al-ḥurriyya*) with socialism, claiming that the principles of liberalism would eventually lead to the rise of materialist socialism (*ahl al-ishtirāk*, *arbāb al-kumūn*, *māddiyya*, *dahriyya*). *Al-Bashīr* argued that the demand of liberals for freedom outside the limitations posed by the church made liberalism, like Protestantism, responsible for the heresy of materialism.[66]

The replacement of the metaphysics of revelation by a metaphysics originating in nature was the subject of a famous treatise

[65] *Al-Bashīr*, March 27, 1878; *al-Bashīr*, January 31, 1879; *al-Bashīr*, May 5, 1881.

[66] *Al-Bashīr*, September 2, 1871, 478–480; *al-Bashīr*, April 20, 1872; *al-Bashīr*, March 27, 1878.

by Jamal al-Din al-Afghani. Around 1880 he wrote his *Refutation of the Materialists*, first in Persian, followed in 1885 by a translation into Arabic by his disciple Muhammad ʿAbdu. The word materialism (*matiryālism*, *māddiyya*) is used as synonymous with naturalism (*nīshariyya*, *ṭabīʿiyya*) and worldly (*dahriyya*), which referred to a group or sect that rejects the idea of metaphysics and divinity and believes that existence can be conceived only by the senses.[67] Al-Afghani attributes the ideas of materialism to philosophers in ancient Greece, contending that these "germs" and "evil" ideas took different shapes, spread in great empires throughout history, and caused their weakness, decline, and destruction. Among the nations that had attached themselves to these destructive ideas, he counts the Greeks, the Persians, the Muslims, the French, and the Ottomans. In his discussion of Islam, he relates the weakness of the Islamic nation to the rise of Muslim sects that believe in the hidden, inner meaning of the Qur'an (*bāṭin*, esoteric as opposed to *ẓāhir*, exoteric meaning), usually referring to sects with esoteric knowledge. He associates the spread of these ideas with the decline that had struck the nation before the Mongol and Crusader invasions.[68]

Under the influence of Freemasonry, al-Afghani does not advocate merely the religion of Islam but the idea of a universal divinity.[69] The universal idea of religion, he argues, stands on three principles that constitute the fundamental motives for the development of civilizations: the belief that human beings are the greatest of all creations; the belief of each religious nation that it alone possesses religious truth; and the belief that human beings come to the world in order to become

[67] Jamal al-Din al-Afghani, *fī Ibṭāl Madhhab al-Dahriyyīn wa-Bayān Mafāsiduhum wa-Ithbāt Anna al-Dīn Asās al-Madaniyya wal-Kufr Fasād al-ʿUmmrān*, trans. Muhammad ʿAbdu (Beirut: Maṭbaʿat Bairut, 1885), 3, 12.

[68] Ibid., 34–35.

[69] Thus, for instance, his use of the term *al-ṣāniʿ al-aqdass* (divine creator) to denote a universal God. Al-Afghani was one of the most prominent leaders of the Masonic movement in Egypt. During his stay in Egypt (he arrived in 1871) he switched between a few Masonic lodges (the most prominent was the British-influenced *Kawkab al-Sharq*), and in 1878 he was appointed to the position of chairman. For more details about his Masonic activity in Egypt, see Karim Wissa, "Freemasonry in Egypt 1798–1921: A Study in Cultural and Political Encounters," *British Journal of Middle Eastern Studies* 16, no. 2 (1989): 148–149; al-Afghani, *fī Ibṭāl Madhhab al-Dahriyyīn wa-Bayān Mafāsiduhum wa-Ithbāt Anna al-Dīn Asās al-Madaniyya wal-Kufr Fasād al-ʿUmmrān*, 12.

experienced and prepare for the next world. Materialism, he argues, consistently undermines these three principles.[70]

He ascribes modern materialism to Darwin, Jean-Jacques Rousseau, and Voltaire, and among the Ottomans, to those who promoted the ideas of the "new age" (*abnāʾ al-ʿaṣr al-jadīd*).[71] All these are enemies of religion. Among followers of the political ideologies that he claims are underpinned by the destructive philosophy of materialism, he names the socialists (*ijtimāʿiyyūn*), anarchists or nihilists (*ʿadamiyyūn*), and communists (*kumūnist, ishtirākiyyūn*). Al-Afghani attacks their ideas of equality, equal sharing of wealth, and their cancellation of privilege.[72] He contends that their consistent aim is libertinism (*ibāḥa*) because they believe that their participation in wealth (*ishtirtāk*) can be achieved only by the cancellation of the three principles of religion.[73]

In its review the Catholic *al-Bashīr* praises al-Afghani's *Refutation of the Materialists*. The conservative newspaper supported al-Afghani's thesis that religion is the basis of civilization and that infidelity is the reason for its corruption. The newspaper presents a summary of al-Afghani's treatise and quotations from critics of Darwin, ending by glorifying al-Afghani's argument and ʿAbdu's high-quality translation.[74]

To a large extent the reaction to and reception of the principles of materialism by conservative Muslim and Catholic scholars was similar. In both cases the metaphysical dimension of materialism was outlined, and in both cases the revolutionary tendency was highlighted. From their perspective, the manifestation of these metaphysical principles drew great challenges; socially, individualization of religious belief was viewed as dangerous for the bonds that form the basis of religious communities, while politically, the idea of political freedom and the principle of "sovereignty of the people" was regarded as the secularization of political governance.

## Theorizing Freedom: Ideologies of Tolerance, Autocratic Constitutionalism, and Liberalism

The radical ideologies of freedom had a relatively minor political impact on Arabic-speaking scholars and did not acquire any prominent

70 Al-Afghani, *fī Ibṭāl Madhhab al-Dahriyyīn wa-Bayān Mafāsiduhum wa-Ithbāt Anna al-Dīn Asās al-Madaniyya wal-Kufr Fasād al-ʿUmmrān*, 14–15.

71 Ibid., 8–13, 35–37.

72 Ibid., 24, 38.

73 Ibid., 25, 35, 38, 40, 46–47.

74 *Al-Bashīr*, July 22, 1886.

adherents. The vast influence of freedom was approached from other angles that related to liberal traditions of civic solidarity and constitutionalism, and the liberal idea of freedom acquired morphological expression in Arabic around 1860. The subject of liberalism made use of two signifiers, the first is the word *ḥurriyya* (freedom), and the second is *tasāmuḥ/tasāhul* (tolerance).

An early use of the first signifier for the word "liberal" appeared in *'Uṭārid*,[75] which in 1859 translated the name of the British Liberal Party as *ḥizb al-librāl* (until the 1860s the formal name of the British liberal party was the Whig Party), interpreting the neologism to its Arabic readers as "adherents of freedom" (*muḥibīn al-ḥurriyya*).[76] *Ḥizb al-librāl* and *librāliyyūn* (liberal group or party and liberals) were coined in Arabic and were frequently used for British, German, and Italian political streams.[77] The neologism *librāl* was rapidly Arabized and replaced by *ḥurr*, and *ḥizb al-librāl* was replaced by *al-ḥizb al-ḥurr* or *ḥizb al-ḥurriyya* (and less frequently by *ḥizb al-aḥrār*). Following these morphological developments, *wazāra librāliyya* or *wazāra ḥurra* came into use to mean a government ruled by a liberal party.[78] Prominent newspapers in Arabic used the word in a Western context to distinguish between two political camps: liberal or leftist as opposed to conservative or rightist. Hence, liberal and leftist newspapers were *jarā'id librāliyya* and *jarā'id ḥurra* (liberal newspapers),[79] *ṣuḥuf*

[75] This newspaper was a semiformal voice of the French and their policies. It advocated ideas such as freedom, progress, and constitutionalism and constantly attacked the ideas stemming from traditionalism (*afkār qadīma, 'ādāt qadīma*). As with other contemporary Arabic periodicals in France, one of its declared aims was to "distribute civilization around the world [*mad al-tamaddun fī al-'ālam*]." *'Uṭārid*, July 2, 1859, 2; *'Uṭārid*, July 13, 1859, 3.

[76] *'Uṭārid*, July 2, 1859, 2.

[77] In the context of the politics in the United States, the words *ḥizb al-librāl* denoted the Democratic Party. For selected examples employing these neologisms, see *Mir'āt al-Aḥwāl*, March 5, 1877; *al-Ahrām*, January 19, 1877; *al-Bashīr*, December 13, 1878; *al-Baṣṣīr*, May 26, 1881; *al-Baṣṣīr*, June 16, 1881; *al-Baṣṣīr*, February 16, 1882.

[78] For selected examples of *al-ḥizb al-ḥurr*, *ḥizb al-ḥurriyya*, or *ḥizb al-aḥrār* as meaning a liberal party, see *al-Ahrām*, December 30, 1876; *al-Ahrām*, January 19, 1877; *al-Ahrām*, February 24, 1877; *al-Ahrām*, May 16, 1877; *al-Ahrām*, February 15, 1878; *al-Ahrām*, April 8, 1880; *al-Jinān* 8 (1880): 23–24; *al-Ahrām*, April 22, 1880; *al-Ahrām*, September 22, 1880; *al-Baṣṣīr*, June 16, 1881; *al-Ahrām*, September 23, 1880; *al-Bashīr*, June 11, 1890; *al-Bashīr*, October 28, 1891; *al-Muqtaṭaf* 1, no. 19 (1895): 236.

[79] *Al-Bashīr*, May 23, 1879; *al-Ahrām*, May 25, 1877; *al-Bashīr*, October 26, 1877.

*al-thawra* (revolutionary newspapers),[80] and *jarāʾid ibāḥiyya* (libertarian newspapers),[81] denoting newspapers advocating political groups that contested conservativism and clericalism.

Another Arabic signifier for liberal was the word *tasāhul* (tolerance). During the 1860s, *al-Jawāʾib* extensively covered the Reform War and the French intervention in Mexico, focusing on the political polarization between liberals and conservatives. In an article from 1867, al-Shidyaq translated Benito Juarez's Liberal Party (*El Partido Liberal*) as *ḥizb al-librāls*. In his definition of the word liberal, al-Shidyaq wrote that it means "proponents of tolerance" (*musāmihīn*).[82] This perception of the ideology of liberalism was rooted in the texts published from 1860 through the 1880s and documented in lexicons published during the same period. The English words "liberal" and "liberalism" were translated as *mutasāhil* and *dhū ḥurriyya*, while "adherents of liberal ideas" and a "liberal party" appeared as *ḥizb al-mutasāhilīn* and *ḥizb al-ḥurriyya*. Liberalism was translated as *uṣūl al-ḥurriyya*, *al-taʿaṣṣub lil-ḥurriyya*, and *uṣūl al-afkār al-mutasāhila*.[83]

All the Arabic lexicography of the period emphasized two aspects of the ideological implications of freedom: social tolerance and political freedom. All these morphological developments attracted different levels of interest among Arabic-speaking scholars. Of the two words *tasāhul* and *ḥurriyya*, the first underwent the earliest systematic construction.[84] The theorization and politicization of tolerance first appeared in Arabic in the context of reporting about the religious clashes in Syria by two prominent journalists, Rashid al-Dahdah and Butrus al-Bustani, both of whom studied foreign languages in the well-known school of ʿAyn Warqa. Al-Dahdah was secretary to Bashir II and left for France in 1845 to work in commerce. There he established *Birjīs Barīs*, one of the earliest private Arabic newspapers.[85]

80 *Al-Bashīr*, January 7, 1871, 150.
81 *Al-Bashīr*, February 8, 1882; *al-Bashīr*, April 6, 1882.
82 Al-Shidyaq, *Kanz al-Raghāʾib fī Muntakhabāt al-Jawāʾib*, 1877, 5:118–119, 130.
83 George Percy Badger, "Liberal, Liberalism," *An English Arabic Lexicon* (London: C. K. Paul & Co., 1881), 569.
84 Yuhanna Abkariyus, "Liberal, Liberalize, Liberate, Liberation, Liberator," *Qāmūs Inklīzī wa-ʿArabī* (Beirut, 1887), 370; Yuhanna Abkariyus, "Liberal, Liberalism, Liberalize, Liberate, Liberation, Liberator," *English-Arabic Reader's Dictionary* (Beirut: Librairie du Liban, 1974), 400.
85 For more details about his biography, see Tarrazi, *Taʾrīkh al-Ṣiḥāfa al-ʿArabiyya*, 1913, 1:100–101.

In the pages of his newspaper, al-Dahdah, assuming that the lack of true reforms was the reason for the massacres of Christians in Syria, wrote in 1859 that "it's a stain on the honor of a state when everything rests on the will of one man who does whatever he likes."[86] Al-Dahdah identifies the source of the violence in Syria, using the word *taʿaṣṣub* (fanaticism), a problem that the state, in his opinion, failed to solve.[87]

The association of religious fanaticism with politics and a political program stood to a large extent at the center of the theorization of this group. Al-Dahdah argues in *Birjīs Barīs* that the source of the failed politics of the Ottoman Empire lay in two related principles: absolutism – a lack of freedom and rights for the subjects, who are treated without any legal constraints "as slaves" – and the lack of any true desire to implement any reforms that were imposed, owing to "external pressures." Fanaticism, violence, and the eradication of groups, he contends, are the natural outcome of the complete failure of the empire in the political field.[88]

Al-Dahdah presents a comprehensive method for reforming the empire and eventually overcoming religious fanaticism. He advocates the idea of civil rights in which Ottoman subjects would be treated as citizens having equal rights because they are "all human beings and not sheep [*quṭʿān*]." In addition he emphasizes the importance of individual freedom in his request that an individual's religion be considered a private matter and that the "creed of nationality" (*dīn al-jinsiyya*) should instead take precedence, which would overcome the differences between the various religions and sects (*adyān wa-madhāhib*). He associates his political attitude with the idea of progress: These principles, he writes, are a precondition for prosperity, progress, and civilization in the societies of the Ottoman Empire.[89]

Al-Dahdah's political criticism of the Ottoman state's persecutions of Christians and his support for the French intervention in the Syrian crisis attracted the reaction of Faris al-Shidyaq in his *al-Jawāʾib*.[90] Al-Shidyaq attacked al-Dahdah, contending that his real goal was to denounce the Ottoman Empire and the Muslim population. Al-Dahdah reacted by arguing that if al-Shidyaq really meant to defend

[86] *Birjīs Barīs*, October 10, 1860. [87] Ibid.
[88] *Birjīs Barīs*, April 25, 1860. [89] Ibid.
[90] *Birjīs Barīs*, March 27, 1861; *Birjīs Barīs*, May 22, 1861.

Muslim interests, he should tell the Muslims to put a halt to the fanaticism (*ta'aṣṣub*) that was the reason for the destruction of the region.[91]

The critique of religious fanaticism and the idea that social tolerance is key for prosperity and progress had already been used extensively by the philosophers of the Enlightenment in the eighteenth century. Echoes of these arguments were presented in the Arabic translations and their appended material in the 1830s. Rafa'a al-Tahtawi used the Arabic *tasāhul* to argue that tolerance was what stood behind the law and order achieved by the ancient Greeks.[92] In the translated works of Voltaire, religious fanaticism was presented as the reason for endless religious conflicts.[93] Nevertheless, Ernest Renan, another French contemporary of al-Dahdah (who was familiar with Renan's ideas), theorized the idea of tolerance and its use in the Arab context. In his 1852 work, *Averroes et l'averroisme*, Renan uses the case of the persecution of Ibn Rushd to argue that Islamic orthodoxy had hindered the spirit of free intellectual inquiry. Renan attributes the decline of Arab philosophy, sciences, and progress to religious fanaticism.[94]

Arabic-speaking scholars of the 1860s knew Renan's work,[95] and his thesis had a strong influence on the Christian and Muslim scholars of the nineteenth century. In the Arabic summarizations of Renan's thesis, Ibn Rushd was presented as a proponent of free thinking (*al-fikr al-ḥurr*) and a model of the enlightened "Arab" scholar who is affiliated with the "Arab nation" (*al-umma al-'Arabiyya*) and eventually

[91] For *al-Jawā'ib*'s critique and *Birjīs*'s response, see *Birjīs Barīs*, October 22, 1862; *Birjīs Barīs*, October 29, 1862.

[92] For additional use of the word in translated sources, see al-Tahtawi and al-Zarabi, *Bidāyat al-Qudamā' wa-Hidāyat al-Ḥukamā'*, 71; Voltaire, *Maṭāli' Shumūs al-Siyar fī Waqā'i' Karlūs al-Thānī 'Ashar*, 43, 72; Robertson, *Kitāb Itḥāf Mulūk al-Zamān bi-Tārīkh al-Imbirāṭūr Sharlakān*, 2:41.

[93] Voltaire, *Rawḍ al-Azhar fī Tārīkh Buṭrus al-Akbar*, 59–66.

[94] Ernest Renan, *Averroes et L'averroïsme: Essai Historique* (Paris: A. Durand, 1852).

[95] See an early critical review in Arabic of Renan's biography of Jesus in *Birjīs Barīs*, July 6, 1864. Early editions of Ibn Rushd in Arabic and Hebrew were printed in Europe prior to 1860, including his known work *Faṣl al-Maqāl*. Ibn Rushd's debate with al-Ghazali, in their works *Tahāfut al-Falāsifa* and *Tahāfut al-Tahāfut*, was printed in one volume in Cairo in 1885. See: Abu al-Walid Ibn Rushd, *Thalāth Rasā'il* (Munich: Commission Bei G. Franz, 1859); Abu al-Walid Ibn Rushd and Muhammad bin Muhammad al-Ghazali, *Majmū'... Thalāthat Kutub* (Egypt: Al-Maṭba'a al-I'lāmiyya, 1885).

falls victim to religious fanaticism (*al-taʿaṣṣub al-dīnī*).[96] The ideological impact and the repercussions of these ideas, especially the relationship of Islam with the Enlightenment, ignited controversies between Ernest Renan and Jamal al-Din al-Afghani in 1883 and later the debate between Muhammad ʿAbdu and Farah Antun in 1902–1903.[97]

About one year after al-Dahdah's criticism in *Birjīs Barīs*, another Syrian publication followed suit and considered the idea of tolerance a key concept for ending the religious conflict. In a series of articles published by Butrus al-Bustani[98] between September 29, 1860 and April 22, 1861, under the title *Nafīr Sūriyya*, he presents a systematic analysis of the subject of religious conflict in his region. In his attempt to explore the reasons for the conflict and suggest solutions that would guide the Syrians toward avoiding another round of violence in the future, he contributes significantly to the theorization of individual freedoms as the ideological basis of his political theory. In his argument he presents an ideological conception that analyzes the social forces as being separated by two world views: the first is identified with progress and civilization (*tamaddun*) and includes ideas such as tolerance, freedom, natural rights, humanism, civilization, science, and civil solidarity, while the other comprises religious fanaticism (*taʿaṣṣub*), tyranny, ignorance, and barbarism. Two major points summarize the revolutionary aspect of this approach: The first is civil law, which is derived from the idea of human rights (*ḥuqūq al-insāniyya*), and the second is the redefinition of the Syrian sociopolitical contract's foundations. Al-Bustani constructs the liberal idea of tolerance in Arabic by

[96] See early reviews of Renan's book about Ibn Rushd in Arabic: Butrus al-Bustani, "Ibn Rushd (Averroes)," *Kitāb Dāʾirat al-Maʿārif* (Beirut: Dār al-Maʿrifa, 1876), 489–490; *al-Muqtaṭaf* 9, no. 10 (1886): 649–653. For another nineteenth-century biography of Ibn Rushd, see Salim al-Khuri and Salim Shihada, "Ibn Rushd," *Kitāb Āthār al-Adhār: Al-Qism al-Tārīkhī* (Beirut: Al-Maṭbaʿa al-Sūriyya, 1877), 221–228.

[97] For further details on the debate between Muhammad ʿAbdu and Farah Antun on the subject of tolerance, see Wael Abu-ʿUksa, "Liberal Tolerance in Arab Political Thought: Translating Farah Antun (1874–1922)," *Journal of Levantine Studies* 3, no. 2 (Winter 2013): 151–157; Farah Antun, "The Meaning of 'Tolerance,' Which Is the Basis of Modern Civilization," ed. Wael Abu-ʿUksa, trans. Zakia Pormann, *Journal of Levantine Studies* 3, no. 2 (Winter 2013): 159–172.

[98] For further details of al-Bustani's biography, see Abu-Manneh, "The Christians between Ottomanism and Syrian Nationalism: The Ideas of Butrus al-Bustani," 289.

emphasizing the contradiction between the medieval Islamic concept of hierarchical relations – upon which the theological Muslim-dhimmi relationship relied – and the modern concept of tolerance, which is based on the ideas of individual freedom, natural rights, and equality before the law. Regarding the first subject, he criticizes the common perception of the religious laws, as they are ahistoric, disconnected from the influence of time and change. Anything related to politics, he argues, refers to earthly matters and therefore changes constantly with the continuous alterations of time.[99] Al-Bustani argues that the state should establish a new body of law (*sharāʾiʿ*) that suits the "[particular] situations, places, and times, and that is detached from religious law." Furthermore, it should refer "during court to the specific case and not to the person's [religious background]" in an implied criticism of the Islamic law that ascribes importance to religious identity, especially in relation to witnesses.[100] Al-Bustani suggests a clear definition of the political/civil realm (*madanī*) by separating it entirely from the religious (*dīnī*): Religion should be limited to the relation between individuals and God, while the civil sphere is defined by the interrelations between individuals who live in the same political community and the same homeland (*waṭan*). He contends that the unification of political authority (*sulṭa zamaniyya*) and religious authority (*sulṭa rūḥiyya*) would harm the purity of religion and cause endless conflicts, including the one the world was witnessing in Syria.[101]

In his argument for overcoming the challenge of religious fanaticism (*al-taʿaṣṣub al-madhhabī*), al-Bustani goes beyond the subject of laws to the sociopolitical foundations of social solidarity. In his articles he suggests transforming the concept of collective solidarity from one based on religious ties to one predicated on the civil bonds manifested in the idea of patriotism (*ḥubb al-waṭan*). He addresses all the Syrians as a unified nation (*umma*):[102] "Those who replace the love of homeland with religious fanaticism and sacrifice the best of their homeland for personal interests do not deserve to belong to the homeland, and they are its enemies."[103] Al-Bustani elaborates his concept of freedom: The subjects have the right to the protection of their lives, honor, and property without regard to their religious affiliation or ethnicity. He indicates that their civil rights also include freedom of the press,

[99] Al-Bustani, *Nafīr Sūriyya*, 38, 57–59. [100] Ibid., 38.
[101] Ibid., 49. [102] Ibid., 50. [103] Ibid., 22.

religion, and conscience (*ḥurriyyat al-ḍamīr*), including the right to choose their creed (*madhhab*).[104]

The religious clashes provided an exceptional opportunity for discussion and criticism of social and religious taboos. Against this background al-Bustani developed his theory of civil identity,[105] contesting the politicization of any sectarian or religious bonds, which he identified as a great evil that struck his society and hindered its progress. He identifies backwardness and fanaticism with religious, sectarian, and tribal sociopolitical loyalties, and he identifies patriotism, reason, freedom, and equality with the spirit of the age and with *tamaddun*. Al-Bustani considers the separation between the state/political and the religious realms to be a precondition for any progress, prosperity, and social success. Only if this concept were to be assimilated in Syria would religious wars stop; otherwise it would be only a matter of time before Syria would experience another round of destructive and bloody clashes.[106]

Al-Bustani combines national principles concerned with solidarity, unity, and power with liberal ideas that address social and political norms. His political thought revolves around the concept of individual freedom, especially freedom of religion. The ideology of tolerance in that sense disconnects this concept from the medieval hierarchical meaning by integrating it with civil ideas that are related to secular law and sociopolitical loyalties. Thus, tolerance comprising individualization of religious belief and fortified with civil laws and bonds would

[104] Aware of the socioreligious constraints on the subject of "freedom of belief," al-Bustani uses the ambiguous word *madhhab*. This word could refer to both freedom to choose religion or freedom to choose a religious school of thought or sect.

[105] See Stephen Paul Sheehi's analysis of al-Bustani's discourse in *Nafīr Sūriyya*. He contends that al-Bustani's discourse is a representation of subjective reform that "existed in the minds of native activists." In a similar postcolonial approach, Ussama Makdisi distinguishes between Butrus al-Bustani's ideas and the formal approach manifested by the ideas of Ottoman Foreign Minister Fuad Pasha, who was sent to investigate the 1860 massacres in Syria. Makdisi argues that al-Bustani "resisted the authoritarian implications of Ottoman modernization." For further details, see Stephen Paul Sheehi, "Inscribing the Arab Self: Butrus al-Bustani and Paradigms of Subjective Reform," *British Journal of Middle Eastern Studies* 27, no. 1 (2000): 7–24; Ussama Makdisi, "After 1860: Debating Religion, Reform, and Nationalism in the Ottoman Empire," *International Journal of Middle East Studies* 34, no. 4 (2002): 602.

[106] Al-Bustani, *Nafīr Sūriyya*, 9–11, 21, 48–49.

guarantee overcoming inequality. Al-Bustani's theorization largely followed the spirit of the Tanzimat, which transformed the concept of rights, transferring their former association with religious affiliation to affiliation with the civil community (Ottomanism).[107] After al-Bustani, the concept of *waṭaniyya* (civil loyalty) was used, at least among Christian scholars, in contrast to religious fanaticism and theocracy.[108] His perception of the subject of tolerance preoccupied intellectual discourse among the Christian Arabic-speaking intelligentsia of the nineteenth and twentieth centuries.

After al-Bustani's criticism, religious fanaticism was marked among Christian scholars of the nineteenth century as the greatest enemy of *tamaddun*. In January 1881 *al-Ahrām* articulated this spirit in an article that begins thus: "Fanaticism is the misfortune of the East and the plague of its societies, which will bring about their destruction and failure. This plague was born of ignorance in the time of slavery and despotism."[109] The ideology of tolerance that stresses the principle of individual freedom provided Christian scholars with a particular viewpoint on the general subject of freedom. The premise that tolerance is a precondition for any progress toward *tamaddun* influenced to a large extent the interest of this social group on the subject of political freedom. In al-Bustani's account of the substantive rights for his imagined civil community, political freedom was entirely ignored. In an entry in the 1883 volume of his encyclopedia (published the same year in which he died) and dedicated to the concept of "freedom," al-Bustani elaborates the variety of ideas that freedom comprises. There he defines freedom as the foundation of rationalism and one of the superior qualities of humanity. In his discussion he defines civil freedom (*ḥurriyya madaniyya*) as the freedom to do that which is permitted by the law, while he defines political freedom (*ḥurriyya siyāsiyya*) as "the rights that the regime gives to each citizen (*waṭanī*)."[110] Not only does he

107 Al-Bustani was a strong proponent of Ottomanism. The authorities amply rewarded him upon the publication of his dictionary, *Muḥīṭ al-Muḥīṭ*, with 25,000 qirsh, and he was awarded the Majidi Order, third class, a military and knightly order. See Abu-Manneh, "The Christians between Ottomanism and Syrian Nationalism: The Ideas of Butrus al-Bustani," 287, 294.

108 See, for instance, the use of *waṭaniyya* in the work of Khalil Ghanim: Al-*Baṣṣīr*, October 6, 1881.

109 *Al-Ahrām*, January 26, 1881.

110 Al-Bustani, "Ḥurriyya," *Kitāb Dā'irat al-Ma'ārif* (Beirut: Maṭba'at al-Ma'ārif, 1883), 3–4.

ignore the idea of sovereignty of the people but he also defines it as a privilege that is bestowed by the ruler, the absolute sovereign.

Early systematic work by Muslim scholars on the subject of freedom appears in 1867 with the publication of Khayr al-Din al-Tunisi's work, *Aqwam al-Masālik*. Al-Tunisi strove to present his position on the idea of change, eventually posting a counterargument to the conservative opponents of the Tanzimat. Using Ibn Khaldun's arguments, he analyzes the reasons for the rise and decline of çivilizations in light of the European experience, arguing that Muslims should not reject all the characteristics of non-Islamic civilizations. Al-Tunisi followed earlier conceptions of freedom, equating it with the traditional idea of *ʿadl* (justice). By adopting the argument that justice is the basic value for the flourishing of civilizations, he advocated the premise that the reforms are the basis for justice and freedom and that they correlate with the divine laws of Islam. In his book he advocates the thesis that freedom and a constitution, the main aim of the reforms, are the keys to strength, prosperity, and progress.[111]

Al-Tunisi assumed that among the fundamental reasons for Europe's progress was their political system, which relied on "worldly justice" (*al-ʿadl al-siyāsī*).[112] In his elaboration of the meaning of "freedom" in Europe, he argues that they use the word in two ways. "Individual freedom" (*ḥurriyya shakhṣiyya*) includes the right to property, security, equality, and the rule of law (which means not judging a citizen by laws not legislated by representatives). This variant of freedom, he continues, exists in all European countries except the Papal States and Russia, which were both autocracies. The second meaning of freedom is "political freedom" (*ḥurriyya siyāsiyya*), which means that people have the right to be involved in politics.[113]

Assessing the theoretical application of these two components of freedom in the Ottoman Empire, al-Tunisi comments on the principle of "political freedom," contending that "bestowing this kind of freedom [*iʿṭāʾ al-ḥurriyya*]"[114] could lead to anarchy and social conflict, which is why it was replaced with the election of representatives. Al-Tunisi continues, completely rejecting the idea of applying this principle and its institutional offshoots in Islamic countries. What the

111 Al-Tunisi, *Aqwam al-Masālik fī Maʿrifat Aḥwāl al-Mamālik*, 149–150, 246–247.

112 Ibid., 155–156. 113 Ibid., 243–244. 114 Ibid., 244.

Europeans call parliament, he argues, is what the Muslims call *ahl al-ḥall wal-ʿaqd* (the influential leaders in Muslim society), even though this last institution is not an elected body. Al-Tunisi defends his position of exempting the masses from any involvement in politics by using an Islamic argument: Changing the forbidden is a communal obligation (*farḍ kifāya*) for Muslims; therefore, if some of them are engaged in this activity, the rest are not obligated to participate.[115] Al-Tunisi elevated the importance of consultation (*shūra*) in making political decisions, referring to a ruler who does not execute this principle as a *mustabid* (autocrat). While he advocates using the medieval Islamic concept of *shūra*, he rejects the idea of sovereignty of the people as a basis for governance.

Ahmad ibn Abi al-Diyaf (known as Bin Diyaf), another Tunisian bureaucrat and al-Tunisi's contemporary, wrote about the best model for governance. He rejects two models – absolute monarchy, because it brings injustice, and the republican, because it ignores the Islamic principle of religious leadership (*imāma sharʿiyya*) – instead advocating for constitutional monarchy. As part of his accounting for the roots of Islamic constitutionalism, he argues that the Muslim ʿulama, who were responsible in the past for directing the ruler's decisions toward justice, had neglected their position. Bin Diyaf contends that this change in the state of the ʿulama eventually led to injustice, which weakened the Muslim nation. Following al-Tunisi, he argues that the way to restore justice is to implement a constitutional monarchy. This is the best model for the Muslims after the caliphate. He suggests limiting the power of Muslim rulers by using *qānūn*, edicts or laws legislated by the rulers, which was used in the early stages of the Ottoman Empire. Bin Diyaf argues that the *qānūn* is the Islamic equivalent of the Western parliaments. Its aim in the Islamic state is to ensure that the ruler implements justice by acting on the advice of the ʿulama and the laws of Islam. This, according to Bin Diyaf, is the most efficient way to sustain a just government, to attain a civilized state, and to restore power to the Muslims.[116] Although he acknowledges the benefits of political

[115] Ibid., 243–244.

[116] For further details about Bin Diyaf's political ideas, see Brown's summary in the introduction to Ibn Abi al-Diyaf, *Consult Them in the Matter*, 11–21; Ibn Abi al-Diyaf, *Itḥāf Ahl al-Zamān bi-Akhbār Mulūk Tūnis wa-ʿAhd al-Amān*, 1:7–88.

freedom in Europe, he completely ignores this principle in his Islamic model.

Another contemporary, Rafaʿa al-Tahtawi, presented an attempt to use Islamic reasoning (*ijtihād*) to develop an Islamic theory derived from his vision of progress and civilization (*tamaddun*).[117] In his works from the 1860s and the beginning of the 1870s (he died in 1873), al-Tahtawi theorized the concept of freedom, considering it a fundamental principle for progress in Egypt and in Islamic societies. In his later works al-Tahtawi widely utilizes Platonist medieval Muslim traditions,[118] emphasizing the importance of the idea of natural law: "Natural law relies on reason and is universal in its origin, which means that it existed before it was used as a foundation for legislation. [Natural law] is the order that was installed by the divine wisdom in all human forces, equally between all of them, for characterizing the permitted [and the forbidden], without regard to any particular country or law."[119] He uses the universality of the idea in his theorization of civil activities and education. There he indicates three primary principles that should form the character of the citizenry. The first is the natural principle, which assumes the "equality of human beings as slaves of God" and includes all members of the polity. The second, religious brotherhood, pertains to the particular religious traditions of each group. All duties between brothers in faith are equal to the duties between brothers of the same civil community because they have the same goal: the improvement of their homeland and its course toward

117 Theoretical attempts to understand the modern experience through local concepts, or local experience through modern concepts, had already appeared in his early works, at the end of the 1820s and the beginning of the 1830s. In his translation of Georges-Bernard Depping, he added the following comment to a translated phrase saying that human beings naturally tend toward freedom: "and that's why the Prophet advocates freedom." Additionally, in the first edition of his journey to Paris (published in 1834) he contends that Lower Egypt under the *humamiyya* dynasty constituted a republican regime. In the second edition of the same book, he argues that Islamic law includes all three models of governance: the absolute, the constitutional, and the republican. See Depping, *Kitāb Qalāʾid al-Mafākhir fī Gharīb ʿAwāʾid al-Awāʾil wal-Awākhir*, 81–82; Depping, *Aperçu Historique Sur Les Mœurs et Coutumes Des Nation*, 221; al-Tahtawi, *Takhlīṣ al-Ibrīz fī Talkhīṣ Bārīz aw al-Dīwān al-Nafīs bi-Īwān Bārīs*, 157; al-Tahtawi, *al-Dīwān al-Nafīs fī Īwān Bārīs aw, Takhlīṣ al-Ibrīz fī Talkhīṣ Bārīz*, 221.

118 Al-Tahtawi, "Kitāb al-Murshid al-Amīn lil-Banāt wal-Banīn," 458.

119 Ibid., 511.

progress and prosperity. The third principle relates to tailoring education to the particular needs of each individual so that citizens can be of benefitto their country.[120] Despite his recognition of "natural law," in his political application of it, al-Tahtawi argues in favor of subordinating reason to shari'a: "People should be taught politics [*siyāsa*] by the methods of divine law and not by pure reason [*al-'aql al-mujarad*]," stressing that shari'a does not contradict the principle of benefiting from "positive" innovations produced by reason.[121]

Al-Tahtawi's religious reasoning is manifested in the construction of an Islamic political theory that assumed a general state of harmony between two spheres of reference: divine Islamic law and the realm of pure reason and *siyāsa*. In his last published work, he elaborates the relation between the two realms:

> All the deductions that civilized nations reached by reason and that they made the foundations of their laws and civilization rarely deviate from the principles [*uṣūl*] underpinning the branches [*furū'*] of Islamic jurisprudence that discuss human activity [*mu'āmalāt*]. What we [the Muslims] call principles of jurisprudence ['*ilm usūl al-fiqh*] is similar to what they call natural rights or natural laws, which means rational principles – in relation to what to accept and what to reject – that underpin their civil laws. What we refer to as branches of jurisprudence they call civil rights or civil laws, and what we call justice and virtue [*al-'adl wal-iḥsān*] they express with the terms freedom and equality, and what the Muslim calls the love of religion and protecting it... they refer to as patriotism [*maḥabat al-waṭan*]. Patriotism in Islam is only one of the branches of the faith, while protecting religion is the main obligation. Every Islamic state is a homeland for all its Muslim inhabitants, and therefore it comprises religion and patriotism.[122]

This passage reveals the ideational orientation on which al-Tahtawi's syncretistic approach to the subject of politics was based. With his Islamic orientation as a starting point, he theorizes both the political community and the norms needed to maintain the social organization in a polity. Reusing the medieval word *madīna* to denote his

[120] Ibid., 398–400; Rifa'a Rafi' al-Tahtawi, "Kitāb Manāhij al-Albāb al-Miṣriyya fī Mabāhij al-Ādāb al-'Aṣriyya," in *al-A'māl al-Kāmila li-Rifā'a Rāfi' al-Ṭahṭawī*, ed. Muammad 'Imara, vol. 1 (Cairo: Dār al-Shurūq, 2010), 398–399.

[121] Al-Tahtawi, "Kitāb al-Murshid al-Amīn lil-Banāt wal-Banīn," 508–510, 513.

[122] Ibid., 501–502.

political community, al-Tahtawi constructs the concept of the "Egyptian nation" (*al-umma al-Miṣriyya*), regarding political communities that are affiliated with a political regime as the most advanced social organizations.[123] In his discussion in his last publication on political principles (1873), al-Tahtawi dedicates an entry to the subject of freedom. There he divides the principles of freedom into five categories: natural freedom, freedom of behavior, religious freedom, civil freedom, and political freedom. He interprets "natural freedom" as expressing natural needs such as eating and walking, while he equates the "freedom of behavior" with good manners. He defines religious freedom as the right to believe, within the limits of the principles of religion (*aṣl al-dīn*) and the schools of law (*madhāhib*). "Civil freedom" is elaborated as the right that stems from the social solidarity within the same political society (*madīna*), and it means the individual's duty to help others to do any action that is not prevented by the laws of the country. He indicates that "political freedom" means the state's obligation to protect the individual's natural freedom, including his right to and noninterference with property.[124] In his theorization of the subject of freedom, al-Tahtawi follows his earlier interpretations and eventually reaches conclusions similar to the earlier works of progressive Christian and Muslim scholars.[125] His conception of freedom revolves around the idea of individual freedom, nursing social solidarity and tolerance while ignoring or rejecting the political principle of freedom.[126]

In their theorizations of freedom, all the aforementioned scholars emphasized the subject of individual freedom and the principle of the rule of law as being the most crucial components of their thought. In their work *ḥurriyya* is a mercy that is vouchsafed by the ruler. On the morphological level this state of subordination manifested in the use of words such as *i'ṭā' al-ḥurriyya* (bestowing freedom). Al-Tahtawi expresses this meaning in his definition of the word, in which he states that *ḥurriyya* "is the permission [*rukhṣa*] to do [what laws] permit

123 Ibid., 457–458. 124 Ibid., 505–507.

125 For further details about al-Tahtawi's concept of political freedom, see Leon Zolondek, "al-Ṭahṭawi and Political Freedom," *The Muslim World* 54, no. 2 (1964): 90–97.

126 Al-Tahtawi criticized the idea of "religious fanaticism" (*al-ta'aṣṣub al-dīnī*) but without being critical of religious social bonds. He uses the word *ta'aṣṣub* to mean interference, arguing that rulers should not interfere in the religious beliefs of their subjects: Al-Tahtawi, "Kitāb Manāhij al-Albāb al-Miṣriyya fī Mabāhij al-Ādāb al-'Aṣriyya," 709.

[*mubāḥ*]."[127] This was al-Tahtawi's rephrasing of Montesquieu's statement, which he had read during his stay in Paris,[128] that "liberty is the right to do everything the laws permit."[129] Al-Tahtawi, however, replaced the words "right" with "permission" embracing a definition that preceded the French Revolution and modern democratic thought. Montesquieu, who influenced al-Tahtawi's perceptions of freedom and liberty, published his composition *The Spirit of the Laws* in 1748 under the French absolute monarchy and died before becoming acquainted with some of the political writings that would later have a great impact on the outbreak of the French Revolution, especially Rousseau's *The Social Contract* (1762). Furthermore, Montesquieu was not a proponent of the idea of direct democracy (representative democracy had not yet become relevant) or of the principle of the sovereignty of the people.[130]

The concept of freedom constructed among those who maintained stances similar to that of al-Tahtawi was based on the assumption that the authority for practicing freedom lay outside of the individual: Freedom is bestowed by the sovereign, whether the absolute ruler or God. In contrast to the significance of the principle of "individual freedoms" in the previously mentioned works in Arabic, a "political freedom" that ascribes political sovereignty to citizens of a polity is absent. The subjects have no right to demand political authority or to shape it. In their model, the subjects' freedom is confined within borders that are determined by laws over which they have no authority to legislate. "Freedom," in that sense, paves the way for constitutional autocracy.

Despite these theoretical conclusions, there were still vast political differences between the scholars. The Christian scholars stressed the importance of facing religious fanaticism and creating equality and a just civil community, while their Muslim counterparts emphasized the establishment of a unified civil community that would preserve the laws both of Islam and of their proto-nation-states and that would lead their countries to prosperity and power. In this regard the sociocultural

127 Al-Tahtawi, "Kitāb al-Murshid al-Amīn lil-Banāt wal-Banīn," 505.

128 Al-Tahtawi indicated in his journey account that he had read Montesquieu's *The Spirit of the Laws*: al-Tahtawi, *Takhlīṣ al-Ibrīz fī Talkhīṣ Bārīz aw al-Dīwān al-Nafīs bi-Īwān Bārīs*, 150.

129 Montesquieu, *The Spirit of the Laws*, 155.

130 Montesquieu, *The Spirit of the Laws*, 10–15.

environment of Greater Syria imposed a different set of requirements on Christian scholars than did the milieu in Egypt on al-Tahtawi or Tunisia on al-Tunisi and Bin Diyaf. While both Egypt and Tunisia comprised relatively homogeneous populations (the majority in each case were Sunni Muslims), Greater Syria was heterogeneous. Furthermore, while al-Tahtawi, al-Tunisi, and Bin Diyaf were active in political environments that sustained older traditions of central semi-independent authority, Greater Syria was divided into many districts that endured ongoing conflicts until after the 1860s. Patriotism there did not evolve together with a unified political entity as it did in Egypt and Tunisia, where political communities were defined not only by unified territory but also by legal affiliation with a monarchy. In the case of Syria, the establishment of shared memory and a homogeneous group was much more complicated, and questions related to social solidarity and tolerance attained crucial significance among Syrian scholars. This difference between the two models might partially explain why ethnicity and "Arab blood" (*al-jins al-ʿArabi, al-dam al-ʿArabi*)[131] received so much more political emphasis in Syria than they did in Egypt and Tunisia.

All the political thinkers of this generation were strongly influenced by religious thought, and therefore their theorization of political ideas was attached to theological or legal conventions. Al-Tahtawi had always distinguished between rational and irrational religions and religious schools of thought. Unlike the "corrupted" religions, he argued, Islam is a religion that correlates with reason, progress, and natural law. This belief accompanied him from his first translation until his last publication, and it dominated his theorizations of modern ideas. Throughout his career al-Tahtawi believed that a rational state that embeds these ideas and brings happiness and prosperity to its citizens in worldly life does not contradict the principles of Islam.[132] Based on this religious conviction, he assumed that there is harmony between natural and religious law.

Butrus al-Bustani was born a Maronite and converted to Protestantism under the influence of the American mission in Beirut in the

131 Al-Bustani, *Nafīr Sūriyya*, 21, 42, 60.
132 Depping, *Kitāb Qalāʾid al-Mafākhir fī Gharīb ʿAwāʾid al-Awāʾil wal-Awākhir*, 85–94; *Rawḍat al-Madāris* 13, no. 1 (October 1869): 2–4; *Rawḍat al-Madāris* 14, no. 1 (October 1870): 2–10.

early 1840s. His transformation from Catholicism to Protestantism deeply impacted his political perceptions, especially his advocacy of the application of natural law. His attack on the idea of divine laws and his stress on the importance of separation between the civil and religious spheres were deeply influenced by his religious background and by the contemporary debates in Arabic between Catholics and Protestants throughout the nineteenth century. The Christian background to his political thought was expressed in the ongoing discussions of the relationship between religion and politics. After the establishment of the private press, these debates covered the pages of the Jesuit *al-Bashīr* (founded in 1870) and other progressive periodicals and newspapers such as *al-Jinān* and the Protestant *al-Nashra al-Usbū'iyya* and its successor *al-Nashra al-Shahriyya*.[133] The Catholic journal presented the most systematic arguments against the ideas of Protestant reformation, including the separation between the divine and civil spheres. *Al-Bashīr* consistently attacked Protestantism, arguing that it is the reason for the establishment of the "corrupted" movement of "those who call themselves the generation of enlightenment [*jīl al-anwār*]."[134] Principles such as the superiority of logic and reason over theology, the idea of the sovereignty of the people, republicanism, freedom of religion, freedom of education, and the idea of revolution were all criticized and rejected by *al-Bashīr* for contradicting the Catholic faith. The conservative Jesuit newspaper advocated clericalism, knowledge that is based in revelation, and the defense of the idea of "God's rights [*ḥuqūq Allah*]" as opposed to "human rights [*ḥuqūq al-insān*]."[135] Like the Christian scholars' debates about Islamic fanaticism, this subject was also approached in internal Christian controversies. Khalil al-Khuri, the editor of *Ḥadīqat al-Akhbār* (founded in 1858), criticized the Jesuits for their religious fanaticism (*ta'aṣṣub*) in a debate that revolved around the subject of the Italian annexation of Rome, which had been under papal authority.[136]

133 For selected examples, see *al-Bashīr*, April 22, 1871, 284.
134 *Al-Bashīr*, September 3, 1870, 2.
135 For selected articles, see *al-Bashīr*, January 7, 1871, 148–150; *al-Bashīr*, July 22, 1871; *al-Bashīr*, April 8, 1871, 265–266; *al-Bashīr*, October 8, 1870, 42–44.
136 See a summary of this debate and *al-Bashīr*'s response in: Al-*Bashīr*, January 28, 1871, 169–171.

The influence of al-Bustani's Protestantism went beyond his belief in the separation of the religious and civil spheres to the idea of universal equality and natural law. In his discussion on religious values, he indicates that the superiority of Christianity relies on the value of universal equality.[137] This idea, which constituted an early statement of the Hobbesian philosophy of natural law,[138] was rephrased in Thomas Jefferson's Declaration of Independence in 1776 ("all men are created equal"), and apparently was well known to al-Bustani, who worked in the Protestant mission in Beirut (he filled the position of dragoman in the American consulate in Beirut between the end of the 1840s and 1862).[139] For many Catholic Arabic-speaking scholars of the time, and their Muslim counterparts, the reception of the idea of universal equality and natural law faced theological constraints and was strongly advocated in the late 1870s by Catholic anticlericalists such as Adib Ishaq.[140]

Despite the vast differences in background and political stances, these Arabic-speaking scholars were responsible for the emergence of reformative thought in Arabic. Their ideas largely corresponded to the spirit of the Tanzimat edicts and to the reformist activity of the "Young Ottomans," who attained prominence between 1867 and 1878. This group was deeply influenced by the constitutionalist ideas of western Europe, and their efforts to reform the empire stemmed from their civil orientation. The members of this group were strong proponents of progressive ideas such as patriotism, Ottomanism, and legal equality between the different subjects of the empire. Their ideas had a direct impact on the Arabic-speaking provinces, especially on prominent activists such as the Egyptian prince and son of Ibrahim Pasha, Mustafa Fadil Pasha, who supported the group financially and was one of its leaders.[141]

137 Al-Bustani, "Tamaddun," 215.

138 Cary J. Nederman, "Individualism," *New Dictionary of the History of Ideas* (Detroit, MI: Charles Scribner's Sons, 2005), 1113–1117.

139 Abu-Manneh, "The Christians between Ottomanism and Syrian Nationalism: The Ideas of Butrus al-Bustani," 289.

140 For an article on his attack on clericalism and the Jesuits, see Ishaq, *Adīb Ishāq: Al-Kitābāt al-Siyāsiyya wal-Ijtimāʿiyya*, 384–385.

141 For the constitutional ideas of Fadil Pasha, see the letter he sent to the sultan in 1866, in which he argues that the reason for the weakness of the empire lay in its political system. The historian Şerif Mardin summarizes the Young Ottomans' importance by stating that they are "the first men to make the idea

The inflation of the political concepts during these years was perhaps the most significant contribution of this generation; approaching individuals from a political perspective as components of a political community reopened the way for the emergence of political philosophy in Arabic. Their theoretical position on the subject of an individual's state of being affected the use of words. In addition to the use of the medieval word *ra'iyya* (subjects), these scholars used newly invented forms that attempted to emphasize the civil state of citizens. Al-Tahtawi conceptualizes this political state in his use of the word *waṭanī*, which combines the concept of belonging to a certain country with the idea of civil rights, using it to mean something close to "citizen," which denotes individuals affiliated with a political community.[142] Another newly coined word was *ahlī* (pl. *ahlīn/ahālī/ahlūn/ahliyyīn*),[143] which pertains to belonging to a community (*ahl*). Al-Tahtawi defined *waṭanī* and *ahlī* in the beginning of the 1870s as one who "enjoys the rights of his country."[144] These two words were added to the medieval *madanī* in an attempt to express the natural political state of the human being.

of enlightenment part of the intellectual equipment of the Turkish reading public and the first thinkers to try to work out a synthesis between these ideas and Islam." For further details, see Mustafa Fadil Pasha, *Min Amīr ila Sulṭān* (Cairo: Al-Maṭba'a al-Raḥmāniyya, 1922); Şerif Mardin, *The Genesis of Young Ottoman Thought: A Study in the Modernization of Turkish Political Ideas* (Syracuse, NY: Syracuse University Press, 2000), 3–4; Davison, *Essays in Ottoman and Turkish History, 1774–1923: The Impact of the West*, 125–126.

142 This term, *waṭanī*, as meaning "citizen" was short lived, and it was replaced later by *muwāṭin*. The most common use of *waṭanī* in the second half of the nineteenth century primarily denoted one who was affiliated with a "homeland." See in this regard its use in the account of Amin Fikri's trip to Europe in 1889 (published in 1892): Muhammad Amin Fikri, *Irshād al-Alibbā ila Maḥāsin Ūrūbā* (Cairo: 'Ayn lil-Dirāsāt wal-Buḥūth, 2008), 140–141.

143 In addition to their frequent political meaning, these words referred to a local inhabitant as opposed to foreigners or settlers. For the temporal and early use of the word, see Robertson, *Kitāb Itḥāf Mulūk al-Zamān bi-Tārīkh al-Imbirāṭūr Sharlakān Masbūqan bi-Muqaddimatihi al-Musammā Itḥāf al-Mulūk al-Alibbā' bi-Taqaddum al-Jam'iyyāt fī Ūrūbā Mundhu Inqirāḍ al-Dawla al-Rūmāniyya*, 1:155; Robertson, *Kitāb Itḥāf Mulūk al-Zamān bi-Tārīkh al-Imbirāṭūr Sharlakān*, 2:38; *al-Jawā'ib*, September 1, 1875; *al-Jawā'ib*, June 22, 1875, 310; al-Shidyaq, *Kanz al-Raghā'ib fī Muntakhabāt al-Jawā'ib*, 1877, 5:6–20; *al-Baṣṣīr*, October 1, 1882; Ibn Abi al-Diyaf, *Itḥāf Ahl al-Zamān bi-Akhbār Mulūk Tūnis wa-'Ahd al-Amān*, 1:83.

144 Al-Tahtawi, "Kitāb al-Murshid al-Amīn lil-Banāt wal-Banīn," 457–458.

One of the most significant aspects of those involved in this intellectual stream is their different positions on political freedom and individual freedoms. Their attitude toward political freedom was demonstrated by their reception of the principle of republicanism – which stemmed from the idea of popular sovereignty – and revolution. All these scholars rejected the idea of republicanism, though their arguments varied. Rashid al-Dahdah, a dedicated Catholic[145] who wrote from monarchic France, translated the word "republic" as *fawḍa*, anarchy.[146] Butrus al-Bustani considered the republican model of governance to be "the first stage," the most basic of political developments, and in some cases a reason for instability and anarchy.[147] Muslim and Christian scholars alike assumed that enlightenment, which first of all involves education and the distribution of knowledge, is a precondition for the advancement of freedoms.[148] Al-Tahtawi articulated this position by stating that "progress in education that relates to the particular state of nations, qualifies them for the acquisition of freedom, which is the opposite of nations that do not invest in education. There, the progress of their civilization [*tamaddun*] could be delayed as long as their education [remains undeveloped]."[149] All these scholars believed

145 Al-Dahdah belonged to a well-known Maronite family. He received the title of "count" from Pope Pius IX in 1867. Tarrazi, *Ta'rīkh al-Ṣiḥāfa al-'Arabiyya*, 1913, 1:100–101.

146 Thus, for instance, he stated that the regimes of the United States of America, Columbia, and Mexico are republican, "*dawlatuhā fawḍa*." See *Birjīs Barīs*, October 26, 1859; *Birjīs Barīs*, November 9, 1859; *Birjīs Barīs*, January 18, 1860.

147 Al-Bustani, "Jumhūriyya," 534. The idea that the republican form of governance is primitive or negative was most common in western Europe by the end of the eighteenth century and the beginning of the nineteenth century (as, for instance, in the political philosophy of Edmund Burke). In a similar, historically well-rooted way, the idea that democracy is a dangerous form of governance that could lead to anarchy, factionalism, and eventually to despotism was common throughout history, including in the works of prominent ancient Greek philosophers such as Plato and Aristotle and medieval philosophers such as Ibn Rushd. For more details on the criticism of democracy in nineteenth-century France, see Michael Drolet, "Democracy, Self, and the Problem of the General Will in Nineteenth-Century French Political Thought," in *Re-imagining Democracy in the Age of Revolutions: America, France, Britain, Ireland, 1750–1850*, 69–82.

148 See in this regard al-Tunisi's argument against those who rejected the Tanzimat because of the state of knowledge in society: al-Tunisi, *Aqwam al-Masālik fī Ma'rifat Aḥwāl al-Mamālik*, 200.

149 Al-Tahtawi, "Kitāb al-Murshid al-Amīn lil-Banāt wal-Banīn," 317–318.

in the primary urgency of developing modern education, assuming that an enlightened society and social progress were most urgent. They rejected the idea of revolution, instead perceiving themselves as reformers. Although the thought produced by this political stream was far from being depicted as national, the influence from their liberal Western counterparts might be summed up as a civic component of nationalism. This ideological perception assumed the existence of harmony between the quest for liberal rights – such as equality, tolerance, and individual rights – and national solidarity, which was perceived as necessary for acquiring these rights. However, the similarities with Western liberals such as Ernest Renan and John Stuart Mill extended, for the most part, only this far.

The perception these scholars had of freedom was formulated against the background of contemporary challenges such as the political weakness of the central authority, its difficulty in imposing its political will – both internally, as a result of social anarchy, and externally, because of ongoing military challenges. This context drew attention to subjects that these scholars perceived as most urgent, such as fortifying social solidarity, a unified culture, developing education for the masses, and establishing the rule of law. Despite the fact that the Turkish and Arab intelligentsia and the Western powers, the French and the British, considered absolutism (*al-taḥakum al-muṭklaq*) to be a primary reason for the hindrance of progress,[150] the subject of autocracy was approached using traditional ideas, such as consultation (*shūra*), that balanced mass engagement in politics with preserving the absolute sovereign and empowering the central authority.

Although these ideas dominated the intellectual discourse between 1860 and 1882, the 1870s witnessed unprecedented freedom that was accompanied by significant events such as the inauguration of the Ottoman parliament (closed down by ʿAbd al-Hamid II in February 1878). During this decade many journalists inside the territories of the Ottoman Empire publicly criticized the local autocratic system by associating it with cultural deterioration and backwardness. The Syrian Lebanese editors of *al-Ahrām* (founded in 1875), Bishara and Salim Taqla, write in an 1879 article dedicated to the subject of freedom in Egypt that the greatest enemy of freedom in the East is the popular belief in determinism, which maintains the legitimacy of autocracy.

[150] *Al-Jawāʾib*, June 25, 1875, 2.

This type of regime grows in a social environment of ignorance, its greatest ally. The two journalists articulate their position on the idea of sovereignty in their discussion of political changes in Egypt: "In every civilized state, the ruler followed the ruled, and the ruled did not follow the ruler. The parliament is the best guarantee of this principle [the rule of the people]."[151]

During the 1870s this political concept became increasingly refined. *Jumhūr*, the general term used to express a broader set of connotations – including republican, liberal, constitutional, and democratic – became less frequently used, and it was replaced by political idioms that more clearly indicated particular ideologies. This transition is reflected in an 1878 article published in *al-Bashīr* that attempts to define the relationship between "liberal" and "republican": "Amply, the republicans express their honest love of freedom and even impudently contend that they are solely responsible for it and the supporters of freedom in the civilized world. This is why they referred to themselves using the word liberal [*librāl*]."[152] Although the use of the word *ḥurr/librāl* during the 1870s was identified with republican and constitutional forces, the use of these words developed more focused content.[153] Two independent meanings in Arabic crystallized as a result of vast historical changes: The republican autocratic experience under Napoleon in the past, together with the Napoleonic party active at that time in France, emphasized that despotism can occur in the name of the republic, which stood in clear contradiction to the common phrase "republic that is based on the principles of freedom."[154] Against this background the meaning of *ḥurr/librāl* primarily indicated liberal politics identified with constitutionalism. Contemporary journalism in Arabic elucidates this aspect with the use of the phrase *ḥukūmat*

[151] For selected examples, see the report in *al-Ahrām* attacking the Egyptian government by using the terms "autocratic governments" (*ḥukūma istibdādiyya*) and "giving freedom [to the people]" (*i'ṭā' al-ḥurriyya*). See the report on the replacement by the khedive of the "absolute and autocratic" governance with a constitutional government, "the first step toward civilized governance and moderate freedom." *Al-Ahrām*, May 22, 1879; *al-Ahrām*, February 27, 1879; *al-Ahrām*, March 13, 1879.

[152] *Al-Bashīr*, September 27, 1878.

[153] Ibid.; *al-Baṣṣīr*, August 18, 1881; *al-Baṣṣīr*, October 13, 1881.

[154] The phrase in Arabic is "*jumhūriyya rasikha 'ala uṣūl al-ḥurriyya.*" See al-Shidaq's criticism of the French republic: Al-*Jawā'ib*, November 7, 1877; *al-Jawā'ib*, December 5, 1877.

*al-ḥurriyya* (liberal government) to indicate agovernment ruled by proponents of constitutionalism.[155] These developments in political language were accompanied by the use of *ḥurriyya* as a subject of individual political identification, and phrases such as *abnāʾ al-waṭan al-aḥrār* (free patriots),[156] *aḥrār fī ārāʾihim* (free thinkers),[157] and *abnāʾ al-ḥurriyya* (proreform thinkers) appeared more frequently.[158]

Despite the fact that the vast majority of the progressive scholars supported constitutional autocracy, they rejected the idea of revolution and neglected or rejected the idea of sovereignty of the people. A few prominent voices in Arabic among the scholars who wrote from outside the borders of the empire presented different stances. This group presented a close systematic concept of freedom that correlates with the liberal perception of their Western counterparts, who approached the problem of freedom from the angle of absolutism. Among Arabic speakers the most prominent scholar identified with liberal ideas was politician and journalist Khalil Ghanim.

Khalil Ghanim was born to a Maronite family in Beirut. In his youth he studied Arabic under Nasif al-Yaziji, in addition to French, English, and Turkish. He began his political career in the early 1860s with his appointment as a member of the court of commerce. Following this, he was appointed as a dragoman in the Mutasarrifate, and after that he filled the same position under the vali of Syria, Rashid Pasha, and his successor, Isad Pasha. With the appointment of Isad Pasha to the position of grand vizier, Ghanim moved with him to Istanbul, where he became chief dragoman in the grand vizierate, a position that preceded his election as a deputy of Beirut. During his service Ghanim

155 This phrase was particularly used in the British context. In an attempt to elucidate the political platform of the British political parties, the progressive periodical *al-Muqtaṭaf* dedicated an article that quoted a British politician distinguishing between the conservatives and the liberals: The liberal party relied on the will of the people, assuming that this political force leads to the common good, while the conservative party feared politicizing the people, assuming that it would lead to destruction. The liberals assume that people are good by nature, while the conservatives fear that the opposite is true. *Al-Baṣṣīr*, August 18, 1881; *al-Muqtaṭaf* 1, no. 10 (1885): 5–8.

156 *Al-Ahrām*, March 7, 1882.

157 *Al-Ahrām*, January 27, 1877; *al-Ahrām*, February 12, 1881.

158 The group published their demands for reforms in an open letter from Beirut signed by "the sons of freedom" (*naḥnu abnāʾ al-ḥurriyya*), addressing them to Midhat Pasha, who was appointed the governor of Syria in November 1878. *Al-Ahrām*, February 21, 1879.

was a prominent deputy, and in the second session of the parliament, he became the leader of the opposition faction. After the prorogation of the first Ottoman parliament, he was requested on February 15, 1878, to appear before the minister of police with nine of the opposition members. There they were informed that they had to leave Istanbul for their homes by the first available ship, formally ending Midhat's parliament. This decision was a refined version of ʿAbd al-Hamid II's request to arrest and punish the opposition members. Ghanim left for Marseille, and afterward Paris, where he established his first newspaper – the first among many that he founded later in France and Switzerland, in French, Arabic, and Turkish. In Paris, Ghanim received French citizenship, was honored by the *Légion d'honneur*, and married a Frenchwoman.[159] He became famous and established close relationships with prominent French politicians and intellectuals, and he was the one who introduced Jamal al-Din al-Afghani to Ernest Renan, a meeting that later led to their famous exchange in 1883.[160]

Ghanim's political activity in the Ottoman parliament and for a few years afterward was referred to by some contemporaries as "liberal" (*ḥurr*).[161] One of the contemporary newspapers indicated that during his political career as a deputy he adopted the "radical" ideas of the liberal party (*dhahaba madhhab al-ḥizb al-ḥur*).[162] Other politicians who received the same appellation were his counterparts: the twelve parliament opposition members who served the same ideas, including Yusif Diyyaʾ Khalidi Efindi, the representative of Jerusalem, ʿAbd al-Rahim Badran Efindi, the representative of Syria, and Manuk Efindi,

159 For further details of his biography, see Tarrazi, *Taʾrīkh al-Ṣiḥāfa al-ʿArabiyya*, 1914, 2:268–271; Robert Devereux, *The First Ottoman Constitutional Period: A Study of the Midhat Constitution and Parliament* (Baltimore, MD: Johns Hopkins Press, 1963), 246–248, 275.

160 Kedourie argues that he worked for the French government. See Elie Kedourie, *Afghani and ʿAbduh: An Essay on Religious Unbelief and Political Activism in Modern Islam* (London: Frank Cass, 1997), 40–41.

161 Arabic newspapers published in Europe used "liberal" more frequently to refer to some constitutional statesmen, including Midhat Pasha, who was known as a "proponent of freedom of conscience and of democratic government" and as "a liberal and a reformist." In Arabic the phrases are "*min aṣḥāb madhhab ḥurriyyat al-ḍamīr wal-ḥukūma al-jumhūriyya*" and "*ishtahara bi-madhhab al-ḥurriyya wal-munādah bil-iṣlāḥ*." *Al-Baṣṣīr*, May 26, 1881.

162 *Al-Baṣṣīr*, June 16, 1881. The government supporters were four deputies from Istanbul and two deputies from Salonica. For the complete list of names of the opposition and the supporters, see: Devereux, *The First Ottoman Constitutional Period*, 151.

the representative of Aleppo. These members, and Ghanim himself, were ordered to leave Istanbul with the close of parliament.[163]

Ghanim, the most prominent politician among this liberal group, was known during the time of his parliamentary activity as being anti-autocratic. Like many Arabic and Turkish speakers, he was convinced that corruption, cultural deterioration, and political weakness are all symptoms of autocracy. After the prorogation of the parliament, he stated that "the sultan advocated freedom of speech by law. When the sultan has decided to grant a constitution, he has no right to retreat from his decision and his formal confirmation. The sultan is subordinate to the constitution and not above it."[164] Ghanim explained his choice to flee to France as resulting from his political convictions and love of freedom: "In this country the tree of freedom had grown and borne fruit."[165]

In France, Ghanim founded *al-Baṣṣir*, a newspaper that followed the formal French foreign policies and was a most critical voice of ʿAbd al-Hamid II's autocracy. In his works from between 1878 and 1882, Ghanim advocates for the idea of freedom, expressing antiautocratic and anticonservative tendencies. He presents a theoretical model that is based on a premise that connects three concepts: freedom, reason, and sovereignty of the people. He argues that reason necessarily leads to the conclusion that freedom is the greatest fortress of individualism. Furthermore, it is a precondition for a peaceful society because the method of elections avoids internal conflicts by giving the right to all social components to choose the regime that fits their needs. He continues by advocating the idea of civil rights. Citizens, he argues, are the body of the state, and they should be treated with respect because they are the reason for its success and prosperity: "Today, all citizens [*raʿāyyā*] of the civilized countries consent to support liberal governments [*hukūmāt ḥurriyya*] that are elected by them and authorized to act according to their will."[166] He was among the earliest of the Arabic-speaking scholars to ascribe central significance to the ideas of "public

[163] For the biographies of these three deputies and for the activity of the Syrian deputies in the Ottoman parliaments, see *Al-Baṣṣīr*, June 16, 1881; Malek Sharif, "A Portrait of Syrian Deputies in the First Ottoman Parliament," in *The Ottoman Experiment in Democracy*, ed. Malek Sharif and Christoph Herzog (Würzburg: Ergon in Kommission, 2010), 285–311.

[164] Tarrazi, *Taʾrīkh al-Ṣiḥāfa al-ʿArabiyya*, 1914, 2:269.

[165] *Al-Baṣṣīr*, June 16, 1881. [166] *Al-Baṣṣīr*, September 1, 1881.

opinion" and "power of the people." To indicate these two democratic ideas, he used two Arabic phrases, "*ra'ī 'ām*" (public opinion)[167] and "*sulṭat al-sha'b*" (power of the people),[168] two concepts whose function in a democracy is to inspect the political process and regulate its development. A free political process (*siyāsa ḥurra*), he argues, is the most important condition for preserving the public interest: "Freedom is the model for perfect politics, a powerful tool shining light that dispels the darkness of suspicion, ignorance, and error."[169] Despite his Catholic background he was a republican, a strong opponent of royalist conservativism, and a proponent of maintaining the separation between religion and worldly affairs.[170] On the subject of religion, he possessed a secular concept of religious tolerance that was based on the principle of freedom of belief. Tolerance was his main interest in both his early and late works, which were apparently written under the influence of the works of Ernest Renan, whom he knew personally. In one of his articles he denounces attacks against the Jewish communities in a few European countries, claiming that this is a black stain that deforms the face of the civilized nations. In the name of freedom of belief, he defends their right to practice their traditions freely.[171] During his activity in the Young Turks movement, and in later work that he published in French about the Ottoman sultans,[172] he connects the deterioration of the "Ottoman nation" with the loss of tolerance and claims that tolerance is conditional upon the restoration of the constitution.[173] In addition to his political ideas, Ghanim was one of the earliest Arabic-speaking scholars to write about the subject of political economy, a field that occupied central importance with the rise of the socialist left during the 1870s.[174]

167 Ibid. 168 *Al-Baṣṣīr*, September 27, 1881.

169 *Al-Baṣṣīr*, September 1, 1881; *al-Baṣṣīr*, July 28, 1881.

170 *Al-Baṣṣīr*, August 11, 1881; *al-Baṣṣīr*, August 25, 1881; Khalil Ghanim, *Kitāb al-Iqtiṣād al-Siyāsī aw Fann Tadbīr al-Manzil* (Alexandria: Maṭba'at Jarīdat Miṣr, 1879), 66–69.

171 *Al-Baṣṣīr*, August 25, 1881; *al-Baṣṣīr*, January 19, 1882.

172 For his activity in the Young Turks, see Ernest Edmondson Ramsaur, *The Young Turks: Prelude to the Revolution of 1908* (Beirut: Khayats, 1965), 14–51; Hourani, *Arabic Thought in the Liberal Age, 1798–1939*, 1970, 263–266.

173 Halil Ganem, *Education Des Princes Ottomans* (Bulle, Suisse: Imprimerie Emile Lenz, 1895).

174 Ghanim, *Kitāb al-Iqtiṣād al-Siyāsī aw Fann Tadbīr al-Manzil.*

Ghanim's liberal democratic ideas were not the only ones that stood apart from the general sphere of political ideas in Arabic during the 1870s. During this decade readers of Arabic were exposed to works that presented the French Revolution using historical methodology, including its being a political and universal symbol of the liberation of mankind. Systematic works on this topic were published as a series of articles by Khattar al-Dahdah in *al-Jinān* between the years 1871 and 1880,[175] in addition to the article by Adib Ishaq, a Syrian of Armenian origin, who wrote enthusiastically about the idea of "revolution," presenting it as both a method for applying freedom and a "cure" for political and social injustice.[176] During this decade "revolution" became a controversial concept, and conservative publications in Arabic, especially in Syria, alerted people to its destructive impact.[177]

Despite this intellectual engagement, "revolution" was rejected by the vast majority of scholars, including Adib Ishaq himself. He, who wrote emphatically about this concept, adopted a reformist stance regarding internal Ottoman affairs, fearing violence and chaos, and making the time for revolution conditional upon a fundamental change of ideas and a "revolution of souls" (*thawrat al-anfus*).[178] Another exceptional thinker was Rizq Allah Hassun. Hassun, also of Armenian origin, a Catholic Arabic speaker from Aleppo, was born to a wealthy father who worked in commerce and as a dragoman in the Austrian consulate in Aleppo. He had a religious education in addition to learning Turkish, French, Arabic, and Armenian in Dair Bizmar, an Armenian Catholic monastery in Keserwan, Lebanon. He founded the earliest Arabic nonofficial newspaper in Istanbul and became connected with Turkish statesmen. In 1860, during the religious clashes in Syria, he accompanied Fuad Pasha, who had been dispatched to Syria to investigate the massacres. After Hassun's return to Istanbul, he was appointed to a position in the tobacco customs office, where he acquired many enemies and was accused of misappropriating funds. This affair was apparently related to his Arabic-speaking rival, Faris al-Shidyaq, who inherited Hassun's position in Istanbul's Arabic

175 Leon Zolondek, "The French Revolution in Arabic Literature of the Nineteenth Century," *The Muslim World* 57, no. 3 (1967): 207–208.
176 Ishaq, *Adīb Ishāq: Al-Kitābāt al-Siyāsiyya wal-Ijtimāʿiyya*, 143–145.
177 See the report in *Al-Bashīr*, April 8, 1871, 266.
178 Ishaq, *Adīb Ishāq: Al-Kitābāt al-Siyāsiyya wal-Ijtimāʿiyya*, 35–42, 143–145.

journalism.[179] He fled to Russia and afterward to France and London. In Great Britain he began publishing his newspaper *Mir'āt al-Aḥwāl* anew; it became one of the most critical voices against the Ottoman Empire, and he became a proponent of Russian foreign policy.[180]

Hassun was one of the rare scholars who did not hold any hope that the Tanzimat and the first Ottoman parliament would bring any improvement in the social or political state of the Ottoman Empire's inhabitants. He accused the constitutional government of chaotic management of the state and of oppressing its non-Muslim subjects. He argued that the non-Muslims did not gain equal rights and equal representation in the parliament, despite being approximately "half of the empire's population."[181] Hassun wrote consistently in his newspaper about Ottoman injustice: critical articles on the heavy burden of taxes that the Ottomans imposed on peasants;[182] the fanaticism of the Muslim ʿulama, their impact on politics, and the use of religion in state affairs;[183] the irrelevance of the past concept of justice and laws (the rule of shariʿa) in the modern era;[184] and critical articles against the slave trade in the Muslim countries, North Africa, and the territories of the Ottoman Empire.[185]

Hassun was convinced that the only way to bring about a fundamental improvement in the state of the Ottoman Empire's subjects was to completely destroy Ottoman rule. He was very critical of the Turkish

179 Hassun and al-Shidyaq were the most powerful Arab journalists in Istanbul, and both had Christian origins. Hassun continued to defame al-Shidyaq, apparently on the ground of his encounters with the Ottoman authorities. For further details about their literary debates, see Kamran Rastegar, *Literary Modernity between the Middle East and Europe: Textual Transactions in Nineteenth-Century Arabic, English, and Persian Literatures* (London: Routledge, 2007), 120–123.

180 In one of the earliest biographies published about him (1910), Hassun is depicted as a "free journalist" and a "free politician." The author explains that information about Hassun's life was rare because of fear of the Ottoman authorities, who persecuted him. For further details about his biography, see *al-Muqtaṭaf* 3, no. 36 (January 3, 1910): 224–231; *al-Muqtaṭaf* 4, no. 36 (January 4, 1910): 321–327; Tarrazi, *Ta'rīkh al-Ṣiḥāfa al-ʿArabiyya*, 1913, 1:105–110; Salma Khadra Jayyusi, *Trends and Movements in Modern Arabic Poetry* (Leiden: E. J. Brill, 1977), 33–34; Philip Charles Sadgrove, "Ḥassūn, Rizq Allah (1825–80)," *Encyclopedia of Arabic Literature* (London: Routledge, 1998), 276.

181 *Mir'āt al-Aḥwāl*, March 22, 1877.

182 Ibid.

183 Ibid.; *Mir'āt al-Aḥwāl*, February 5, 1877.

184 *Mir'āt al-Aḥwāl*, March 22, 1877.

185 *Mir'āt al-Aḥwāl*, March 29, 1877; *Mir'āt al-Aḥwāl*, June 6, 1877.

rulers, who in his opinion managed their interior political situation by oppressing and exploiting their subjects in barbaric and savage ways. He referred to the Turks as "foreigners in the land of civilization" (*dukhalā' 'ala arḍ al-tamaddun*),[186] criticizing with no less incisiveness the European powers that did not invest much effort in helping the Ottomans' oppressed subjects. He was most critical of the British, who with their policies protected the Ottoman sovereignty and managed "to keep [the Ottoman subjects] under slavery" in return for the Ottomans staying away from the British struggle with other Western powers over British commercial and political interests in India.[187] These mutual interests were, in his opinion, rooted in the cruel Turkish internal policies and supported them indirectly by preventing any Western intervention. The outcome of the British policies was the oppression of the Christian nations and "the victory of Turkish barbarism over civilization, and the principles of savageness over humanism."[188]

Hassun consistently attempted to convince the European powers to replace their policies promoting the Ottoman reform by supporting the idea of revolution and the destruction of the sultanate. He used the Arabic term *thawra*, which would become the most widely accepted term in modern Arabic to indicate modern revolutions. Hassun was convinced that the Tanzimat reforms were enacted due to external pressures on the Ottoman government. He dedicated a few satirical articles to mocking the inauguration of the Turkish parliament, contending that it was a comedy; he argued that the Turks utilized the Western demands for reform to gain time and allies and that these "civilized" principles were foreign to the Turks and their savage culture. He believed that the seed of freedom could not develop under Turkish rule: "Neither their culture and traditions nor their language embed any minimal conditions for limited government that has a constitution and representatives."[189]

Hassun's writings present an obsessive fear of massacres. He criticizes the foreign policy of Great Britain, which supported the Ottomans against the Russians, contending that if the civilized world did not condemn the Turks for their massacres, and if they did not produce

[186] *Mir'āt al-Aḥwāl*, March 29, 1877. [187] *Mir'āt al-Aḥwāl*, March 22, 1877.
[188] Ibid.; *Mir'āt al-Aḥwāl*, March 29, 1877.
[189] *Mir'āt al-Aḥwāl*, March 22, 1877; *Mir'āt al-Aḥwāl*, June 4, 1877.

a mechanism to protect the Christian nations, the Turks would continue killing their subjects. He criticizes British hypocrisy on the subject of revolution: On the one hand, they supported the revolution in and union of Italy, and on the other, they stood against the revolutions in the Ottoman Empire.[190] They objected to the slave trade, yet they opposed the liberation of nations under the Ottomans. Above all, they claimed to be the protectors of freedom in the world.[191] He argues for the necessity of revolution by portraying the circular relationship between the Turkish structural failures and massacres: The Turks would continue in their attempt to implement reforms, their failure would lead to revolutions, and the reaction to that would be massacres. He was convinced that this bloody circle could end either internally by revolution or externally by an invasion that would have to impose an end to the "Turkish" seizure of territories. Although his works do not present a clear national perception, Hassun was anti-Turk. Unlike his critical works on the Ottomans, he excludes the semi-independent countries, Egypt and Tunisia, which were ruled by "non-Turks," from his attack.[192] He argues that Islam was not the reason for Turkish cruelty; rather, it stemmed from their national culture and traditions. In their violence, he continues, they did not preserve even the divine Islamic laws that command Muslims to protect the "the people of the book."[193] Hassun followed other Christian journalists, such as al-Bustani, by arguing that divine laws are not ahistoric and that the human concept of justice should be subject to change over time: "The way of justice that made this kingdom great in the past is not applicable now, and it should be replaced because it has become impossible in this age that considers the justice of the past to be unjust [*ẓulm*]."[194]

Unlike most of his mainstream contemporaries, Hassun was a critical scholar, presenting an early observation of the failure of Ottomanism, the reforms, and the constitution. He observed the failure of the Tanzimat during its peak, when high hopes were raised with the inauguration of the first Ottoman parliament. Hassun's satirical articles on the superficial implementation of reforms put him in conflict with the

190 *Mir'āt al-Aḥwāl*, April 26, 1877.

191 *Mir'āt al-Aḥwāl*, May 17, 1877.

192 *Mir'āt al-Aḥwāl*, April 26, 1877.

193 See his summary of an article from the British newspaper *The Times*: *Mir'āt al-Aḥwāl*, May 24, 1877.

194 *Mir'āt al-Aḥwāl*, March 22, 1877.

mainstream of the freethinkers and advocates of reform. The intellectual function of scholars who were exposed to the private journalism of the end of the 1850s and to the short-lived experience of free politicians in the 1870s was to present new models whose outlines were exposed by Hassun's conflict with his greatest enemy, Faris al-Shidyaq;[195] while the first functioned as a critical revolutionary, the second acted as the voice of the existing institution.[196] In an illuminating note, al-Shidyaq elaborated on his social function as a scholar: "I am not like those [scholars] who criticize changing laws or royal decisions. I am not like those who criticize rulers either, because I am afraid that they might discharge me from using my pen."[197] Hassun died in London in 1880, apparently poisoned by agents of Sultan ʿAbd al-Hamid II.

Among the formative theoretical models presented between 1860 and 1882, that of the mainstream had the greatest impact on the development of the concept of freedom. This model espoused civil tolerance and autocratic constitutionalism, and it presented "freedom" as both a utopian ideal of the program of progress and a practical political idea that shaped formal edicts and documents. Contemporary journalists and politicians constantly employed this particular perception of freedom in their language. The constitution was presented by the Ottoman deputies as a declaration for the "emancipation of Ottomans" (*farmān ḥurriyyat al-ʿUthmāniyyīn*).[198] Authoritarianism (*al-ḥukm al-istibdādī*) was recognized in the sultan's declarations as a major cause for the deterioration of the empire,[199] while a civil community (*al-hayʾa al-ijtimāʿiyya al-madaniyya*)[200] combined with Islamic

[195] Despite the fact that he was a strong proponent of the idea of a constitution when the idea was promoted by the state, his newspaper, *al-Jawāʾib*, supported ʿAbd al-Hamid II's decision to close down the parliament, arguing that it was not the proper time for parliamentary discussions; rather, the time was right for defending the state's territories. *Al-Jawāʾib*, February 20, 1878, 1.

[196] Much of Hassun's writing after his departure from Istanbul focused on al-Shidyaq's works. Their debates are characterized by the use of vilifying language. Hassun, for example, accused al-Shidyaq of unbelief (*kufr*). For selected examples, see Rizq Allah Hassun, *al-Nafathāt* (London: Trübner & Co., 1867), 80–83.

[197] Al-Shidyaq, *al-Wāsiṭa ila Maʿrifat Aḥwāl Mālṭa wa-Kashf al-Mukhabbāʾ ʿan Funūn Ūrūbā*, 61–62.

[198] See the response in the chamber of deputies to the sultan's speech: Ahmad Faris al-Shidyaq, *Kanz al-Raghāʾib fī Muntakhabāt al-Jawāʾib*, ed. Salim al-Shidyaq, vol. 6 (Istanbul: Maṭbaʿat *al-Jawāʾib*, 1878), 173.

[199] Ibid., 6:2–4. [200] *Al-Jawāʾib*, January 4, 1877, 2.

consultation (*shūra*) was used as the particular Islamic perception of civil society and constitutionalism. These intellectual conventions formulated the political language used in the Ottoman constitution. This important document, which was published and discussed in a series of articles in many Arabic newspapers and periodicals at the end of the 1870s, indicates that the Ottoman sultan is the caliph who is responsible for both Islam and for the non-Muslim Ottoman subjects (Article 4), in attempt to maintain balance between civil principles and the religious Islamic function of the state. Similarly, the constitution grants Islam the official status of state religion in addition to stating that all affiliated with recognized religions had the right to freely practice their religious beliefs, while recognizing civic equality among all Ottomans (Articles 11 and 17).[201] The use of the word "freedom" in this document presents the common perception among the mainstream scholars that ascribes the right to freedom to the absolute sovereign, the sultan. The word *ḥurriyya* is used to indicate the freedom of the Ottoman dynasty (*ḥurriyyat sulālat āll ʿUthmān*) and their divine rights (Articles 6 and 7), which include the right of the divine sultan to open and to disperse the parliament, to announce war or peace, to sign treaties with foreign states, to approve and discharge deputies, and the responsibility of the sultan to implement shariʿa law (Article 7). The relation between the two principles, sovereignty and freedom, is also determined: On the one hand, the subjects (*tabaʿat al-dawla*) enjoy individual freedoms (Articles 9 and 10), and on the other hand, the sultan is the absolute sovereign, and the parliament is elected pending his approval.[202] In practice these ideas came to an end in ʿAbd al-Hamid II's era, in February 1878, with his order to close down the parliament, but the particular balance between the components of the formative concept of freedom as they crystallized during this period would accompany Arab history during and after the twentieth century.

201 Ibid., 2–3; *al-Jawāʾib*, January 10, 1877, 3; *al-Ahrām*, January 13, 1877; *al-Ahrām*, January 27, 1877; *al-Ahrām*, February 2, 1877; *al-Ahrām*, February 10, 1877; *al-Jinān* 2 (1877): 37–45.

202 The Arabic translation of the articles of the constitution in *al-Jawāʾib* were collected and republished in al-Shidyaq, *Kanz al-Raghāʾib fī Muntakhabāt al-Jawāʾib*, 1878, 6:5–27.

# *Conclusion*

Ideas might emerge in one particular cultural environment and be transferred to and developed in another, but this development is fully imbued with complexities that emanate from the particular topographies of culture and systems of values in which that development takes place. Conceptual history demonstrates how ideas and traditions are summoned and constructed at distinct points in time and in contexts in which they are regarded as essential. The intensity of these dynamics is clearly manifested in how concepts developed during the period between 1820 and 1860, in which their linguistic signifiers experienced instability and uncertainty that determined the survival of some, the submersion of others, or the minting of new terms and the recycling of old ones. These decades, however, were rich in "semantic turning points" in the Arabic language, which in their significance could be compared to major transitions in European history such as the Renaissance or the Enlightenment.

The reorganization of the realm of ideas and its invigoration in the nineteenth century were generated by a broad intellectual movement that was conceptualized by its adherents as *tamaddun*. This movement emerged against a background that was dominated by a sense of cultural crisis and regression, manifesting an urgent need for advancement, refinement, and the acquisition of social solidarity and political power. Above all, this intellectual movement emphasized the subject of the enlightenment of society through the distribution of knowledge and the acquisition of education as a key for making progress. It is within this framework of *tamaddun* that ideas later considered by historians to be modern emerged, evolved, and were conceptualized. The intellectual endeavor that contributed to the construction of these ideas involved thinking from within the temporal language through which ideas were filtered and sometimes formulated within the particular parameters of the local culture.

Arabic-speaking scholars became acquainted with the political concept and the political practice of freedom beginning in the late eighteenth century. The individual and collective political aspects of the concept were, however, constructed in Arabic and transformed into a focal idea in cultural discourse only later: This took place mainly between the years 1820 and 1860. It was only then that Arabic-speaking scholars began to rethink their political and social institutions in a context that comprised policies of centralization implemented by authorities from above and social tensions that endangered the existence of some minority communities, technological developments, economic transitions, and cultural shifts that left a deep impact on the subject of identity from below. "Freedom" and associated concepts such as "progress," "civilization," "politics," "reason," "equality," "tolerance," "citizenship," and "justice" expanded semantically and were reorganized as systems of ideas in political and social future-oriented doctrines or ideological structures that stabilized in language between 1860 and 1882. Terms such as *ḥurriyya* and *tasāhul* (derived from liberalism) were thematized and used as theoretical programs for developing the sociopolitical state in correlation with the ideals of *tamaddun*. Less attractive but also stable content was acquired during the same period by idioms such as *ishtirākiyya* (derived from socialism) and *ʿadamiyya* (derived from anarchism). These ideologies were received critically and perceived as radical interpretations of "freedom" that did not suit the values and the aspirations of the contemporary Arabic-speaking scholars.

The scholars' preoccupation with the subject of freedom produced a variety of interpretations. Conceptual history provides some illuminating insights regarding the relation between the components of this concept, emphasizing its particularities through looking at their inter-dynamics, especially between the principles of "political freedom" and "individual freedoms." The majority of scholars living under Ottoman rule assessed the idea of freedom as an alienable value that is bestowed by the sovereign, whether the absolute monarch or God. In this respect their major focus addressed freedom through the aspect of "individual freedoms," ignoring or entirely rejecting the principle of "political freedom" that ascribes political sovereignty to "citizens." The manifestations of these ideas appear in the broad stances that progressive scholars assumed by supporting constitutional autocracy and rejecting the modern idea of revolution as a violent quest to implement popular sovereignty. Their conceptualization of individual freedom was the perspective they used to assess the subject of political identity. The theoretical engagement that refined the inherited perception of solidarity in an attempt to establish a new perception of community preserved the hierarchic political patterns of subjectivity while striving for social equality. The vast interest in the individual rather than the political aspect of freedom manifested in a state of thought in which the idea of "democracy" did not acquire an independent meaning and in 1882 continued to be commonly conceived as an integral part of the concept "republic." Different perceptions, however, were voiced by a few prominent Christians who wrote from outside the borders of the Ottoman Empire and possessed a close systematic concept of freedom that correlated with the liberal-democratic perception common in western Europe.

The most frequently embraced concept of freedom in Arabic constitutes one of the main differences between the components of nationalism and liberalism in western Europe and the local discourse about collective solidarity and civil rights. By the end of the 1870s, neither the politicization of the community (*waṭaniyya*) nor the politicization of individuals had evolved in Arabic in contrast with absolutism. A variety of motives influenced the formation of the concept of freedom in Arabic: the social function of most of the Muslim scholars involved, who served as civil servants who were selected by the political authorities to perform specific tasks; the belief that the principle of the sovereignty of the people contradicts the Islamic principle of religious leadership (*imāma sharʿiyya*); the impact of the revived political thought inherited from medieval Islamic philosophy, which was dominated by Platonic hierarchical political perceptions that rejected democratic principles; and motives derived from contemporary affairs such as the belief that political freedom or revolution might lead to chaos, thus endangering social stability. Nevertheless, the scholarly endeavor of this intellectual stream created particular ideological forms that stemmed from local experience.

In Arabic the modern concept of freedom evolved against the landscape of the particular sociopolitical and religious topographies of Ottoman societies. When the Spring of Nations broke out in 1848 in most of the European capitals where national and liberal slogans calling for the sovereignty of the people were in use, the Arabic-speaking scholars were preoccupied with different issues that were related to the weakness of the state and the fragility of social solidarity. They ascribed scant importance to the subject of political rights in relation to individual rights and communal unity. While Western national and liberal ideas evolved in contrast with absolutism, the idea of freedom evolved in the Arabic-speaking provinces in contrast to a lack of order, anarchy, inequality, and a sense of injustice. In an analogy with European thought, the political concept of freedom in Arabic would be closer to the principle of the "rule of law" than to liberal constitutionalism.

# *Bibliography*

## Lexicons, Dictionaries, and Glossaries

Abkariyus, Yuhanna. *Qāmūs Inklīzī wa-'Arabī*. Beirut, 1887.

*English-Arabic Reader's Dictionary*. Beirut: Librairie du Liban, 1974.

Ahmadnakri, 'Abd al-Nabi bin 'Abd al-Rasul. *Jāmi' al-'Ulūm fī Iṣṭilāḥāt al-Funūn al-Mulaqqab bi-Dustūr al-'Ulamā'*. 4 vols. Beirut: Mu'assasat al-A'lamī lil-Maṭbū'āt, 1975.

Badger, George Percy. *An English-Arabic Lexicon*. London: C. K. Paul & Co., 1881.

Berggren, Jacob. *Guide Français-Arabe Vulgaire Des Voyageurs et Des Francs En Syrie et En Égypte: Avec Carte Physique et Géographique de La Syrie et Plan Géométrique de Jérusalem Ancien et Moderne, Comme Supplément Aux Voyages En Oreint*. Upsal: Leffler et Sebell, 1844.

Bianchi, Thomas Xavier, and Jean Daniel Kieffer. *Dictionnaire Turc-Français: À L'usage Des Agents Diplomatiques et Consulaires, Des Commerçants, Des Navigateurs, et Autres Voyageurs Dans Le Levant*. 2 vols. Paris: Impr. royale, 1835, 1837.

Biberstein-Kazimirski, Albert de. *Dictionnaire Arabe-Français*. 2 vols. Paris: Barrois, 1850.

Bocthor, Ellious. *Dictionnaire Français-Arabe*. 2 vols. Paris: Chez Firmin Didot Freres, 1828–1829.

al-Bustani, Butrus. *Muḥīṭ al-Muḥīṭ*. Beirut: Maktabat Lubnān, 1998.

Cañes, Francisco. *Gramatica Arabigo-Española, Vulgar, Y Literal: Con Un Diccionario Arabigo-Español, En Que Se Ponen Las Voces Mas Usuales Para Una Conversacion Familiar, Con El Texto de La Doctrina Cristiana En El Idioma Arabigo*. Madrid: En la imprenta de don Antonio Perez de Soto, 1775.

*Diccionario Español-Latino-Arabigo*. 3 vols. Madrid: Impr. de A. Sancha, 1787.

Dozy, Reinhart Pieter Anne. *Takmilat al-Ma'ājim al-'Arabiyya*. 11 vols. Baghdad: Dār al-Shu'ūn al-Thaqāfiyya al-'Āmma, 1978–2001.

*Dictionnaire Français-Arabe*. Beirut: Imprimerie Catholique, 1857.

Firuzabadi, Muhammad Ibn Ya'qub. *Al-Qāmūs al-Muḥīṭ*. Beirut: Mu'assasat al-Risāla, 2005.

Golius, Jacobus. *Lexicon Arabico-Latinum*. Lugduni Batavorum: typis Bonaventurae and Abrahami, Elseviriorum, prostant Amstelodami apud Johannem Ravesteynivm, 1653.

Handjéri, Alexandre. *Dictionnaire Français-Arabe-Persan et Turc: Enrichi D'examples En Langue Turque Avec Des Variantes, et de Beaucoup de Mots D'arts et Des Sciences*. 3 vols. Moscow: Impr. de l'Université impériale, 1840–1841.

Hopkins, David. *A Vocabulary, Persian, Arabic, and English; Abridged from the Quarto Edition of Richardson's Dictionary*. London: Printed for F. and C. Rivingson, 1810.

Ibn Manzur, Muhammad Ibn Mukarram. *Lisān al-ʿArab*. 18 vols. Beirut: Dār al-Ṣādir, 2004.

Jahn, Johann. *Lexicon Arabico-Latinum*. Vindobonae: Apud C. F. Wappler et Beck, 1802.

Johnson, Francis. *A Dictionary, Persian, Arabic, and English*. London: Wm. H. Allen and Co., 1852.

al-Juhari, Ismaʿil Ibn Hamad. *Al-Ṣiḥāḥ fī al-Lugha: Tāj al-Lugha wa-Ṣiḥāh al-ʿArabiyya*. 7 vols. Beirut: Dār al-ʿIlm lil-Malāyīn, 1990.

Kaffawi, Abi al-Baqaʾ Ayyub ibn Musa. *Al-Kulliyāt: Muʿjam fī al-Muṣṭalaḥāt wal-Furūq al-Lughawiyya*. Beirut: Muʾassasat al-Risāla, 1998.

Kirkpatrick, William. *A Vocabulary, Persian, Arabic, and English*. London: Printed by Joseph Cooper, Drury-Lane, 1785.

Mallouf, Nassif. *Dictionnaire Français-Turc*. Paris: Maisonneuve et Cie, 1856.

Meninski, Francisci. *Lexicon Arabico-Persico-Trucicum: Adiecta Ad Singulas Voces et Phrases Significatione Latina, Ad Usitatiores Etiam Italica*. 4 vols. Viennae: Nunc secundis curis recognitum et auctum, 1780.

Nashwan, Ibn Saʿid al-Himyari. *Shams al-ʿUlūm wa-Dawāʾ Kalām al-ʿArab min al-Kulūm*. 12 vols. Damascus: Dār al-Fikr al-Muʿāṣir, 1999.

Raphelengius, Franciscus. *Lexicon Arabicum*. Leiden: Ex Officina Auctoris, 1613.

Richardson, John. *A Dictionary, Persian, Arabic, and English: with a Dissertation on the Languages, Literature, and Manners of Eastern Nations*. London: William Bulmer, 1806.

Ruphy, Jacques Français. *Dictionnaire Abrégé Français-Arabe*. Paris: Impr. de la République, 1802.

al-Saghani, al-Hassan bin Muhammad al-Hassan. *Al-ʿIbāb al-Zākhir wal-Libāb al-Fākhir*. 4 vols. Iraq: Dār al-Rashīd, 1977–1981.

Spiro, Socrates. *An English Arabic Vocabulary of the Modern and Colloquial Arabic of Egypt*. Cairo: Al-Muqaṭṭam Printing Office, 1905.

al-Tahanawi, Muhammad ʿAli. *Kashshāf Iṣṭilāḥāt al-Funūn wal-ʿUlūm*. 2 vols. Beirut: Nāshirūn, 1996.

Zakhur, Rufa'il. *Dizionario Italiano E Arabo*. Bolacco: Dalla Stamperia Reale, 1822.

al-Zubaydi, Muhammad Murtada al-Husayni. *Tāj al-'Arūs min Jawāhir al-Qāmūs*. 40 vols. Kuwait: Maṭba'at Ḥukūmat al-Kūwayt, 1965–2001.

## Pre–Nineteenth-Century Sources

Averroes [Ibn Rushd]. *Averroes' Commentary on Plato's Republic*. Translated by Erwin Isak Jakob Rosenthal and Samuel bin Yehuda. Cambridge: Cambridge University Press, 1956.

Burayk, Mikha'il. *Wathā'iq Tārīkhiyya lil-Kursī al-Malakī al-Anṭākī*. Harisa: Maṭba'at al-Qiddīss Būluṣ, 1930.

al-Farabi, Abu Nasr Muhammad ibn Muhammad. *Fuṣūl al-Madanī: Aphorisms of the Statesman*. Translated by D. M. Dunlop. Cambridge: Cambridge University Press, 1961.

*Kitāb al-Siyāsa al-Madaniyya*. Beirut: Al-Maṭba'a al-Kāthūlīkiyya, 1998.

*Rasāyil Falsafiyya*. Bonn, 1831.

*Hādhihi Sharḥ Fuṣūl al-Ḥikam lil-Mu'allim al-Thānī Abī Naṣr al-Fārābī*. Bulaq: Dār al-Ṭibā'a al-'Āmira, 1874.

Hashi, Salim Hassan. *Al-Murāsalāt al-Ijtimā'iyya wal-Iqtiṣādiyya li-Zu'amā' Jabal Lubnān Khilāl Thalāthat Qurūn (1600–1900)*. 4 vols. Beirut: Dār al-Bāḥith, 1985.

Ibn al-Muqaffa', Sawirus. *Tārīkh Baṭārikat al-Kanīsa al-Miṣriyya*. 3 vols. Cairo: Jam'iyyat al-Āthār al-Miṣriyya, 1943–1974.

*The Lamp of the Intellect of Severus Ibn al-Muqaffa'*. Louvain: Secrétariat du CorpusSCO, 1975.

Ibn Bajja, Abu Bakr. *Rasā'il Falsafiyya li-Abī Bakr bin Bajja*. Beirut: Dār al-Thaqāfa, 1983.

Ibn Khaldun, 'Abd al-Rahman. *Muqaddimat al-'Allāma Ibn Khaldūn al-Musamma Dīwān al-Mubtada' wal-Khabarr fī Ta'rīkh al-'Arab wal-Barbar wa-man 'Āṣarahum min Dhawī al-Sha'n al-Akbarr*. Beirut: Dār al-Fikr, 2004.

*The Muqaddimah: An Introduction to History*. Translated by Franz Rosenthal. 3 vols. Princeton, NJ: Princeton University Press, 1967.

Ibn Rushd, Abu al-Walid. *Thalāth Rasā'il*. Munich: Commission Bei G. Franz, 1859.

*Majmū' . . . Thalāthat Kutub*. Egypt: Al-Maṭba'a al-I'lāmiyya, 1885.

Ibn Tufail, Muhammad ibn 'Abd al-Malik. *Ḥayy Ibn Yaqẓān*. Cairo: Kalimāt, 2011.

Laertius, Diogenes. *Les Vies Des plus Illustres Philosophes de L'antiquité*. Paris: Richard, 1769.

Montesquieu, Charles de Secondat. *The Spirit of the Laws*. Cambridge: Cambridge University Press, 1989.

## Nineteenth-Century Sources: Arabic, Turkish, and French

### *Newspapers and Periodicals*

*al-Ahrām* (Examined between 1876 and 1888)
*al-Bashīr* (Examined between 1870 and 1890)
*al-Baṣṣīr* (Examined between 1881 and 1882)
*Birjīs Barīs* (Examined between 1859 and 1865)
*al-I'lām* (Examined in 1885)
*al-Ittiḥād* (Examined in 1880)
*al-Jawā'ib* (Examined between 1860 and 1876)
*al-Jinān* (Examined between 1870 and 1886)
*Kawkab al-Mashriq* (Examined between 1882 and 1883)
*al-Laṭā'if* (Examined between 1886 and 1891)
*Mir'āt al-Aḥwāl* (Examined in 1877)
*al-Muqtaṭaf* (Examined between 1867 and 1910)
*al-Naḥla* (Examined in 1870)
*al-Naẓẓārāt al-Miṣriyya* (Examined between 1879 and 1880)
*Rawḍat al-Madāris* (Examined between 1870 and 1877)
*'Uṭārid* (Examined in 1859)

### *Books, Encyclopedias, and Manuscripts*

Abkariyus, Iskandar. *Kitāb Nihayat al-Irab fī Akhbār al-'Arab*. Marseille: Maṭba'at al-Fa'la, 1852.

Abkariyus, Iskandar. *Nawādir al-Zamān fī Waqā'i' Jabal Lubnān*. London: Riyāḍ al-Rayyis lil-Kutub wal-Nashr, 1987.

Abu al-Su'ud, 'Abd Allah. *Kitāb Naẓm al-La'ālī' fī al-Sulūk fī man Ḥakama Faransā wa-man Qābalahum 'Ala Miṣr min al-Mulūk*. Cairo: Maṭba'at Ṣāḥib al-Sa'āda, 1841.

al-Afghani, Jamal al-Din. *Fī Ibṭāl Madhhab al-Dahriyyīn wa-Bayān Mafāsiduhum wa-Ithbāt anna al-Dīn Asās al-Madaniyya wal-Kufr Fasād al-'Ummrān*. Translated by Muhammad 'Abdu. Beirut: Maṭba'at Bairut, 1885.

al-Afghani, Jamal al-Din, and Muhammad 'Abdu. "Al-'Urwa al-Wuthqa." In *al-Āthār al-Kāmila: al-Sayyid Jamāl al-Dīn al-Ḥusainī al-Afghānī*, edited by Sayyid Hadi Khusru Shahi. 9 vols. Cairo: Maktabat al-Shurūq al-Duwaliyya, 2002.

Aḥad Kutāb al-Ḥukūma al-Dīmashqiyyīn. *Mudhakarāt Taʾrīkhiyya*. Edited by Qustantin al-Basha. Harisa: Maṭbaʿat al-Qiddīss Būluṣ, 1926.

ʿAqiqi, Antun Dahir. *Thawra wa-Fitna fī Lubnān: Ṣafḥa Majhūla min Tārīkh al-Jabal min 1841 ila 1873*. Beirut: Al-*Ittiḥād*, 1939.

al-Bustani. "Ḥurriyya." In *Kitāb Dāʾirat al-Maʿārif*. Beirut: Maṭbaʿat al-Maʿārif, 1883.

"Rusu." In *Kitāb Dāʾirat al-Maʿārif*. Beirut: Al-Adabiyya, 1887.

al-Bustani, Butrus. *Al-Jamʿiyya al-Sūriyya lil-ʿUlūm wal-Funūn, 1847–1852*. Beirut: Dār al-Ḥamrāʾ, 1990.

"Ibn Rushd (Averroes)." In *Kitāb Dāʾirat al-Maʿārif*. Beirut: Dār al-Maʿrifa, 1876.

"Jumhūriyya." In *Kitāb Dāʾirat al-Maʿārif*. Beirut: Dār al-Maʿārif, 1882.

*Maʿārik al-ʿArab fī al-Sharq wal-Gharb*. Beirut: Dār al-Makshūf, 1944.

*Nafīr Sūriyya*. Beirut: Dār al-Fikr, 1990.

"Tamaddun." In *Kitāb Dāʾirat al-Maʿārif*. Beirut: Dār al-Maʿārif, 1882.

"Taqlīd." In *Kitāb Dāʾirat al-Maʿārif*. Beirut: Maṭbaʿat al-Maʿārif, 1882.

*Udabāʾ al-ʿArab fī al-Jāhiliyya wa-Ṣadr al-Islām*. Beirut: Maktabat Ṣādir, 1953.

Bustrus, Salim ibn Musa. *Al-Nuzha al-Shahiyya fī al-Riḥla al-Salīmiyya, 1855*. Beirut: Al-Muʾassasa al-ʿArabiyya lil-Dirāsāt wal-Nashr, 2003.

Depping, Georges-Bernard. *Aperçu Historique Sur Les Moeurs et Coutumes Des Nation*. Paris: Mairet et fournier, 1842.

*Kitāb Qalāʾid al-Mafākhir fī Gharīb ʿAwāʾid al-Awāʾil wal-Awākhir*. Translated by Rifaʿa Rafiʿ al-Tahtawi. Bulaq: Dār al-Ṭibāʿa al-ʿĀmira, 1833.

al-Dimashqi, Mikhail. *Taʾrīkh Ḥawādith al-Shām wa-Lubnān*. Beirut: Maṭbaʿat al-Kāthūlīk lil-Ābāʾ al-Yasuʿiyyīn, 1912.

Dumarsais, César Chesneau. *Tanwīr al-Mashriq bi-ʿIlm al-Manṭiq*. Translated by Khalifa Mahmud. Bulaq: Al-Maṭbaʿa al-ʿĀmira, 1838.

Fadil Pasha, Mustafa. *Min Amīr ila Sulṭān*. Cairo: Al-Maṭbaʿa al-Raḥmāniyya, 1922.

Fandik, Karniliyus. "Fī Faḍl al-Mutaʾakhkhirīn ʿala al-Mutaqaddimīn." In *al-Jamʿiyya al-Sūriyya lil-ʿUlūm wal-Funūn, 1847–1852*, edited by Butrus al-Bustani, 79–82. Beirut: Dār al-Ḥamrāʾ, 1990.

"Fī Lidhat al-ʿIlm wa-Fawaʾiduhu." In *al-Jamʿiyya al-Sūriyya lil-ʿUlūm wal-Funūn, 1847–1852*, edited by Butrus al-Bustani, 27–32. Beirut: Dār al-Ḥamrāʾ, 1990.

Fikri, Muhammad Amin. *Irshād al-Alibbā ila Maḥāsin Ūrūbā*. Cairo: ʿAyn lil-Dirāsāt wal-Buḥūth, 2008.

Fourier, Joseph. "Priface Hisforique." In *Description de l'Égypte, Ou, Recueil de Observations et Des Recherches Qui Ont Été Faites En*

*Égypte Pendant L'éxpédition de L'armée Française*, edited by Commission des monuments d'Égypte, 2nd ed. Paris: Imprimerie de C. L. F. Panckoucke, 1826.

Ganem, Halil. *Education Des Princes Ottomans*. Bulle, Suisse: Imprimerie Emile Lenz, 1895.

Ghanim, Khalil. *Kitāb al-Iqtiṣād al-Siyāsī aw Fann Tadbīr al-Manzil*. Alexandria: Maṭba'at Jarīdat Miṣr, 1879.

Habicht, Maximilan. *Epistolae Quaedam Arabicae*. Wroclaw: Typis Universitatis Regis, 1824.

Hassun, Rizq Allah. *Al-Nafathāt*. London: Trübner & Co., 1867.

al-Hatuni, Mansur Tanus. *Nabdha Tārīkhiyya fī al-Muqāṭa'a al-Kisrwāniyya*. Beirut, 1884.

Hegel, Georg W. F. *The Philosophy of History*. Translated by J. Sibree. Kitchener: Batoche Books, 2001.

Ibn Abi al-Diyaf, Ahmad. *Consult Them in the Matter: A Nineteenth-Century Islamic Argument for Constitutional Government*. Edited by Leon Carl Brown. Fayetteville: The University of Arkansas Press, 2005.

*Itḥāf Ahl al-Zamān bi-Akhbār Mulūk Tūnis wa-'Ahd al-Amān*. 8 vols. Tunis: Al-Dār al-Tūnisiyya lil-Nashr, 1989.

al-Īji, 'Adad al-Din. *Kitāb al-Mawāqif*. Constantinople: Dār al-Ṭibā'a al-'Āmira, 1824.

Ishaq, Adib. *Adīb Ishāq: al-Kitābāt al-Siyāsiyya wal-Ijtimā'iyya*. Edited by Naji 'Alush. Beirut: Dār al-Ṭalī'a, 1978.

Jabarti, Abd al-Rahman. *'Abd al-Raḥmān al-Jabartī's History of Egypt: 'Ajā'ib al-Āthār fī 'l-Tarājim wa'l-Akhbār*. Edited by Thomas Philipp and Moshe Perlmann. 5 vols. Stuttgart: Franz Steiner Verlag, 1994.

*Maẓhar al-Taqdīs bi-Zawāl Dawlat al-Faransīs*. Cairo: Dār al-Kutub al-Miṣriyya, 1998.

*'Ajā'ib al-Āthār fī al-Tarājim wal-Akhbār*. 4 vols. Cairo: Dār al-Kutub al-Miṣriyya, 1998.

Jalal, Iman al-Sa'id. *Alfāẓ al-Ḥaḍāra fī Miṣr bil-Qarn al-Tāsi' 'Ashar: Ruṣidat min Kitāb Rifā'a al-Ṭahṭawī Qalā'id al-Mafākhir fī Gharīb 'Awā'id al-Awā'il wal-Awākhir, ma'a al-Naṣṣ al-Kāmil lil-Kitāb*. Cairo: Maktabat al-Ādāb, 2008.

Kafafi, Muhammad. "Al-Ḥamla al-Faransiyya 'ala Miṣr fī Riwayat Aḥad al-Mu'āṣirīn." In *Ila Ṭaha Ḥusayn fī 'Īd Mīlādihi al-Sab'īn: Dirāsāt Muhdā min Aṣdiqā'ihi wa-Talāmīdhihi*, edited by 'Abd al-Rahman Badawi, 369–96. Cairo: Dār al-Ma'ārif, 1962.

al-Kalanbawi, Isma'il. *al-Burhān*. Constantinople: Dār al-Ṭibā'a al-'Āmira, 1837.

Kalivaris, Lewis. *Kitāb Sirat al-Mu'aẓam al-Murafa' al-Kabīr Nabulyūn al-Awwal Imbaratūr al-Farānsawiyya*. Paris, 1855.

al-Kawakibi, 'Abd al-Rahman. *Umm al-Qura: aī Ḍabṭṭ Mufāwaḍāt wa-Muqararāt Mu'tamar al-Nahḍa al-Islāmiyya al-Mun'aqid fī Makka Sant 1316*. Egypt: Al-Sayyid al-Furātī, n.d.

al-Khashab, Isma'il. *Khulāṣat mā Yurād min Akhbār al-Amīr Murād*. Cairo: Dār al-'Arabī lil-Nashr wal-Tawzī', 1992.

*Akhbār Aḥl al-Qarn al-Thāni 'Ashar: Ta'rīkh al-Mamālīk fī al-Qāhira*. Cairo: Al-Nāshir al-'Arabī, 1990.

*Al-Tārīkh al-Musalsal fī Ḥawādith al-Zamān wa-Waqāyi' al-Dīwān, 1800–1801*. Cairo: Al-Ma'had al-'Ilmī al-Faransī lil-Āthār al-Sharqiyya, 2003.

al-Khazin, Philippe, and Farid al-Khazin, eds. *Majmū'at al-Muḥarrarāt al-Siyāsiyya wal-Mufāwaḍāt al-Duwaliyya 'an Sūriyya wa-Lubnān min Sanat 1840 ila Sanat 1910*. 3 vols. Beirut: Dār al-Rā'id al-Lubnānī, 1983.

al-Khuri, Salim, and Salim Shihada, "Ibn Rushd." *Kitāb Āthār al-Adhār: al-Qism al-Tārīkhī*. Beirut: Al-Maṭba'a al-Sūriyya, 1877.

*Kitāb al-Kanz al-Mukhtār fī Kashf al-Arāḍī wal-Biḥār*. Malta, 1836.

*Kitāb Majmū' Ḥawādith al-Ḥarb al-Wāqi' bayna al-Faransāwiyya wal-Namsāwiyya fī Awākhir Sant 1802 al-Masīḥiyya*. Paris, 1807.

*Kitāb al-Muḥāwara al-Unsiyya fī al-Lughatayn al-Inklīziyya wal-'Arabiyya*. Malta, 1840.

Korkut, Besim. *Al-Wathā'iq al-'Arabiyya fī Dār al-Maḥfūẓāt bi-Madīnat Dubrūnik*. Sarajevo: Orijentalni Institu u Sarajevu, 1960.

Laertius, Diogenes. *Mukhtaṣar Tarjamāt Mashāhīr Qudamā' al-Falāsifa*. Translated by Husain 'Abd Allah al-Misri. Bulaq: Dār al-Ṭibā'a al-'Āmira, 1836.

Laurens, Henry. *L'expedition d'Egypte, 1798–1801*. Paris: A. Colin, 1989.

Malte-Brun, Conrad. *Al-Jughrāfiyya al-'Umūmiyya*. Translated by Rifa'a Rafi' al-Tahtawi. 4 vols. Bulaq, 1838.

Marrash, Fransis Fathalah. *Riḥlat Bārīs 1867*. Beirut: Al-Mu'assasa al-'Arabiyya lil-Dirāsāt wal-Nashr, 2004.

Markham, Henry. *Hadhā Kitāb Siyāḥat Amrīqa*. Translated by Sa'd Na'am. Bulaq: Dār al-Ṭibā'a, 1846.

Mazlum, Maksimus. *Nabdha Tārīkhiyya: fīmā Jara li-Ṭā'ifat al-Rūm al-Kāthūlīk Mundhu Sant 1837 Famā Ba'dahā*. Edited by Qustantin al-Basha. n.p.: 1907.

Mishaqa, Mikha'il. *Al-Risāla al-Maūsūma bil-Dalīl ila Ṭā'at al-Injīl*. Beirut, 1849.

Mithat, Ahmet. *Uss-I Inkılap*. Istanbul, 1877.

al-Munayyir, Hananiya. *Al-Durr al-Marṣūf fī Tārīkh al-Shūf*. Lebanon: Jrus Press, n.d.

al-Muwaylihi, Ibrahim. *Ibrāhīm al-Mūwaylihi: al-A'māl al-Kāmila*. Edited by Roger M. A. Allen. Cairo: Al-Majlis al-A'la lil-Thaqāfa, 2007.

Nakhlah, Salih. *Al-Kanz al-Mukhabbā lil-Siyāḥa fī Ūrūbā*. Cairo, 1876.

Nawfal, Na'm Allah, trans. *Al-Dustūr*. Beirut: Naẓārat al-Ma'ārif al-Jalīla, 1883.

Perron, Nicolas. *Al-Azhār al-Badī'a fī 'ilm al-Ṭabī'a: Kitāb al-Ṭabī'a*. Translated by Yuhanna Anhuri. Bulaq: Maṭba'at Ṣāḥib al-Sa'āda al-Khidīwiyya, 1838.

al-Qalawi, Mustafa al-Safawi. *Ṣafwat al-Zamān fī man Tawalla 'ala Miṣr min Amīr wa-Sulṭān*. Alexandria: Dār al-Ma'rifa al-Jāmi'iyya, 2006.

*Qiṣat Martin Luthir*. Falta, 1840.

Renan, Ernest. *Averroes et L'averroïsme: Essai Historique*. Paris: A. Durand, 1852.

Robertson, William. *Kitāb Itḥāf Mulūk al-Zamān bi-Tārīkh al-Imbirāṭūr Sharlakān Masbūqan bi-Muqaddimatihi al-Musammā Itḥāf al-Mulūk al-Alibbā' bi-Taqaddum al-Jam'īyyāt fī Ūrūbā Mundhu Inqirāḍ al-Dawla al-Rūmāniyya*. Translated by Khalifa Ibn Mahmud. 3 vols. Bulaq: Al-Maṭba'a al-'Āmira, 1844–1850.

Rustum, Asad. *Al-Maḥfūẓāt al-Malakiyya al-Miṣriyya*. 4 vols. Beirut: Al-Maṭba'a al-Amrīkiyya, 1940–1943.

*Al-Uṣūl al-'Arabiyya li-Tārīkh Sūriyya fī 'Ahd Muḥammad 'Ali Bāshā*. 5 vols. Beirut: Al-Maṭba'a al-Amīrikāniyya and Manshurāt al-Maktaba al-Bulisiyya, 1987–1988.

al-Sabbagh, Mikha'il. *Al-Risāla al-Tāmma fī Kalām al-'Āmma: wal-Manāhij fī Aḥwāl al-Kalām al-Dārij*. Strassburg: Trübner, 1886.

*Musābaqat al-Barq wal-Ghamām fī Su'āt al-Ḥamām*. Paris: Dār al-Maṭba'a al-Ṣulṭāniyya, 1805.

*Nashīd Qaṣīdat Tahāni li-Sa'ādat al-Qayṣar al-Mu'aẓam Nabūlyūn Sulṭān Faransā fī Mauwlid Bikrihi Sa'ādat Malik Rummiyya Nabūlyūn al-Thānī*. Paris: Dār al-Maṭba'a al-Ṣulṭāniyya, 1811.

Salih, 'Adil. *Suṭūr min al-Risāla: Tārīkh Ḥaraka Istiqlāliyya Qāmat fī al-Mashriq al-'Arabī Sant 1877*. Beirut, 1966.

Salih, Majdi. *Ḥilyat al-Zamān bi-Manāqib Khādim al-Waṭan*. Cairo: Al-Bāb al-Ḥalabī, 1958.

al-Sharqawi, 'Abd Allah. *Tuḥfat al-Nāẓirīn fī-man Waliya Miṣr min al-Mulūk wal-Salāṭīn*. Cairo: Maktabat Madbūlī, 1996.

al-Shidyaq, Ahmad Faris. *Al-Sāq 'ala al-Sāq fī mā huwa al-Fāryāq*. Beirut: Dār Maktabat al-Ḥayā, 1966.

*Al-Wāsiṭa ila Ma'rifat Aḥwāl Mālṭa wa-Kashf al-Mukhabbā' 'an Funūn Ūrūbā*. Beirut: Kutub, 2002.

*Kanz al-Raghā'ib fī Muntakhabāt al-Jawā'ib*. Edited by Salim al-Shidyaq. 7 vols. Istanbul: Maṭba'at al-Jawā'ib, 1871–1880 or 1881.

*Mukhtārāt min Āthār Aḥmad Fāris al-Shidyāq*. Beirut: Al-Mu'assasa al-Sharqiyya lil-Nashr, 2001.

al-Shidyaq, Tanus. *Kitāb Akhbār al-A'yān fī Jabal Lubnān*. 2 vols. Beirut: Al-Maktaba al-Sharqiyya, 1970.

al-Shihabi, Haydar. "Kitāb Nuzhat al-Zamān fī Ḥawādith 'Arabistān." Cambridge, 1849.

*Qiṣat Aḥmad Bāsha al-Jazzār bayna Miṣr wal-Shām wa-Ḥawādithuhu ma' Nābulyūn Būnābart*. Cairo: Maktabat Madbūlī, 2008.

Shumail, Shibli. *Kitāb Falsafat al-Nushū' wal-Irtiqā'*. Cairo: Maṭba'at *al-Muqtaṭaf*, 1910.

al-Tahtawi, Rifa'a Rafi'. *Takhlīṣ al-Ibrīz fī Talkhīṣ Bārīz aw al-Dīwān al-Nafīs bi-Īwān Bārīs*. Bulaq: Dār al-Ṭibā'a al-Khidīwiyya, 1834.

*Al-Dīwān al-Nafīs fī Īwān Bārīs aw, Takhlīṣ al-Ibrīz fī Talkhīṣ Bārīz*. Beirut: Dār al-Suwaydī lil-Nashr wal-Tawzī', 2002.

trans. *Al-Ta'rībāt al-Shāfiya li-Murīd al-Jughrāfiyya*. Bulaq: Dār al-Ṭibā'a al-Khidīwiyya, 1834.

"Anwār Tawfīq al-Khalīl fī Akhbār Miṣr wa-Tawthīq Banī Ismā'īl." In *al-A'māl al-Kāmila li-Rifā'a Rāfi' al-Ṭahṭawī*, edited by Muammad 'Imara, Vol. 3. Cairo: Dār al-Shurūq, 2010.

"Kitāb Manāhij al-Albāb al-Miṣriyya fī Mabāhij al-Ādāb al-'Aṣriyya." In *al-A'māl al-Kāmila li-Rifā'a Rāfi' al-Ṭahṭawī*, edited by Muammad 'Imara, Vol. 1. Cairo: Dār al-Shurūq, 2010.

"Kitāb al-Murshid al-Amīn lil-Banāt wal-Banīn." In *al-A'māl al-Kāmila li-Rifā'a Rāfi' al-Ṭahṭawī*, edited by Muammad 'Imara, Vol. 2. Cairo: Dār al-Shurūq, 2010.

*Muqaddima Waṭaniyya Miṣriyya*. Bulaq: Maṭba'at Bulaq, 1866.

al-Tahtawi, Rifa'a Rafi', and Mustafa al-Zarabi, trans. *Bidāyat al-Qudamā' wa-Hidāyat al-Ḥukamā'*. Bulaq: Dār al-Ṭibā'a al-'Āmira, 1838.

al-Tunisi, Khayr al-Din. *Aqwam al-Masālik fī Ma'rifat Aḥwāl al-Mamālik*. Edited by Ma'an Ziyada. Beirut: Al-Mu'assasa al-Jāmi'iyya lil-Dirāsāt wal-Nashr, 1985.

al-Turk, Niqula. *Dhikr Tamalluk Jumhūr al-Fransāwiyya al-Aqṭār al-Miṣriyya wal-Bilād al-Shāmiyya, aw, al-Ḥamla al-Faransiyya 'ala Miṣr wal-Shām*. Beirut: Dār al-Fārābī, 1990.

Van Dyck, Cornelius. *Kitāb al-Mir'ā al-Waḍ'iyya fī al-Kura al-Arḍiyya*. Beirut, 1852.

Voltaire. *Maṭāli' Shumūs al-Siyar fī Waqā'i' Karlūs al-Thānī 'Ashar*. Translated by Muhammad Mustafa Bashjawish. Bulaq: Maṭba'at Ṣāḥib al-Sa'āda, 1841.

*Rawḍ al-Azhar fī Tārīkh Buṭrus al-Akbar*. Translated by Ahmad Muhammad 'Aubaid al-Tahtawi. Cairo: Dār al-Ṭibā'a al-'Āmira, 1850.

al-Yaziji, Nasif. *Risāla Tārīkhiya fī Aḥwāl Jabal Lubnān fī 'Ahdihi al-Iqṭā'ī.* Beirut: Dār Ma'n, 2002.

## Secondary Sources

Abu-Manneh, Butrus. "The Christians between Ottomanism and Syrian Nationalism: The Ideas of Butrus al-Bustani." *International Journal of Middle East Studies* 11, no. 3 (1980): 287–304.

Abu-'Uksa, Wael. "Liberal Tolerance in Arab Political Thought: Translating Farah Antun (1874–1922)." *Journal of Levantine Studies* 3, no. 2 (Winter 2013): 151–57.

Adams, Charles C. *Islam and Modernism in Egypt: A Study of the Modern Reform Movement Inaugurated by Muhammad Abduh.* London: Oxford University Press, 1933.

al-'Arawi, 'Abd Allah. *Mafhūm al-Ḥurriyya.* Casablanca: Al-Markaz al-Thaqāfī al-'Arabī, 1981.

Alwan, Mohammed. "The History and Publications of al-Jawā'ib Press." *MELA Notes*, no. 11 (1977): 4–7.

Antun, Farah. "The Meaning of 'Tolerance,' Which Is the Basis of Modern Civilization." Edited by Wael Abu-'Uksa. Translated by Zakia Pormann. *Journal of Levantine Studies* 3, no. 2 (Winter 2013): 159–72.

Antonius, George. *The Arab Awakening: The Story of the Arab National Movement.* London: Hamish Hamilton, 1938.

al-'Aqad, 'Abas Mahmud. *Rijāl 'Araftuhum.* Cairo: Nahḍat Miṣr, 1992.

Atiya, Aziz Suryal, ed. "Ilyas Buqtur." In *The Coptic Encyclopedia.* New York: Macmillan, 1991.

ed. "Ya'qub, General." In *The Coptic Encyclopedia.* New York: Macmillan, 1991.

Ayalon, Ami. *Language and Change in the Arab Middle East: The Evolution of Modern Political Discourse.* New York: Oxford University Press, 1987.

"Semantics and the Modern History of Non-European Societies: Arab 'Republics' as a Case Study." *The Historical Journal* 28, no. 4 (1985): 821–34.

"'Sihafa': The Arab Experiment in Journalism." *Middle Eastern Studies* 28, no. 2 (1992): 258–80.

Baer, Gabriel. "Social Change in Egypt: 1800–1914." In *Political and Social Change in Modern Egypt: Historical Studies from the Ottoman Conquest to the United Arab Republic*, edited by Peter M. Holt, 135–61. London: Oxford University Press, 1968.

Baycroft, Timothy. "Nationalism." In *New Dictionary of the History of Ideas.* Detroit, MI: Charles Scribner's Sons, 2005.

Bödeker, Hans Erich. "Concept – Meaning – Discourse. Begriffsgeschichte Reconsidered." In *History of Concepts: Comparative Perspectives*, edited by Iain Hampsher-Monk, Karin Tilmans, and Frank Van Vree. 51–64. Amsterdam: Amsterdam University Press, 1998.

Bosworth, Clifford Edmund. "Siyāsa: In the Sense of Statecraft." In *The Encyclopedia of Islam*. Leiden: E. J. Brill, 1997.

Böwering, Gerhard. "The Concept of Time in Islam." *Proceedings of the American Philosophical Society* 141, no. 1 (1997): 55–66.

Ceylan, Ebubekir. *The Ottoman Origins of Modern Iraq: Political Reform, Modernization and Development in the Nineteenth Century Middle East*. London: I. B. Tauris, 2011.

Cheikho, Louis. *Kitāb Shu'arā' al-Naṣrāniyya Ba'da al-Islām: Shu'arā' al-Dawla al-'Abbāsiyya*. Vol. 3. Beirut: Maṭba'at al-Ābā' al-Yasū'iyyīn, 1926.

Cole, Juan. *Napoleon's Egypt: Invading the Middle East*. New York: Palgrave Macmillan, 2007.

Coller, Ian. *Arab France: Islam and the Making of Modern Europe, 1798–1831*. Berkeley: University of California Press, 2011.

Couland, Jacques. "Waṭaniyya." *The Encyclopedia of Islam*. Leiden: Brill, 2002.

Crook, Malcolm. "Elections and Democracy in France, 1789–1848." In *Re-imagining Democracy in the Age of Revolutions: America, France, Britain, Ireland, 1750–1850*, edited by Joanna Innes and Mark Philp, 83–97. Oxford: Oxford University Press, 2013.

Curtis, Michael. *Orientalism and Islam: European Thinkers on Oriental Despotism in the Middle East and India*. Cambridge: Cambridge University Press, 2009.

Dalacoura, Katerina. *Islam, Liberalism and Human Rights: Implications for International Relations*. London: I. B. Tauris, 2007.

Darling, Linda T. *A History of Social Justice and Political Power in the Middle East: The Circle of Justice from Mesopotamia to Globalization*. London: Routledge, 2013.

Davison, Roderic. *Essays in Ottoman and Turkish History, 1774–1923: The Impact of the West*. Austin: University of Texas Press, 1990.

Denny, Frederick Mathewson. "Umma." In *The Encyclopedia of Islam*. Leiden: E. J. Brill, 2000.

Devereux, Robert. *The First Ottoman Constitutional Period: A Study of the Midhat Constitution and Parliament*. Baltimore, MD: Johns Hopkins Press, 1963.

Dodds, Eric Robertson. "Progress in Classical Antiquity." In *Dictionary of the History of Ideas: Studies of Selected Pivotal Ideas*. New York: Scribner, 1973–1974.

Douglas, Elmer. "The Muslim Concept of Freedom by Franz Rosenthal." *Middle East Journal* 15, no. 4 (1961): 470–72.

Drolet, Michael. "Democracy, Self, and the Problem of the General Will in Nineteenth-Century French Political Thought." In *Re-imagining Democracy in the Age of Revolutions: America, France, Britain, Ireland, 1750–1850*, edited by Joanna Innes and Mark Philp, 69–82. Oxford: Oxford University Press, 2013.

*Dustūr: A Survey of the Constitutions of the Arab and Muslim States*. Leiden: Brill, 1966.

Esenwein, George. "Socialism." In *New Dictionary of the History of Ideas*. Detroit, MI: Charles Scribner's Sons, 2005.

Esposito, John L., ed. "Aql." *The Oxford Dictionary of Islam*. Oxford: Oxford University Press, 2003.

Evans, Robert John Weston. "Liberalism, Nationalism, and the Coming of the Revolution." In *The Revolutions in Europe 1848–1849: From Reform to Reaction*, edited by Robert John Weston Evans and Hartmut Pogge von Strandmann, 9–26. Oxford: Oxford University Press, 2002.

Gellner, Ernest. "The Muslim Concept of Freedom Prior to the 19th Century." *Philosophy* 39, no. 147 (1964): 85–86.

Gershoni, Israel. "Egyptian Liberalism in an Age of 'Crisis of Orientation': al-Risala's Reaction to Fascism and Nazism, 1933–39." *International Journal of Middle East Studies* 31, no. 4 (November 1999): 551–576.

Gershoni, Israel, and James P. Jankowski. *Confronting Fascism in Egypt: Dictatorship Versus Democracy in the 1930s*. Stanford, CA: Stanford University Press, 2010.

Gibb, Hamilton A. *Modern Trends in Islam*. Chicago: University of Chicago Press, 1947.

Ginsberg, Morris. "Progress in the Modern Era." In *Dictionary of the History of Ideas: Studies of Selected Pivotal Ideas*. New York: Scribner, 1974.

Godlewska, Anne. "Map, Text and Image. The Mentality of Enlightened Conquerors: A New Look at the Description de l'Egypte." *Transactions of the Institute of British Geographers* 20, no. 1 (1995): 5–28.

Goldziher, Ignác, and Amélie Marie Goichon. "Dahriyya." In *The Encyclopedia of Islam*. Leiden: E. J. Brill, 1965.

Haarmann, Ulrich. "Waṭan." In *The Encyclopedia of Islam*. Leiden: Brill, 2002.

Haddad, George A. "A Project for the Independence of Egypt, 1801." *Journal of the American Oriental Society* 90, no. 2 (1970): 169–83.

Haddad, George M. "The Historical Work of Niqula El-Turk 1763–1828." *Journal of the American Oriental Society* 81, no. 3 (1961): 247–51.

Hampsher-Monk, Iain, Karin Tilmans, and Frank Van Vree. "A Comparative Perspective on Conceptual History – An Introduction." In *History of Concepts: Comparative Perspectives*, edited by Iain Hampsher-Monk, Karin Tilmans, and Frank Van Vree. 1–9. Amsterdam: Amsterdam University Press, 1998.

Hatina, Meir. *Identity Politics in the Middle East: Liberal Thought and Islamic Challenge in Egypt*. London: Tauris Academic Studies, 2007.

Heyworth-Dunne, James. "Rifāʿah Badawī Rāfiʿ aṭ-Ṭahṭāwī: The Egyptian Revivalist." *Bulletin of the School of Oriental Studies, University of London* 9, no. 4 (1939): 961–67.

Hill, Peter. "The First Arabic Translations of Enlightenment Literature: The Damietta Circle of the 1800s and 1810s." *Intellectual History Review*, 2015, 1–25.

Holt, Peter M. "Arabic Thought in the Liberal Age, 1798–1939." *Bulletin of the School of Oriental and African Studies* 27, no. 1 (1964): 222–23.

Hourani, Albert. *Arabic Thought in the Liberal Age, 1798–1939*. London: Oxford University Press, 1970.

*Arabic Thought in the Liberal Age, 1798–1939*. Cambridge: Cambridge University Press, 1983.

Hurewitz, Jacob Coleman. *Diplomacy in the Near and Middle East: A Documentary Record*. New York: Octagon Books, 1972.

Innes, Joanna, and Mark Philp. "Introduction." In *Re-imagining Democracy in the Age of Revolutions: America, France, Britain, Ireland, 1750–1850*, edited by Joanna Innes and Mark Philp, 1–10. Oxford: Oxford University Press, 2013.

Innes, Joanna, and Mark Philp. "Synergies." In *Re-imagining Democracy in the Age of Revolutions: America, France, Britain, Ireland, 1750–1850*, edited by Joanna Innes and Mark Philp, 191–212. Oxford: Oxford University Press, 2013.

Ahmed, Jamal. *The Intellectual Origins of Egyptian Nationalism*. London: Oxford University Press, 1960.

Jayyusi, Salma Khadra. *Trends and Movements in Modern Arabic Poetry*. Leiden: E. J. Brill, 1977.

Johansen, Baber. *Muhammad Husain Haikal: Europa und der Orient in Weltbild eines Ägyptischen Liberalen*. Beirut: In Kommission bei F. Steiner, Wiesbaden, 1967.

Jones, Eric. *The European Miracle: Environments, Economies, and Geopolitics in the History of Europe and Asia*. Cambridge: Cambridge University Press, 1981.

Kassab, Elizabeth Suzanne. *Contemporary Arab Thought: Cultural Critique in Comparative Perspective*. New York: Columbia University Press, 2010.

Kedourie, Elie. *Afghani and ʿAbduh: An Essay on Religious Unbelief and Political Activism in Modern Islam*. London: Frank Cass, 1997.

"Arabic Thought in the Liberal Age, 1798–1939." *The Political Quarterly* 34, no. 2 (1963): 217–19.

Kennedy, Emmet. "'Ideology' from Destutt De Tracy to Marx." *Journal of the History of Ideas* 40, no. 3 (1979): 353–68.

Kerr, Malcolm. "Arabic Thought in the Liberal Age, 1798–1939." *Journal of the American Oriental Society* 84, no. 4 (1964): 427–29.

*Islamic Reform: The Political and Legal Theories of Muḥammad ʿAbdu and Rashīd Riḍā*. Berkeley: University of California Press, 1966.

Khadduri, Majid. *Political Trends in the Arab World: The Role of Ideas and Ideals in Politics*. Baltimore, MD: Johns Hopkins Press, 1970.

Khuri-Makdisi, Ilham. *The Eastern Mediterranean and the Making of Global Radicalism, 1860–1914*. Berkeley, CA: University of California Press, 2010.

Khuri, Raʾif. *Al-Fikr al-ʿArabī al-Ḥadīth*. Beirut: Dār al-Makshūf, 1943.

Koselleck, Reinhart. *The Practice of Conceptual History: Timing History, Spacing Concepts*. Palo Alto, CA: Stanford University Press, 2002.

Leonhard, Jorn. "From European Liberalism to the Languages of Liberalisms: The Semantics of 'Liberalism' in European Comparison." *Redescriptions: Yearbook of Political Thought and Conceptual History*, no. 8 (2004): 17–51.

Lewis, Bernard. "Ḥurriyya: The Ottoman Empire and After." In *The Encyclopedia of Islam*. Leiden: E. J. Brill, 1991.

"Ifrandj." *The Encyclopedia of Islam*. Leiden: E. J. Brill, 1986.

*Political Words and Ideas in Islam*. Princeton, NJ: Markus Wiener Publishers, 2008.

*The Emergence of Modern Turkey*. London: Oxford University Press, 1968.

"The Muslim Discovery of Europe." *Bulletin of the School of Oriental and African Studies* 20, no. 1/3 (1957): 409–16.

Livingston, John W. "Western Science and Educational Reform in the Thought of Shaykh Rifaa al-Tahtawi." *International Journal of Middle East Studies* 28, no. 4 (1996): 543–64.

Maghraoui, Abdeslam. *Liberalism without Democracy: Nationhood and Citizenship in Egypt, 1922–1936*. Durham, NC: Duke University Press, 2006.

Makdisi, Ussama. "After 1860: Debating Religion, Reform, and Nationalism in the Ottoman Empire." *International Journal of Middle East Studies* 34, no. 4 (2002): 601–17.

Maoz, Moshe. "Attempts at Creating a Political Community in Modern Syria." *Middle East Journal* 26, no. 4 (1972): 389–404.

*Ottoman Reform in Syria and Palestine, 1840–1861: The Impact of the Tanzimat on Politics and Society*. Oxford: Clarendon Press, 1968.

Mardin, Şerif. *The Genesis of Young Ottoman Thought: A Study in the Modernization of Turkish Political Ideas*. Syracuse, NY: Syracuse University Press, 2000.

Mustafa, Ahmed Abdel-Rahim. "The Breakdown of the Monopoly System in Egypt After 1840." In *Political and Social Change in Modern Egypt: Historical Studies from the Ottoman Conquest to the United Arab Republic*, edited by Peter M. Holt, 291–307. London: Oxford University Press, 1968.

Nadolski, Dora Glidewell. "Ottoman and Secular Civil Law." *International Journal of Middle East Studies* 8, no. 4 (1977): 517–43.

Nederman, Cary J. "Individualism." In *New Dictionary of the History of Ideas*. Detroit, MI: Charles Scribner's Sons, 2005.

Netton, Ian Richard. "Siyāsa: In the Context of Political Philosophy." In *The Encyclopedia of Islam*. Leiden: E. J. Brill, 1997.

Newman, Daniel L. "Introduction." In *An Imam in Paris*, 17–97. London: Saqi Books, 2011.

Nietzsche, Friedrich. "On the Genealogy of Morals." In *On the Genealogy of Morals; Ecce Homo*, trans. Walter Kaufmann (New York: Vintage Books, 1989).

Nikki, R. Keddie. "Secularization and Secularism." In *New Dictionary of the History of Ideas*. New York: Charles Scribner's Sons, 2005.

Philipp, Thomas. "Identities and Loyalties in Bilad al-Sham at the Beginning of the Early Modem Period." In *From The Syrian Land to the States of Syria and Lebanon*, edited by Thomas Philipp and Christoph Schumann, 9–26. Würzburg: Ergon in Kommission, 2004.

Pilbeam, Pamela. *Saint-Simonians in Nineteenth-Century France*. New York: Palgrave Macmillan, 2014.

Rahman, Fazlur. "ʿAkl." *The Encyclopedia of Islam*. Leiden: E. J. Brill, 1986.

Ramsaur, Ernest Edmondson. *The Young Turks: Prelude to the Revolution of 1908*. Beirut: Khayats, 1965.

Rastegar, Kamran. *Literary Modernity between the Middle East and Europe: Textual Transactions in Nineteenth-Century Arabic, English, and Persian Literatures*. London: Routledge, 2007.

Reid, Donald. "Arabic Thought in the Liberal Age: Twenty Years After." *International Journal of Middle East Studies* 14, no. 4 (November 1982): 541–57.

"The Syrian Christians and Early Socialism in the Arab World." *International Journal of Middle East Studies* 5, no. 2 (1974): 177–93.

Richter, Melvin, and Michaela W. Richter. "Introduction: Translation of Reinhart Koselleck's 'Krise' in Geschichtliche Grundbegriffe." *Journal of the History of Ideas* 67, no. 2 (April 2006): 343–56.

Roper, Geoffrey. "Aḥmad Fāris al-Shidyāq and the Libraries of Europe and the Ottoman Empire." *Libraries & Culture* 33, no. 3 (1998): 233–48.

Rosenthal, Franz. *The Muslim Concept of Freedom Prior to the Nineteenth Century*. Leiden: E. J. Brill, 1960.

Sadgrove, Philip Charles. "Ḥassūn, Rizq Allah (1825–80)." In *Encyclopedia of Arabic Literature*. London: Routledge, 1998.

Safran, Nadav. *Egypt in Search of Political Community: An Analysis of the Intellectual and Political Evolution of Egypt, 1804–1952*. Cambridge, MA: Harvard University Press, 1961.

Sarkis, Yusuf Ilyan. *Muʿjam al-Maṭbūʿāt al-ʿArabiyya wal-Muʿarraba*. Cairo: Āyyāt Allah al-ʿUẓma, 1928.

Sawaie, Mohammed. "Rifaʿa Rafiʿ al-Tahtawi and His Contribution to the Lexical Development of Modern Literary Arabic." *International Journal of Middle East Studies* 32, no. 3 (2000): 395–410.

al-Sayyid, Ahmad Lutfi. *Turāth Aḥmad Luṭfī al-Sayyīd*. 2 vols. Cairo: Maṭbaʿat Dār al-Kutub wal-Wathāʾiq al-Qawmiyya, 2008.

al-Sayyid, Radwan. "Taqdīm." In *Mafhūm al-Ḥurriyya fī al-Islām: Dirāsa fī Mushkilāt al-Muṣṭalaḥ wa-Abʿāduhu fī al-Turāth al-ʿArabī al-Islāmī*. Beirut: Dār al-Madār al-Islāmī, 2007.

Schaebler, Birgit. "Civilizing Others: Global Modernity and Local Boundaries (French/German/Ottoman and Arab) of Savagery." In *Globalization and the Muslim World: Culture Religion and Modernity*, edited by Birgit Schaebler and Leif Stenberg, 3–31. New York: Syracuse University Press, 2004.

Schumann, Christoph. "Introduction." In *Liberal Thought in the Eastern Mediterranean: Late 19th Century until the 1960s*, edited by Christoph Schumann, 1–11. Leiden: Brill, 2008.

"Introduction." In *Nationalism and Liberal Thought in the Arab East: Ideology and Practice*, edited by Christoph Schumann, 1–10. London: Routledge, 2010.

Sharabi, Hisham. *Arab Intellectuals and the West: The Formative Years, 1875–1914*. Baltimore, MD: Johns Hopkins Press, 1970.

"The Burden of the Intellectuals of the Liberal Age." *Middle East Journal* 20, no. 2 (1966): 227–32.

Sharif, Malek. "A Portrait of Syrian Deputies in the First Ottoman Parliament." In *The Ottoman Experiment in Democracy*, edited by Malek Sharif and Christoph Herzog, 285–311. Würzburg: Ergon in Kommission, 2010.

Shaw, Stanford J. "The Nizam-I Cedid Army under Sultan Selim III 1789–1807." *Oriens* 18/19 (1965–1966): 168–84.

al-Shayyal, Jamal al-Din. *Tārīkh al-Tarjama wal-Ḥaraka al-Thaqāfiyya fī ʿAṣr Muḥammad ʿAli*. Cairo: Dār al-Fikr al-ʿArabī, 1951.

Sheehi, Stephen Paul. "Inscribing the Arab Self: Butrus al-Bustani and Paradigms of Subjective Reform." *British Journal of Middle Eastern Studies* 27, no. 1 (2000): 7–24.

Shogimen, Takashi. "Liberty." *New Dictionary of the History of Ideas*. Detroit, MI: Charles Scribner's Sons, 2005.

Silvera, Alain. "The First Egyptian Student Mission to France under Muhammad Ali." *Middle Eastern Studies* 16, no. 2 (1980): 1–22.

Smith, Wilfred Cantwell. *Islam in Modern History*. Princeton, NJ: Princeton University Press, 1957.

Streich, Gregory. "Equality." In *New Dictionary of the History of Ideas*. Detroit, MI: Charles Scribner's Sons, 2005.

Suleiman, Yasir. *The Arabic Language and National Identity: A Study in Ideology*. Washington, DC: Georgetown University Press, 2003.

Tarrazi, Filib. *Ta'rīkh al-Ṣiḥāfa al-'Arabiyya*. 2 vols. Beirut: Al-Maṭba'a al-Adabiyya, 1913–1914.

Thompson, Elizabeth. *Justice Interrupted: The Struggle for Constitutional Government in the Middle East*. Cambridge, MA: Harvard University Press, 2013.

Thomson, David. *Europe since Napoleon*. New York: Knopf, 1957.

Tyan, Emile. "'Adl." In *The Encyclopedia of Islam*. Leiden: E. J. Brill, 1986.

Vatikiotis, Panayiotis J. *The Modern History of Egypt*. London: Weidenfeld and Nicolson, 1969.

"Ishtirakiyya." In *The Encyclopedia of Islam*. Leiden: E. J. Brill, 1978.

Vogel, Frank E. "Siyāsa: In the Sense of Siyasa Shar'iyya." In *The Encyclopedia of Islam*. Leiden: E. J. Brill, 1997.

Wahba, Mourad Magdi. "The Meaning of Ishtirakiyah: Arab Perceptions of Socialism in the Nineteenth Century." *Alif: Journal of Comparative Poetics*, no. 10 (1990): 42–55.

Weber, Max. *Wirtschaft und Gesellschaft: Grundriss der verstehenden Soziologie*. Tübingen: J. C. B. Mohr, 1976.

Weinberger, Jerry. "Idea of Progress." In *New Dictionary of the History of Ideas*. Detroit, MI: Charles Scribner's Sons, 2005.

Wissa, Karim. "Freemasonry in Egypt 1798–1921: A Study in Cultural and Political Encounters." *British Journal of Middle Eastern Studies* 16, no. 2 (1989): 143–61.

Woolf, Stuart. "French Civilization and Ethnicity in the Napoleonic Empire." *Past and Present* 124, no. 1 (August 1, 1989): 96–120.

Zachs, Fruma. "Cultural and Conceptual Contributions of Beiruti Merchants to the Nahḍa." *Journal of the Economic and Social History of the Orient* 55 (2012): 153–82.

"Mīkhā'īl Mishāqa-The First Historian of Modern Syria." *British Journal of Middle Eastern Studies* 28, no. 1 (May 2001): 67–87.

*The Making of a Syrian Identity: Intellectuals and Merchants in Nineteenth Century Beirut*. Leiden: Brill, 2005.

"Toward a Proto-Nationalist Concept of Syria? Revisiting the American Presbyterian Missionaries in the Nineteenth-Century Levant." *Die Welt Des Islams* 41, no. 2 (2001): 145–73.

Zachs, Fruma, and Sharon Halevi. *Gendering Culture in Greater Syria: Intellectuals and Ideology in the Late Ottoman Period*. London: I. B. Tauris, 2015.

Zolondek, Leon. "Al-Ṭahṭawi and Political Freedom." *The Muslim World* 54, no. 2 (1964): 90–97.

"The French Revolution in Arabic Literature of the Nineteenth Century." *The Muslim World* 57, no. 3 (1967): 202–11.

# Index